The Waning of
the Middle Ages

J(OHAN) HUIZINGA was born in Holland in 1872. He became professor of history at the University of Leiden in 1915, and taught there until the university was closed under the Nazi occupation. He died in 1945. Huizinga was the author of many books, four of which have been translated and are available in English: *In the Shadow of Tomorrow, Homo Ludens, A Study of the Play Element in Culture, Erasmus of Rotterdam*, and *The Waning of the Middle Ages*, which was first published in 1924.

The Waning of the Middle Ages

A STUDY OF THE FORMS OF LIFE,
THOUGHT AND ART IN FRANCE AND
THE NETHERLANDS IN THE XIVTH
AND XVTH CENTURIES

J. HUIZINGA

ANCHOR BOOKS
DOUBLEDAY
NEW YORK   LONDON   TORONTO   SYDNEY   AUCKLAND

Aን ANCHOR BOOK
PUBLISHED BY DOUBLEDAY
a division of Bantam Doubleday Dell Publishing Group, Inc.
1540 Broadway, New York, New York 10036

ANCHOR BOOKS, DOUBLEDAY, and the portrayal of an anchor are
trademarks of Doubleday, a division of Bantam Doubleday Dell
Publishing Group, Inc.

The Waning of the Middle Ages was originally published in hard-
cover by St. Martin's Press, Inc., in 1949. The Anchor Books edition is published by arrangement with St. Martin's Press, Inc.

ISBN 0-385-09288-1
ANCHOR BOOKS EDITIONS: 1954, 1989
36   35   34   33   32   31   30   29

PREFACE

History has always been far more engrossed by problems of origins than by those of decline and fall. When studying any period, we are always looking for the promise of what the next is to bring. Ever since Herodotus, and earlier still, the questions imposing themselves upon the mind have been concerned with the rise of families, nations, kingdoms, social forms or ideas. So, in medieval history, we have been searching so diligently for the origins of modern culture, that at times it would seem as though what we call the Middle Ages had been little more than the prelude to the Renaissance.

But in history, as in nature, birth and death are equally balanced. The decay of overripe forms of civilization is as suggestive a spectacle as the growth of new ones. And it occasionally happens that a period in which one had, hitherto, been mainly looking for the coming to birth of new things, suddenly reveals itself as an epoch of fading and decay.

The present work deals with the history of the fourteenth and fifteenth centuries regarded as a period of termination, as the close of the Middle Ages. Such a view of them presented itself to the author of this volume, whilst endeavouring to arrive at a genuine understanding of the art of the brothers Van Eyck and their contemporaries, that is to say, to grasp its meaning by seeing it in connection with the entire life of their times. Now the common feature of the various manifestations of civilization of that epoch proved to be inherent rather in that which links them to the past than in the germs which they contain of the future. The significance, not of the artists alone, but also of theologians, poets, chroniclers, princes and statesmen, could be best appreciated by considering them, not as the harbingers of a coming culture, but as perfecting and concluding the old.

This English edition is not a simple translation of the original Dutch (second edition 1921, first 1919), but the result of a work of adaptation, reduction and consolidation under the author's directions. The references, here left out, may be found in full in the original.

Verse quotations are given in the original French throughout the work. In order to avoid an undue increase in length, quotations in prose are, as a rule, given in translations only, except in the concluding chapters where the literary expression as such is discussed, and the actual language becomes important. Here the old French prose also is set out in full.

The author wishes to express his sincere thanks to Sir J. Rennell Rodd, whose kind interest in the book gave rise to this edition, and to the translator, Mr. F. Hopman, of Leiden, whose clear insight into the exigencies of translation rendered the recasting possible, and whose endless patience with the wishes of an exacting author made the difficult task a work of friendly co-operation.

Leiden, J. H.
April, 1924.

CONTENTS

Chapter I

THE VIOLENT TENOR OF LIFE

To the world when it was half a thousand years younger, the outlines of all things seemed more clearly marked than to us. The contrast between suffering and joy, between adversity and happiness, appeared more striking. All experience had yet to the minds of men the directness and absoluteness of the pleasure and pain of child-life. Every event, every action, was still embodied in expressive and solemn forms, which raised them to the dignity of a ritual. For it was not merely the great facts of birth, marriage and death which, by the sacredness of the sacrament, were raised to the rank of mysteries; incidents of less importance, like a journey, a task, a visit, were equally attended by a thousand formalities: benedictions, ceremonies, formulæ.

Calamities and indigence were more afflicting than at present; it was more difficult to guard against them, and to find solace. Illness and health presented a more striking contrast; the cold and darkness of winter were more real evils. Honours and riches were relished with greater avidity and contrasted more vividly with surrounding misery. We, at the present day, can hardly understand the keenness with which a fur coat, a good fire on the hearth, a soft bed, a glass of wine, were formerly enjoyed.

Then, again, all things in life were of a proud or cruel publicity. Lepers sounded their rattles and went about in processions, beggars exhibited their deformity and their misery in churches. Every order and estate, every rank and profession, was distinguished by its costume. The great lords never moved about without a glorious display of arms and liveries, exciting fear and envy. Executions and other public acts of justice, hawking, marriages and funerals, were all announced by cries and processions, songs and music.

The lover wore the colours of his lady; companions the
emblem of their confraternity; parties and servants the
badges or blazon of their lords. Between town and country,
too, the contrast was very marked. A medieval town did
not lose itself in extensive suburbs of factories and villas;
girded by its walls, it stood forth as a compact whole,
bristling with innumerable turrets. However tall and
threatening the houses of noblemen or merchants might be,
in the aspect of the town the lofty mass of the churches
always remained dominant.

The contrast between silence and sound, darkness and
light, like that between summer and winter, was more
strongly marked than it is in our lives. The modern town
hardly knows silence or darkness in their purity, nor the
effect of a solitary light or a single distant cry.

All things presenting themselves to the mind in violent
contrasts and impressive forms, lent a tone of excitement
and of passion to everyday life and tended to produce that
perpetual oscillation between despair and distracted joy,
between cruelty and pious tenderness which characterize
life in the Middle Ages.

One sound rose ceaselessly above the noises of busy life
and lifted all things unto a sphere of order and serenity:
the sound of bells. The bells were in daily life like good
spirits, which by their familiar voices, now called upon the
citizens to mourn and now to rejoice, now warned them of
danger, now exhorted them to piety. They were known
by their names: big Jacqueline, or the bell Roland. Every
one knew the difference in meaning of the various ways of
ringing. However continuous the ringing of the bells, people would seem not to have become blunted to the effect of
their sound.

Throughout the famous judicial duel between two citizens of Valenciennes, in 1455, the big bell, "which is
hideous to hear," says Chastellain, never stopped ringing.
What intoxication the pealing of the bells of all the
churches, and of all the monasteries of Paris, must have
produced, sounding from morning till evening, and even

during the night, when a peace was concluded or a pope elected.

The frequent processions, too, were a continual source of pious agitation. When the times were evil, as they often were, processions were seen winding along, day after day, for weeks on end. In 1412 daily processions were ordered in Paris, to implore victory for the king, who had taken up the oriflamme against the Armagnacs. They lasted from May to July, and were formed by ever-varying orders and corporations, going always by new roads, and always carrying different relics. The Burgher of Paris calls them "the most touching processions in the memory of men." People looked on or followed, "weeping piteously, with many tears, in great devotion." All went barefooted and fasting, councillors of the Parlement as well as the poorer citizens. Those who could afford it, carried a torch or a taper. A great many small children were always among them. Poor country-people of the environs of Paris came barefooted from afar to join the procession. And nearly every day the rain came down in torrents.

Then there were the entries of princes, arranged with all the resources of art and luxury belonging to the age. And, lastly, most frequent of all, one might almost say, uninterrupted, the executions. The cruel excitement and coarse compassion raised by an execution formed an important item in the spiritual food of the common people. They were spectacular plays with a moral. For horrible crimes the law invented atrocious punishments. At Brussels a young incendiary and murderer is placed in the centre of a circle of burning fagots and straw, and made fast to a stake by means of a chain running round an iron ring. He addresses touching words to the spectators, "and he so softened their hearts that every one burst into tears and his death was commended as the finest that was ever seen." During the Burgundian terror in Paris in 1411, one of the victims, Messire Mansart du Bois, being requested by the hangman, according to custom, to forgive him, is not only ready to do so with all his heart, but begs the executioner to embrace him. "There was a great multitude of people, who nearly all wept hot tears."

When the criminals were great lords, the common people had the satisfaction of seeing rigid justice done, and at the same time finding the inconstancy of fortune exemplified more strikingly than in any sermon or picture. The magistrate took care that nothing should be wanting to the effect of the spectacle: the condemned were conducted to the scaffold, dressed in the garb of their high estate. Jean de Montaigu, grand maître d'hôtel to the king, the victim of Jean sans Peur, is placed high on a cart, preceded by two trumpeters. He wears his robe of state, hood, cloak, and hose half red and half white, and his gold spurs, which are left on the feet of the beheaded and suspended corpse. By special order of Louis XI, the head of maître Oudart de Bussy, who had refused a seat in the Parlement, was dug up and exhibited in the market-place of Hesdin, covered with a scarlet hood lined with fur "selon la mode des conseillers de Parlement," with explanatory verses.

Rarer than processions and executions were the sermons of itinerant preachers, coming to shake people by their eloquence. The modern reader of newspapers can no longer conceive the violence of impression caused by the spoken word on an ignorant mind lacking mental food. The Franciscan friar Richard preached in Paris in 1429 during ten consecutive days. He began at five in the morning and spoke without a break till ten or eleven, for the most part in the cemetery of the Innocents. When, at the close of his tenth sermon, he announced that it was to be his last, because he had no permission to preach more, "great and small wept as touchingly and as bitterly as if they were watching their best friends being buried; and so did he." Thinking that he would preach once more at Saint Denis on the Sunday, the people flocked thither on Saturday evening, and passed the night in the open, to secure good seats.

Another Minorite friar, Antoine Fradin, whom the magistrate of Paris had forbidden to preach, because he inveighed against the bad government, is guarded night and

day in the Cordeliers monastery, by women posted around
the building, armed with ashes and stones. In all the towns
where the famous Dominican preacher Vincent Ferrer is
expected, the people, the magistrates, the lower clergy,
and even prelates and bishops, set out to greet him with
joyous songs. He journeys with a numerous and ever-increasing following of adherents, who every night make a
circuit of the town in procession, with chants and flagella-
tions. Officials are appointed to take charge of lodging and
feeding these multitudes. A large number of priests of
various religious orders accompany him everywhere, to assist him in celebrating mass and in confessing the faithful.
Also several notaries, to draw up, on the spot, deeds em-
bodying the reconciliations which this holy preacher everywhere brings about. His pulpit has to be protected by a
fence against the pressure of the congregation which wants
to kiss his hand or habit. Work is at a stand-still all the time
he preaches. He rarely fails to move his auditors to tears.
When he spoke of the Last Judgment, of Hell, or of the
Passion, both he and his hearers wept so copiously that
he had to suspend his sermon till the sobbing had ceased.
Malefactors threw themselves at his feet, before every one,
confessing their great sins. One day, while he was preaching, he saw two persons, who had been condemned to death
—a man and a woman—being led to execution. He begged
to have the execution delayed, had them both placed under
the pulpit, and went on with his sermon, preaching about
their sins. After the sermon, only some bones were found
in the place they had occupied, and the people were convinced that the word of the saint had consumed and saved
them at the same time.

After Olivier Maillard had been preaching Lenten
sermons at Orléans, the roofs of the houses surrounding the
place whence he had addressed the people had been so
damaged by the spectators who had climbed on to them,
that the roofer sent in a bill for repairs extending over sixty-
four days.

The diatribes of the preachers against dissoluteness and
luxury produced violent excitement which was translated

into action. Long before Savonarola started bonfires of
"vanities" at Florence, to the irreparable loss of art, the
custom of these holocausts of articles of luxury and amusement was prevalent both in France and in Italy. At the
summons of a famous preacher, men and women would
hasten to bring cards, dice, finery, ornaments, and burn
them with great pomp. Renunciation of the sin of vanity
in this way had taken a fixed and solemn form of public
manifestation, in accordance with the tendency of the age
to invent a style for everything.

All this general facility of emotions, of tears and spiritual
upheavals, must be borne in mind in order to conceive
fully how violent and high-strung was life at that period.

Public mourning still presented the outward appearance
of a general calamity. At the funeral of Charles VII, the
people are quite appalled on seeing the cortège of all the
court dignitaries, "dressed in the deepest mourning, which
was most pitiful to see; and because of the great sorrow and
grief they exhibited for the death of their master, many
tears were shed and lamentations uttered throughout the
town." People were especially touched at the sight of six
pages of the king mounted on horses quite covered with
black velvet. One of the pages, according to a rumour, had
neither eaten nor drunk for four days. "And God knows
what doleful and piteous plaints they made, mourning for
their master."

Solemnities of a political character also led to abundant
weeping. An ambassador of the king of France repeatedly
bursts into tears while addressing a courteous harangue to
Philip the Good. At the meeting of the kings of France
and of England at Ardres, at the reception of the dauphin
at Brussels, at the departure of John of Coïmbre from the
court of Burgundy, all the spectators weep hot tears. Chastellain describes the dauphin, the future Louis XI, during
his voluntary exile in Brabant, as subject to frequent fits of
weeping.

Unquestionably there is some exaggeration in these descriptions of the chroniclers. In describing the emotion
caused by the addresses of the ambassadors at the peace

congress at Arras, in 1435, Jean Germain, bishop of Chalons,
makes the auditors throw themselves on the ground, sobbing and groaning. Things, of course, did not happen thus,
but thus the bishop thought fit to represent them, and the
palpable exaggeration reveals a foundation of truth. As
with the sentimentalists of the eighteenth century, tears
were considered fine and honourable. Even nowadays an
indifferent spectator of a public procession sometimes feels
himself suddenly moved to inexplicable tears. In an age
filled with religious reverence for all pomp and grandeur,
this propensity will appear altogether natural.

A simple instance will suffice to show the high degree of
irritability which distinguishes the Middle Ages from our
own time. One can hardly imagine a more peaceful game
than that of chess. Still like the *chansons de gestes* of some
centuries back, Olivier de la Marche mentions frequent
quarrels arising over it: "le plus saige y pert patience."

A scientific historian of the Middle Ages, relying first
and foremost on official documents, which rarely refer to
the passions, except violence and cupidity, occasionally
runs the risk of neglecting the difference of tone between
the life of the expiring Middle Ages and that of our own
days. Such documents would sometimes make us forget the
vehement pathos of medieval life, of which the chroniclers,
however defective as to material facts, always keep us in
mind.

In more than one respect life had still the colours of a
fairy-story; that is to say, it assumed those colours in the
eyes of contemporaries. The court chroniclers were men of
culture, and they observed the princes, whose deeds they
recorded, at close quarters, yet even they give these records a somewhat archaic, hieratic air. The following story,
told by Chastellain, serves to prove this. The young count
of Charolais, the later Charles the Bold, on arriving at
Gorcum, in Holland, on his way from Sluys, learns that his
father, the duke, has taken all his pensions and benefices
from him. Thereupon he calls his whole court into his
presence, down to the scullions, and in a touching speech

imparts his misfortune to them, dwelling on his respect for
his ill-informed father, and on his anxiety about the welfare
of all his retinue. Let those who have the means to live,
remain with him awaiting the return of good fortune; let the
poor go away freely, and let them come back when they
hear that the count's fortune has been re-established: they
will all return to their old places, and the count will reward them for their patience. "Then were heard cries and
sobs, and with one accord they shouted: 'We all, we all,
my lord, will live and die with thee.'" Profoundly touched,
Charles accepts their devotion: "Well, then, stay and suffer,
and I will suffer for you, rather than that you should be in
want." The nobles then come and offer him what they possess, "one saying, I have a thousand, another, ten thousand;
I have this, I have that to place at thy service, and I am
ready to share all that may befall thee." And in this way
everything went on as usual, and there was never a hen
the less in the kitchen.

Clearly this story has been more or less touched up.
What interests us is that Chastellain sees the prince and
his court in the epic guise of a popular ballad. If this is a
literary man's conception, how brilliant must royal life have
appeared, when displayed in almost magic splendour, to
the naïve imagination of the uneducated!

Although in reality the mechanism of government had
already assumed rather complicated forms, the popular
mind pictures it in simple and fixed figures. The current
political ideas are those of the Old Testament, of the
romaunt and the ballad. The kings of the time are reduced
to a certain number of types, every one of which corresponds, more or less, to a literary motif. There is the wise
and just prince, the prince deceived by evil counsellors,
the prince who avenges the honour of his family, the un-
fortunate prince to whom his servants remain faithful. In
the mind of the people political questions are reduced to
stories of adventure. Philip the Good knew the political
language which the people understands. To convince the
Hollanders and Frisians that he was perfectly able to conquer the bishopric of Utrecht, he exhibits, during the

festivities of the Hague, in 1456, precious plate to the value
of thirty thousand silver marks. Everybody may come and
look at it. Amongst other things, two hundred thousand
gold lions have been brought from Lille contained in two
chests which every one may try to lift up. The demon-
stration of the solvency of the state took the form of an
entertainment at a fair.

Often we find a fantastic element in the life of princes
which reminds us of the caliph of the *Arabian Nights*.
Charles VI, disguised and mounted with a friend on a
single horse, witnesses the entrance of his betrothed and is
knocked about in the crowd by petty constables. Philip
the Good, whom the physicians ordered to have his head
shaved, issues a command to all the nobles to do likewise,
and charges Pierre de Hagenbach with the cropping of
any whom he finds recalcitrant. In the midst of coolly calculated enterprises princes sometimes act with an impetu-
ous temerity, which endangers their lives and their policy.
Edward III does not hesitate to expose his life and that of
the prince of Wales in order to capture some Spanish
merchantmen, in revenge for deeds of piracy. Philip the
Good interrupts the most serious political business to make
the dangerous crossing from Rotterdam to Sluys for the
sake of a mere whim. On another occasion, mad with rage
in consequence of a quarrel with his son, he leaves Brussels
in the night alone, and loses his way in the woods. The
knight Philippe Pot, to whom fell the delicate task of
pacifying him on his return, lights upon the happy phrase:
"Good day, my liege, good day, what is this? Art thou
playing King Arthur, now, or Sir Lancelot?"

The custom of princes, in the fifteenth century, frequently to seek counsel in political matters from ecstatic
preachers and great visionaries, maintained a kind of religious tension in state affairs which at any moment might
manifest itself in decisions of a totally unexpected character.

At the end of the fourteenth century and at the beginning of the fifteenth, the political stage of the kingdoms of
Europe was so crowded with fierce and tragic conflicts

that the peoples could not help seeing all that regards royalty as a succession of sanguinary and romantic events: in England, King Richard II dethroned and next secretly murdered, while nearly at the same time the highest monarch in Christendom, his brother-in-law Wenzel, king of the Romans, is deposed by the electors; in France, a mad king and soon afterwards fierce party strife, openly breaking out with the appalling murder of Louis of Orléans in 1407, and indefinitely prolonged by the retaliation of 1419 when Jean sans Peur is murdered at Montereau. With their endless train of hostility and vengeance, these two murders have given to the history of France, during a whole century, a sombre tone of hatred. For the contemporary mind cannot help seeing all the national misfortunes which the struggle of the houses of Orléans and of Burgundy was to unchain, in the light of that sole dramatic motive of princely vengeance. It finds no explanation for historic events save in personal quarrels and motives of passion.

In addition to all these evils came the increasing obsession of the Turkish peril, and the still vivid recollection of the catastrophe of Nicopolis in 1396, where a reckless attempt to save Christendom had ended in the wholesale slaughter of French chivalry. Lastly, the great schism of the West had lasted already for a quarter of a century, unsettling all notions about the stability of the Church, dividing every land and community. Two, soon three, claimants contending for the papacy! One of them, the obstinate Aragonese Peter of Luna, or Benedict XIII, was commonly called in France "le Pappe de la Lune." What can an ignorant populace have imagined when hearing such a name?

The familiar image of Fortune's wheel from which kings are falling with their crowns and their sceptres took a living shape in the person of many an expelled prince, roaming from court to court, without means, but full of projects and still decked with the splendour of the marvellous East whence he had fled—the king of Armenia, the king of Cyprus, before long the emperor of Constantinople. It is not surprising that the people of Paris should have believed in the tale of the Gipsies, who presented themselves in

1427, "a duke and a count and ten men, all on horseback,"
while others, to the number of 120, had to stay outside
the town. They came from Egypt, they said; the pope had
ordered them, by way of penance for their apostasy, to
wander about for seven years, without sleeping in a bed;
there had been 1,200 of them, but their king, their queen
and all the others had died on the way; as a mitigation
the pope had ordered that every bishop and abbot was to
give them ten pounds tournois. The people of Paris came in
great numbers to see them, and have their fortunes told
by women who eased them of their money "by magic art
or in other ways."

The inconstancy of the fortune of princes was strikingly
embodied in the person of King René. Having aspired to
the crowns of Hungary, of Sicily, and of Jerusalem, he had
lost all his opportunities, and reaped nothing but a series
of defeats, and imprisonments, chequered by perilous
escapes. The royal poet, a lover of the arts, consoled himself for all his disappointments on his estates in Anjou and
in Provence; his cruel fate had not cured him of his predilection for pastoral enjoyment. He had seen all his children die but one, a daughter for whom was reserved a fate
even harder than his own. Married at sixteen to an imbecile
bigot, Henry VI of England, Margaret of Anjou, full of wit,
ambition and passion, after living for many years in that
hell of hatred and of persecution, the English court, lost
her crown when the quarrel between York and Lancaster
at last broke out into civil war. Having found refuge, after
many dangers and suffering, at the court of Burgundy, she
told Chastellain the story of her adventures: how she had
been forced to commit herself and her young son to the
mercy of a robber, how at mass she had had to ask a
Scotch archer a penny for her offering, "who reluctantly
and with regret took a groat scots for her out of his purse
and lent it her." The good historiographer, moved by so
much misfortune, dedicated to her "a certain little treatise
on fortune, based on its inconstancy and deceptive nature,"
which he entitled *Le Temple de Bocace*. He could not
guess that still graver calamities were in store for the un-

fortunate queen. At the battle of Tewkesbury, in 1471, the fortunes of Lancaster went down for ever. Her only son perished there, probably slaughtered after the battle. Her husband was secretly murdered; she herself was imprisoned in the Tower of London, where she remained for five years, to be at last given up by Edward IV to Louis XI, who made her renounce her father's inheritance as the price of her liberty.

An atmosphere of passion and adventure enveloped the lives of princes. It was not popular fancy alone which lent it that colour.

A present-day reader, studying the history of the Middle Ages based on official documents, will never sufficiently realize the extreme excitability of the medieval soul. The picture drawn mainly from official records, though they may be the most reliable sources, will lack one element: that of the vehement passion possessing princes and peoples alike. To be sure, the passionate element is not absent from modern politics, but it is now restrained and diverted for the most part by the complicated mechanism of social life. Five centuries ago it still made frequent and violent irruptions into practical politics, upsetting rational schemes. In princes this violence of sentiment is doubled by pride and the consciousness of power, and therefore operates with a twofold impetus. It is not surprising, says Chastellain, that princes often live in hostility, "for princes are men, and their affairs are high and perilous, and their natures are subject to many passions, such as hatred and envy; their hearts are veritable dwelling-places of these, because of their pride in reigning."

In writing the history of the house of Burgundy, the *leitmotiv* should constantly keep before our minds the spirit of revenge. Nobody, of course, will now seek the explanation of the whole conflict of power and interests, whence proceeded the secular struggle between France and the house of Austria, in the family feud between Orléans and Burgundy. All sorts of causes of a general nature—political, economic, ethnographic—have contributed to the genesis of that great conflict. But we should never forget that the apparent origin of it, and the central motive dominating it, was, to the men of the fifteenth century and even later, the thirst for revenge. To them Philip the Good is always, in the first place, the avenger, "he who, to avenge the outrage done to the person of Duke John, sustained the war for sixteen years." He had undertaken it as a sacred duty: "with the most violent and deadly hatred he would give himself up to revenge the dead, as far as ever God would permit him, as he would devote to it body and soul, substance and lands, submitting everything to Fortune, considering it more a salutary task and agreeable to God to undertake it, than to leave it."

Read the long list of expiatory deeds which the treaty of Arras demanded in 1435—chapels, monasteries, churches, chapters to be founded, crosses to be erected, masses to be chanted—then one realizes the immensely high rate at which men valued the need of vengeance and of reparations to outraged honour. The Burgundians were not alone in thinking after this fashion; the most enlightened man of his century, Aeneas Sylvius, in one of his letters praises Philip above all the other princes of his time, for his anxiety to avenge his father.

According to La Marche, this duty of honour and revenge was to the duke's subjects also the cardinal point of policy. All the dominions of the duke, he says, were clamouring for vengeance along with him. We shall find it difficult to believe this, when we remember, for instance, the commercial relations between Flanders and England, a more important political factor, it would seem, than the honour of the ducal family. But to understand the sentiment of the age itself, one should look for the avowed and conscious political ideas. There can be no doubt that no other political motive could be better understood by the people than the primitive motives of hatred and vengeance. Attachment to princes had still an emotional character; it was based on the innate and immediate sentiments of fidelity and fellowship, it was still feudal sentiment at bottom. It was rather party feeling than political. The last three centuries of the Middle Ages are the time of the great party struggles. From the thirteenth century onward inveterate party quarrels arise in nearly all countries: first in Italy, then in France, the Netherlands, Germany and England. Though economic interests may sometimes have been at the bottom of these quarrels, the attempts which have been made to disengage them often smack somewhat of arbitrary construction. The desire to discover economic causes is to some degree a craze with us, and sometimes leads us to forget a much simpler psychological explanation of the facts.

In the feudal age the private wars between two families have no other discernible reason than rivalry of rank and covetousness of possessions. Racial pride, thirst of vengeance, fidelity, are their primary and direct motives. There are no grounds to ascribe another economic basis to them than mere greed of one's neighbour's riches. Accordingly as the central power consolidates and extends, these isolated quarrels unite, agglomerate to groups; large parties are formed, are polarized, so to say; while their members know of no other grounds for their concord or enmity than those of honour, tradition and fidelity. Their economic differences are often only a consequence of their relation towards their rulers.

Every page of medieval history proves the spontaneous and passionate character of the sentiments of loyalty and devotion to the prince. At Abbeville, in 1462, a messenger comes at night, bringing the news of a dangerous illness of the duke of Burgundy. His son requests the good towns to pray for him. At once the aldermen order the bells of the church of Saint Vulfran to be rung; the whole population wakes up and goes to church, where it remains all night in prayer, kneeling or prostrate on the ground, with "grandes allumeries merveilleuses," while the bells keep tolling.

It might be thought that the schism, which had no dogmatic cause, could hardly awaken religious passions in countries distant from Avignon and of Rome, in which the two popes were only known by name. Yet in fact it immediately engendered a fanatical hatred, such as exists between the faithful and infidels. When the town of

Bruges went over to the "obedience" of Avignon, a great
number of people left their house, trade or prebend, to
go and live according to their party views in some diocese
of the Urbanist obedience: Liège, Utrecht, or elsewhere.
In 1382 the oriflamme, which might only be unfurled in a
holy cause, was taken up against the Flemings, because
they were Urbanists, that is, infidels. Pierre Salmon, a
French political agent, arriving at Utrecht about Easter,
could not find a priest there willing to admit him to the
communion service, "because they said I was a schismatic
and believed in Benedict the anti-pope."

The emotional character of party sentiments and of
fidelity was further heightened by the powerfully suggestive effect of all the outward signs of these divergences:
liveries, colours, badges, party cries. During the first years
of the war between the Armagnacs and the Burgundians,
these signs succeeded each other in Paris with a dangerous
alternation: a purple hood with a cross of Saint Andrew,
white hoods, then violet ones. Even priests, women and
children wore distinctive signs. The images of saints were
decorated with them; it was asserted that certain priests,
during mass and in baptizing, refused to make the sign
of the cross in the orthodox way, but made it in the form
of a Saint Andrew cross.

In the blind passion with which people followed their
lord or their party, the unshakable sentiment of right, characteristic of the Middle Ages, is trying to find expression.
Man at that time is convinced that right is absolutely fixed
and certain. Justice should prosecute the unjust everywhere
and to the end. Reparation and retribution have to be extreme, and assume the character of revenge. In this
exaggerated need of justice, primitive barbarism, pagan at
bottom, blends with the Christian conception of society.
The Church, on the one hand, had inculcated gentleness
and clemency, and tried, in that way, to soften judicial
morals. On the other hand, in adding to the primitive need
of retribution the horror of sin, it had, to a certain extent,
stimulated the sentiment of justice. And sin, to violent and
impulsive spirits, was only too frequently another name for

what their enemies did. The barbarous idea of retaliation was reinforced by fanaticism. The chronic insecurity made the greatest possible severity on the part of the public authorities desirable; crime came to be regarded as a menace to order and society, as well as an insult to divine majesty. Thus it was natural that the late Middle Ages should become the special period of judicial cruelty. That the criminal deserved his punishment was not doubted for a moment. The popular sense of justice always sanctioned the most rigorous penalties. At intervals the magistrate undertook regular campaigns of severe justice, now against brigandage, now against sorcery or sodomy.

What strikes us in this judicial cruelty and in the joy the people felt at it, is rather brutality than perversity. Torture and executions are enjoyed by the spectators like an entertainment at a fair. The citizens of Mons bought a brigand, at far too high a price, for the pleasure of seeing him quartered, "at which the people rejoiced more than if a new holy body had risen from the dead." The people of Bruges, in 1488, during the captivity of Maximilian, king of the Romans, cannot get their fill of seeing the tortures inflicted, on a high platform in the middle of the market-place, on the magistrates suspected of treason. The unfortunates are refused the deathblow which they implore, that the people may feast again upon their torments.

Both in France and in England, the custom existed of refusing confession and the extreme unction to a criminal condemned to death. Sufferings and fear of death were to be aggravated by the certainty of eternal damnation. In vain had the council of Vienne in 1311 ordered to grant them at least the sacrament of penitence. Towards the end of the fourteenth century the same custom still existed. Charles V himself, moderate though he was, had declared that no change would be made in his lifetime. The chancellor Pierre d'Orgemont, whose "forte cervelle," says Philippe de Mézières, was more difficult to turn than a mill-stone, remained deaf to the humane remonstrances of the latter. It was only after Gerson had joined his voice to that of Mézières that a royal decree of the 12th of February, 1397,

ordered that confession should be accorded to the condemned. A stone cross erected by the care of Pierre de
Craon, who had interested himself in the decree, marked
the place where the Minorite friars might assist penitents
going to execution. And even then the barbarous custom
did not disappear. Etienne Ponchier, bishop of Paris, had
to renew the decree of 1311 in 1500.

In 1427 a noble brigand is hanged in Paris. At the moment when he is going to be executed, the great treasurer
of the regent appears on the scene and vents his hatred
against him; he prevents his confession, in spite of his
prayers; he climbs the ladder behind him, shouting insults, beats him with a stick, and gives the hangman a
thrashing for exhorting the victim to think of his salvation.
The hangman grows nervous and bungles his work; the
cord snaps, the wretched criminal falls on the ground,
breaks a leg and some ribs, and in this condition has to
climb the ladder again.

The Middle Ages knew nothing of all those ideas which
have rendered our sentiment of justice timid and hesitat-
ing: doubts as to the criminal's responsibility; the conviction that society is, to a certain extent, the accomplice of
the individual; the desire to reform instead of inflicting
pain; and, we may even add, the fear of judicial errors.
Or rather these ideas were implied, unconsciously, in the
very strong and direct feeling of pity and of forgiveness
which alternated with extreme severity. Instead of lenient
penalties, inflicted with hesitation, the Middle Ages knew
but the two extremes: the fulness of cruel punishment, and
mercy. When the condemned criminal is pardoned, the
question whether he deserves it for any special reasons is
hardly asked; for mercy has to be gratuitous, like the mercy
of God. In practice, it was not always pure pity which
determined the question of pardon. The princes of the
fifteenth century were very liberal of "lettres de rémission"
for misdeeds of all sorts, and contemporaries thought it
quite natural, that they were obtained by the intercession
of noble relatives. The majority of these documents, however, concern poor common people.

The contrast of cruelty and of pity recurs at every turn
in the manners and customs of the Middle Ages. On the
one hand, the sick, the poor, the insane, are objects of
that deeply moved pity, born of a feeling of fraternity akin
to that which is so strikingly expressed in modern Russian
literature; on the other hand, they are treated with incredible hardness or cruelly mocked. The chronicler Pierre
de Fenin, having described the death of a gang of brigands,
winds up naïvely: "and people laughed a good deal, because they were all poor men." In 1425, an "esbatement"
takes place in Paris, of four blind beggars, armed with
sticks, with which they hit each other in trying to kill a pig,
which is a prize of the combat. On the evening before they
are led through the town, "all armed, with a great banner
in front, on which was pictured a pig, and preceded by a
man beating a drum."

In the fifteenth century, female dwarfs were objects of
amusement, as they still were at the court of Spain when
Velazquez painted their infinitely sad faces. Madame d'Or,
the blond dwarf of Philip the Good, was famous. She was
made to wrestle, at a court festival, with the acrobat Hans.
At the wedding-feasts of Charles the Bold, in 1468, Madame de Beaugrant, the female dwarf of Mademoiselle of
Burgundy, enters dressed like a shepherdess, mounted on
a golden lion, larger than a horse; she is presented to the
young duchess and placed on the table. As to the fate of
these small creatures, the account-books are more eloquent
for us than any sentimental complaint could be. They tell
us of a dwarf-girl whom a duchess caused to be fetched
from her home, and how her parents came to visit her
from time to time and receive a gratuity. "Au père de Belon
la folle, qui estoit venu veoir sa fille. . . . 27s. 6d." The
poor fellow perhaps went home well pleased and much
elated about the court function of his daughter. That same
year a locksmith of Blois furnished two iron collars, the
one "to make fast Belon, the fool, and the other to put
round the neck of the monkey of her grace the Duchess."

In the harshness of those times there is something ingenuous which almost forbids us to condemn it. When the

massacre of the Armagnacs was in full swing in 1418, the
Parisians founded a brotherhood of Saint Andrew in the
church of Saint Eustache: every one, priest or layman, wore
a wreath of red roses, so that the church was perfumed
by them, "as if it had been washed with rose-water." The
people of Arras celebrate the annulment of the sentences
for witchcraft, which during the whole year 1461 had in-
fested the town like an epidemic, by joyous festivals and
a competition in acting "folies moralisées," of which the
prizes were a gold fleur-de-lis, a brace of capons, etc.; nobody, it seems, thought any more of the tortured and executed victims.

So violent and motley was life, that it bore the mixed
smell of blood and of roses. The men of that time always
oscillate between the fear of hell and the most naïve joy,
between cruelty and tenderness, between harsh asceticism
and insane attachment to the delights of this world, between hatred and goodness, always running to extremes.

After the close of the Middle Ages the mortal sins of
pride, anger and covetousness have never again shown the
unabashed insolence with which they manifested themselves in the life of preceding centuries. The whole history
of the house of Burgundy is like an epic of overweening and
heroic pride, which takes the form of bravura and ambition
with Philippe le Hardi, of hatred and envy with Jean sans
Peur, of the lust of vengeance and fondness for display
with Philip the Good, of foolhardy temerity and obstinacy
with Charles the Bold.

Medieval doctrine found the root of all evil either in the
sin of pride or in cupidity. Both opinions were based on
Scripture texts: *A superbia initium sumpsit omnis perditio.
—Radix omnium malorum est cupiditas.* It seems, nevertheless, that from the twelfth century downward people begin
to find the principle of evil rather in cupidity than in pride.
The voices which condemn blind cupidity, "la cieca
cupidigia" of Dante, become louder and louder. Pride
might perhaps be called the sin of the feudal and hierarchic
age. Very little property is, in the modern sense, liquid,
while power is not yet associated, predominantly, with

money; it is still rather inherent in the person and depends
on a sort of religious awe which he inspires; it makes itself felt by pomp and magnificence, or a numerous train
of faithful followers. Feudal or hierarchic thought expresses the idea of grandeur by visible signs, lending to it
a symbolic shape, of homage paid kneeling, of ceremonial
reverence. Pride, therefore, is a symbolic sin, and from the
fact that, in the last resort, it derives from the pride of
Lucifer, the author of all evil, it assumes a metaphysical
character.

Cupidity, on the other hand, has neither this symbolic
character nor these relations with theology. It is a purely
worldly sin, the impulse of nature and of the flesh. In the
later Middle Ages the conditions of power had been
changed by the increased circulation of money, and an il-
limitable field opened to whosoever was desirous of satisfy-
ing his ambitions by heaping up wealth. To this epoch
cupidity becomes the predominant sin. Riches have not
acquired the spectral impalpability which capitalism,
founded on credit, will give them later; what haunts the
imagination is still the tangible yellow gold. The enjoyment
of riches is direct and primitive; it is not yet weakened by
the mechanism of an automatic and invisible accumulation
by investment; the satisfaction of being rich is found either
in luxury and dissipation, or in gross avarice.

Towards the end of the Middle Ages feudal and hierarchic pride had lost nothing, as yet, of its vigour; the relish
for pomp and display is as strong as ever. This primitive
pride has now united itself with the growing sin of cupidity,
and it is this mixture of the two which gives the expiring
Middle Ages a tone of extravagant passion that never appears again.

A furious chorus of invectives against cupidity and avarice rises up everywhere from the literature of that period.
Preachers, moralists, satirical writers, chroniclers and poets
speak with one voice. Hatred of rich people, especially of
the new rich, who were then very numerous, is general.
Official records confirm the most incredible cases of unbridled avidity told by the chronicles. In 1436 a quarrel

between two beggars, in which a few drops of blood had
been shed, had soiled the church of the Innocents at Paris.
The bishop, Jacques du Châtelier, "a very ostentatious,
grasping man, of a more worldly disposition than his station
required," refused to consecrate the church anew, unless
he received a certain sum of money from the two poor men,
which they did not possess, so that the service was interrupted for twenty-two days. Even worse happened under
his successor, Denys de Moulins. During four months of the
year 1441, he prohibited both burials and processions in
the cemetery of the Innocents, the most favoured of all,
because the church could not pay the tax he demanded.
This Denys de Moulins was reputed "a man who showed
very little pity to people, if he did not receive money or
some equivalent; and it was told for truth that he had
more than fifty lawsuits before the Parlement, for nothing
could be got out of him without going to law."

A general feeling of impending calamity hangs over all.
Perpetual danger prevails everywhere. To realize the continuous insecurity in which the lives of great and small alike
were passed, it suffices to read the details which Monsieur
Pierre Champion has collected regarding the persons mentioned by Villon in his *Testament*, or the notes of Monsieur
A. Tuetey to the diary of a Burgher of Paris. They present
to us an interminable string of lawsuits, crimes, assaults
and persecutions. A chronicle like that of Jacques du
Clercq, or a diary such as that of the citizen of Metz,
Philippe de Vigneulles, perhaps lay too much stress on the
darker side of contemporary life, but every investigation of
the careers of individual persons seems to confirm them, by
revealing to us strangely troubled lives.

In reading the chronicle of Mathieu d'Escouchy, simple,
exact, impartial, moralizing, one would think that the
author was a studious, quiet and honest man. His character was unknown before Monsieur du Fresne de Beaucourt had elicited the history of his life from the archives.
But what a life it was, that of this representative of
"colérique Picardie." Alderman, then, towards 1445 provost, of Péronne, we find him from the outset engaged in a

family quarrel with Jean Froment, the city syndic. They
harass each other reciprocally with lawsuits, for forgery and
murder, for "excès et attemptaz." The attempt of the provost to get the widow of his enemy condemned for witchcraft costs him dear. Summoned before the Parlement of
Paris himself, d'Escouchy is imprisoned. We find him again
in prison as an accused on five more occasions, always in
grave criminal causes, and more than once in heavy chains.
A son of Froment wounds him in an encounter. Each of
the parties hires brigands to assail the other. After this long
feud ceases to be mentioned in the records, others arise of
similar violence. All this does not check the career of
d'Escouchy: he becomes bailiff, provost of Ribemont,
"procureur du roi" at Saint Quentin; he is ennobled. He
is taken prisoner at Montlhéry, then comes back maimed
from a later campaign. Next he marries, but not to settle
down to a quiet life. Once more, he appears accused of
counterfeiting seals, conducted to Paris "comme larron et
murdrier," forced into confessions by torture, prevented
from appealing, condemned; then rehabilitated and again
condemned, till the traces of this career of hatred and persecutions disappear from the records.

Is it surprising that the people could see their fate and
that of the world only as an endless succession of evils?
Bad government, exactions, the cupidity and violence of
the great, wars and brigandage, scarcity, misery and pestilence—to this is contemporary history nearly reduced in
the eyes of the people. The feeling of general insecurity
which was caused by the chronic form wars were apt to
take, by the constant menace of the dangerous classes, by
the mistrust of justice, was further aggravated by the obsession of the coming end of the world, and by the fear of
hell, of sorcerers and of devils. The background of all
life in the world seems black. Everywhere the flames of
hatred arise and injustice reigns. Satan covers a gloomy
earth with his sombre wings. In vain the militant Church
battles, preachers deliver their sermons; the world remains
unconverted. According to a popular belief, current towards the end of the fourteenth century, no one, since the

beginning of the great Western schism, had entered Paradise.

Chapter II

PESSIMISM AND THE IDEAL OF THE SUBLIME LIFE

At the close of the Middle Ages, a sombre melancholy weighs on people's souls. Whether we read a chronicle, a poem, a sermon, a legal document even, the same impression of immense sadness is produced by them all. It would sometimes seem as if this period had been particularly unhappy, as if it had left behind only the memory of violence, of covetousness and mortal hatred, as if it had known no other enjoyment but that of intemperance, of pride and of cruelty.

Now in the records of all periods misfortune has left more traces than happiness. Great evils form the groundwork of history. We are perhaps inclined to assume without much evidence that, roughly speaking, and notwithstanding all calamities, the sum of happiness can have hardly changed from one period to another. But in the fifteenth century, as in the epoch of romanticism, it was, so to say, bad form to praise the world and life openly. It was fashionable to see only its suffering and misery, to discover everywhere signs of decadence and of the near end—in short, to condemn the times or to despise them.

We look in vain in the French literature of the beginning of the fifteenth century for the vigorous optimism which will spring up at the Renaissance—though, by the way, the optimist tendency of the Renaissance is sometimes exaggerated. The exulting exclamation of Ulrich von Hutten, which has become trite from much quoting, "O saeculum, O literae! juvat vivere!" [1] expresses the enthusiasm of the

[1] "O world, O letters, it is a delight to live!"

scholar rather than that of the man. With the humanists
optimism is still tempered by the ancient contempt, both
Christian and Stoic, for the world. A passage extracted
from a letter written by Erasmus in 1518, may serve better
than Hutten's exclamation to show the average valuation
put upon life by a humanist. "I am not so greatly attached
to life; having entered upon my fifty-first year, I judge I
have lived long enough; and on the other hand, I see in
this life nothing so excellent or agreeable that a man might
wish for it, on whom the Christian creed has conferred
the hope of a much happier life, in store for those who have
attached themselves closely to piety. Nevertheless, at
present, I could almost wish to be rejuvenated for a few
years, for this only reason that I believe I see a golden
age dawning in the near future." He then describes the
concord reigning among the princes of Christendom and
their inclination to peace—which was so dear to him personally—then he continues: "Everything confirms my hope
that not only good morals and Christian piety will be re-
born and flourish, but also pure and true literature and
good learning." Thanks to the protection of princes, be it
understood. "It is to their pious feelings that we are in-
debted for seeing everywhere, as at a given signal, illustrious spirits awakening and conspiring to restore good learning."

In short, the appreciation of the joys of life, which
Erasmus manifests, is fairly cool; moreover, he soon
changed his mood of hopeful expectation, never to find it
again. However, compared with current feeling in the preceding century, except in Italy, Erasmus's appreciation
might rather be called warm. The men of letters at the
court of Charles VII, or at that of Philip the Good, never
tire of inveighing against life and the age. The note of
despair and profound dejection is predominantly sounded
not by ascetic monks, but by the court poets and the
chroniclers—laymen, living in aristocratic circles and amid
aristocratic ideas. Possessing only a slight intellectual and
moral culture, being for the most part strangers to study
and learning, and of only a feebly religious temper, they

were incapable of finding consolation or hope in the
spectacle of universal misery and decay, and could only
bewail the decline of the world and despair of justice and
of peace.

No one has been so lavish of complaints of this nature as
Eustache Deschamps:

> "Temps de doleur et de temptacion,
> Aages de plour, d'envie et de tourment,
> Temps de langour et de dampnacion,
> Aages meneur près du definement,
> Temps plains d'orreur qui tout fait faussement,
> Aage menteur, plain d'orgueil et d'envie,
> Temps sanz honeur et sanz vray jugement,
> Aage en tristesse qui abrege la vie." [2]

The ballads he has composed in this spirit may be
counted by the dozen: monotonous and gloomy variations
of the same dismal theme. There must have prevailed
among the nobility a general disposition to melancholy;
otherwise we could not account for the manifest popularity
of these poems.

> "Toute léesse deffaut,
> Tous cueurs ont prins par assaut
> Tristesse et merencolie." [3]

Towards the end of the fifteenth century, the tone is
still unchanged; Jean Meschinot sighs as did Deschamps.

> "O miserable et très dolente vie! . . .
> La guerre avons, mortalité, famine;
> Le froid, le chaud, le jour, la nuit nous mine;
> Puces, cirons et tant d'autre vermine

[2] Time of mourning and of temptation, Age of tears, of
envy and of torment, Time of languor and of damnation,
Age of decline nigh to the end, Time full of horror which
does all things falsely, Lying age, full of pride and of envy,
Time without honour and without true judgment, Age of
sadness which shortens life.

[3] All mirth is lost, All hearts have been taken by storm
By sadness and melancholy.

Nous guerroyent. Bref, miserere domine
Noz meschans corps, dont le vivre est très court." [4]

He too is convinced that all goes wrong in the world;
there is no justice any more; the great exploit the small,
and the small exploit each other. He pretends to have
been led by his hypochondria within an ace of suicide. He
depicts himself in the following terms:

> "Et je, le pouvre escrivain,
> Au cueur triste, faible et vain,
> Voyant de chascun le deuil,
> Soucy me tient en sa main;
> Toujours les larmes à l'œil,
> Rien fors mourir je ne vueil." [5]

All that we get to know of the moral state of the nobles
points to a sentimental need of enrobing their souls with the
garb of woe. There is hardly one who does not come forward to affirm that he has seen nothing but misery during
his life and expects only worse things from the future.
Georges Chastellain, the historiographer of the dukes of
Burgundy and chief of the Burgundian rhetorical school,
speaks thus of himself in the prologue to his chronicle: "I,
man of sadness, born in an eclipse of darkness, and thick
fogs of lamentation." His successor, Olivier de la Marche,
chooses for his device the lament, "tant a souffert La
Marche." [6] It would be interesting to study from the point
of view of physiognomy the portraits of that time, which
for the most part strike us by their sad expression.

It is curious to notice the variation of meaning which

[4] O miserable and very sad life! . . . We suffer from
warfare, death and famine; Cold and heat, day and night,
sap our strength; Fleas, scabmites and so much other vermin Make war upon us. In short, have mercy, Lord, upon
our wicked persons, whose life is very short.

[5] And I, poor writer, With the sad, feeble and vain heart,
When I see every one mourning, Then Affliction holds me
in her hand; I have always tears in my eye, I wish for
nothing but to die.

[6] So much has La Marche suffered.

the word melancholy shows in the fourteenth century. The
ideas of sadness, of reflection, and of fancy, are blended in
the term. For example, in speaking of Philip of Artevelde,
lost in thought, in consequence of a message he had just
received, Froissart expresses himself thus: "Quant il eut
merancoliet une espasse, il s'avisa que il rescriproit aus com-
missaires dou roi de France." [7] Deschamps says of something that is uglier than could be imagined: no artist is
"merencolieux" enough to be able to paint it. The change
of meaning evidently shows a tendency to identify all serious occupation of the mind with sadness.

The poetry of Eustache Deschamps is full of petty re-
viling of life and its inevitable troubles. Happy is he who
has no children, for babies mean nothing but crying and
stench; they give only trouble and anxiety; they have to
be clothed, shod, fed; they are always in danger of falling
and hurting themselves; they contract some illness and die.
When they grow up, they may go to the bad and be put
in prison. Nothing but cares and sorrows; no happiness
compensates us for our anxiety, for the trouble and expenses of their education. Is there a greater evil than to
have deformed children? The poet has no word of pity
for their misfortune; he holds

> "Que homs de membre contrefais
> Est en sa pensée meffais,—
> Plains de pechiez et plains de vices." [8]

Happy are bachelors, for a man who has an evil wife has
a bad time of it, and he who has a good one always fears
to lose her. In other words, happiness is feared together
with misfortune. In old age the poet sees only evil and disgust, a lamentable decline of the body and the mind,
ridicule and insipidity. It comes soon, at thirty for a woman,
at fifty for a man, and neither lives beyond sixty, for the

[7] When he had reflected for a space, he resolved to answer the emissaries of the king of France.
[8] That a man with deformed limbs is misshapen of mind,
—Full of sins and full of vices.

most part. It is a far cry to the serene ideality of Dante's conception of noble old age in the *Convivio*!

The world, says Deschamps, is like an old man fallen into dotage. He has begun by being innocent, then he has been wise for a long time, just, virtuous and strong:

> "Or est laches, chetis et molz,
> Vieulx, convoiteux et mal parlant:
> Je ne voy que foles et folz. . . .
> La fin s'approche, en vérité. . . .
> Tout va mal." [9]

In another place he laments:

> "Pour quoy est si obscurs le temps,
> Que li uns l'autre ne cognoist,
> Mais muent les gouvernements
> De mal en pis, si comme on voit?
> Le temps passé trop mieulx valoit.
> Qui règne? Tristesse et Ennuy;
> Il ne court justice ne droit;
> Je ne scé mais desquelz je suy." [10]

And again:

> "Se ce temps tient, je deviendray hermite,
> Car je n'i voys fors que dueil et tourment." [11]

Pessimism of this kind has hardly anything to do with religion. Deschamps only gives an off-hand pious purport to his reflections. Despondency and spleen are at the bottom of them, not piety. A contempt of the world, which is

[9] Now the world is cowardly, decayed and weak, Old, covetous, confused of speech: I see only female and male fools. . . . The end approaches, in sooth. . . . All goes badly.

[10] Why are the times so dark That men do not know each other, But governments move From bad to worse, as we see? The past was much better. Who reigns? Affliction and annoyance; Justice nor law are current; I know no more where I belong.

[11] If the times remain so, I shall become a hermit, For I see nothing but grief and torment.

dominated by fear of weariness and of sorrow, of disease and of old age, is but an asceticism of the blasé, born of disillusion and of satiety. It has nothing in common with religion but its terminology.

Even in ascetic utterances of a purer and loftier kind such fear of life, such recoiling before its inevitable sorrows, is not seldom mingled. The series of arguments which Jean Gerson propounds in his *Discours de l'excellence de Virginité*, written for his sisters, with a view to keep them from marrying, does not essentially differ from Deschamps' gloomy lamentations. All the evils attaching to wedlock are found there. The husband may be a drunkard, a spendthrift, a miser. If he be honest and good, bad harvests, death of cattle, a shipwreck may occur, robbing him of all he possesses. What misery it is to be pregnant! How many women die in childbed. The woman who suckles her baby knows neither rest nor pleasure. Children may be deformed or disobedient; the husband may die, and leave his widow behind in care and poverty.

Thus, always and everywhere in the literature of the age, we find a confessed pessimism. As soon as the soul of these men has passed from childlike mirth and unreasoning enjoyment to reflection, deep dejection about all earthly misery takes their place and they see only the woe of life. Still this very pessimism is the ground whence their soul will soar up to the aspiration of a life of beauty and serenity. For at all times the vision of a sublime life has haunted the souls of men, and the gloomier the present is, the more strongly this aspiration will make itself felt.

Three different paths, at all times, have seemed to lead to the ideal life. Firstly, that of forsaking the world. The perfection of life here seems only to be reached beyond the domain of earthly labour and delight, by a loosening of all ties. The second path conducts to amelioration of the world itself, by consciously improving political, social and moral institutions and conditions. Now, in the Middle Ages, Christian faith had so strongly implanted in all minds the ideal of renunciation as the base of all personal and social perfection, that there was scarcely any room left for en-

tering upon this path of material and political progress. The
idea of a purposed and continual reform and improvement
of society did not exist. Institutions in general are considered as good or as bad as they can be; having been
ordained by God, they are intrinsically good, only the sins
of men pervert them. What therefore is in need of remedy
is the individual soul. Legislation in the Middle Ages never
aims consciously and avowedly at creating a new organism;
professedly it is always opportunistic, it only restores good
old law (or at least thinks it does no more) or mends
special abuses. It looks more towards an ideal past than
towards an earthly future. For the true future is the Last
Judgment, and that is near at hand.

It goes without saying that this mental disposition must
have greatly contributed to the general pessimism. If in all
that regards the things of this world there is no hope of
improvement and of progress, however slow, those who
love the world too much to give up its delights, and who
nevertheless cannot help aspiring to a better order of
things, see nothing before them but a gulf. We will have
to wait till the eighteenth century—for even the Renaissance does not truly bring the idea of progress—before
men resolutely enter the path of social optimism;—only
then the perfectibility of man and society is raised to the
rank of a central dogma, and the next century will only
lose the naïveté of this belief, but not the courage and
optimism which it inspired.

It would be a mistake to think that the medieval mind,
lacking the ideas of progress and conscious reform, had
only known the religious form of the aspiration to ideal life.
For there is a third path to a world more beautiful, trodden
in all ages and civilizations, the easiest and also the most
fallacious of all, that of the dream. A promise of escape
from the gloomy actual is held out to all; we have only to
colour life with fancy, to enter upon the quest of oblivion,
sought in the delusion of ideal harmony. After the religious
and the social solution we here have the poetical.

A simple tune suffices for the enrapturing fugue to develop itself; an outlook on the heroism, the virtue or the

happiness of an ideal past is all that is wanted. The themes are few in number, and have hardly changed since antiquity; we may call them the heroic and the bucolic theme. Nearly all the literary culture of later ages has been built upon them.

But *was* it only a question of literature, this third path to the sublime life, this flight from harsh reality into illusion? Surely it has been more. History pays too little attention to the influence of these dreams of a sublime life on civilization itself and on the forms of social life. The content of the ideal is a desire to return to the perfection of an imaginary past. All aspiration to raise life to that level, be it in poetry only or in fact, is an imitation. The essence of chivalry is the imitation of the ideal hero, just as the imitation of the ancient sage is the essence of humanism. Strongest and most lasting of all is the illusion of a return to nature and its innocent charms by an imitation of the shepherd's life. Since Theocritus it has never lost its hold upon civilized society.

Now, the more primitive a society is, the more the need of conforming real life to an ideal standard overflows beyond literature into the sphere of the actual. Modern man is a worker. To work is his ideal. The modern male costume since the end of the eighteenth century is essentially a workman's dress. Since political progress and social perfection have stood foremost in general appreciation, and the ideal itself is sought in the highest production and most equitable distribution of goods, there is no longer any need for playing the hero or the sage. The ideal itself has become democratic. In aristocratic periods, on the other hand, to be representative of true culture means to produce by conduct, by customs, by manners, by costume, by deportment, the illusion of a heroic being, full of dignity and honour, of wisdom and, at all events, of courtesy. This seems possible by the aforesaid imitation of an ideal past. The dream of past perfection ennobles life and its forms, fills them with beauty and fashions them anew as forms of art. Life is regulated like a noble game. Only a small aristocratic group can come up to the standard of this

artistic game. To imitate the hero and the sage is not everybody's business. Without leisure or wealth one does not
succeed in giving life an epic or idyllic colour. The aspiration to realize a dream of beauty in the forms of social life
bears as a *vitium originis* the stamp of aristocratic exclusiveness.

Here, then, we have attained a point of view from which
we can consider the lay culture of the waning Middle
Ages: aristocratic life decorated by ideal forms, gilded by
chivalrous romanticism, a world disguised in the fantastic
gear of the Round Table.

The quest of the life beautiful is much older than the
Italian *quattrocento*. Here, as elsewhere, the line of demarcation between the Middle Ages and the Renaissance has
been too much insisted upon. Florence had but to adopt
and develop ancient motifs which the Middle Ages had
known. In spite of the æsthetic distance separating the
Giostre of the Medici from the barbarous pageantry of the
dukes of Burgundy, the inspiration is the same. Italy, indeed, discovered new worlds of beauty, and tuned life to a
new tone; but the impulse itself to force it up to a thing
of art, generally taken as typical of the Renaissance, was
not its invention.

In the Middle Ages the choice lay, in principle, only between God and the world, between contempt or eager acceptance, at the peril of one's soul, of all that makes up the
beauty and the charm of earthly life. All terrestrial beauty
bore the stain of sin. Even where art and piety succeeded
in hallowing it by placing it in the service of religion, the
artist or the lover of art had to take care not to surrender to
the charms of colour and line. Now, all noble life was in its
essential manifestations full of such beauty tainted by sin.
Knightly exercises and courteous fashions with their worship of bodily strength; honours and dignities with their
vanity and their pomp, and especially love;—what were
they but pride, envy, avarice and lust, all condemned by
religion! To be admitted as elements of higher culture all
these things had to be ennobled and raised to the rank
of virtue.

It was here that the path of fancy proved its civilizing value. All aristocratic life in the later Middle Ages is a wholesale attempt to act the vision of a dream. In cloaking itself in the fanciful brilliance of the heroism and probity of a past age, the life of the nobles elevated itself towards the sublime. By this trait the Renaissance is linked to the times of feudalism.

The need of high culture found its most direct expression in all that constitutes ceremonial and etiquette. The actions of princes, even daily and common actions, all assume a quasi-symbolic form and tend to raise themselves to the rank of mysteries. Births, marriages, deaths, are framed in an apparatus of solemn and sublime formalities. The emotions which accompany them are dramatized and amplified. Byzantinism is nothing but the expression of the same tendency, and to realize that it survived the Middle Ages, it is sufficient to remember the Roi-Soleil.

The court was pre-eminently the field where this æstheticism flourished. Nowhere did it attain to greater development than at the court of the dukes of Burgundy, which was more pompous and better arranged than that of the kings of France. It is well known how much importance the dukes attached to the magnificence of their household. A splendid court could, better than anything else, convince rivals of the high rank the dukes claimed to occupy among the princes of Europe. "After the deeds and exploits of war, which are claims to glory," says Chastellain, "the household is the first thing that strikes the eye, and which it is, therefore, most necessary to conduct and arrange well." It was boasted that the Burgundian court was the richest and best regulated of all. Charles the Bold, especially, had the passion of magnificence. The archaic and idyllic function of justice administered by the prince in person, even to the humblest of his subjects, was practised by the duke, who was in the habit of sitting in audience with great solemnity two or three times a week, when every one might tender his petition. He would deliver judgment in the presence of all the noblemen of his household, seated on a "hautdos" covered with gold-cloth, and assisted by two "maîtres des requêtes," the warrant-officer and the clerk kneeling before him. The noblemen were a good deal bored, but there was no help for it, says Chastellain, who expresses some doubt as to the use of these audiences. "It seemed to be a magnificent and very praiseworthy thing, whatever fruit it might bear. But I have neither heard nor seen such a thing done in my time by a prince or a king."

For amusements, too, Charles felt the need of solemn and showy forms. "He was in the habit of devoting part of his day to serious occupations, and, with games and laughter mixed, pleased himself with fine speeches and with exhorting his nobles, like an orator, to practise virtue. And in this regard he was often seen sitting in a chair of state, with his nobles before him, remonstrating with them according to time and circumstances. And always, as the prince and chief of all, he was richly and magnificently dressed, more so than all the others."

This "haute magnificence de cœur pour estre vu et regardé en singulières choses," [12] is it not altogether according to the spirit of the Renaissance, in spite of its naïve and somewhat stiff outward appearance?

The meals of the duke were ceremonies of a dignity that was almost liturgic. The descriptions by the master of ceremonies, Olivier de la Marche, are well worth reading. His treatise, *L'Etat de la Maison du duc Charles de Bourgogne*, composed at the request of the king of England, Edward IV, to serve him for a model, expounds the complicated service of breadmasters, carvers, cup-bearers, cooks, and the ordered course of the banquet, which was crowned by all the noblemen filing past the duke, who was still seated at table, "pour lui donner gloire."

The kitchen regulations are truly Pantagruelistic. We may picture them in operation in the kitchen of heroic dimensions, with its seven gigantic chimneys, which can still be seen in the ducal palace of Dijon. The chief cook is seated on a raised chair, overlooking the whole apart-

[12] High magnificence of heart to be seen and regarded in extraordinary things.

ment; "and he must hold in his hand a big wooden ladle which serves him for a double purpose: on the one hand to taste soup and broth, on the other to chase the scullions from the kitchen to their work, and to strike them, if need be."

La Marche speaks of the ceremonies which he describes, in as respectful and quasi-scholastic a tone as if he were treating of sacred mysteries. He submits to his readers grave questions of precedence and of service, and answers them most knowingly.—Why is the chief-cook present at the meals of his lord and not the "écuyer de la cuisine"? How does one proceed to nominate the chief-cook? To which he replies in his wisdom: When the office of chief-cook falls vacant at the court of the prince, the "maîtres d'hôtel" call the "écuyers" and all the kitchen servants to them one by one. Each one solemnly gives his vote, attested by an oath, and in this way the chief-cook is elected. —Who is to take the chief-cook's place in case he is absent: the "spit-master," or the "soup-master"?—Answer: Neither; the substitute will be designated by election.—Why do the "panetiers" and cup-bearers form the first and second ranks, above the carvers and cooks?—Because they are in charge of bread and wine, to which the sanctity of the sacrament gives a holy character.

The extreme importance which attaches to questions of precedence and etiquette can only be explained by the almost religious significance ascribed to them wherever tradition is strong, and where a primitive spirit still prevails. They contain, so to say, a ritualistic element. All forms of etiquette are elaborated so as to constitute a noble game, which, although artificial, has not yet degenerated altogether into a vain parade. Sometimes the polite form takes such an importance that the gravity of the matter in hand is lost sight of.

Before the battle of Crécy, four French knights returned from reconnoitring the English lines. The incident is told by Froissart. Impatient to hear the news they bring, the king rides forward to meet them and stops as soon as he sees them. They force their way through the ranks of the

men-at-arms and reach the king. "What news, my lords?"
asks the king. Then they look at each other without speaking a word, for not one is willing to speak before his companions. And one said to the other: "Lord, do you say it,
speak to the king. I shall not speak before you." So, for a
time they were debating, as none would begin to speak
"par honneur." Till at last the king ordered Sir Monne de
Basele to tell what he knew.

Messire Gaultier Rallart, "chevalier du guet" at Paris,
in 1418, was in the habit of never going his rounds without
being preceded "by three or four musicians playing brass
instruments, which appeared a strange thing to the people,
for they said that it seemed that he said to malefactors:
'Get away, for I am coming.'" This case, reported by the
Burgher of Paris, of a chief of police warning malefactors
of his approach, is not an isolated one. Jean de Roye tells
the same thing of Jean Balue, bishop of Evreux in 1465.
At night he went his rounds, "with clarions, trumpets and
other instruments of music, through the streets and on the
walls, which was not a customary thing to do for men of
the watch."

Even on the scaffold the honours due to rank are strictly
observed. Thus the scaffold mounted by the Constable of
Saint Pol is richly shrouded with black velvet strewn with
fleurs-de-lis; the cloth with which his eyes are bandaged,
the cushion on which he kneels, are of crimson velvet, and
the hangman is a fellow who has never yet executed a
single criminal—rather a doubtful privilege for the noble
victim.

The struggles of politeness, which some forty years ago
were still characteristic of lower-middle-class etiquette,
were extraordinarily developed in the court life of the
fifteenth century. A person of fashion would have considered himself dishonoured by not according to a superior
the place which belonged to him. The dukes of Burgundy
give precedence scrupulously to their royal relations of
France. Jean sans Peur never fails to show exaggerated
respect to his daughter-in-law, the young princess Michelle
of France; he calls her Madame; he bends his knee to the

earth before her and at table always tries to help her, which she will not suffer him to do. When Philip the Good learns that his cousin, the dauphin, in consequence of a quarrel with his father, has removed to Brabant, he at once raises the siege of Deventer, which formed the first step to his very important scheme of conquering Friesland. He travels in hot haste to Brussels, there to receive his royal guest. As the moment of the meeting approaches, there follows a veritable race to be the first in doing homage to the other. At the news that the dauphin is coming to meet him, the old duke is extremely vexed; he sends him "three, four messages, one after the other, to tell him, that if he should ride forward to meet him, he had taken an oath, he would quickly return to where he came from, and would retire before him so quickly and so far, that the other would not find him for a whole year, nor would see him, whatever he did; for, he said, it would mean to him, the duke, ridicule and shame, which would never cease, but be imputed to him throughout the world, to all eternity as a great outrage and a foolish thing; which he was very anxious to avoid." Out of reverence for the blood of France, the duke, although in the territory of the Empire, prohibits his sword to be carried before him, on entering Brussels; before reaching the palace, he hastily alights from his horse, enters the court and passes on quickly on perceiving the king's son, "who has come down from his apartment, holding the duchess by the hand, and rapidly goes to him in the inner court with wide-open arms." At once the old duke bares his head, kneels down for a moment and passes on quickly. The duchess holds the dauphin to prevent his advancing a step, the dauphin vainly seizes the duke to prevent him from kneeling, and makes a fruitless attempt to make him rise. Both cried with emotion, says Chastellain, and so did all the spectators.

In the royal receptions of modern times we undoubtedly find ceremonies bordering on the ludicrous, but we shall look in vain for this passionate anxiety about formalities, which attests that towards the close of the Middle Ages a moral significance still attached to them.

After the young count of Charolais, out of modesty, has
obstinately refused to use the wash-basin before a meal at
the same time with the queen of England, the court talks
the whole day of the incident; the duke, to whom the case
is submitted, charges two noblemen to argue the case on
both sides. Humble refusals to take precedence of another
last upwards of a quarter of an hour; the longer one resists,
the more one is praised. People hide their hands to avoid
the honour of a hand-kiss; the queen of Spain does so on
meeting the young archduke Philippe le Beau; the latter
waits patiently, for a moment of inattentiveness on the part
of the queen, to seize her hand and kiss it. For once Spanish gravity was at fault; the court laughed.

All the trifling amenities of social intercourse are minutely
regulated. Etiquette not only prescribes which ladies of
the court may hold each other by the hand, but also which
lady is entitled to encourage others to this mark of intimacy, by beckoning them. This right of beckoning,
"hucher," is a technical question for the old court lady
Aliénor de Poitiers, who has described the ceremonial of
the court of Burgundy. The departure of a guest is opposed with troublesome insistence. Philip the Good refuses
to let the queen of France go on the day fixed by the
king, in spite of the fear which the poor queen and her
train felt for the anger of Louis XI.

Goethe has said that there is not an outward sign of
politeness which has not a profound moral foundation, and
Emerson expresses almost the same thought when calling
politeness "virtue gone to seed." It would, perhaps, be an
exaggeration to say that at the end of the Middle Ages
people were still fully conscious of the ethical value of
politeness; but surely people still felt its æsthetic value,
which marks the transition of these forms from sincere professions of affection to arid formalities of civility.

It is obvious that this rich adornment of life flourished
nowhere so much as at the court of princes, where people
could devote time to it and had room for it. This same cult
of forms, however, spread downwards from the nobility to
the middle classes, where they lingered on, after having

become obsolete in higher circles. Customs such as that of urging a guest to have another helping of a dish, or to prolong his visit, of refusing to take precedence, now hardly fashionable, were in full bloom in the fifteenth century, scrupulously observed, though at the same time an object of satire.

Above all, public worship offered ample occasion for lengthy displays of civility. In the first place, there is the "offrande"; no one is willing to be the first to place his alms on the altar:

> "Passez.—Non feray.—Or avant!
> Certes si ferez, ma cousine.
> —Non feray.—Huchez no voisine,
> Qu'elle doit mieux devant offrir.
> —Vous ne le devriez souffrir."
> Dist la voisine; "n'appartient
> A moy; offrez, qu'a vous ne tient
> Que li prestres ne se delivre." [13]

When at last the person of highest rank has led the way, the same debate will be repeated in connection with the "pax," a disc of wood, silver or ivory, that was kissed after the *Agnus Dei*. Amid polite refusals to kiss first, the "pax" went from hand to hand among the notabilities, with the result of a prolonged interruption of the service.

> "Respondre doit la juene fame:
> —Prenez, je ne prendray pas, dame.
> —Si ferez, prenez, douce amie.
> —Certes, je ne le prandray mie;
> L'en me tendroit pour une sote.
> —Baillez, damoiselle Marote.
> —Non feray, Jhesucrist m'en gart!
> Portez a ma dame Ermagart.

[13] "Go on—I shall not—Come forward! Certainly, you will do so, cousin—I shall not—Call to our neighbour, That she should offer before you—You should not suffer it," the neighbour says: "it does not belong To me; offer, only for you The priest has to wait."

—Dame, prenez.—Saincte Marie,
Portez la paix a la baillie
—Non, mais a la gouverneresse." [14]

Even a holy man like François de Paule thought it his
duty to take part in these childish observances; the witnesses in the process for his canonization considered this
behaviour a mark of great humility and merit, which shows
that satire can have hardly exaggerated and that the ethical idea of these forms had not completely disappeared.

With all this business of compliments, attending public
worship became almost like dancing a minuet. For on leaving the church similar scenes are enacted, in getting a
superior to walk on the right hand, or to be the first to
cross a plank-bridge or enter a narrow lane. Arrived at
home, the whole company has to be invited to enter and
drink some wine (as Spanish courtesy demands to this
day). The company excuse themselves politely, upon
which it becomes requisite to accompany them part of the
way, in spite of their repeated protestations.

These futile forms become touching, and their moral and
civilizing value is better understood, on remembering they
emanated from the passionate soul of a savage race, struggling to tame its pride and its anger. Quarrels and acts of
violence go hand in hand with the ceremonious abdication
of all pride, of which they are the reverse. Noble families
disputed fiercely for that same precedence in church by
which they courteously pretended to set little store.

Often enough native rudeness pierces through the thin
veneer of politeness. Duke John of Bavaria, the elect of
Liège, is a guest at Paris. At the festivities given in his
honour by the great nobles, he wins all their money from
them in gaming. One of the princes cannot restrain himself

[14] The young woman should answer, Take it, I shall not,
lady—Yes, do, take it, dear friend—I shall certainly not take
it, dear; People would take me for a fool—Pass it, miss
Marote—I shall not, Jesus Christ forbid! Take it to the lady
Ermagart—Lady, take it—Holy Mary, Take the pax to the
bailiff's wife—No, but to the governor's wife.

any longer, and exclaims: "What devil of a priest have we got here?" (It is the chronicler of Liège, Jean de Stavelot, who reports the fact.) "What, is he to win all our money? Whereupon my lord of Liège rose from the table and said angrily: I am not a priest and I do not want your money. And he took it and threw it all about the room, and many marvelled greatly at his liberality."

The magnificent order maintained at the court of Burgundy, praised by Christine de Pisan, by Chastellain, and by the Bohemian nobleman Leon of Rozmital, acquires its full significance only when compared with the disorder which reigned at the court of France, Burgundy's older and more illustrious model. In a number of his ballads Eustache Deschamps complains of the misery at court, and these complaints are not merely variations on the familiar theme of disparagement of court life. Bad fare and poor lodgings; continual noise and disorder; swearing and quarrels; jealousies and injuries; in short, the court is an abyss of sins, the gate of hell.

Neither the sacred respect for royalty, nor the almost sacramental value attaching to ceremonies, could prevent decorum from being occasionally ignominiously thrust aside on the most solemn occasions. At the coronation banquet of Charles VI, in 1380, the duke of Burgundy seeks, by force, to take the place to which he is entitled, as doyen of the peers, between the king and the duke of Anjou. Already the train of the duke begins to thrust aside their opponents; threatening cries arise, a scuffle is breaking out when the king prevents it, by doing justice to the claims of the duke of Burgundy.

Even the infractions of solemn forms tended to become forms themselves. It seems that it was more or less a custom for the funeral of a king of France to be interrupted by a quarrel, of which the object was the possession of the utensils of the ceremony. In 1422 the corporation of the "henouars," or salt-weighers, of Paris, whose privilege it was to carry the king's corpse to Saint-Denis, came to blows with the monks of the abbey, as both parties claimed the pall covering the bier of Charles VI.

An analogous case occurred in 1461, at the funeral of
Charles VII. In consequence of an altercation with the
monks, the "henouars" put down the coffin when they have
come halfway and refuse to carry it any further, unless
they are paid ten pounds Paris. The Lord Grand Master of
the Horse quiets them by promising to pay them out of his
own pocket, but the delay had been so long that the cortège arrives at Saint-Denis only towards eight at night.
After the interment, a new conflict arises with regard to
the pall of gold-cloth, between the monks and the Grand
Master of the Horse himself.

The great publicity which it was customary to give to all
important events in the life of a king, and which survived to
the times of Louis XIV, sometimes led to a pitiable break-
down of discipline on the most solemn occasions. At the
coronation banquet of 1380, the throng of spectators, guests
and servants was such that the constable and the marshal of
Sancerre had to serve up the dishes on horseback. At the
coronation of Henry VI of England at Paris, in 1431, the
people force their way at daybreak into the great hall
where the feast was to take place, "some to look on, others
to regale themselves, others to pilfer or to steal victuals or
other things." The members of the Parlement and of the
University, the provost of the merchants and the aldermen,
after having succeeded with great difficulty in entering the
hall, find the tables assigned to them occupied by all sorts
of artisans. An attempt is made to remove them, "but when
they had succeeded in driving away one or two, six or
eight sat down on the other side." At the inauguration of
Louis XI, in 1461, the precaution had been taken of closing
the doors of the cathedral of Reims early and placing a
guard there, so that not more persons should enter the
church than the choir could hold. Nevertheless, the spectators so pressed round the altar where the king was
anointed, that the prelates assisting the archbishop could
scarcely move, and the princes of the blood were nearly
squeezed to death in their seats of honour.

The passionate and violent soul of the age, always vacillating between tearful piety and frigid cruelty, between respect and insolence, between despondency and wantonness, could not dispense with the severest rules and the strictest formalism. All emotions required a rigid system of conventional forms, for without them passion and ferocity would have made havoc of life. By this sublimating faculty each event became a spectacle for others; mirth and sorrow were artificially and theatrically made up. For want of the faculty to express emotions in a simple and natural way, recourse must needs be had to æsthetic representations of sorrow and of joy.

The ceremonies accompanying birth, marriage and death fully assumed this character of spectacles. Æsthetic values have here taken the place of their old religious (pagan for the most part) or magic signification.

Nowhere does the formalizing of the emotions assume a more suggestive appearance than in the sphere of mourning rites. There is a tendency in primitive times to exaggerate the expression of grief, like that of joy. Pompous mourning is the counterpart of immoderate rejoicings and of insane luxury. At the death of Jean sans Peur the mourning is organized with incomparable magnificence, in which there was, no doubt, also a political by-purpose. The retinue escorting Philip of Burgundy, who went out to meet the kings of France and of England, carry two thousand black vanes, to say nothing of the standards and banners seven yards long, of the same colour. The carriage of the duke and also the state seats have been painted black for the occasion. At the meeting of Troyes, Philip wears a mantle of black velvet which is so long as to hang down from his horse to the ground. For a long time afterwards he and his court only show themselves dressed in black.

Amidst the general black of court mourning the red worn only by the king of France (not even by the queen) must have made a most startling contrast. In 1393 the Parisians had the surprise of a pompous funeral all in white: that of the king of Armenia, Léon de Lusignan, who died in exile.

The manifestations of sorrow at the death of a prince, if at times purposely exaggerated, undoubtedly often enfolded a deep and unfeigned grief. The general instability of the soul, the extreme horror of death, the fervour of family attachment and loyalty, all contributed to make the decease of a king or a prince an afflicting event. A savage exuberance of grief breaks out when the news is brought to Ghent of the murder of Jean sans Peur. All chronicles confirm it; Chastellain is diffuse on the subject. His heavy and trailing style is wonderfully well adapted for reporting the long harangue of the bishop of Tournay to prepare the young duke for the awful tidings, as well as for the majestic lamentations of Philip and of Michelle of France, his consort. Half a century later we see Charles the Bold, at the death-bed of his father, weeping, crying out, wringing his hands, falling on the ground, "so as to make every one wonder at his unmeasured grief."

Whatever may be the share of the court style in these narratives, what they tell us fits in too well with the overstrung sensibility of the epoch, and at the same time with the craving for clamorous mourning as an edifying thing, not to be substantially true. Primitive custom demanding that the dead should be publicly and loudly lamented still survived in considerable strength in the fifteenth century. Noisy manifestations of sorrow were thought fine and becoming, and all things connected with a deceased person had to bear witness to unmeasured grief.

The extreme fear of announcing a death likewise bears testimony to the same intermingling of primitive ritual and passionate emotionalism. The death of her father is kept a secret from the countess of Charolais, who is pregnant. During an illness of Philip the Good, the court does not dare to announce to him a single death touching him at all nearly; Adolphus of Cleves is forbidden to go into mourning for his wife, out of consideration for the duke, who is ill. The chancellor Nicolas Rolin dies: the duke is left in ignorance of his decease. Yet he begins to suspect it and asks the bishop of Tournay, who has come to visit him, to tell him the truth. "My liege, says the bishop—in sooth, he is dead, indeed, for he is old and broken, and cannot live long.— Déa! says the duke, I do not ask that. I ask if he is truly dead and gone.—Hà! my liege—the bishop retorts, he is not dead, but paralysed on one side, and therefore practically dead.—The duke grows angry.—Vechy merveilles! Tell me clearly, now, whether he is dead. Only then says the bishop: Yes, truly, my liege, he is really dead."

Does not this curious way of announcing a death suggest some trace of ancient superstition, more even than the wish to spare a sick man? The anxiety to exclude systematically the thought of death denotes a state of mind analogous to that of Louis XI, who would never again wear the dress he had on, nor use the horse he was riding at the moment when evil tidings were announced to him, and who even had a part of the forest of Loches cut down where the tidings of the death of a new-born son were brought to him. "Monsieur the Chancellor," the king writes on May 25, 1483, "I thank you for the letters etc., but I beg you to send me no more by him who brought them, for I found his face terribly changed since I last saw him, and I tell you on my word that he made me much afraid, and farewell."

The cultural value of mourning is that it gives grief its form and rhythm. It transfers actual life to the sphere of the drama. It shoes it with the cothurnus. Mourning at the court of France or of Burgundy, at the time with which we are concerned, has to be regarded as a sort of acted elegy. Funeral ceremonial and funeral poetry, which in primitive civilizations are still undistinguished (in Ireland, for instance), had not yet been completely separated. Mourning still continued a remnant of its poetical functions. It dramatized the effects of grief.

The nobler the deceased and the survivors are, the more heroic the mourning. For a whole year the queen of France may not leave the room in which the death of her consort was announced to her. For the princesses the seclusion lasts six weeks. During all the time that Madame de Charolais is in mourning for her father, she remains in bed, propped up by cushions and dressed in bands, coif and mantle. The rooms are upholstered in black; the floor is covered with a large black cloth. Aliénor de Poitiers has described for us all the gradations of the ceremonial, varying according to rank.

Under this fine outward show the feelings which are thus exhibited and formalized often tend to disappear. The pathetic posture belies itself behind the scenes. "State" and real life are clearly and naïvely distinguished. Aliénor, having described the sumptuous mourning of the countess of Charolais, adds: "When Madame was 'en son particulier' she by no means always lay in bed, nor confined herself to one room."

Next to mourning, the lying-in chamber affords ample opportunity for fine ceremonial and differentiation according to rank. The colours and materials of coverings and clothes all have a meaning. Green is the privilege of queens and of princesses, whereas it was white in preceding ages. "La chambre verde" was forbidden even to countesses. During the lying-in of Isabelle de Bourbon, mother of Mary of Burgundy, five large state beds, all draped with an artful fabric of green curtain, remain empty, like state coaches at funerals, only to serve for ceremonious use at the baptism, while the mother reposes on a low couch near the fire. The blinds are kept closed all the time, and the room is lighted by candles.

Through all the ranks of society a severe hierarchy of material and colour kept classes apart, and gave to each estate or rank an outward distinction, which preserved and exalted the feeling of dignity.

Moreover, outside the sphere of birth, marriage and death, a strongly felt æsthetic need tends to create a solemn and decorous form for every event and every notable deed. A sinner who humbles himself, a condemned prisoner who repents, a holy person sacrificing himself, all afford a kind of public spectacle. Public life in this way almost presents the appearance of a perpetual "morale en action."

Even intimate relations in medieval society are rather paraded than kept secret. Not only love, but friendship too, has its finely made up forms. Two friends dress in the same way, share the same room, or the same bed, and call one another by the name of "mignon." It is good form for the prince to have his minion. We must not let the well-known case of Henry III of France affect for us the ordinary acceptance of the word "mignon" in the fifteenth century. There have been princes and favourites in the Middle Ages too who were accused of culpable relations—Richard II of England and Robert de Vere, for instance—but minions would not have been spoken of so freely, if we had to regard this institution as connoting anything but sentimental friendship. It was a distinction of which the friends boasted in public. On the occasion of solemn receptions the prince leans on the shoulder of the minion, as Charles V at his abdication leaned on William of Orange. To understand the duke's sentiment towards Cesario in *Twelfth Night,* we must recall this form of sentimental friendship, which maintained itself as a formal institution till the days of James I and George Villiers.

The complex of all these fine forms, veiling cruel reality under apparent harmony, made life an art. This art leaves no traces, and it is for this reason that its cultural importance has been noticed too little. The tenderness of compliments, the charming fiction of modesty and altruism, the hieratic pomp of ceremonies, the pageant of marriage, all this is ephemeral and may seem culturally sterile. That which gives them their style and expression is fashion, not art, and fashion leaves no monuments behind.

And yet, at the close of the Middle Ages, the connections between art and fashion were closer than at present. Art had not yet fled to transcendental heights; it formed an integral part of social life. In the domain of costume art and fashion were still inextricably blended, style in dress stood nearer to artistic style than later, and the function of costume in social life, that of accentuating the strict order of society itself, almost partook of the liturgic. The amazing extravagance of dress during the last centuries of the Middle Ages was, as it were, the expression of an overflowing æsthetic craving, which art alone did not suffice to satisfy.

All relations, all dignities, all actions, all sentiments, had found their style. The higher the moral value of a social function, the nearer its form of expression approached to pure art. Whereas ceremony and courtesy have no other expression than conversation and luxury, and pass away without visible residue, the rites of mourning do not exhaust themselves in funeral pomp and fictions of etiquette, but leave a durable and artistic expression in the sepulchral monument. As in the case of marriage and baptism, the link of mourning with religion heightens its cultural value.

Still, the richest flower of beautiful forms was reserved for three other elements of life—courage, honour and love.

Chapter III

THE HIERARCHIC CONCEPTION OF SOCIETY

When, somewhat more than a hundred years ago, medieval history began to assert itself as an object of interest and admiration, the first element of it to draw general attention and to become a source of enthusiasm and inspiration was chivalry. To the epoch of romanticism the Middle Ages and Chivalry were almost synonymous terms. Historical imagination dwelt by preference on crusades, tournaments, knights-errant. Since then history has become democratic. Chivalry is now only seen as a very special efflorescence of civilization, which, far from having controlled the course of medieval history, has been rather a secondary factor in the political and social evolution of the epoch. For us the problems of the Middle Ages lie first of all in the development of communal organization, of economic conditions, of monarchic power, of administrative and judicial institutions; and, in the second place, in the domain of religion, scholasticism and art. Towards the end of the period our attention is almost entirely occupied by the genesis of new forms of political and economic life (absolutism, capitalism), and new modes of expression (Renaissance). From this point of view feudalism and chivalry appear as little more than a remnant of a superannuated order already crumbling into insignificance, and, for the understanding of the epoch, almost negligible.

Nevertheless, an assiduous reader of the chronicles and literature of the fifteenth century will hardly resist the impression that nobility and chivalry occupy a much more considerable place there than our general conception of the epoch would imply. The reason of this disproportion lies in the fact, that long after nobility and feudalism had ceased to be really essential factors in the state and in society, they continued to impress the mind as dominant forms of life. The men of the fifteenth century could not understand that the real moving powers of political and social evolution might be looked for anywhere else than in the doings of a warlike or courtly nobility. They persisted in regarding the nobility as the foremost of social forces and attributed a very exaggerated importance to it, undervaluing altogether the social significance of the lower classes.

So the mistake, it may be argued, is theirs, and our conception of the Middle Ages is right. This would be so if, to understand the spirit of an age, it sufficed to know its real and hidden forces and not its illusions, its fancies and its errors. But for the history of civilization every delusion or opinion of an epoch has the value of an important fact. In the fifteenth century chivalry was still, after religion, the strongest of all the ethical conceptions which dominated the mind and the heart. It was thought of as the crown of the whole social system. Medieval political speculation is imbued to the marrow with the idea of a structure of society based upon distinct orders. This notion of "orders" is itself by no means fixed. The words "estate" and "order," almost synonymous, designate a great variety of social realities. The idea of an "estate" is not at all limited to that of a class; it extends to every social function, to every profession, to every group. Side by side with the French system of the three estates of the realm, which in England, according to Professor Pollard, was only secondarily and theoretically adopted after the French model, we find traces of a system of twelve social estates. The functions or groupings, which the Middle Ages designated by the words "estate" and "order," are of very diverse natures. There are, first of all, the estates of the realm, but there are also the trades, the state of matrimony and that of virginity, the state of sin. At court there are the "four estates of body and mouth": bread-masters, cup-bearers, carvers, and cooks. In the Church there are sacerdotal orders and monastic orders. Finally, there are the different orders of chivalry. That which, in medieval thought, establishes unity in the very dissimilar meanings of the word, is the conviction that every one of these groupings represents a divine institution, an element of the organism of Creation emanating from the will of God, constituting an actual entity, and being, at bottom, as venerable as the angelic hierarchy.

Now, if the degrees of the social edifice are conceived as the lower steps of the throne of the Eternal, the value assigned to each order will not depend on its utility, but on its sanctity—that is to say, its proximity to the highest place. Even if the Middle Ages had recognized the diminishing importance of the nobility as a limb of the social body, that would not have changed the conception they had of its high value, no more than the spectacle of a violent and dissipated nobility ever hindered the veneration of the order in itself. To the catholic soul the unworthiness of the persons never compromises the sacred character of the institution. The morals of the clergy, or the decadence of chivalrous virtues, might be stigmatized, without deviating for a moment from the respect due to the Church or the nobility as such. The estates of society cannot but be venerable and lasting, because they all have been ordained by God. The conception of society in the Middle Ages is statical, not dynamical.

The aspect which society and politics assume under the influence of these general ideas is bound to be a strange one. The chroniclers of the fifteenth century have, nearly all, been the dupes of an absolute misappreciation of their times, of which the real moving forces escaped their attention. Chastellain, the historiographer of the dukes of Burgundy, may serve as an instance. A Fleming by birth, he had been face to face, in the Netherlands, with the power and the wealth of the commoners, nowhere stronger and more self-conscious than there. The extraordinary fortune of the Burgundian branch of Valois transplanted to Flanders was in reality based on the wealth of the Flemish and Brabant towns. Nevertheless, dazzled by the splendour and magnificence of an extravagant court, Chastellain imagined that the power of the house of Burgundy was especially due to the heroism and the devotion of knighthood.

God, he says, created the common people to till the earth and to procure by trade the commodities necessary for life; he created the clergy for the works of religion; the nobles that they should cultivate virtue and maintain justice, so that the deeds and the morals of these fine personages might be a pattern to others. All the highest tasks in the state are assigned by Chastellain to the nobility; notably those of protecting the Church, augmenting the faith, defending the people from oppression, maintaining public prosperity, combating violence and tyranny, confirming peace. Veracity, courage, integrity, liberality, appertain properly to the noble class, and French nobility, according to this pompous panegyrist, comes up to this ideal image. In spite of his general pessimism, Chastellain does his best to see his times through the tinted glasses of this aristocratic conception.

This failing to see the social importance of the common people, which is proper to nearly all authors of the fifteenth century, may be regarded as a kind of mental inertia, which is a phenomenon of frequent occurrence and vital importance in history. The idea which people had of the third estate had not yet been corrected and remodelled in accordance with altered realities. This idea was simple and summary, like those miniatures of breviaries, or those bas-reliefs of cathedrals, representing the tasks of the year in the shape of the toiling labourer, the industrious artisan, or the busy merchant. Among archaic types like these there is neither place for the figure of the wealthy patrician encroaching upon the power of the nobleman, nor for that of the militant representative of a revolutionary craft-guild. Nobody perceived that the nobility only maintained itself, thanks to the blood and the riches of the commoners. No distinction in principle was made, in the third estate, between rich and poor citizens, nor between townsmen and country-people. The figure of the poor peasant alternates indiscriminately with that of the wealthy burgher, but a sound definition of the economic and political functions of these different classes does not take shape. In 1412 the reform programme of an Augustinian friar demanded in all earnest that every non-noble person in France should either devote himself to some handicraft or to labour, or be banished from the kingdom, evidently considering commerce and law as useless occupations.

Chastellain, who is very naïve in political matters and very susceptible to ethical delusions, attributes sublime virtues only to the nobility, and only inferior ones to the common people. "Coming to the third estate, making up the kingdom as a whole, it is the estate of the good towns, of merchants and of labouring men, of whom it is not becoming to give such a long exposition as of the others, because it is hardly possible to attribute great qualities to them, as they are of a servile degree." Humility, diligence, obedience to the king, and docility in bowing "voluntarily to the pleasure of the lords," those are the qualities which bring credit to "cestuy bas estat de François." [1]

May not this strange infatuation, by preventing them from foreseeing future times of economic expansion have contributed to engender pessimism in minds such as that of Chastellain, who could only expect the good of mankind from the virtues of the nobility?

Chastellain still calls the rich burghers simply villeins. He has not the slightest notion of middle-class honour. Duke Philip the Good was wont to abuse his power by marrying his archers or other servants of lesser gentility to rich burgher widows or heiresses. To avoid those alliances, the

[1] This low estate of Frenchmen.

parents on their side married their daughters as soon as
they reached marriageable age. Jacques du Clercq mentions the case of a widow, who for this reason remarried
two days after the burial of her husband. Once the duke,
while engaged in such marriage-broking, met with an obstinate refusal from a rich brewer of Lille, who felt affronted
at such an alliance for his daughter. The duke secured the
person of the young girl; the father removed with all his
possessions to Tournay, outside the ducal jurisdiction, in
order to be able to bring the matter before the Parlement
of Paris. This brought him nothing but vexation, and he fell
ill with grief. At last he sent his wife to Lille "in order to
beg mercy of the duke and give up his daughter to him."
The latter, in honour of Good Friday, gave her back to
the mother, but with scornful and humiliating words.—
Chastellain's sympathies are all on the side of his master,
though, on other occasions, he did not at all fear to record
his disapproval of the duke's conduct. For the injured
father he has no other terms than "this rebellious rustic
brewer," "and such a naughty villein too."

There are in the sentiments of the aristocratic class towards the people two parallel currents. Side by side with
this haughty disdain of the small man, already a little out
of date, we notice a sympathetic attitude in the nobility,
which seems in absolute contrast with it. Whereas feudal
satire goes on expressing hatred mixed with contempt and
sometimes with fear, as in the *Proverbes del Vilain* and in
the *Kerelslied*, the song of the Flemish villagers, the code
of aristocratic ethics teaches, on the other hand, a sentimental compassion for the miseries of the oppressed and
defenceless people. Despoiled by war, exploited by the
officials, the people live in the greatest distress.

> "Si fault de faim perir les innocens
> Dont les grans loups font chacun jour ventrée,
> Qui amassent à milliers et à cens
> Les faulx trésors; c'est le grain, c'est le blée,
> Le sang, les os qui ont la terre arée

Des povres gens, dont leur esperit crie
Vengence à Dieu, vé à la seignourie." [2]

They suffer in patience. "The prince knows nothing of
this." If, at times, they murmur, "poor sheep, poor foolish
people," a word from the prince will suffice to appease
them. The devastation and insecurity which in consequence
of the Hundred Years' War had finally spread over almost
all France, gave these laments a sad actuality. From the
year 1400 downwards there is no end to the complaints
about the fate of the peasants, plundered, squeezed, mal-
treated by gangs of enemies or friends, robbed of their
cattle, driven from their homes. They are expressed by the
great Churchmen who favoured reform, such as Nicolas de
Clemanges, in his *Liber de lapsu et reparatione justitiæ,*
or Gerson in his political sermon *Vivat rex,* preached on
November 7, 1405, in the queen's palace at Paris, before
the regents and the court. "The poor man"—said the brave
chancellor—"will not have bread to eat, except perhaps a
handful of rye or barley; his poor wife will lie in and they
will have four or six little ones about the hearth or the
oven, which perchance will be warm; they will ask for
bread, they will scream, mad with hunger. The poor
mother will but have a very little salted bread to put
into their mouths. Now such misery ought to suffice; but
no:—the plunderers will come, who will seek everything.
. . . Everything will be taken and snapped up; and we
need not ask who pays."

Statesmen, too, make themselves the spokesmen of the
miserable people, and utter their complaints. Jean Jouvenel
laid them before the States of Blois in 1433, and those of
Orléans in 1439. In a petition presented to the king at the
meeting of the States of Tours in 1484, these complaints
take the direct form of a political "remonstrance."

[2] The innocents must starve With which the big wolves
fill their belly every day, Who by thousands and hundreds
hoard Ill-gotten treasures; it is the grain, it is the corn, The
blood, the bones of poor people, which have ploughed the
earth And therefore their souls call Upon God for vengeance and woe to lordship.

The chroniclers could not help reverting to the subject again and again: it was bound up with their subject-matter.

The poets in their turn took hold of the motif. Alain Chartier treats it in his *Quadriloge Invectif*, and Robert Gaguin in his *Debat du Laboureur, du Prestre et du Gendarme,* inspired by Chartier. A hundred years after *La Complainte du povre Commun et des povres Laboureurs de France* of about 1400, Jean Molinet was to compose a *Resource du petit Peuple*. Jean Meschinot never tires of reminding the ruling classes of the fact that the common people are being neglected.

> "O Dieu, voyez du commun l'indigence,
> Pourvoyez-y à toute diligence:
> Las! par faim, froid, paour et misere tremble.
> S'il a peché ou commis negligence
> Encontre vous, il demande indulgence.
> N'est-ce pitié des biens que l'on lui emble?
> Il n'a plus bled pour porter au molin,
> On lui oste draps de laine et de lin,
> L'eaue, sans plus, lui demeure pour boire." [3]

This pity, however, remains sterile. It does not result in acts, not even in programmes, of reform. The felt need of serious reform is wanting to it and will be wanting for a long time. In La Bruyère, in Fénelon, perhaps in the elder Mirabeau, the theme is still the same; even they have not yet got beyond theoretical and stereotyped commiseration.

It is natural that the belated chivalrous spirits of the fifteenth century join in this chorus of pity for the people. Was it not the knight's duty to protect the weak? The ideal of chivalry implied, after all, two ideas which might seem to concur in forbidding a haughty contempt for the small

[3] O God, see the indigence of the common people, Provide for it with all speed: Alas! with hunger, cold, fear and misery they tremble, If they have sinned or are guilty of negligence Toward Thee, they beg indulgence. Is it not a pity that they are bereft of their goods? They have no more corn to take to the mill, Woollen and linen goods are taken from them, Only water is left to them to drink.

man; the ideas, namely, that true nobility is based on virtue,
and that all men are equal.

We should be careful not to overrate the importance of
these two ideas. They were equally stereotyped and theoretical. To acknowledge true chivalry a matter of the
heart should not be considered a victory over the spirit of
feudalism or an achievement of the Renaissance. This medieval notion of equality is by no means a manifestation of
the spirit of revolt. It does not owe its origin to radical
reformers. In quoting the text of John Ball, who preached
the revolt of 1381, "When Adam delved and Eve span, who
was then the gentleman?" one is inclined to fancy that the
nobles must have trembled on hearing it. But, in fact, it
was the nobility themselves who for a long time had been
repeating this ancient theme.

The two ideas of the equality of men and of the nature
of true nobility were commonplaces of courteous literature,
just as they were in the salons of the "ancien régime." Both
derived from antiquity. The poetry of the troubadours had
sung and popularized them. Every one applauded them.

"Dont vient a tous souveraine noblesse?
Du gentil cuer, paré de nobles mours.
. . . Nulz n'est villains se du cuer ne lui muet."[4]

The notion of equality had been borrowed by the Fathers of the Church from Cicero and Seneca. Gregory the
Great, the great initiator of the Middle Ages, had given a
text for coming ages in his *Omnes namque homines natura
aequales sumus.* It had been repeated in all keys, but an
actual social purport was not attached to it. It was a moral
sentence, nothing more; to the men of the Middle Ages it
meant the approaching equality of death, and was far from
holding out, as a consolation for the iniquities of this world,
a deceptive prospect of equality on earth. The thought of
equality in the Middle Ages is closely akin to a *memento*

[4] Whence comes to all sovereign nobility? From a gentle
heart, adorned by noble morals. . . . No one is a villein
unless it comes from his heart.

mori. Thus we find it in a ballad by Eustache Deschamps, where Adam addresses his posterity:

"Enfans, enfans, de moy, Adam, venuz,
Qui après Dieu suis peres premerain
Créé de lui, tous estes descenduz
Naturelment de ma coste et d'Evain;
Vo mere fut. Comment est l'un villain
Et l'autre prant le nom de gentillesce
De vous, freres? dont vient tele noblesce?
Je ne le sçay, se ce n'est des vertus,
Et les villains de tout vice qui blesce:
Vous estes tous d'une pel revestuz.

"Quant Dieu me fist de la boe ou je fus,
Homme mortel, faible, pesant et vain,
Eve de moy, il nous crea tous nuz,
Mais l'esperit nous inspira a plain
Perpetuel puis eusmes soif et faim,
Labour, dolour, et enfans en tristesce;
Pour noz pechiez enfantent a destresce
Toutes femmes; vilment estes conçuz.
Vous estes tous d'une pel revestuz.

"Les roys puissans, les contes et les dus,
Le gouverneur du peuple et souverain,
Quant ilz naissent, de quoy sont ilz vestuz?
D'une orde pel.
. . . Prince, pensez, sans avoir en desdain
Les povres gens, que la mort tient le frain." [5]

[5] Children, descended from me, Adam, Who am the first father, after God, Created by him, you are all born Naturally of my rib and of Eve; She was your mother. How is it that one is a villein And the other assumes the name of gentility, Of you, brothers? Whence comes such nobility? I do not know, unless it springs from virtues And the villeins from all vice, which wounds: You are all covered by the same skin.

When God made me out of the mud where I lay, A mortal man, feeble, heavy and vain, Eve out of me, he

Jean le Maire de Belges, in *Les Chansons de Namur*, purposely mentions the exploits of rustic heroes, to acquaint the nobles with the fact that those whom they treat as villeins are sometimes animated by the greatest gallantry. For the reason of these poetical admonitions on the subject of true nobility and human equality generally lies in the stimulus they impart to the nobles to adapt themselves to the true ideal of knighthood, and thereby to support and to purify the world. In the virtues of the nobles, says Chastellain, lies the remedy for the evils of the time; the weal of the kingdom, the peace of the Church, the rule of justice, depend on them.—"Two things," it is said in *Le Livre des Faicts du Mareschal Boucicaut*, "have, by the will of God, been established in the world, like two pillars to sustain the order of divine and human laws . . . and without which the world would be like a confused thing and without any order . . . these two flawless pillars are Chivalry and Learning, which go very well together." "Learning, Faith and Chivalry" are the three flowers of the *Chapel des Fleurs-de-lis* of Philippe de Vitri; it is the duty of knighthood to preserve and protect the two others.

Long after the Middle Ages a certain equivalence of knighthood and a doctor's degree was generally acknowledged. This parallelism indicates the high ethical value attaching to the idea of chivalry. The two dignities of a knight and of a doctor are conceived as the sacred forms of two superior functions, that of courage and of knowledge. By being knighted the man of action is raised to an ideal level;

created us quite nude, But the spirit fully inspired us, Afterwards we were perpetually thirsty and hungry, We laboured, suffered, children were born in sorrow; For our sins, all women bear children In pain; vilely you are conceived. Whence then comes this name: villein that wounds the hearts? You are all covered by the same skin.
The mighty kings, the counts and the dukes, The governor of the people and sovereign, When they are born, with what are they clothed? By a dirty skin. . . . Prince, remember, without disdaining The poor people, that death holds the reins.

by taking his doctor's degree the man of knowledge receives a badge of superiority. They are stamped, the one as a hero, the other as a sage. The devotion to a higher life-work is expressed by a ceremonial consecration. If as an element of social life the idea of chivalry has been of much greater importance, it was because it contained, besides its ethical value, an abundance of æsthetic value of the most suggestive kind.

Chapter IV

THE IDEA OF CHIVALRY

Medieval thought in general was saturated in every part with the conceptions of the Christian faith. In a similar way and in a more limited sphere the thought of all those who lived in the circles of court or castle was impregnated with the idea of chivalry. Their whole system of ideas was permeated by the fiction that chivalry ruled the world. This conception even tends to invade the transcendental domain. The primordial feat of arms of the archangel Michael is glorified by Jean Molinet as "the first deed of knighthood and chivalrous prowess that was ever achieved." From the archangel "terrestrial knighthood and human chivalry" take their origin, and in so far are but an imitation of the host of the angels around God's throne.

This illusion of society based on chivalry curiously clashed with the reality of things. The chroniclers themselves, in describing the history of their time, tell us far more of covetousness, of cruelty, of cool calculation, of well-understood self-interest, and of diplomatic subtlety, than of chivalry. None the less, all, as a rule, profess to write in honour of chivalry, which is the stay of the world. Froissart, Monstrelet, d'Escouchy, Chastellain, La Marche,

Molinet, all, with the exception only of Philippe de Commines and Thomas Basin, open their works by high-sounding declarations of their purpose of glorifying knightly bravery and virtues, of recording "noble enterprises, conquests, feats of heroism and of arms," "the great marvels and the fine feats of arms that have come to pass because of the great wars." History, to them, is illumined throughout by this their ideal. Later, when writing, they forget it more or less. Froissart, himself the author of a superromantic epic of chivalry, *Méliador,* narrates endless treasons and cruelties, without being aware of the contradiction between his general conceptions and the contents of his narrative. Molinet, in his chronicle, from time to time remembers his chivalrous intention, and interrupts his matter-of-fact account of events, to unbosom himself in a flood of high-flown terms.

The conception of chivalry constituted for these authors a sort of magic key, by the aid of which they explained to themselves the motives of politics and of history. The confused image of contemporaneous history being much too complicated for their comprehension, they simplified it, as it were, by the fiction of chivalry as a moving force (not consciously, of course). A very fantastic and rather shallow point of view, no doubt. How much vaster is ours, embracing all sorts of economic and social forces and causes. Still, this vision of a world ruled by chivalry, however superficial and mistaken it might be, was the best they had in the matter of general political ideas. It served them as a formula to understand, in their poor way, the appalling complexity of the world's way. What they saw about them looked primarily mere violence and confusion. War in the fifteenth century tended to be a chronic process of isolated raids and incursions; diplomacy was mostly a very solemn and very verbose procedure, in which a multitude of questions about juridical details clashed with some very general traditions and some points of honour. All notions which might have enabled them to discern in history a social development were lacking to them. Yet they required a form for their political conceptions, and here the idea of chivalry came in. By this traditional fiction they succeeded in explaining to themselves, as well as they could, the motives and the course of history, which thus was reduced to a spectacle of the honour of princes and the virtue of knights, to a noble game with edifying and heroic rules.

As a principle of historiography, this point of view is a very inferior one. History thus conceived becomes a summary of feats of arms and of ceremonies. The historians *par excellence* will be heralds and kings-at-arms—Froissart thinks so—for they are the witnesses of these sublime deeds; they are experts in matters of honour and of glory, and it is to record honour and glory that history is written. The statutes of the Golden Fleece enjoined that the feats of arms of the knights be noted down. Types of this combination of herald and historiographer are the king-at-arms of the Golden Fleece, Lefèvre de Saint Remy, and Gilles le Bouvier, dit le héraut Berry.

The conception of chivalry as a sublime form of secular life might be defined as an æsthetic ideal assuming the appearance of an ethical ideal. Heroic fancy and romantic sentiment form its basis. But medieval thought did not permit ideal forms of noble life, independent of religion. For this reason piety and virtue have to be the essence of a knight's life. Chivalry, however, will always fall short of this ethical function. Its earthly origin draws it down. For the source of the chivalrous idea is pride aspiring to beauty, and formalized pride gives rise to a conception of honour, which is the pole of noble life. The sentiment of honour, says Burckhardt, this strange mixture of conscience and of egotism, "is compatible with many vices and susceptible to extravagant delusions; nevertheless, all that has remained pure and noble in man may find support in it and draw new strength from it." Is not this almost what Chastellain tried to say, when he expressed himself thus:

"Honneur semont toute noble nature

D'aimer tout ce qui noble est en son estre.
Noblesse aussi y adjoint sa droiture." [1]

And again:

"La gloire des princes pend en orgueil et en haut peril
emprendre; toutes principales puissances conviengnent en
un point estroit qui se dit orgueil." [2]

According to the celebrated Swiss historian, the quest
of personal glory was the characteristic attribute of the
men of the Renaissance. The Middle Ages proper, according to him, knew honour and glory only in collective
forms, as the honour due to groups and orders of society,
the honour of rank, of class, or of profession. It was in Italy,
he thinks, under the influence of antique models, that the
craving for individual glory originated. Here, as elsewhere, Burckhardt has exaggerated the distance separating Italy from the Western countries and the Renaissance
from the Middle Ages.

The thirst for honour and glory proper to the men of the
Renaissance is essentially the same as the chivalrous ambition of earlier times, and of French origin. Only it has
shaken off the feudal form and assumed an antique garb.
The passionate desire to find himself praised by contemporaries or by posterity was the source of virtue with the
courtly knight of the twelfth century and the rude captain
of the fourteenth, no less than with the beaux-esprits of the
quattrocento. When Beaumanoir and Bamborough fix the
conditions of the famous combat of the Thirty, the English
captain, according to Froissart, expresses himself in these
terms: "And let us right there try ourselves and do so much
that people will speak of it in future times in halls, in
palaces, in public places and elsewhere throughout the

[1] Honour urges every noble nature To love all that is
noble in being. Nobility also adds its uprightness to it.
[2] The glory of princes is in their pride and in undertaking great peril; all principal forces meet in a small point,
which is called pride.

world." The saying may not be authentic, but it teaches us what Froissart thought.

The quest of glory and of honour goes hand in hand with a hero-worship which also might seem to announce the Renaissance. The somewhat factitious revival of the splendour of chivalry that we find everywhere in European courts after 1300 is already connected with the Renaissance by a real link. It is a naïve prelude to it. In reviving chivalry the poets and princes imagined that they were returning to antiquity. In the minds of the fourteenth century, a vision of antiquity had hardly yet disengaged itself from the fairy-land sphere of the Round Table. Classical heroes were still tinged with the general colour of romance. On the one hand, the figure of Alexander had long ago entered the sphere of chivalry; on the other, chivalry was supposed to be of Roman origin. "And he maintained the discipline of chivalry well, as did the Romans formerly," thus a Burgundian chronicler praised Henry V of England. The blazons of Cæsar, of Hercules, and of Troilus, are placed in a fantasy of King René, side by side with those of Arthur and of Lancelot. Certain coincidences of terminology played a part in tracing back the origin of chivalry to Roman antiquity. How could people have known that the word *miles* with Roman authors did not mean a *miles* in the sense of medieval Latin, that is to say, a knight, or that a Roman *eques* differed from a feudal knight? Consequently, Romulus, because he raised a band of a thousand mounted warriors, was taken to be the founder of chivalry.

The life of a knight is an imitation; that of princes is so too, sometimes. No one was so consciously inspired by models of the past, or manifested such desire to rival them, as Charles the Bold. In his youth he made his attendants read out to him the exploits of Gauvain and of Lancelot. Later he preferred the ancients. Before retiring to rest, he listens for an hour or two to the "lofty histories of Rome." He especially admires Cæsar, Hannibal and Alexander, "whom he wished to follow and imitate." All his contemporaries attach great importance to this eager-

ness to imitate the heroes of antiquity, and agree in regarding it as the mainspring of his conduct. "He desired
great glory"—says Commines—"which more than anything
else led him to undertake his wars; and longed to resemble
those ancient princes who have been so much talked of
after their death." The anecdote is well known of the jester
who, after the defeat of Granson, called out to him: "My
lord, we are well Hannibaled this time!" His love of the
"beau geste" in antique style was observed by Chastellain
at Mechlin in 1467, when he made his first entry there as
duke. He had to punish a rising. He sat down facing the
scaffold erected for the leader of the insurgents. Already
the hangman has drawn the sword and is preparing to
strike the blow. "Stop," said the duke then, "take the
bandage from his eyes and help him up." "And then I
perceived"—says Chastellain—"that he had set his heart on
high and singular purposes for the future, and on acquiring
glory and renown by extraordinary works."

Thus the aspiration to the splendour of antique life,
which is the characteristic of the Renaissance, has its roots
in the chivalrous ideal. Between the ponderous spirit of
the Burgundian and the classical instinct of an Italian of
the same period there is only a difference of nuance. The
forms which Charles the Bold affected are still flamboyant
Gothic, and he still read his classics in translations.

The chivalrous element and the Renaissance element are
also confounded in the cult of the Nine Worthies ("les neuf
preux"). The grouping of three pagans, three Jews, and
three Christians in a sort of gallery of heroism is found for
the first time in a work of the beginning of the fourteenth
century, *Les Vœux du Paon*, by Jacques de Longuyon.
The choice of the heroes betrays a close connection with
the romances of chivalry. They are Hector, Cæsar, Alexander, Joshua, David, Judas Maccabæus, Arthur, Charlemagne, Godfrey of Bouillon. Eustache Deschamps adopted
the idea of the "neuf preux" from his master, Guillaume
de Machaut, and devoted many of his ballads to the subject.
The craving for symmetry, so strong in the Middle Ages,
demanded that the series should be completed by counter-

parts of the female sex. Deschamps satisfied the demand
by choosing from fiction and history a group of rather
bizarre heroines. Among them we find Penthesilea,
Tomyris, Semiramis. His idea was successful. Literature
and tapestry popularized the female as well as the male
worthies. Blazons were invented for them. On the occasion of his entry into Paris, in 1431, the English king, Henry
VI, is preceded by all the eighteen worthies of both sexes.
How popular the idea was, is attested by the parody which
Molinet composed of the "nine worthies of gluttony."
Francis I still occasionally dressed himself "in the antique
style," in order to represent one of the worthies.

Deschamps went further. He completed the series of
the nine worthies by adding a tenth, Bertrand du Guesclin,
the brave and prudent Breton warrior to whom France
owed her recovery from Crécy and Poitiers. In this way he
linked the cult of ancient heroes to the budding sentiment
of national military glory. His idea was generally adopted.
Louis of Orléans had the statue of Du Guesclin, as tenth
of the "preux," erected in the great hall of the castle of
Coucy. His special reason for honouring the constable's
memory was the fact that the latter had held him at the
baptismal font and put a sword into his little hand.

The inventories of the Burgundian dukes enumerate
curious relics of ancient and modern heroes, such as "the
sword of Saint George," with his coat of arms; "another
war-sword which belonged to Messire Bertran de Clai-
quin"; "a big boar's fang, said to be the fang of the boar
of Garin le Loherain"; "the psalter of Saint Louis, out of
which he learned in his childhood." How curiously the
spheres of imagination of chivalrous romance, and of religious veneration, blend here with the coming spirit of
the Renaissance!

About 1300 the sword of Sir Tristram, with an inscription in French verse, was said to have been discovered in
Lombardy, in an ancient tomb.[3] Here we are only a step

[3] A sword of Tristram figures also among King John's
jewels lost in the Wash in 1216.

from Pope Leo X, who accepted solemnly, as though it were a relic, a humerus of Livy, offered him by the Venetians.

This hero-worship of the declining Middle Ages finds its literary expression in the biography of the perfect knight. In this genre the figures of recent history gradually superseded the legendary ones like that of Gillon de Trazegnies. Three of these lives of contemporary and illustrious knights are characteristic, although very different from each other: those of Marshal Boucicaut, of Jean de Bueil, and of Jacques de Lalaing.

The military career of Jean le Meingre, surnamed the Marshal Boucicaut, had led him from the defeat of Nicopolis to that of Agincourt, where he was taken prisoner, to die in captivity, six years later. As early as 1409 one of his admirers wrote his biography from reliable information, but with the intention of producing, not a book of contemporary history, but a mirror of chivalrous life. The real facts of this hard life of a captain and statesman disappear beneath the appearances of ideal heroism. The marshal is depicted as the type of a frugal and pious knight, at once courtly and well read. He is not rich. His father would neither augment nor diminish his possessions, saying: "If my children are honest and brave, they will have enough; if they are worthless, it would be a pity to leave them much." Boucicaut's piety has a Puritan flavour. He rises early and remains in prayer for three hours. However occupied or hurried he may be, he hears, on his knees, two masses a day. On Fridays he dresses in black. On Sundays and festal days he makes pilgrimages on foot, discourses of holy matters, or has some life of a saint read out to him or some story of "the valiant dead—Roman or other." He lives soberly, he speaks little, and when he speaks it is of God and the saints, or of chivalry and virtue. He has accustomed his servants to practise piety and observe decency; they have given up the habit of swearing. We shall find him again as one of the propagandists of faithful and chaste love, and as the founder of the order of "l'escu vert à la dame blanche," for the defence of women, for which

THE IDEA OF CHIVALRY

Christine de Pisan praised him. At Genoa, as a regent of the king of France, one day he courteously returned the curtsy of two ladies whom he met. "My lord"—said his squire—"who are those two women to whom you bowed so deeply?"—"Huguenin," said he, "I do not know." Then he said to him: "My lord, they are harlots." "Harlots," said he. "Huguenin, I would rather have paid my salutations to ten harlots than have omitted them to one respectable woman." His device, resigned and enigmatical, is "What you will."

Such are the colours of piety, austerity and fidelity in which the ideal image of a knight is painted. The real Boucicaut did not altogether resemble this portrait; no one would have expected it. He was neither free from violence nor from avarice, common faults in his class.

There are, however, patterns of chivalry of another type. The biographical romance about Jean de Bueil, entitled *Le Jouvencel*, was written half a century after *Le Livre des Faicts* of Boucicaut, which partly explains the differences. Jean de Bueil had fought under the banner of Joan of Arc. He had taken part in the rising called the Praguerie and in the war "du bien public"; he died in 1477. Fallen in disgrace with the king, he dictated, or rather suggested, about 1465, an account of his life to three of his servants. In contrast with the *Life* of Boucicaut, of which the historical form hardly conceals the romantic purpose, *Le Jouvencel* contains in fictitious garb a great deal of simple realism; this is so, at least, in the first part, for further on the authors have lost themselves in very insipid romanticism.

Jean de Bueil must have given his scribes a very lively narrative of his exploits. It would hardly be possible to quote in the literature of the fifteenth century another work giving as sober a picture as *Le Jouvencel* of the wars of those times. We find the small miseries of military life, its privations and boredom, gay endurance of hardships and courage in danger. A castellan musters his garrison; there are but fifteen horses, lean and old beasts, most of them unshod. He puts two men on each horse, but of the men also most are blind of one eye or lame. They set out to seize the enemy's laundry in order to patch the captain's clothes. A captured cow is courteously returned to a hostile captain at his request. Reading the description of a nocturnal march, one feels as though surrounded by the silence and the freshness of the night. It is not saying too much that here military France is announcing herself in literature, which will give birth to the types of the "mousquetaire," the "grognard," and the "poilu." The feudal knight is merging into the soldier of modern times; the universal and religious ideal is becoming national and military. The hero of the book releases his prisoners without a ransom, on condition that they shall become good Frenchmen. Having risen to great dignities, he yearns for the old life of adventure and liberty.

Le Jouvencel is an expression of true French sentiment. Literature in the Burgundian sphere, being more old-fashioned, more feudal and more solemn, would not have been able as yet to create so realistic a type of a knight. By the side of the Jouvencel, the figure of the Hainaut pattern knight of the fifteenth century, Jacques de Lalaing, is an antique curiosity, more or less modelled on the knights-errant of a preceding age. *Le Livre des Faits du bon Chevalier Messire Jacques de Lalaing* is far more concerned with tournaments and jousts than with real war.

In the *Jouvencel* we find a remarkable portrayal, hardly to be surpassed, of the psychology of warlike courage of a simple and touching kind. "It is a joyous thing, is war. . . . You love your comrade so in war. When you see that your quarrel is just and your blood is fighting well, tears rise to your eye. A great sweet feeling of loyalty and of pity fills your heart on seeing your friend so valiantly exposing his body to execute and accomplish the command of our Creator. And then you prepare to go and die or live with him, and for love not to abandon him. And out of that there arises such a delectation, that he who has not tasted it is not fit to say what a delight it is. Do you think that a man who does that fears death? Not at all; for he feels so strengthened, he is so elated, that he does not know where he is. Truly he is afraid of nothing."

These sentiments have nothing specifically chivalrous or medieval. The words might have been spoken by a modern soldier. They show us the very core of courage: man, in the excitement of danger, stepping out of his narrow egotism, the ineffable feeling caused by a comrade's bravery, the rapture of fidelity and of sacrifice,—in short, the primitive and spontaneous asceticism, which is at the bottom of the chivalrous ideal.

Chapter V

THE DREAM OF HEROISM AND OF LOVE

A conception of military life resembling that of medieval chivalry is found nearly everywhere, notably with the Hindus of the *Mahābhārata* and in Japan. Warlike aristocracies need an ideal form of manly perfection. The aspiration to a pure and beautiful life, expressed in the *Kalokagathia* of the Hellenes, in the Middle Ages gives birth to chivalry. And during several centuries that ideal remains a source of energy, and at the same time a cloak for a whole world of violence and self-interest.

The ascetic element is never absent from it. It is most accentuated in the times when the function of knighthood is most vital, as in the times of the early crusades. The noble warrior has to be poor and exempt from worldly ties. "This ideal of the well-born man without possessions"—says William James—"was embodied in knight-errantry and templardom, and, hideously corrupted as it has always been, it still dominates sentimentally, if not practically, the military and aristocratic view of life. We glorify the soldier as the man absolutely unincumbered. Owning nothing but his bare life, and willing to toss that up at any moment when the cause commands him, he is the representative of unhampered freedom in ideal directions." Medieval chivalry, in its first bloom, was bound to blend with monachism. From this union were born the military orders of the Templars, of Saint John, of the Teutonic knights, and also those of Spain. Soon, however, or rather from the very beginning, reality gives the lie to the ideal, and accordingly the ideal will soar more and more towards the regions of fantasy, there to preserve the traits of asceticism and sacrifice too rarely visible in real life. The knight-errant, fantastic and useless, will always be poor and without ties, as the first Templars had been. ·

It would thus be unjust to regard as factitious or superficial the religious elements of chivalry, such as compassion, fidelity, justice. They are essential to it. Yet the complex of aspirations and imaginings, forming the idea of chivalry, in spite of its strong ethical foundation and the combative instinct of man, would never have made so solid a frame for the life beautiful if love had not been the source of its constantly revived ardour.

These very traits, moreover, of compassion, of sacrifice, and of fidelity, which characterize chivalry, are not purely religious; they are erotic at the same time. Here, again, it must be remembered that the desire of bestowing a form, a style, on sentiment, is not expressed exclusively in art and literature; it also unfolds in life itself: in courtly conversation, in games, in sports. There, too, love incessantly seeks a sublime and romantic expression. If, therefore, life borrows motifs and forms from literature, literature, after all, is only copying life. The chivalrous aspect of love had somehow to make its appearance in life before it expressed itself in literature.

The knight and his lady, that is to say, the hero who serves for love, this is the primary and invariable motif from which erotic fantasy will always start. It is sensuality transformed into the craving for self-sacrifice, into the desire of the male to show his courage, to incur danger, to be strong, to suffer and to bleed before his lady-love.

From the moment when the dream of heroism through love has intoxicated the yearning heart, fantasy grows

and overflows. The first simple theme is soon left behind,
the soul thirsts for new fancies, and passion colours the
dream of suffering and of renunciation. The man will not
be content merely to suffer, he will want to save from
danger, or from suffering, the object of his desire. A more
vehement stimulus is added to the primary motif: its chief
feature will be that of defending imperilled virginity—
in other words, that of ousting the rival. This, then, is the
essential theme of chivalrous love poetry: the young hero,
delivering the virgin. The sexual motif is always behind it,
even when the aggressor is only an artless dragon; a glance
at Burne-Jones's famous picture suffices to prove it.

One is surprised that comparative mythology should
have looked so indefatigably to meteorological phenomena
for the explanation of such an immediate and perpetual
motif as the deliverance of the virgin, which is the oldest
of literary motifs, and one which can never grow antiquated. It may from time to time become stale from over-
much repetition, and yet it will reappear, adapting itself
to all times and surroundings. New romantic types will
arise, just as the cowboy has succeeded the corsair.

The Middle Ages cultivated these motifs of a primitive
romanticism with a youthful insatiability. Whereas in some
higher genres of literature, such as lyrical poetry, the expression of desire and fulfilment became more refined, the
romance of adventure always preserved it in its crude and
naïve form, without ever losing its charm to its contemporaries. We might have expected that the last centuries
of the Middle Ages would have lost their relish for these
childish fancies. We are inclined to suppose that *Méliador*,
the super-romantic novel by Froissart, or *Perceforest*, those
belated fruits of chivalrous romance, were anachronisms
even in their own day. They were no more so than the
sensational novel is at present. Erotic imagination always
requires similar models, and it finds them here. In the hey-
day of the Renaissance we see them revive in the cycle of
Amadis of Gaul. When, a good while after the middle of
the sixteenth century, François de la Noue affirms that
the novels of Amadis had caused "un esprit de vertige"

among his generation—the generation of the Huguenots, which had passed through humanism with its vein of rationalism—we can imagine what must have been the romantic susceptibility of the ill-balanced and ignorant generation of 1400.

Literature did not suffice for the almost insatiable needs of the romantic imagination of the age. Some more active form of expression was required. Dramatic art might have supplied it, but the medieval drama in the real sense of the word treated love matters only exceptionally; sacred subjects were its substance. There was, however, another form of representation, namely, noble sports, tourneys and jousts. Sportive struggles always and everywhere contain a strong dramatic element and an erotic element. In the medieval tournament these two elements had so much got the upper hand, that its character of a contest of force and courage had been almost obliterated by its romantic purport. With its bizarre accoutrements and pompous staging, its poetical illusion and pathos, it filled the place of the drama of a later age.

The life of aristocracies when they are still strong, though of small utility, tends to become an all-round game. In order to forget the painful imperfection of reality, the nobles turn to the continual illusion of a high and heroic life. They wear the mask of Lancelot and of Tristram. It is an amazing self-deception. The crying falsehood of it can only be borne by treating it with some amount of raillery. The whole chivalrous culture of the last centuries of the Middle Ages is marked by an unstable equilibrium between sentimentality and mockery. Honour, fidelity and love are treated with unimpeachable seriousness; only from time to time the solemn rigidity relaxes into a smile, but downright parody never prevails. Even after the *Morgante* of Pulci and the *Orlando Innamorato* of Boiardo had made the heroic pose ridiculous, Ariosto recaptured the absolute serenity of chivalrous sentiment.

In French circles, of about 1400, the cult of chivalry was treated with perfect gravity. It is not easy for us to understand this seriousness, and not to be startled by the contrast between the literary note of a Boucicaut and the facts of his career. He is represented as the indefatigable defender of courtesy and of chivalry, serving his lady according to the old rules of courteous love. "He served all, he honoured all, for the love of one. His speech was graceful, courteous and diffident before his lady." During his travels in the Near East in 1388, he and his companions in arms amuse themselves by composing a poetical defence of the the faithful and chaste love of a knight—the *Livre des Cent Ballades*. One might have supposed him cured of all chivalrous delusions after the catastrophe of Nicopolis. There he had seen the lamentable consequences of statecraft recklessly embarking on an enterprise of vital import in the spirit of a chivalrous adventure. His companions of the *Cent Ballades* had perished. That would suffice, one would think, to make him turn his back on old-fashioned forms of courtesy. Yet he remains devoted to them and resumes his moral task in founding the order "de la dame blanche à l'escu vert."

Like all romantic forms that are worn out as an instrument of passion, this apparatus of chivalry and of courtesy affects us at first sight as a silly and ridiculous thing. The accents of passion are heard in it no more save in some rare products of literary genius. Still, all these costly elaborated forms of social conduct have played their part as a decoration of life, as a framework for a living passion. In reading this antiquated love poetry, or the clumsy descriptions of tournaments, no exact knowledge of historical details avails without the vision of the smiling eyes, long turned to dust, which at one time were infinitely more important than the written word that remains.

Only a stray glimmer now reminds us of the passionate significance of these cultural forms. In the *Vœu du Héron* the unknown author makes Jean de Beaumont speak:

"Quant sommes ès tavernes, de ces fors vins buvant,
 Et ces dames delès qui nous vont regardant,
 A ces gorges polies, ces coliés tirant,
 Chil œil vair resplendissent de biauté souriant,

Nature nous semont d'avoir cœur désirant,
. . . Adonc conquerons-nous Yaumont et Agoulant
Et li autre conquierrent Olivier et Rollant.
Mais, quant sommes as camps sus nos destriers courans,
Nos escus à no col et nos lansses bais(s)ans,
Et le froidure grande nous va tout engelant,
Li membres nous effondrent, et derrière et devant,
Et nos ennemies sont envers nous approchant,
Adonc vorrièmes estre en un chélier si grant
Que jamais ne fussions veu tant ne quant." [1]

Nowhere does the erotic element of the tournament appear more clearly than in the custom of the knight's wearing the veil or the dress of his lady. In *Perceforest* we read how the lady spectators of the combat take off their finery, one article after another, to throw them to the knights in the lists. At the end of the fight they are bareheaded and without sleeves. A poem of the thirteenth century, the work of a Picard or a Hainaut minstrel, entitled *Des trois Chevaliers et del Chainse*,[2] has worked out this motif in all its force. The wife of a nobleman of great liberality, but not very fond of fighting, sends her shirt to three knights who serve her for love, that one of them at the tournament which her husband is going to give may wear it as a coat-armour, without any mail underneath. The first and the second knights excuse themselves. The third, who is poor, takes the shirt in his arms at night, and kisses it passionately. He appears at the tournament, dressed in the

[1] When we are in the tavern, drinking strong wines, And the ladies pass and look at us, With those white throats, and tight bodices, Those sparkling eyes resplendent with smiling beauty, Then nature urges us to have a desiring heart, . . . Then we could overcome Yaumont and Agoulant And the others would conquer Oliver and Roland. But when we are in camp on our trotting chargers, Our bucklers round our necks and our lances lowered, And the great cold is congealing us altogether, And our limbs are crushed before and behind, And our enemies are approaching us, Then we should wish to be in a cellar so large That we might never be seen by any means.
[2] Of the three knights and the shirt.

shirt and without a coat of mail; he is grievously wounded, the shirt, stained with his blood, is torn. Then his extraordinary bravery is perceived and he is awarded the prize. The lady gives him her heart. The lover asks something in his turn. He sends back the garment, all blood-stained, to the lady, that she may wear it over her gown at the meal which is to conclude the feast. She embraces it tenderly and shows herself dressed in the shirt as the knight had demanded. The majority of those present blame her, the husband is confounded, and the minstrel winds up by asking the question: Which of the two lovers sacrificed most for the sake of the other?

The Church was openly hostile to tournaments; it repeatedly prohibited them, and there is no doubt that the fear of the passionate character of this noble game, and of the abuses resulting from it, had a great share in this hostility. Moralists were not favourably disposed towards tournaments, neither were the humanists. Where do we read, Petrarch asks, that Cicero or Scipio jousted? The burghers thought them useless and ridiculous. Only the world of the nobility continued to cultivate all that regarded tournaments and jousts, as things of the highest importance. Monuments were erected on the sites of famous combats, as the Pélerine Cross near Saint Omer, in remembrance of the Passage of Arms of la Pélerine, and of the exploits of the bastard of Saint Pol and a Spanish knight. Bayard piously went to visit this cross, as if on a pilgrimage. In the church of Notre Dame of Boulogne were preserved the decorations of the Passage of Arms of the Fontaine des Pleurs, solemnly dedicated to the Holy Virgin.

The warlike sports of the Middle Ages differ from Greek and modern athletics by being far less simple and natural. Pride, honour, love and art give additional stimulus to the competition itself. Overloaded with pomp and decoration, full of heroic fancy, they serve to express romantic needs too strong for mere literature to satisfy. The realities of court life or a military career offered too little opportunity for the fine make-believe of heroism and love, which filled the soul. So they had to be acted. The staging of the tournament, therefore, had to be that of romance; that is to say, the imaginary world of Arthur, where the fancy of a fairy-tale was enhanced by the sentimentality of courtly love.

A Passage of Arms of the fifteenth century is based on a fictitious case of chivalrous adventure, connected with an artificial scene called by a romantic name, as, for instance, *La fontaine des pleurs, L'arbre Charlemagne*. A fountain is expressly constructed, and beside it a pavilion, where during a whole year a lady is to reside (in effigy, be it understood), holding a unicorn which bears three shields. The first day of each month knights come to touch the shields, and in this way to pledge themselves for a combat of which the "Chapters" of the Passage of Arms lay down the rules. They will find horses in readiness, for the shields have to be touched on horseback. Or, in the case of the *Emprise du dragon*, four knights will be stationed at a cross-road where, unless she gives a gage, no lady may pass without a knight breaking two lances for her. There is an unmistakable connection between these primitive forms of warlike and erotic sport and the children's play of forfeits. One of the rules of the "Chapters" of the *Fontaine des pleurs* runs thus: he who, in a combat, is unhorsed, will during a year wear a gold bracelet, until he finds the lady who holds the key to it and who can free him, on condition that he shall serve her.

The nobles liked to throw a veil of mystery and melancholy over the procedure. The knight should be unknown. He is called "le blanc chevalier," "le chevalier mesconnu," or he wears the crest of Lancelot or Palamedes. The shields of the Fount of Tears are white, violet and black, and overspread with white tears; those of the Tree of Charlemagne are sable and violet, with gold and sable tears. At the *Emprise du dragon*, celebrated on the occasion of the departure of his daughter Margaret for England, King René was present, dressed all in black, and his whole outfit, caparison, horse and all, down to the wood of his lance, was of the same colour.

Chapter VI

ORDERS OF CHIVALRY AND VOWS

The ideal of courage, of honour, and of fidelity found other forms of expression, besides those of the tournament. Apart from martial sport, the orders of chivalry opened an ample field where the taste for high aristocratic culture might expand. Like the tournaments and the accolade, the orders of chivalry have their roots in the sacred rites of a very remote past. Their religious origins are pagan, only the feudal system of thought had Christianized them. Strictly speaking, the several orders of chivalry are only ramifications of the order of knighthood itself. For knighthood was a sacred brotherhood, into which admittance was effected by means of solemn rites of initiation. The more elaborate form of these rites shows a most curious blending of Christian and heathen elements: the shaving, the bath, and the vigil of arms undoubtedly go back to pre-Christian times. Those who had gone through these ceremonies were called Knights of the Bath, in distinction from those who were knighted by the simple accolade. The term afterwards gave rise to the legend of a special Order of the Bath instituted by Henry IV, and thus to the establishment of the real one by George I.

The first great orders, those of the Temple, of Saint John, and of the Teutonic Knights, born of the mutual penetration of monastic and feudal ideas, early assumed the character of great political and economic institutions. Their aim was no longer in the first place the practice of chivalry; that element, as well as their spiritual aspirations, had been more or less effaced by their political and financial importance. It was in the orders of more recent origin that the primitive conception of a club, of a game, of an aristocratic federation, reappeared. In the fourteenth and fifteenth centuries the real importance of chivalrous orders, which were founded in great numbers, was very slight, but the aspirations professed in founding them were always those of the very highest ethical and political idealism. Philippe de Mézières, an unrivalled political dreamer, wishes to remedy all the evils of the century by a new order of chivalry, that of the Passion, which is to unite Christendom in a common effort to expel the Turks. Burgesses and labourers are to find a place in it, side by side with the nobles. The three monastic vows are to be modified for practical reasons: instead of celibacy he only requires conjugal fidelity. Mézières adds a fourth vow, unknown to preceding orders, that of individual, moral perfection, *summa perfectio.* He confided the task of propagating the *Militia Passionis Jhesu Christi* to four "messaiges de Dieu et de la chevalerie" (among whom was the celebrated Othe de Granson), who were to go to "divers lands and kingdoms to preach and to announce the aforesaid holy chivalry, like four evangelists."

The word "order" thus still preserved much of its spiritual meaning; it alternates with "religion," which usually designated a monastic order. We hear of the "religion" of the Golden Fleece, of a "knight of the religion of Avys." The rules of the Golden Fleece are conceived in a truly ecclesiastical spirit; mass and obsequies occupy a large place in them; the knights are seated in choir-stalls like canons. The membership of an order of chivalry constituted a sacred and exclusive tie. The knights of the Star of John the Good are required to withdraw from every other order. Philip the Good declines the honour of the Garter, in spite of the urgency of the duke of Bedford, in order not to tie himself too closely to England. Charles the Bold, on accepting it, was accused by Louis XI of having broken the peace of Péronne, which forbade alliance with England without the king's consent.

In spite of these serious airs, the founders of new orders had to defend themselves from the reproach of pursuing merely a vain amusement. The Golden Fleece, says the poet Michault, was instituted,

"Non point pour jeu ne pour esbatement,
Mais à la fin que soit attribuée
Loenge à Dieu trestout premièrement,
Et aux bons gloire et haulte renommée."[1]

Similarly, Guillaume Fillastre writes his book of the Golden Fleece to demonstrate the high interest and the sacred importance of the order, that it might not be regarded as a work of vanity. It was not superfluous to draw attention to the high objects of the duke, so that his creation might be distinguished from the numerous orders of recent foundation. There was not a prince or great noble who did not desire to have his own order. Orléans, Bourbon, Savoie, Hainaut-Bavière, Lusignan, Coucy, all eagerly exerted themselves in inventing bizarre emblems and striking devices. The chain of Pierre de Lusignan's Sword-order was made of gold S's, which meant "silence." The Porcupine of Louis of Orléans threatens Burgundy with its spines, which it shoots, according to popular belief, *cominus et eminus*.

If the Golden Fleece eclipsed all the other orders, it is because the dukes of Burgundy placed at its disposal the resources of their enormous wealth. In their view, the order was to serve as the symbol of their power. The fleece was primarily that of Colchis; the fable of Jason was familiar to all. Jason, however, was, as an eponymous hero, not absolutely irreproachable. Had he not broken his word? There was an opening here for nasty allusions to the policy of the dukes towards France. *La Ballade de Fougères* of Alain Chartier is an instance:

"A Dieu et aux gens detestable
Est menterie et trahison,
Pour ce n'est point mis à la table
Des preux l'image de Jason,
Qui pour emporter la toison

---

[1] Not for amusement, nor for recreation, But for the purpose that praise shall be given To God, in the first place, And glory and high renown to the good.

De Colcos se veult parjurer.
Larrecin ne se peult celer." [2]

It was, therefore, a very happy inspiration of the
learned bishop of Chalons, chancellor of the order, to substitute for the fleece of the ram that carried Helle another,
far more venerable, namely, that which Gideon spread to
receive the dew of Heaven. The fleece of Gideon was one
of the most striking symbols of the Annunciation. Thus the
Old Testament judge more or less eclipses the pagan hero,
as a patron of the order. Guillaume Fillastre, the successor
of Jean Germain as chancellor of the order, discovered four
more fleeces in Scripture, each of them denoting a special
virtue. But this was plainly overdoing it, and, as far as we
can see, was not successful. "Gedeonis signa" remained the
most revered appellation of the Golden Fleece.

To describe the solemn pomp of the Golden Fleece, or
of the Star, would only be adding new instances to the
subject-matter of a preceding chapter. Let it suffice here to
point out a single trait common to all the orders of chivalry,
in which the original character of a primitive and sacred
game is particularly conspicuous, namely, the technical
appellations of their officials. The kings-at-arms are called
Golden Fleece, Garter. The heralds bear names of countries: Charolais, Zealand. The first of the pursuivants is
called "Fusil," after the duke's emblem, the flint-and-steel.
The names of the other pursuivants are of a romantic or
moral character, as Montreal, Perseverance, or allegorical,
as Humble Request, Sweet Thought, Lawful Pursuit, des-
ignations borrowed from the *Romaunt of the Rose*. At the
feasts of the order, the pursuivants are baptized in these
names by sprinkling them with wine. Nicolas Upton, a
herald of Humphrey of Gloucester, has described the
ceremonial of such a baptism.

[2] To God and to men detestable Is lying and treason,
For this reason the image of Jason Is not placed in the
gallery of worthies. Who, to carry off the fleece Of Colchis,
was willing to commit perjury, Larceny cannot remain hidden.

The very essence of the conception of an order of chivalry appears in its knightly vows. Every order presupposes vows, but the chivalrous vow exists also outside the orders, under an individual and occasional form. Here the barbarous character, testifying that chivalry has its roots in primitive civilization, comes to the surface. We find parallels in the India of the *Mahâbhârata,* in ancient Palestine, and in the Iceland of the *Sagas.*

What remained, at the end of the Middle Ages, of the cultural value of these chivalrous vows? We find them very near akin to purely religious vows, serving to accentuate or to fix a lofty moral aspiration. We also find them supplying romantic and erotic needs and degenerating into an amusement and a theme for raillery. It is not easy to determine accurately the degree of sincerity belonging to them. We should not judge them from the impression of silliness and untruthfulness which we derive from the *Vœux du Faisan,* to mention the best known and most historical example. As in the case of tournaments and passages of arms, we only see the dead form of the thing: the cultural significance of the custom has disappeared with the passion animating those to whom these forms were the realization of a dream of beauty.

In the vows we find once more that mixture of asceticism and eroticism which we found underlying the idea of chivalry itself, and so clearly expressed in the tournaments. The Chevalier de la Tour Landry, in his curious book of admonition to his daughters, speaks of a strange order of amorous men and women of noble birth which existed in Poitou and elsewhere, in his youth. They called themselves Galois and Galoises, and had "very savage regulations." In summer they dressed themselves in furs and furlined hoods, and lighted a fire on the hearth, whereas in winter they were only allowed to wear a simple coat without fur; neither mantles, nor hats, nor gloves. During the most severe cold they hid the hearth behind evergreen sprigs, and had only very light bed-clothes. It is not surprising that a great many members died of cold. The husband of a Galoise receiving a Galois under his roof was bound, under penalty of dishonouring himself, to give up his house and his wife to him. Here is a very primitive trait, which the author could hardly have invented, although he may have exaggerated this strange aberration in which we divine a wish to exalt love by ascetic excitement.

The savage spirit of the vows of knights manifests itself very clearly in *Le Vœu du Héron,* a poem of the fourteenth century, of little historical value, describing the feasts given at the court of Edward III at the moment when Robert d'Artois urges the king to declare war on France. The earl of Salisbury is seated at the feet of his lady. When called upon to formulate a vow, he begs her to place a finger on his right eye. Two, if necessary, she replies, and she closes his eye by placing two fingers on it. "Belle, is it well closed?" asks the knight. "Yes, certainly."

> "A dont, dist de le bouche, du cuer le pensement;
> Et je veu et prometh à Dieu omnipotent,
> Et à sa douche mère que de beauté resplent,
> Qu'il n'est jamais ouvers, pour oré, ne pour vent,
> Pour mal, ne pour martire, ne pour encombrement,
> Si seray dedans Franche, où il a bonne gent,
> Et si aray le fu bouté entièrement
> Et serai combatus à grand efforchement
> Contre les gens Philype, qui tant a hardement.
> . . . Or, aviegne qu'aviegne, car il n'est autrement.
> A donc osta son doit la puchelle au cors gent,
> Et li iex clos demeure, si ques virent la gent." [3]

The literary motif is not without a real foundation.

[3] Well then, he said by the mouth the thought of the heart; And I vow and I promise to Almighty God, And to his sweet mother of resplendent beauty, That it will never be opened, for storm nor for wind, By evil, nor by torture, nor by hindrance, Until I shall be in France, where there are good people, And until I shall have lighted the fire And I shall have battled with great exertion Against the people of Philip who is so hardy. . . . Now come what may, for it is not otherwise. Then the gentle girl took away her finger And the eye remained shut, as people saw.

Froissart actually saw English gentlemen who had covered one eye with a piece of cloth, to redeem a pledge to use only one eye, till they should have achieved some deed of bravery in France.

The extreme of savagery is reached in the vow of the queen, which ends the series in *The Vow of the Heron.* She takes an oath not to give birth to the child of which she is pregnant before the king has taken her to the enemy's country and to kill herself "with a big steel knife," if the confinement announces itself too early.

"I shall have lost my soul and the fruit will perish."

Le Vœu du Héron shows us the literary conception of these vows, the barbarous and primitive character they had in the minds of that time. Their magical element betrays itself in the part which the hair and the beard play in them, as in the case of Benedict XIII, imprisoned at Avignon, who made the very archaic vow not to have his beard shaved before he recovered his liberty.

In making a vow, people imposed some privation upon themselves as a spur to the accomplishment of the actions they were pledged to perform. Most frequently the privation concerns food. The first of the knights whom Philippe de Mézières admitted to his Chivalry of the Passion was a Pole, who during nine years had only eaten and drunk standing. Bertrand du Guesclin was dangerously prone to utter vows of this kind. He will not undress till he has taken Montcontour; he will not eat till he has effected an encounter with the English.

It goes without saying that a nobleman of the fourteenth century understood nothing of the magical meaning implied in these fasts. To us this original meaning is clear. It is equally so in the custom of wearing foot-irons as signs of a vow. As early as the eighteenth century, La Curne de Sainte Palaye remarked that the usage of the Chatti, described by Tacitus, corresponded exactly with the fashion which medieval chivalry had preserved. In 1415 Jean de Bourbon vowed, and sixteen knights and squires with him, that each Sunday during two years they would wear on the left leg foot-irons—the knights of gold, the

squires of silver—till they should find sixteen adversaries
ready to fight them to the death. The "adventurous
knight," Jean de Boniface, arriving at Antwerp from Sicily
in 1445, wears an "emprise" of the same sort, so does Sir
Loiselench in *Le petit Jehan de Saintré*. The prospensity to
vow to perform some thing, when in danger or in violent
emotion, undoubtedly always remains a powerful one. It
has very deep psychological roots, and does not belong to
any particular religion or civilization. Nevertheless, as a
form of chivalrous culture, the vow was dying out at the
end of the Middle Ages.

When, at Lille, in 1454, Philip the Good, preparing for
his crusade, crowns his extravagant feasts by the celebrated Vows of the Pheasant, it is like the last manifestation of a dying usage, which has become a fantastic
ornament, after having been a very serious element of
earlier civilization. The old ritual, such as chivalrous tradition and romance taught it, is carefully observed. The
vows are taken at the banquet; the guests swear by the
pheasant served up, one "bluffing" the other, just as the
old Norsemen vied with each other in fool-hardy vows
sworn in drunkenness by the boar served up. There are
pious vows, made to God and to the Holy Virgin, to the
ladies and to the bird, and others in which the Deity is
not mentioned. They contain always the same privations
of food or of comfort: not to sleep in a bed on Saturday,
not to take animal food on Friday, etc. One act of asceticism
is heaped upon another: one nobleman promises to wear
no armour, to drink no wine one day in every week, not to
sleep in a bed, not to sit down to meals, to wear the hair-
shirt. The method of accomplishing the vowed exploit is
minutely specified and registered.

Are we to take all this seriously? The actors of the play
pretend to do so. In connection with the vow of Philippe
Pot to fight with his right arm bare, the duke, as though
he feared real danger for his favourite, orders this addition
to the registered promise: "It is not the pleasure of my
very redoubted lord, that Messire Philippe Pot undertakes,
in his company, the holy votive journey with his arm bare;

but he desires that he shall travel with him well and sufficiently armed, as beseems." As regards the vow of the duke himself, to fight the Grand Turk with his own hand, it provokes general emotion. Among the vows there are conditional ones, betraying the intention of escaping, in case of danger, by a pretext.. There are those resembling a fillipeen. And in fact this game, still in fashion some forty years ago, may be regarded as a pale survival of the chivalrous vow.

Yet a vein of mocking pleasantry runs through the superficial pomp. At the Vow of the Heron, Jean de Beaumont takes an oath to serve the lord from whom he may expect the greatest liberality. At those of the Pheasant, Jennet de Rebreviettes swears that unless he wins the favour of his lady before the expedition, he will marry, on his return from the East, the first lady or girl possessing twenty thousand gold pieces, "if she be willing." Yet the same Rebreviettes, in spite of his cynicism, set out as a "poor squire," seeking adventures in the wars against the Moors of Granada.

Thus a blasé aristocracy laughs at its own ideal. After having adorned its dream of heroism with all the resources of fantasy, art and wealth, it bethinks itself that life is not so fine, after all—and smiles.

Chapter VII

THE POLITICAL AND MILITARY VALUE OF CHIVALROUS IDEAS

In tracing the picture of the declining Middle Ages, the scholars of our days, generally speaking, take little account of the surviving chivalrous ideas. They are regarded by common consent as a more or less artificial revival of ideas, whose real value had long since disappeared. They would seem to be an ornament of society and no more. The men

who made the history of those times, princes, nobles, prelates, or burghers, were no romantic dreamers, but dealt in
solid facts. Still, nearly all paid homage to the chivalrous
bias, and it remained to consider to what extent this bias
modified the course of events. For the history of civilization the perennial dream of a sublime life has the value of
a very important reality. And even political history itself,
under penalty of neglecting actual facts, is bound to take
illusions, vanities, follies, into account. There is not a more
dangerous tendency in history than that of representing
the past, as if it were a rational whole and dictated by
clearly defined interests.

We have, therefore, to estimate the influence of chivalrous ideas on politics and on war at the close of the
Middle Ages. Were the rules of chivalry taken into account in the councils of kings and in those of war? Were
resolutions sometimes inspired by the chivalrous point of
view? Without any doubt. If medieval politics were not
governed for the better by the idea of chivalry, surely they
were so sometimes for the worse. Chivalry during the
Middle Ages was, on the one hand, the great source of
tragic political errors, exactly as are nationalism and racial
pride at the present day. On the other, it tended to disguise well-adjusted calculations under the appearance of
generous aspirations. The gravest political error which
France could commit was the creation of a quasi-in-
dependent Burgundy, and it had a chivalrous reason for
its avowed motive: King John, that knightly muddle-head,
wished to reward the courage shown by his son at Poitiers
by an extraordinary liberality. The stubborn anti-French
policy of the dukes of Burgundy after 1419, although
dictated by the interests of their house, was justified in the
eyes of contemporaries by the duty of exacting an exem-
plary vengeance for the murder of Montereau. Burgundian
court literature exerts itself to keep up in all political matters the semblance of chivalrous inspiration. The surnames
of the dukes, that of "Sans Peur" given to Jean, of "Hardi"
to the first Philip, of "Qui qu'en hongne" which they did
not succeed in imposing on the second Philip, usually called

"the Good," are inventions calculated to place the prince in
a nimbus of chivalrous romance.

Now there was one among the political aspirations of
the epoch where the chivalrous ideal was implied in the
nature of the enterprise itself, namely, the recovery of the
Holy Sepulchre. The highest political ideal which all the
kings of Europe were obliged to profess was still symbolized by Jerusalem. Here the contrast between the real
interest of Christendom and the form the idea took is most
striking. The Europe of 1400 was confronted by an Eastern
question of supreme urgency: that of repulsing the Turks
who had just taken Adrianople and wiped out the Serbian
kingdom. The imminent danger ought to have concentrated
all efforts on the Balkans. Yet the imperative task of
European politics does not yet disengage itself from the
old idea of the crusades. People only succeeded in seeing
the Turkish question as a secondary part of the sacred
duty in which their ancestors had failed: the conquest of
Jerusalem.

The conquest of Jerusalem could not but present itself
to the mind as a work of piety and of heroism—that is to
say, of chivalry. In the councils on Eastern politics the
heroic ideal preponderated more than in ordinary politics,
and this it is which explains the very meagre success of the
war against the Turks. Expeditions which, before all else,
required patient preparation and minute inquiry, tended,
more than once, to be romanticized, so to speak, from the
very outset. The catastrophe of Nicopolis had proved the
fatal folly of undertaking, against a very warlike enemy, an
expedition of great importance as light-heartedly as if it
were a question of going to kill a handful of heathen
peasants in Prussia or in Lithuania.

In the fifteenth century each king still felt virtually
bound to set out and recapture Jerusalem. When Henry V
of England, dying at Paris in 1422, in the midst of his
career of conquest, was listening to the reading of the
seven penitential psalms, he interrupted the officiating
priest at the words *Benigne fac, domine, in bona voluntate
tua Sion, ut aedificentur muri Jerusalem,* and declared that

he had intended to go and conquer Jerusalem, after having re-established peace in France, "if it had pleased God, his Creator, to let him live to old age." After that he orders the priest to go on reading, and dies.

In the case of Philip the Good, the design of a crusade seems to have been a mixture of chivalrous caprice and political advertising; he wished to pose, by this pious and useful project, as the protector of Christendom, to the detriment of the king of France. The expedition to Turkey was, as it were, a trump-card that he did not live to play.

The chivalrous fiction was also at the back of a peculiar form of political advertisement, to which Duke Philip was much attached—to wit, the duel between two princes, always being announced, but never carried out. The idea of having political differences decided by a single combat between the two princes concerned, was a logical consequence of the conception still prevailing, as if political disputes were nothing but a "quarrel" in the juristic sense of the word. A Burgundian partisan, for instance, serves the "quarrel" of his lord. What more natural means to settle such a case can be imagined than the duel of two princes, the two parties to the "quarrel"? The solution was satisfactory to both the primitive sense of right and the chivalrous imagination. In reading the summary of the carefully arranged preparations for these princely duels, we ask ourselves, if they were not a conscious feint, either to impose upon one's enemy, or to appease the grievances of one's own subjects. Are we not rather to regard them as an inextricable mixture of humbug and of a chimerical, but, after all, sincere, craving to conform to the life heroic, by posing before all the world as the champion of right, who does not hesitate to sacrifice himself for his people?

How, otherwise, are we to explain the surprising persistence of those plans for princely duels? Richard II of England offers to fight, together with his uncles, the dukes of Lancaster, York, and Gloucester, against the king of France, Charles VI, and his uncles, the dukes of Anjou, Burgundy and Berry. Louis of Orléans defies the king of England, Henry IV. Henry V of England challenges the dauphin before marching upon Agincourt. Above all, the duke of Burgundy displayed an almost frenzied attachment to this mode of settling a question. In 1425 he challenges Humphrey, duke of Gloucester, in connection with the question of Holland. The motive, as always, is expressly formulated in these terms: "To prevent Christian bloodshed and destruction of the people, on whom my heart has compassion," I wish "that by my own body, this quarrel may be settled, without proceeding by means of wars, which would entail that many noblemen and others, both of your army and of mine, would end their days pitifully."

All was ready for the combat: the magnificent armour and the state dresses, the pavilions, the standards, the banners, the armorial tabards for the heralds, everything richly adorned with the duke's blazons and with his emblems, the flint-and-steel and the Saint Andrew's cross. The duke had gone in for a course of training "both by abstinence in the matter of food and by taking exercise to keep him in breath." He practised fencing every day in his park of Hesdin with the most expert masters. The detailed expenses entailed by this affair are found in the accounts published by de La Borde, but the combat did not take place.

This did not prevent the duke, twenty years later, from again wishing to decide a question touching Luxembourg by a single combat with the duke of Saxony. Towards the close of his life he is still vowing to engage in a hand-to-hand combat with the Grand Turk.

We find this custom of challenges between sovereigns reappearing as late as the hey-day of the Renaissance. To deliver Italy from Cesare Borgia, Francesco Gonzaga offers to fight the latter with sword and dagger. Charles V himself, on two occasions, in 1526 and in 1536, formally proposes to the king of France to end their differences by a single combat.

The notion of two princes fighting a duel in order to decide a conflict between their countries had nothing impossible about it at an epoch when the judicial duel was still as firmly rooted in practice and in ideas as it was in

the fifteenth century. If a political duel between two real
sovereigns never actually took place, at any rate in 1397
a very great lord, accused of a political crime by a nobleman, fought him in due form and was killed. We refer to
Othe de Granson, an illustrious knight and admired poet,
who perished at Bourg en Bresse by the hand of Gerard
d'Estavayer. The latter had made himself the champion
of the towns of the Pays de Vaud, which were very hostile
to Granson, as he was suspected of complicity in the murder of his lord, Amé VII, of Savoy, surnamed "the Red
Count." This judicial duel caused an immense sensation.

If princes had such a chivalrous conception of their duty,
it is not astonishing that similar ideas constantly exercised
a certain influence on political and military decisions: a
negative influence and scarcely of a decisive nature, taking all in all, but nevertheless real. The chivalrous prejudice often caused resolutions to be retarded or precipi-
tated, opportunities to be lost, and profit to be neglected,
for the sake of a point of honour; it exposed commanders
to unnecessary dangers. Strategical interests were frequently sacrificed in order to keep up the appearances
of the heroic life. Sometimes a king himself would go
forth to seek military adventure, like Edward III attacking a convoy of Spanish ships by night. Froissart asserts
that the knights of the Star had to swear never to
fly more than four acres from the battlefield, through which
rule soon afterwards more than ninety of them lost their
lives. The article is not found in the statutes of the order,
as published by Luc d'Achéry; nevertheless, such formalism tallies well with the ideas of that epoch. Some days
before the battle of Agincourt, the king of England, on his
way to meet the French army, one evening passed by mistake by the village which the foragers of his army had
fixed upon as night-quarters. He would have had time to
return, and he would have done it, if a point of honour
had not prevented him. The king, "as the chief guardian
of the very laudable ceremonies of honour," had just
published an order, according to which knights, while reconnoitring, had to take off their coat-armour, because their

honour would not suffer knights to retreat, when accoutred
for battle. Now, the king himself had put on his coat-
armour, and so, having passed it by, he could not return
to the village mentioned. He therefore passed the night
in the place he had reached and also made the vanguard
advance accordingly, in spite of the dangers that might
have been incurred.

Just as a political conflict was regarded as an action at
law, so there was also but a difference of degree between
a battle and a judicial duel, or the combat of knights in
the lists. In his *Arbre des Batailles*, Honoré Bonet places
them under the same head, although carefully distinguish-
ing "great general battles" and "particular battles." In the
wars of the fifteenth century, and even later, the custom
for two captains or two equal groups to appoint meetings
for a fight, in sight of the two armies, was still kept up.
The Combat of the Thirty has remained the celebrated
type of these fights. It was fought in 1351 at Ploërmel, in
Brittany, between the French of Beaumanoir and a company of thirty men, English, Germans and Bretons, under
a certain Bamborough. Froissart, though full of admiration,
cannot help remarking: "Some held it a prowess, and some
held it a shame and a great overbearing." The uselessness
of these chivalrous spectacles was so evident that those in
authority resented them. It was impossible to expose the
honour of the kingdom to the hazards of a single combat.
When Guy de la Trémoïlle wished to prove in 1386 the
superiority of the French by a duel with an English nobleman, Peter Courtenay, the dukes of Burgundy and Berry
at the last moment issued a formal prohibition. The authors
of the *Jouvencel* disapprove of these competitions of glory.
"They are forbidden things and which people should not
do. In the first place, those who do it, want to take away
the good of others, that is to say, their honour, to procure
themselves vain glory, which is of little value; and, in doing this, he serves none, he spends his money; . . . in being
occupied in doing this, he neglects his part in waging war,
the service of his king and the public cause; and no one
should expose his body, unless in meritorious works."

This is the military spirit, which itself has issued from the spirit of chivalry and is now gradually supplanting it. The custom of these fights outlived the Middle Ages. The French and Spanish armies, in the south of Italy, in 1503, feasted their eyes first upon the Combat of the Eleven, without any fatal result, and then upon the famous duel between Bayard and Sotomayor, which was by no means the last of its sort.

Thus, in warfare, the chivalrous point of honour continues to make itself felt, but when an important question arises for decision, strategic prudence carries the day in the majority of cases. Generals still propose to the enemy to come to an understanding as to the choice of the battlefield, but the invitation is generally declined by the party occupying the better position. In vain did the English in 1333 invite the Scotch to come down from their strong position in order to fight them in the plains; in vain did Guillaume de Hainaut propose an armistice of three days to the king of France, during which a bridge could be built permitting the armies to join battle. Reason, however, is not always victorious. Before the battle of Najera (or of Navarrete), in which Bertrand du Guesclin was taken prisoner, Don Henri de Trastamara desires, at any cost, to measure himself with the enemy in the open field. He voluntarily gives up the advantages offered by the configuration of the ground and loses the battle.

If chivalry had to yield to strategy and tactics, none the less it remained of importance in the exterior apparatus of warfare. An army of the fifteenth century, with its splendid show of rich ornament and solemn pomp, still offered the spectacle of a tournament of glory and honour. The multitude of banners and pennons, the variety of heraldic bearings, the sound of clarions, the war-cries resounding all day long, all this, with the military costume itself and the ceremonies of dubbing knights before the battle, tended to give war the appearance of a noble sport.

After the middle of the century, the drum, of Oriental origin, makes its appearance in the armies of the West, introduced by the lansquenets. With its unmusical hypnotic

effect it symbolizes, as it were, the transition from the epoch
of chivalry to that of the art of modern warfare; together
with fire-arms it has contributed towards rendering war
mechanical.

The chivalrous point of view still presides over the classification of martial exploits by the chroniclers. They take
pains to distinguish, according to technical rules, between
a pitched battle and an encounter, for it is imperative that
every combat has its appropriate place in the records of
glory. "And so, from this day forward"—says Monstrelet—
"this business was called the encounter of Mons en Vimeu.
And it was declared to be no battle, because the parties
met by chance and there were hardly any banners unfurled." Henry V solemnly baptizes his great victory, the
battle of Agincourt, "inasmuch as all battles should bear
the name of the nearest fortress where they are fought."

In spite of the care taken on all hands to keep up the
illusion of chivalry, reality perpetually gives the lie to it,
and obliges it to take refuge in the domains of literature
and of conversation. The ideal of the fine heroic life could
only be cultivated within the limits of a close caste. The
sentiments of chivalry were current only among the members of the caste and by no means extended to inferior
persons. The Burgundian court, which was saturated with
chivalrous prejudice, and would not have tolerated the
slightest infringement of rules in a "combat à outrance" between noblemen, relished the unbridled ferocity of a judicial duel between burghers, where there was no code of
honour to observe. Nothing could be more remarkable in
this respect than the interest excited everywhere by the
combat of two burghers of Valenciennes in 1455. The old
Duke Philip wanted to see the rare spectacle at any cost.
One must read the vivid and realistic description given by
Chastellain in order to appreciate how a chivalrous writer
who never succeeded in giving more than a vaguely fanciful description of a Passage of Arms, made up for it here
by giving full rein to the instincts of natural cruelty. Not
one detail of the "very beautiful ceremony" escaped him.

The adversaries, accompanied by their fencing masters, enter the lists, first Jacotin Plouvier, the plaintiff, next Mahuot. Their heads are cropped close and they are sewn up from head to foot in cordwain dresses of a single piece. They are very pale. After having saluted the duke, who was seated behind lattice-work, they await the signal, seated upon two chairs upholstered in black. The spectators exchange remarks in a low voice on the chances of the combat: How pale Mahuot is as he kisses the Testament! Two servants come to rub them with grease from the neck to the ankles. Both champions rub their hands with ashes and take sugar in their mouths; next they are given quartersticks and bucklers painted with images of saints, which they hold upside down, having, moreover, in their hands "a scroll of devotion."

Mahuot, a small man, begins the combat by throwing sand into Jacotin's face with the point of his buckler. Soon afterwards he falls to the ground under the formidable blows of Jacotin, who throws himself on him, fills his eyes and mouth with sand, and thrusts his thumb into the socket of his eye, to make him let go of a finger which Mahuot has between his teeth. Jacotin wrings the other's arms, jumps upon his back and tries to break it. In vain does Mahuot cry for mercy, and asks to be confessed. "O my lord of Burgundy," he calls out, "I have served you so well in your war of Ghent! O my lord, for God's sake, I beg for mercy, save my life!" . . . Here some pages of Chastellain's chronicle are missing; we learn elsewhere that the dying man was dragged out of the lists and hanged by the executioner.

Did Chastellain end his lively narrative by a moral? It is probable; anyhow, La Marche tells that the nobility were a little ashamed at having been present at such a spectacle. "Because of which God caused a duel of knights to follow, which was irreproachable and without fatal consequences," adds the incorrigible court poet.

As soon as it is a question of non-nobles, the old and deep-rooted contempt for the villein shows us that the ideas of chivalry had availed but little in mitigating feudal bar-

barism. Charles VI, after the battle of Rosebeke, wishes to
see the corpse of Philip of Artevelde. The king does not
show the slightest respect for the illustrious rebel. According to one chronicle, he is said to have kicked the body,
"treating it as a villein." "When it had been looked at, for
some time"—says Froissart—"it was taken from that place
and hanged on a tree."

Hard realities were bound to open the eyes of the nobility and show the falseness and uselessness of their ideal.
The financial side of a knight's career was frankly avowed.
Froissart never omits to enumerate the profits which a successful enterprise procured for its heroes. The ransom of a
noble prisoner was the backbone of the business to the warriors of the fifteenth century. Pensions, rents, governor's
places, occupy a large place in a knight's life. His aim is
"s'avanchier par armes" (to get on in life by arms). Commines rates the courtiers according to their pay, and speaks
of "a nobleman of twenty crowns," and Deschamps makes
them sigh after the day of payment, in a ballad with the
refrain:

"Et quant venra le trésorier?" [1]

As a military principle, chivalry was no longer sufficient.
Tactics had long since given up all thought of conforming
to its rules. The custom of making the knights fight on foot
was borrowed by the French from the English, though the
chivalrous spirit was opposed to this practice. It was also
opposed to sea-fights. In the *Debat des Hérauts d'Armes
de France et d'Angleterre*, the French herald being asked
by his English colleague: Why does the king of France not
maintain a great naval force, like that of England? replies
very naïvely:—In the first place he does not need it, and,
then, the French nobility prefer wars on dry land, for several reasons, "for (on the sea) there is danger and loss of
life and God knows how awful it is when a storm rages and
sea-sickness prevails which many people find hard to bear.

[1] And when will the paymaster come?

Again, look at the hard life which has to be lived, which
does not beseem nobility."

Nevertheless, chivalrous ideas did not die out without
having borne some fruit. In so far as they formed a system
of rules of honour and precepts of virtue, they exercised a
certain influence on the evolution of the laws of war. The
law of nations originated in antiquity and in canon law,
but it was chivalry which caused it to flower. The aspiration after universal peace is linked with the idea of crusades
and with that of the orders of chivalry. Philippe de
Mézières planned his "Order of the Passion" to insure the
good of the world. The young king of France—(this was
written about 1388, when such great hopes were still en-
tertained of the unhappy Charles VI)—will be easily able
to conclude peace with Richard of England, young like
himself and also innocent of bloodshed in the past. Let
them discuss the peace personally; let them tell each other
of the marvellous revelations which have already heralded
it. Let them ignore all the futile differences which might
prevent peace, if negotiations were left to ecclesiastics, to
lawyers, and to soldiers. The king of France may fearlessly
cede a few frontier towns and castles. Directly after the
conclusion of peace the crusade will be prepared. Quarrels
and hostilities will cease everywhere; the tyrannical governments of countries will be reformed; a general council
will summon the princes of Christendom to undertake a
crusade, in case sermons do not suffice to convert the
Tartars, Turks, Jews and Saracens.

The share which the ideas of chivalry have had in the
development of the law of nations is not limited to these
dreams. The notion of a law of nations itself was preceded
and led up to by the ideal of a beautiful life of honour
and of loyalty. In the fourteenth century we find the for-
mulation of principles of international law blending with
the casuistical and often puerile regulations of passages of
arms and combats in the lists. In 1352 Sir Geoffroi de
Charny (who died at Poitiers bearing the oriflamme) addresses to the king, who has just instituted his order of the
Star, a treatise composed of a long list of "demandes," that

is to say, questions of casuistry, concerning jousts, tournaments and war. Jousts and tournaments rank first, but the importance of questions of military law is shown by their far greater number. It should be remembered that this order of the Star was the culmination of chivalrous romanticism, founded expressly "in the manner of the Round Table."

Better known than the "demandes" of Geoffroi de Charny is a work that appeared towards the end of the fourteenth century, and which remained in vogue till the sixteenth: *L'Arbre des Batailles* of Honoré Bonet, prior of Selonnet, in Provence. The influence of chivalry on the development of the law of nations nowhere appears more clearly than here. Though the author is an ecclesiastic, the idea which suggests his very remarkable conceptions to him is that of chivalry. He treats promiscuously questions of personal honour and the gravest questions of the law of nations. For example, "by what right can one wage war against the Saracens or other unbelievers," or, "if a prince may refuse the passage through his country to another." What is especially remarkable is the spirit of gentleness and of humanity in which Bonet solves these problems. May the king of France, waging war with England, take prisoner "the poor English, merchants, labourers of the soil and shepherds who tend their flocks in the fields"? The author answers in the negative; not only do Christian morals forbid it, but also "the honour of the age." He even goes so far as to extend the privilege of safe conduct in the enemy's country to the case of the father of an English student wishing to visit his sick son in Paris.

L'Arbre des Batailles was, unfortunately, only a theoretical treatise. We know full well that war in those times was very cruel. The fine rules and the generous exemptions enumerated by the good prior of Selonnet were too rarely observed. Still, if a little clemency was slowly introduced into political and military practice, this was due rather to the sentiment of honour than to convictions based on legal and moral principles. Military duty was conceived in the first place as the honour of a knight.

Taine said: "In the middle and lower classes the chief motive of conduct is self-interest. With an aristocracy the mainspring is pride. Now among the profound sentiments of man there is none more apt to be transformed into probity, patriotism and conscience, for a proud man feels the need of self-respect, and, to obtain it, he is led to deserve it." Is not this the point of view whence we must consider the importance of chivalry in the history of civilization? Pride assuming the features of a high ethical value, knightly self-respect preparing the way for clemency and right. These transitions in the domain of thought are real. In the passage quoted above from *Le Jouvencel* we noticed how chivalric sentiment passes into patriotism. All the best elements of patriotism—the spirit of sacrifice, the desire for justice and protection for the oppressed—sprouted in the soil of chivalry. It is in the classic country of chivalry, in France, that are heard, for the first time, the touching accents of love of the fatherland, irradiated by the sentiment of justice. One need not be a great poet to say these simple things with dignity. No author of those times has given French patriotism such a touching and also such a varied expression as Eustache Deschamps, whom we can only rate as a mediocre poet. Addressing France, he says:

> "Tu as duré et durras sanz doubtance
> Tant com raisons sera de toy amée,
> Autrement, non; fay donc à la balance
> Justice en toy et que bien soit gardée." [2]

Chivalry would never have been the ideal of life during several centuries if it had not contained high social values. Its strength lay in the very exaggeration of its generous and fantastic views. The soul of the Middle Ages, ferocious and passionate, could only be led by placing far too high the ideal towards which its aspirations should tend. Thus acted the Church, thus also feudal thought. We may apply here

[2] You have endured and will, no doubt, endure So long as reason will be loved by you. Not otherwise; so hold the balance Of justice in yourself, and let it be well kept.

Emerson's words: "Without this violence of direction, which men and women have, without a spice of bigot and fanatic, no excitement, no efficiency. We aim above the mark to hit the mark. Every act hath some falsehood of exaggeration in it." That reality has constantly given the lie to these high illusions of a pure and noble social life, who would deny? But where should we be, if our thoughts had never transcended the exact limits of the feasible?

Chapter VIII

LOVE FORMALIZED

When in the twelfth century unsatisfied desire was placed by the troubadours of Provence in the centre of the poetic conception of love, an important turn in the history of civilization was effected. Antiquity, too, had sung the sufferings of love, but it had never conceived them save as the expectation of happiness or as its pitiful frustration. The sentimental point of Pyramus and Thisbe, of Cephalus and Procris, lies in their tragic end; in the heart-rending loss of a happiness already enjoyed. Courtly poetry, on the other hand, makes desire itself the essential motif, and so creates a conception of love with a negative ground-note. Without giving up all connection with sensual love, the new poetic ideal was capable of embracing all kinds of ethical aspirations. Love now became the field where all moral and cultural perfection flowered. Because of his love, the courtly lover is pure and virtuous. The spiritual element dominates more and more, till towards the end of the thirteenth century, the *dolce stil nuovo* of Dante and his friends ends by attributing to love the gift of bringing about a state of piety and holy intuition. Here an extreme had been reached. Italian poetry was gradually to find its way back to a less exalted expression of erotic sentiment. Petrarch is divided between the ideal of spiritualized love and the more natural charm of antique models. Soon the artificial system of courtly love is abandoned, and its subtle distinctions will not be revived, when the Platonism of the Renaissance, latent, already, in the courtly conception, gives rise to new forms of erotic poetry with a spiritual tendency.

In France the evolution of erotic culture was more complicated. The idea of courtly love was not to be supplanted so easily there. The system is not given up; but the forms are filled by new values. Even before Dante had found the eternal harmony of his *Vita Nuova*, the *Roman de la Rose* had inaugurated a novel phase of erotic thought in France. The work, begun before 1240 by Guillaume de Lorris, was finished, before 1280, by Jean Chopinel. Few books have exercised a more profound and enduring influence on the life of any period than the *Romaunt of the Rose*. Its popularity lasted for two centuries at least. It determined the aristocratic conception of love in the expiring Middle Ages. By reason of its encyclopedic range it became the treasure-house whence lay society drew the better part of its erudition.

The existence of an upper class whose intellectual and moral notions are enshrined in an *ars amandi* remains a rather exceptional fact in history. In no other epoch did the ideal of civilization amalgamate to such a degree with that of love. Just as scholasticism represents the grand effort of the medieval spirit to unite all philosophic thought in a single centre, so the theory of courtly love, in a less elevated sphere, tends to embrace all that appertains to the noble life. The *Roman de la Rose* did not destroy the system; it only modified its tendencies and enriched its contents.

To formalize love is the supreme realization of the aspiration to the life beautiful, of which we traced above both the ceremonial and the heroic expression. More than in pride and in strength, beauty is found in love. To formalize love is, moreover, a social necessity, a need that is the more imperious as life is more ferocious. Love has to be elevated to the height of a rite. The overflowing violence of passion demands it. Only by constructing a system of forms and rules for the vehement emotions can barbarity be escaped. The brutality and the licence of the lower classes was always fervently, but never very efficiently, repressed by the Church. The aristocracy could feel less dependent on religious admonition, because they had a piece of culture of their own from which to draw their standards of conduct, namely, courtesy. Literature, fashion and conversation here formed the means to regulate and refine erotic life. If they did not altogether succeed, they at least created the appearance of an honourable life of courtly love. For, in reality, the sexual life of the higher classes remained surprisingly rude.

In the erotic conceptions of the Middle Ages two diverging currents are to be distinguished. Extreme indecency showing itself freely in customs, as in literature, contrasts with an excessive formalism, bordering on prudery. Chastellain mentions frankly how the duke of Burgundy, awaiting an English embassy at Valenciennes, reserves the baths of the town "for them and for all their retinue, baths provided with everything required for the calling of Venus, to take by choice and by election what they liked best, and all at the expense of the duke." Charles the Bold was reproached with his continence, which was thought unbecoming in a prince. At the royal or princely courts of the fifteenth century, marriage feasts were accompanied by all sorts of licentious pleasantries—a usage which had not disappeared two centuries later. In Froissart's narrative of the marriage of Charles VI with Isabella of Bavaria we hear the obscene grinning of the court. Deschamps dedicates to Antoine de Bourgogne an epithalamium of extreme indecency. A certain rhymer makes a lascivious ballad at the request of the lady of Burgundy and of all the ladies.

Such customs seem to be absolutely opposed to the constraint and the modesty imposed by courtesy. The same circles who showed so much shamelessness in sexual relations professed to venerate the ideal of courtly love. Are we to look for hypocrisy in their theory or for cynical abandonment of troublesome forms in their practice?

We should rather picture to ourselves two layers of civilization superimposed, coexisting though contradictory.

Side by side with the courtly style, of literary and rather recent origin, the primitive forms of erotic life kept all their force; for a complicated civilization like that of the closing Middle Ages could not but be heir to a crowd of conceptions, motives, erotic forms, which now collided and now blended.

The whole of the epithalamic genre may be considered as a heritage of a remote past. In primitive culture marriage and nuptials form but one single sacred rite, converging in the mystery of copulation. Afterwards the Church, by transferring the sacred element of marriage to the sacrament, reserved the mystery for itself, leaving its accessories, to which it objected, to develop freely as popular practices. Thus the epithalamic apparatus, though stripped of its sacred character, nevertheless kept its importance as the main element in the nuptial feasts, thriving there more freely than ever. Licentious expression and gross symbolism were essential to it. The Church was powerless to bridle them. Neither Catholic discipline nor Reformed Puritanism could do away with the quasi-publicity of the marriage-bed, which remained in vogue well into the seventeenth century.

It is therefore from an ethnological point of view, as survivals, that we have to regard the mass of obscenities, equivocal sayings and lascivious symbols which we meet in the civilization of the Middle Ages. They were the remains of mysteries that had degenerated into games and amusements. Evidently the people of that epoch did not feel that, in taking pleasure in them, they were infringing the prescriptions of the courtly code; they felt themselves on different soil where courtesy was not current.

It would be an exaggeration to say that in erotic literature the whole comic genre was derived from the epithalamium. Certainly the indecent tale, the farce and the lascivious song had long formed a genre of their own of which the forms of expression were liable to but little variation. Obscene allegory predominates; every trade lent itself to this treatment; the literature of the time abounds in symbolism borrowed from the tournament, the

chase or music; but most popular of all was the religious
travesty of erotic matters. Besides the grossly comic style
of the *Cent Nouvelles Nouvelles,* punning with homony-
mous words like *saint* and *seins,* or using in an obscene
sense the words for blessing and confession, erotic-
ecclesiastical allegory took a more refined form. The poets
of the circle of Charles d'Orléans compared their amorous
sadness to the sufferings of the ascetic and the martyr.
They call themselves "les amoureux de l'observance," al-
luding to the severe reform which the Franciscan order had
just undergone. Charles d'Orléans begins one of his pieces:

> "Ce sont ici les dix commandemens,
> Vray Dieu d'amours. . . ."[1]

Or, lamenting his dead love, he says:

> "J'ay fait l'obseque de ma dame
> Dedans le moustier amoureux,
> Et le service pour son ame
> A chanté Penser doloreux.
> Mains sierges de soupirs piteux
> Ont esté en son luminaire,
> Aussi j'ay fait la tombe faire
> De regrets. . . ."[2]

All the effects of a sweet and melancholy burlesque are
found together in that very tender and pure poem of the
end of the century called *L'Amant rendu Cordelier de
l'Observance d'Amour,* which describes the reception of an
inconsolable lover in the convent of amorous martyrs. It is
as though erotic poetry even in this perverse way strove
to recover that primitive connection with sacred matters
of which the Christian religion had bereft it.

[1] These are the ten commandments, True God of
love. . . .
[2] I have celebrated the obsequies of my lady In the
church of love, And the service for her soul Was sung by
dolorous Thought. Many tapers of pitiful sighs Have
burned in her illumination, Also I had the tomb made Of
regrets. . . .

French authors like to oppose "l'esprit gaulois" to the
conventions of courtly love, as the natural conception and
expression opposed to the artificial. Now the former is no
less a fiction than the latter. Erotic thought never acquires
literary value save by some process of transfiguration of
complex and painful reality into illusionary forms. The
whole genre of *Les Cent Nouvelles Nouvelles* and the
loose song, with its wilful neglect of all the natural and
social complications of love, with its indulgence towards
the lies and egotism of sexual life, and its vision of a never-
ending lust, implies, no less than the screwed-up system of
courtly love, an attempt to substitute for reality the dream
of a happier life. It is once more the aspiration towards the
life sublime, but this time viewed from the animal side.
It is an ideal all the same, even though it be that of un-
chastity. Reality at all times has been worse and more
brutal than the refined æstheticism of courtesy would have
it be, but also more chaste than it is represented to be by
the vulgar genre which is wrongly regarded as realism.

As an element of literary culture the "genre gaulois"
could only occupy a secondary place, because erotic poetry
is only fit to beautify life and to serve as a source of inspiration and imitation, in so far as it takes for its themes,
not sexual intercourse itself, but the possibility of happiness, the promise, desire, languor, expectation. Only thus
will it be capable of expressing all the different shadings
of love, and of treating it equally from the sad and from
the merry side. By introducing into love's domain the concepts of honour, courage, fidelity, and all the other elements of moral life, it will be of far greater æsthetic and
ethical value. The *Roman de la Rose,* by combining the
passionate character of its sensuous central theme with all
the elaborate fancy of the system of courtly love, satisfied
the needs of erotic expression of a whole age.

In this veritable treasure-house of amorous doctrine,
ritual and legend, systematic and complete, the encyclopedic spirit of the thirteenth century had poured itself out, as
it did in the sterner work of a Vincent of Beauvais. The
extraordinary influence of the book could not but be height-

ened by its ambiguous nature. The work of two poets of
different trends of thought, it joined—it would be more correct to say it juxtaposed—the courtly conception of love
and sensual cynicism of the most daring kind. Texts could
be found in it for all purposes.

Guillaume de Lorris had given it charm of form and
tenderness of accent. The background of vernal landscape,
the bizarre and yet harmonious imagery of allegorical figures, are his work. As soon as the lover has approached the
wall of the mysterious garden of love, the allegorical system is unfolded. Dame Leisure opens the gate for him,
Gaiety conducts the dance, Amor holds by the hand
Beauty, who is accompanied by Wealth, Liberality, Frankness, Courtesy and Youth. After having locked the heart
of his vassal, Amor enumerates to him the blessings of love,
called Hope, Sweet Thought, Sweet Speech, Sweet Look.
Then, when Bel-Accueil, the son of Courtesy, invites him
to come and see the roses, Danger, Malebouche, Fear and
Shame come to chase him away. The dramatic struggle
commences. Reason comes down from its high tower, and
Venus appears upon the scene. The text of Guillaume de
Lorris ends in the middle of the crisis.

Jean Chopinel, or Clopinel, or de Meun, who finished the
work, adding much more than he found, sacrificed the harmony of the composition to his fondness for psychological
and social analysis. The conquest of the castle of the roses
is drowned in a continual flood of digressions, speculations
and examples. The sweet breeze of Guillaume de Lorris
was followed by the east wind of chilling scepticism and
cruel cynicism of his successor. The vigorous and trenchant
spirit of the second tarnished the naïve and lightsome idealism of the first. Jean de Meun is an enlightened man, who
believes neither in spectres nor in sorcerers, neither in faithful love nor in the chastity of woman, who has an inkling
of the problems of mental pathology, and puts into the
mouths of Venus, Nature and Genius the most daring
apology for sensuality.

Venus, requested by her son to come to his aid, swears
not to leave a single woman chaste and makes Amor and

the whole army of assailants take the same vow as regards men. Nature, occupied in her smithy with her task of preserving the various species, her eternal struggle against Death, complains that of all creatures, man alone transgresses her commandments by abstaining from procreation. She charges Genius, her priest, to go and hurl at Love's army, Nature's anathema on those who despise her laws. In sacerdotal dress, a taper in his hand, Genius pronounces the sacrilegious excommunication, in which the boldest sensualism blends with refined mysticism. Virginity is condemned, hell is reserved for those who do not observe the commandments of nature and of love. For the others the flowered field, where the white sheep, led by Jesus, the lamb born of the Virgin, crop the incorruptible grass in endless daylight. At the close Genius throws the taper into the besieged fortress; its flame sets the universe on fire. Venus also throws her torch; then Shame and Fear flee, the castle is taken, and Bel-Accueil allows the lover to pluck the rose.

Here, then, in the *Roman de la Rose*, the sexual motif is again placed in the centre of erotic poetry, but enveloped by symbolism and mystery and presented in the guise of saintliness. It is impossible to imagine a more deliberate defiance of the Christian ideal. The dream of love had taken a form as artistic as it was passionate. The profusion of allegory satisfied all the requirements of medieval imagination. These personifications were indispensable for expressing the finer shades of sentiments. Erotic terminology, to be understood, could not dispense with these graceful puppets. People used these figures of Danger, Evil Mouth, etc., as the accepted terms of a scientific psychology. The passionate character of the central motif prevented tediousness and pedantry.

In theory, the *Roman de la Rose* does not deny the ideal of courtesy. The garden of delights is inaccessible except to the elect, regenerated by love. He who wants to enter must be free from all hatred, felony, villainy, avarice, envy, sadness, hypocrisy, poverty and old age. But the positive qualities he has to oppose to these are no longer ethical, as in the system of courtly love, but simply of an aristocratic character. They are leisure, pleasure, gaiety, love, beauty, wealth, liberality, frankness and courteousness. They are no longer so many perfections brought about by the sacredness of love, but simply the proper means to conquer the object desired. For the veneration of idealized womanhood, Jean Chopinel substituted a cruel contempt for its feebleness.

Now, whatever influence the *Roman de la Rose* may have exercised on the minds of men, it did not succeed in completely destroying the older conception of love. Side by side with the glorification of seduction professed by the *Rose*, the glorification of the pure and faithful love of the knight maintained its ground, both in lyrical poetry and in the romance of chivalry, not to speak of the fantasy of tournaments and passages of arms. Towards the end of the fourteenth century the question which of the two conceptions of love should be held by the perfect nobleman provoked a literary dispute such as French taste loved in later centuries also. The noble Boucicaut had made himself the champion of true courtesy by composing with his travelling companions the *Livre des Cent Ballades*, in which he called on the wits of the court to decide between the honest and self-denying service of a single lady, and fashionable flirtation. Knights or poets who, like Boucicaut, honoured the old ideal of courtesy, were vaunted as models, Othe de Granson and Louis de Sancerre among others. Christine de Pisan took part in the dispute by posing as the intrepid advocate of female honour. Her *Epistre au Dieu d'Amours* formulated the complaints of women about all the deceit and insults of men. With serious indignation she denounces the doctrine of the *Roman de la Rose*.

Then the multitude of fervent admirers of Jean de Meun appeared upon the scene. Among them were men of very varying spiritual bent, even ecclesiastics. The debate lasted for years. The nobility and the court took it up as a means of amusement. Boucicaut—encouraged, perhaps, by the praise of Christine de Pisan, for his defence of ideal courtesy—had already founded his "ordre de l'escu vert à

la dame blanche," for the defence of oppressed women,
when the duke of Burgundy eclipsed him by founding in
Paris, at the "hôtel d'Artois," on February 14, 1401, a court
of love on a very splendid scale. Philippe le Hardi, the old
diplomat, whom one would have supposed to be occupied
with affairs of a very different nature, and Louis de
Bourbon, had begged the king to institute a court of love
to furnish some distraction during an epidemic of the
plague which raged at Paris, "to spend part of the time
more graciously and in order to find awakening of new
joy." The cause of chivalry triumphed in the form of a
literary salon. The court was founded on the virtues of
humility and of fidelity, "to the honour, praise and com-
mendation and service of all noble ladies." The members
were provided with illustrious titles. The two founders and
the king were called the Grands Conservateurs. Among
the conservators we find Jean sans Peur, his brother Antoine, and his six-years-old son, Philippe. A certain Pierre
d'Hauteville, from Hainaut, was Prince of Love; there
were also ministers, auditors, knights of honour, knights
treasurers, councillors, grand-masters of the chase, squires
of love, etc. Burghers and lower clergy were admitted, side
by side with princes and prelates. The business of the
court much resembled that of a "rhetorical chamber." Re-
frains were set to be worked up into "ballades couronnées
ou chapelées," songs, sirventois, complaints, rondels, lays,
virelais, etc. There were debates "in the form of amorous
law-suits to defend different opinions." The ladies dis-
tributed the prizes, and poems attacking the honour of
women were forbidden.

In this pompous and grave apparatus of a graceful
amusement one cannot help feeling the effect of Burgundian style beginning to influence the French court itself.
It is equally obvious that the royal court, archaic like all
courts, must declare in favour of the ancient and severe
ideal of love, and that the 700 known members of the club
were far from conforming their practice to it. By what is
known of their habits, the great lords of that epoch were
rather strange protectors of female honour. The most cu-

rious fact is that we find there the same persons who, in
the debate about love, had defended the *Roman de la Rose*
and attacked Christine de Pisan. Evidently it was merely
a society amusement.

The intimate circle of Jean de Meun's admirers consisted
of men in the service of princes, both priests and laymen.
It is identical with that of the first French humanists. One
of them, Jean de Montreuil, provost of Lille, secretary to
the dauphin and later to the duke of Burgundy, was the
author of a good many Ciceronian epistles, and, like his
friends, Gontier and Pierre Col, he corresponded with
Nicolas de Clemanges, the grave censor of the abuses in
the Church. We now find him devoting his talents to the
defence of the *Roman de la Rose*, and of its author, Jean
de Meun. He asserts that several of the most learned and
enlightened men honour the *Roman de la Rose* so much
that their appreciation resembles a cult (*paene ut
colerent*), and that they would rather do without their
shirt than this book. He exhorts his friends to undertake its
defence, like himself. "The more I study"—he writes to one
of the detractors—"the gravity of the mysteries and the
mystery of the gravity of this profound and famous work
of Master Jean de Meun, the more I am astonished at your
disapprobation." He himself will defend it to his last breath,
and many others will serve this cause with words and
deeds.

The conviction with which Jean de Montreuil speaks,
seems already to indicate that the question of love, after
all, involved graver issues than those of a court amusement,
and this is further proved by the fact that Jean Gerson,
the illustrious chancellor of the university, took part in the
quarrel. He hated the *Roman de la Rose* with implacable
hatred. The book seemed to him to be the most dangerous
pest, the source of all immorality. In his works he reverts
again and again to the pernicious influence "of the vicious
romaunt of the rose." If he had a copy, which was the only
one and worth a thousand pounds, he would rather burn
it than sell it to be published. When Pierre Col had refuted
one of Gerson's polemical writings, the latter replied by a

treatise against the *Roman de la Rose,* which was more
bitter than his former denunciations. He dated it "from my
study, on the evening of the 18th of May, 1402."

Following the example of the author of the *Roman de
la Rose,* he gave his treatise the form of an allegoric vision.
Awakening, one morning, he feels his soul flying far away,
"using the feathers and the wings of various thoughts, from
one place to another, to the sacred court of Christianity,"
where he hears the complaints of Chastity addressed to
Justice, Conscience and Wisdom about the Fool of love,
that is to say, Jean de Meun, who has chased her from the
earth, with all her train. The "good guardians" of Chastity
are precisely the evil personages of the Rose: Shame, Fear
and Danger, "the good porter, who would not dare, who
would not deign to sanction even an impure kiss or dissolute
look, or attractive smile or light speech." Chastity over-
whelms the Fool of love with reproaches. The Fool rails at
marriage and monastic life. He teaches "how all young girls
should sell their persons early and dearly, without fear
and without shame, and that they should make light of
deceit and perjury." He directs the fancy exclusively to
carnal desire, and, to top all perversity, in the speeches of
Venus, of Nature, and of Dame Reason, he blends conceptions of Paradise, and of the mysteries of the Faith, with
those of sensual pleasure.

There, in truth, was the peril. This imposing work, with
its mixture of sensuality, scoffing cynicism and elegant
symbolism, infused a voluptuous mysticism into the mind
which, to an austere man, was simply an abyss of sin. Had
not Gerson's adversary dared to affirm that only the Fool
of love could judge of the value of passion? He who does
not know it sees it only as in a glass, to him it remains a
riddle. Such was the use he had made for his sacrilegious
purposes, of the holy words of Saint Paul! Pierre Col had
not scrupled to affirm that the Song of Solomon was composed in honour of the daughter of Pharaoh. Those who
have defamed the *Roman de la Rose,* he declared, have
bent their knees before Baal. Nature does not wish that a
woman should be content with one single man, and the

genius of Nature is God. He carried his blasphemy so far as to show from the Gospel of Saint Luke that formerly a woman's genitals, the rose of the romance, were sacred. Being convinced of the truth of this impious mysticism, he appealed to the friends of the book, forming a cloud of witnesses, and predicted that Gerson himself would fall madly in love, as had happened to other theologians before him.

Gerson did not succeed in destroying the authority, or, at least, the popularity, of the *Roman de la Rose*. In 1444 a canon of Lisieux, Estienne Legris, composed a *Répertoire du Roman de la Rose*. Towards the end of the century Jean Molinet could assert that its sentences were current like proverbs. He has given himself the trouble of "moralizing" the whole book, in giving its allegories a religious meaning. The nightingale calling to love meant the voice of the preacher, the rose meant Jesus. Even in the hey-day of the Renaissance, Clément Marot considered that the work deserved to be modernized, and Ronsard did not consider the figures of Bel-Accueil and Faus Danger too worn for use in his verse.

Chapter IX

THE CONVENTIONS OF LOVE

It is from literature that we gather the forms of erotic thought belonging to a period, but we should try to picture them functioning as elements of social life. A whole system of amatory conceptions and usages was current in aristocratic conversation of those times. What signs and figures of love which later ages have dropped! Around the god of Love the bizarre mythology of the *Roman de la Rose* was grouped. Then there was the symbolism of colours in costume, and of flowers and precious stones. The meaning of colours, of which feeble traces still obtain, was of extreme importance in amorous conversation during the Middle Ages. A manual of the subject was written about 1458, by the herald Sicily in his *Le Blason des Couleurs,* laughed at by Rabelais. When Guillaume de Machaut meets his beloved for the first time, he is delighted to see her wear a white dress and a sky-blue hood with a design of green parrots, because green signifies new love and blue fidelity. Later, he sees her image in a dream, turning away from him and dressed in green, "signifying novelty," and reproaches her with it in a ballad:

"En lieu de bleu, dame, vous vestez vert." [1]

Rings, veils and bands, all the jewels and presents of courtship had their special function, with devices and enigmatic emblems which sometimes were veritable rebuses. The standard of the dauphin in 1414 bore a gold K, a swan (cygne) and an L, indicating one of his mother's maids of honour, who was called la Cassinelle. The "glorieux de court et transporteurs de noms," at whom Rabelais mocked, represent "espoir" by a sphere, "mélancholie" by a columbine (ancolie). Numerous games served to express the finesses of sentiment, such as The King who does not lie, The Castle of love, Sales of love, Games for sale. In one of them, for instance, the lady mentions a flower; the young man has to answer by a rhymed compliment.

"Je vous vens la passerose.
   —Belle, dire ne vous ose
   Comment Amours vers vous me tire,
   Si l'apercevez tout sanz dire." [2]

The game of Castle of love consisted of a series of allegorical riddles.

"Du chastel d'Amours vous demant:

[1] Instead of in blue, lady, you dress in green.
[2] I sell you the hollyhock.—Belle, I dare not tell How Love draws me towards you, But you perceive it, without saying a word.

Dites le premier fondement!
—Amer loyaument.

"Or me nommez le mestre mur
Qui joli le font, fort et seur!
—Celer sagement.

"Dites moy qui sont li crenel,
Les fenestres et li carrell
—Regart atraiant.

"Amis, nommez moy le portier!
—Dangier mauparlant.

"Qui est la clef qui le puet deffermer?
—Prier courtoisement." [3]

Since the times of the troubadours the casuistry of love
had occupied a large place in courtly conversation. It was,
so to say, curiosity and backbiting raised to the level of a
literary form. At the court of Louis of Orléans people amuse
themselves at meals by "tales, ballads" and "graceful questions." Poets are especially laid under contribution.
Machaut is requested by a company of ladies and noblemen to reply to a series of "partures of love and of its
adventures." Every love-affair is discussed according to
rigorous rules. "Beau sire, which would you prefer: that
people spoke ill of your lady and that you found her good,
or that she were well spoken of and you should find her
bad?" The strict conception of honour obliged a gentleman to answer: "Lady, I should prefer to hear her well
spoken of and that I should find her bad."

Does a lady, neglected by her lover, break faith by

[3] Of the castle of Love I ask you: Tell me the first
foundation!—To love loyally. Now mention the principal
wall Which makes it fine, strong and sure!—To conceal
wisely. Tell me what are the loopholes, The windows and
the stones!—Alluring looks. Friend, mention the porter!—
Ill-speaking danger. Which is the key that can unlock it?
—Courteous request.

choosing another? May a knight bereft of all hope of seeing his lady, whom a jealous husband keeps locked up, seek a new love? One step more and love questions will be treated as lawsuits, as in the *Arrestz d'Amour* of Martial d'Auvergne.

The courtly code did not serve exclusively for making verses; it claimed to be applicable to life, or at least to conversation. It is very difficult to pierce the clouds of poetry and to penetrate to the real life of the epoch. How far did courting and flirtation during the fourteenth and fifteenth centuries come up to the requirements of the courtly system or to the precepts of Jean de Meun? Autobiographical confessions are very rare at that epoch. Even when an actual love-affair is described with the intention of being accurate, the author cannot free himself from the accepted style and technical conceptions. We find an instance of this in the too lengthy narrative of a love-affair of an old poet and a young girl, which Guillaume de Machaut has given us in *Le Livre du Voir-Dit*. He was approaching his sixtieth year, when Peronnelle d'Armentières, of a noble family in Champagne, sent him, in 1362, her first rondel, in which she offered her heart to the celebrated poet, whom she did not know, and invited him to enter with her into a poetical love correspondence. The poor poet, sickly, blind of one eye, gouty, at once kindles. He replies to her rondel and an exchange of letters and of poems begins. Peronnelle is proud of her literary connection; she does not make a secret of it, and begs the poet to put in writing the true story of their love, inserting their letters and their poetry. Machaut readily complies. "I shall make," he says, "to your glory and praise, something that will be well remembered."

"And, my very sweet heart, are you sorry because we have begun so late? By God, so am I; but here is the remedy: let us enjoy life as much as circumstances permit, so that we may make up for the time we have lost; and that people may speak of our love a hundred years hence, and all well and honourably; for if there were evil, you would conceal it from God, if you could."

The narrative connecting the letters and the poetry

teaches us what degree of intimacy was considered compatible with a decent love-affair. The young lady may permit herself extraordinary liberties, provided everything takes place in the presence of third parties, her sister-in-law, her maid or her secretary. At the first interview, which Machaut has been waiting for with misgivings, because of his unattractive appearance, Peronnelle falls asleep, or pretends to sleep, under a cherry tree, with her head on the poet's knees. The secretary covers her mouth with a green leaf and tells Machaut to kiss the leaf. Just when the latter takes courage to do so, the secretary pulls the leaf away.

She grants him other favours. A pilgrimage to Saint Denis, at the time of the fair, provides them with an opportunity of passing some days together. One afternoon, overcome by the heat of mid-June, they fly from the crowd at the fair to take a few hours' rest. A burgher of the town provides them with a double-bedded room. The blinds are closed and the company lies down. The sister-in-law takes one of the two beds. Peronnelle and her maid occupy the other. She orders the bashful poet to lie down between them, which he does, lying very still for fear of disturbing her. On waking, she orders him to kiss her.

At the end of the trip, she permits him to come and wake her, in order to take leave, and the narrative gives us to understand that she refused him nothing. She gives him the golden key of her honour, to guard that treasure, or what was left of it.

The poet's good fortune ended there. He did not see her again, and, for lack of other adventures, he filled the rest of his book with mythological excursions. At last she lets him know that their relations must end, because of a marriage, probably. He resolves to go on loving and revering her till the end of his days. And after their death, he will pray God, to reserve for her, in the glory of Heaven, the name he gave her: *Toute-belle*.

In the *Voir-Dit* of Machaut religion and love are mixed up with a sort of ingenuous shamelessness. We need not be shocked by the fact that the author was a canon of the church of Reims, for, in the Middle Ages, minor orders,

which sufficed for a canon (Petrarch was one), did not
absolutely impose celibacy. The fact that a pilgrimage was
chosen as an occasion for the lovers to meet was not extraordinary either. At this period pilgrimages served all sorts of
frivolous purposes. But what astonishes us is that Machaut,
a serious and delicate poet, claims to perform his pilgrimage "very devoutly." At mass he is seated behind her:

> ". . . Quant on dist: Agnus Dei,
> Foy que je doy à Saint Crepais,
> Doucement me donna la pais,[4]
> Entre deux pilers du moustier.
> Et j'en avoie bien mestier,
> Car mes cuers amoureus estoit
> Troublés, quant si tost se partoit."[5]

He says his hours as he is waiting for her in the garden. He glorifies her portrait as his God on earth. Entering
the church to begin a novene, he takes a mental vow to
compose a poem about his beloved on each of the nine
days—which does not prevent him from speaking about the
great devotion with which he said his prayers.

We shall revert elsewhere to the astonishing ingenuous-
ness with which, before the Council of Trent, worldly occupations were mixed up with works of the Faith.

As regards the tone of the love-affair of Machaut and
Peronnelle, it is soft, cloying, somewhat morbid. The expression of their feelings remains enveloped in arguments
and allegories. But there is something touching in the
tenderness of the old poet, which prevents him from seeing
that "Toute-belle," after all, has but played with him and
with her own heart.

To grasp what little we can of actual love relations, apart
from literature, we should oppose to the *Voir-Dit*, as a
pendant, *Le Livre du Chevalier de la Tour Landry pour*

[4] *Vide* page 37.
[5] When the priest said: Agnus Dei, Faith I owe to
Saint Crepais, Sweetly she gave me the pax Between
two pillars of the church. And I needed it indeed, For my
amorous heart was Troubled that we had to part so soon.

l'Enscignement de ses Filles, written at the same epoch.
This time we are not concerned with an amorous old poet;
we have to do with a father of a rather prosaic turn of
mind, an Angevin nobleman, who relates his reminiscences,
anecdotes and tales "pour mes filles aprandre à roumancier." This might be rendered, "to teach my daughters the
fashionable conventions in love matters." The instruction,
however, does not turn out romantic at all. The moral of
the examples and admonitions which the cautious father
recommends to his daughters tends especially to put them
on their guard against the dangers of romantic flirtations.
Take heed of eloquent people, always ready with their
"false long and pensive looks and little sighs, and wonderful emotional faces, and who have more words at hand
than other people." Do not be too encouraging. He himself, when young, was conducted by his father to a castle
to make the acquaintance of a young lady to whom they
wanted to betroth him. The girl received him very kindly.
He conversed with her on all sorts of subjects, so as to
probe her character somewhat. They got to talk of prisoners, which gave the knight a chance to pay a neat compliment: "'Ma demoiselle, it would be better to fall into
your hands as a prisoner than into many another's, and I
think your prison would not be so hard as that of the English.' She replied that she had recently seen one whom she
could wish to be her prisoner. And then I asked her, if
she would make a bad prison for him, and she said not at
all, and that she would hold him as dear as her own person, and I told her that the man would be very fortunate
in having such a sweet and noble prison. What shall I
say? She could talk well enough, and it seemed, to judge
from her conversation, that she knew a good deal, and
her eyes had also a very lively and lightsome expression."
When they took leave she begged him two or three times
to come back soon, as if she had known him for a long time
already. "And when we had departed my lord my father
said to me: 'What do you think of her whom you have
seen? Tell me your opinion.' 'Monseigneur, she seems to
me all well and good, but I shall never be nearer to her

than I am now, if you please.'" Her lack of reserve left
him without any desire to get better acquainted with her.
So they did not get engaged, and of course the author says
that he afterwards had reason not to repent it.

It is to be regretted that the chevalier has not given
more autobiographical details and fewer moral exhortations, because these personal traits, showing how customs
adapted themselves to the ideal, are very rare in the
traditions of the Middle Ages.

In spite of his avowed intention to teach his girls "à
roumancier," the knight de la Tour Landry thinks, before
all things, of a good marriage; and marriage had little to do
with love. He reports to them a "debate" between his wife
and himself, on the question, whether it is becoming
"d'amer par amours." He thinks that a girl may, in certain
cases, for example, "in the hope of marrying," love honourably. His wife thinks otherwise. It is better that a girl
should not fall in love at all, not even with her betrothed,
otherwise piety would suffer in consequence. "For I have
heard many women say who were in love in their youth,
that when they were in church, their thoughts and fancies
made them dwell more on those nimble imaginations and
delights of their love-affairs than on the service of God, and
the art of love is of such a nature that just at the holiest
moments of the service, that is to say, when the priest
holds our Lord on the altar, the most of these little thoughts
would come to them." Machaut and Peronnelle might have
confirmed this.

It is not easy for us to reconcile the general austerity of
the Chevalier de la Tour Landry with the fact that this
father does not scruple to instruct his daughters by means
of stories which would not have been out of place in the
Cent Nouvelles Nouvelles. Still, even more recent literature, that of the Elizabethan age, for instance, may remind us how completely the world becomes estranged from
the erotic forms of a few centuries back. As for betrothals
and marriages, neither the graceful forms of the courtly
ideal nor the refined frivolity and open cynicism of the
Roman de la Rose had any real hold upon them. In the

very matter-of-fact considerations on which a match between noble families was based there was little room for
the chivalrous fictions of prowess and of service. Thus it
came about that the courtly notions of love were never
corrected by contact with real life. They could unfold
freely in aristocratic conversation, they could offer a literary
amusement or a charming game, but no more. The ideal
of love, such as it was, could not be lived up to, except in a
fashion inherently false.

Cruel reality constantly gave the lie to it. At the bottom
of the intoxicating cup of the *Roman de la Rose* the moralist
exposed the bitter dregs. From the side of religion maledic-
tions were poured upon love in all its aspects, as the sin by
which the world is being ruined. Whence, exclaims Gerson,
come the bastards, the infanticides, the abortions, whence
hatred, whence poisonings?—Woman joins her voice to that
from the pulpit: all the conventions of love are the work
of men: even when it dons an idealistic guise, erotic culture
is altogether saturated by male egotism: and what else is
the cause of the endlessly repeated insults to matrimony,
to woman and her feebleness, but the need of masking this
egotism? One word suffices, says Christine de Pisan, to answer all these infamies: it is not the women who have
written the books.

Indeed, medieval literature shows little true pity for
woman, little compassion for her weakness and the dangers
and pains which love has in store for her. Pity took on a
stereotyped and factitious form, in the sentimental fiction of
the knight delivering the virgin. The author of the *Quinze
Joyes de Mariage,* after having mocked at all the faults of
women, undertakes to describe also the wrongs they have
to suffer. So far as is known, he never performed this task.

Civilization always needs to wrap up the idea of love in
veils of fancy, to exalt and refine it, and thereby to forget
cruel reality. The solemn or graceful game of the faithful
knight or the amorous shepherd, the fine imagery of courtly
allegories, however brutally life belied them, never lost
their charm nor all their moral value. The human mind

needs these forms, and they always remain essentially the
same.

Chapter X

THE IDYLLIC VISION OF LIFE

The lasting vogue of the pastoral genre towards the end of
the Middle Ages implies a reaction against the ideal of
courtesy. Weary of the complicated formalism of chivalrous
love, the aristocratic soul renounces the overstrung pretension of heroism in love, and praises rural life as the escape
from it. The new, or rather revived, bucolic ideal remains
essentially an erotic one. Still there is a strain of bucolic
sentiment, the inspiration of which is rather ethical than
erotic. We may perhaps distinguish it from the pastoral
proper by calling it the idea of the simple life, or of *aurea
mediocritas*. It is continually merging into the other.

The negation of the chivalric ideal arises among the
nobles themselves. It is in court literature that sarcastic or
sentimental criticism of it springs up. The burghers, on the
other hand, are always striving to imitate the forms of the
noble life. Nothing could be falser than to picture the third
estate in the Middle Ages as animated by class hatred, or
scorning chivalry. On the contrary, the splendour of the
life of the nobility dazzles and seduces them. The rich
burghers take pains to adopt the forms and the tone of the
nobility. Philip of Artevelde, the leader of the Flemish insurgents, whom one would like to picture as a simple, sober
revolutionary, kept a state like a prince's. His going in to
dinner is announced by music. His meals are served up on
silver plate like that of a count of Flanders; he goes about
dressed in scarlet and miniver, preceded by his unfurled
pennon showing a sable scutcheon with three silver hats.
The great financier, Jacques Cœur, whom one instinctively
thinks of as a modern, took a lively interest, according to

Jacques de Lalaing's biographer, in the fantastic and useless
projects of that anachronistic knight-errant.

Among those who freed themselves from the chivalric
illusion, seeing the misery and the falsehood of it, we must
begin with those practical and frigid minds which were,
so to say, opposed to it by temperament. Such were
Philippe de Commines and his master, Louis XI. In describing the battle of Montlhéry, Commines abstains from all
heroic fiction: no fine exploits, no dramatic turns; he only
gives us a realistic picture of comings and goings, of
hesitations and fears. He takes pleasure in telling of flights
and noting how courage returned with security. He re-
jects all chivalrous terminology and scarcely mentions
honour, which he treats almost as an inevitable evil.

The ideal of chivalry tallies with the spirit of a primitive
age, susceptible of gross delusion and little accessible to the
corrections of experience. Sooner or later intellectual progress demands a revision of this ideal. It does not disappear,
however, it only sheds its too fantastic tendencies. Chivalry,
far from being completely disavowed, drops its affectation
of a quasi religious perfection, and will be henceforth only
a model of social life. The knight is transformed into the
cavalier, who, though still keeping up a very severe code
of honour and of glory, will no longer claim to be a defender of the Faith or a protector of the oppressed. The
modern gentleman is still ideally linked with the medieval
conception of chivalry.

The requirements of moral, æsthetic and social perfection weighed too heavily on the knight. This highly praised
chivalry, considered from any point of view whatever,
could not conceal its inherent falsity. It was a ridiculous
anachronism, a piece of factitious making up. No social
utility, no moral value, everywhere vanity and sin. Even as
an æsthetic game, the courtly life ended by boring the
players. So they turn to another ideal, that of simplicity
and of repose. Does this mean that the disillusioned nobles
turned to a spiritual life? Sometimes they did. At all times
the lives of many courtiers and soldiers have ended in renunciation of the world. More often, however, they are

content themselves to seek elsewhere the sublime life
which chivalry failed to give. From the days of antiquity a
promise had been held out of an earthly felicity to be
found in rural life. Here true peace seemed attainable without strife, simply by flight. Here was a sure refuge from
envy and hatred, from the vanity of honours, from oppressive luxury and cruel war.

Medieval literature inherited from the classic authors the
theme of the praise of the simple life, which may be called
the negative side of the bucolic sentiment. Court life and
aristocratic pretension are disavowed in favour of solitude,
work and study. In the fourteenth century this theme had
found its typical expression in France in *Le Dit de Franc
Gontier* of Philippe de Vitri, bishop of Meaux, musician and
poet, and a friend of Petrarch.

> "Soubz feuille vert, sur herbe delitable
> Lez ru bruiant et prez clere fontaine
> Trouvay fichee une borde portable,
> Ilec mengeoit Gontier o dame Helayne
> Fromage frais, laict, burre fromaigee,
> Craime, matton, pomme, nois, prune, poire,
> Aulx et oignons, escaillongne froyee
> Sur crouste bise, au gros sel, pour mieux boire." [1]

After the meal they kiss "both the mouth and the nose,
the soft and the shaggy," then Gontier goes off to fell a tree,
while Helayne goes to do the washing.

> "J'oy Gontier en abatant son arbre
> Dieu mercier de sa vie seüre:
> 'Ne sçay,' dit-il, 'que sont pilliers de marbre,
> Pommeaux luisans, murs vestus de paincture;
> Je n'ay paour de traïson tissue

[1] Under green leaves, on delightful grass Near a noisy
brook and a clear fountain I found a portable board, There
Gontier took his meal with dame Helayne On fresh cheese,
milk, cream and cheese, curds, apple, nut, plum, pear,
Garlic and onions, chopped shallots On a brown crust, with
coarse salt, to drink the better.

Soubz beau semblant, ne qu'empoisonné soye
En vaisseau d'or. Je n'ay la teste nue
Devant thirant, ne genoil qui s'i ploye.

'Verge d'uissier jamais ne me deboute,
Car jusques la ne m'esprent convoitise,
Ambicion, ne lescherie gloute.
Labour me paist en joieuse franchise;
Moult j'ame Helayne et elle moy sans faille,
Et c'est assez. De tombel n'avons cure.'
Lors je dy: 'Las! serf de court ne vault maille,
Mais Franc Gontier vault en or jame pure.' " [2]

We observe how here already the motif of the simple
life is coupled with that of natural love.

For later generations the poem of Philippe de Vitri remained the classic expression of the bucolic sentiment and
of the happiness procured by security and independence,
frugality and health, useful labour and conjugal love, without complications.

Eustache Deschamps imitated him in a number of ballads, of which one follows its model very closely.

"En retournant d'une court souveraine
Ou j'avoie longuement sejourné,
En un bosquet, dessus une fontaine
Trouvay Robin le franc, enchapelé;

[2] I heard Gontier in felling his tree Thank God for his
life of security:
"I do not know," he said, "what are pillars of marble,
Shining pommels, walls decorated with paintings; I have no
fear of treason hidden Under fine appearances, nor that I
shall be poisoned In a gold cup. I do not bare my head
Before a tyrant, nor bend my knee.
"No usher's rod ever turns me away, For no covetousness, Ambition, nor lechery entice me (to court). Labour
holds me in joyous liberty; I love Helayne dearly, and she
loves me without fail, And that is enough. We are not
afraid of the grave." Then I said: "Alas! a serf of the court
is not worth a doit, But Franc Gontier is worth a sure gem
set in gold."

Chapeauls de flours avoit cilz afublé
Dessus son chief, et Marion sa drue . . ." etc.[3]

He has enlarged the motif in adding to it an indictment
of a knight's or a soldier's life; there is no worse condition
than that of a warrior; he commits the seven deadly sins
every day; avarice and vainglory are the essence of warfare.

". . . Je vueil mener d'or en avant
Estat moien, c'est mon opinion,
Guerre laissier et vivre en labourant:
Geurre mener n'est que dampnacion."[4]

Generally, however, he simply praises the golden mean.

"Je ne requier à Dieu fors qu'il me doint
En ce monde de lui servir et loer,
Vivre pour moy, cote entiere ou pourpoint,
Aucun cheval pour mon labour porter.
Et que je puisse mon estat gouverner
Moiennement, en grace, sanz envie,
Sanz trop avoir et sanz pain demander,
Car au jour d'ui est la plus seure vie."[5]

The quest of glory or of gain does but entail misery; only
the poor man is happy, he lives tranquilly and long.

". . . Un ouvrier et uns povres chartons
Va mauvestuz, deschirez et deschaulx

---

[3] Returning from a sovereign's court Where I had long
sojourned, In a bush, near a fountain I found Robin the
free, his head crowned; With chaplets of flowers had he
adorned His head, and Marion, his beloved . . .

[4] Henceforth I will take up a Middle station, so I am
resolved To leave off fighting and to live by labour; Waging
war is but damnation.

[5] I only ask of God to give me That I may serve and
praise him in this world, Live for myself, my coat or doublet
whole, One horse to carry my labour, And that I may govern my estate In mediocre style, in grace, without envy,
Without having too much and without begging my bread,
For this day is the safest life.

> Mais en ouvrant prant en gré ses travaulx
> Et liement fait son euvre fenir.
> Par nuit dort bien; pour ce uns telz cueurs loiaulx
> Voit quatre roys et leur regne fenir." [6]

The picture of a working man surviving four kings pleased him so much that he used it several times.

The editor of Deschamps' works, Monsieur Gaston Raynaud, supposes that the poems of this tendency all date from the last period of his life, when, deprived of his functions, forsaken and disappointed, he has at last learned to understand the vanity of court affairs. This is perhaps going too far; these poems would seem rather to be the expression of sentiments, more or less conventional, current among the nobility itself in the midst of court life.

The theme of contempt for a courtier's life enjoyed great favour with a group of scholars who, towards the end of the fourteenth century, mark the beginning of French humanism, and whose circle was connected with that of the leaders of the great councils of the Church. Pierre d'Ailly himself is the author of a poem forming a companion piece with that of *Franc Gontier*: the tyrant, in contrast with the happy rustic, leading the life of a slave in continuous fear. The theme was admirably fit to be treated in the epistolary style, after the model of Petrarch. Jean de Montreuil tried his hand at it; so did Nicolas de Clemanges, three times over. A secretary to the duke of Orléans, the Milanese Ambrose de Miliis, addressed to Gontier Col a Latin letter, in which a courtier dissuades his friend from entering into court service. Translated into French, this letter figures among the works of Alain Chartier, under the title *Le Curial*, and afterwards Robert Gaguin translated it back into Latin.

The theme was even worked out by a certain Charles

[6] A working man and a poor waggoner, Go about ill dressed, in torn clothes and ill shod, But, labouring, he takes pleasure in his work And merrily finishes it. At night he sleeps well; and therefore such a loyal heart Sees four kings and their reigns end.

Rochefort in a long-winded allegorical poem, *L'Abuzé en
Court,* afterwards attributed to King René. Towards the
end of the fifteenth century, Jean Meschinot still rhymes as
follows:

> "La cour est une mer, dont sourt
> Vagues d'orgueil, d'envie orages. . . .
> Ire esmeut debats et outrages,
> Qui les nefs jettent souvent bas:
> Traison y fait son personnage.
> Nage aultre part pour tes ebats." [7]

In the sixteenth century the old motif had lost nothing
of its freshness.

For the most part the praises of a frugal life and of hard
work in the fields are not based on the delights of simplicity
and labour in themselves, nor on the security and independence they seemed to confer; the positive content of
the ideal is the longing for natural love. The pastoral is the
idyllic form assumed by erotic thought. Just like the dream
of heroism which is at the bottom of the ideas of chivalry,
the bucolic dream is somewhat more than a literary genre.
It is a craving to reform life itself. It does not stop at
describing the life of shepherds with its innocent and natural pleasures. People want to imitate it, if not in real life,
at least in the illusion of a graceful game. Weary of
factitious conceptions of love, the aristocracy sought a
remedy for them in the pastoral ideal. Facile and innocent
love amid the delights of nature seemed to be the lot of
country people, theirs to be the truly enviable form of happiness. The villein, in his turn, becomes an ideal type.

The antique form of bucolic life still satisfied the aspirations of the waning Middle Ages. No need is felt to correct
the pastoral fiction in accordance with real life. The new
enthusiasm for nature does not mean a truly deep sense of

[7] The court is a sea, whence come Waves of pride,
thunderstorms of envy. Wrath stirs up quarrels and out-
rages, Which often cause the ships to sink: Treason plays
its part there, Swim elsewhere for your amusement.

reality, not even a sincere admiration for work; it is only an attempt to adorn courteous manners by an array of artificial flowers, playing at shepherd and shepherdess just as people had played at Lancelot and Guinevere.

In the *Pastourelle*, the short poem relating the facile adventure of the knight with the country girl, pastoral fancy is still in touch with reality. In the pastoral proper, however, the lover or poet thinks himself a shepherd too, all contact with reality is lost, all things are transferred to a sunlit landscape full of the singing of birds and playing of reedpipes, where even sadness assumes a sweet sound. The faithful shepherd continues to resemble the faithful knight only too closely; after all, it is courtly love transposed into another key.

However artificial it might be, pastoral fancy still tended to bring the loving soul into touch with nature and its beauties. The pastoral genre was the school where a keener perception and a stronger affection towards nature were learned. The literary expression of the sentiment of nature was a by-product of the pastoral. Out of the simple words of exultation at the joys caused by sunshine and shade, birds and flowers, the loving description of scenery and rural life gradually develops. A poem like *Le Dit de la Pastoure* of Christine de Pisan marks the transition of the pastoral to a new genre.

The bucolic idyll, then, offered itself as a new style for courtly amusement, a supplement to chivalry, as it were. Once received as such, it becomes another mask. The pastoral travesty serves for all sorts of diversions; the domains of pastoral fancy and of chivalric romanticism mingle. Tournaments are held in the apparel of an eclogue, like the "Pas d'armes de la bergère" of King René. These pastoral representations, even if they did not really deceive people, at least seem to have been regarded as important. Among his "Marvels of the World" Chastellain mentions King René's playing at shepherd.

> "J'ay un roi de Cécille
> Vu devenir berger

> Et sa femme gentille
> De ce mesme mestier,
> Portant la pannetière,
> La houlette et chappeau,
> Logeans sur la bruyère
> Auprès de leur trouppeau." [8]

On another occasion, pastoral fancy had to supply a literary form for political satire. It is hard to imagine a more bizarre product than *Le Pastoralet,* a very long poem by a partisan of Burgundy, who, in this pretty disguise, relates the murder of Louis of Orléans for the purpose of exculpating Jean sans Peur and of venting his spleen on the house of Orléans. The two hostile dukes represented by Tristifer and Léonet in an environment of country dances and ornaments of flowers, Tristifer-Orléans robbing the shepherds of their bread and cheese, apples and nuts, shepherd's reeds and bells, and threatening them with his large crook, even the battle of Agincourt described in pastoral guise . . . one would be inclined to think this style rather flamboyant, if we did not remember that Ariosto uses the same machinery for exculpating his patron, the Cardinal d'Este, who was hardly less guilty than Jean sans Peur.

The pastoral element is never absent from court festivities. It was admirably fitted both for masquerades and for political allegories. Here the bucolic conception coalesced with another of Scriptural origin: the prince and his people symbolized by the shepherd and his sheep, the duties of the ruler compared to those of the shepherd. Meschinot sings:

> "Seigneur, tu es de Dieu bergier;
> Garde ses bestes loyaument,
> Mets les en champ ou en vergier,
> Mais ne les perds aucunement,

[8] I have seen a king of Sicily Turn shepherd And his gentle wife Take to the same trade, Carrying the shepherd's pouch, The crook and hat, Dwelling on the heath Near their flock.

> Pour ta peine auras bon paiement
> En bien le gardant, et se non,
> A male heure reçus ce nom." [9]

Represented in actual mummery, these ideas naturally took the outward appearance of the pastoral proper. At the marriage feasts of Charles the Bold and Margaret of York at Bruges in 1468, an "entremets" glorified the princesses of yore as "noble shepherdesses who formerly tended and guarded the sheep of the 'pays de par deça' (the provinces 'over here')." At Valenciennes, in 1493, the revival of the land after the devastations of war was represented, "all in pastoral style." Even in war the pastoral game was kept up. The stone-mortars of the duke of Burgundy before Granson are called "the shepherd and the shepherdess." Philippe de Ravestein takes the field with four-and-twenty noble-men; they are all dressed up as shepherds and carry shep-herds' pouches and crooks.

As the *Roman de la Rose* had done, because of its con-trast with the chivalric ideal, so the bucolic ideal in its turn gave rise to an elegant quarrel. A number of variations had been made on the theme of Franc Gontier: every one had declared that he was sighing for a diet of cheese, apples, onions, brown bread and fresh water, for a woodcutter's work with its liberty and carelessness. But aristocratic life still looked very little like it and sceptics were aware of the inherent falsity of the factitious ideal. Villon unmasked it. In *Les contrediz Franc Gontier* he opposed to the idealized country man and his love under the roses, the fat canon, free from care, tasting good wines and the joys of love in a comfortable room, supplied with an ample hearth and a soft bed. The brown bread and the water of Franc Gontier?

"Tous les oyseaulx d'ici en Babiloine

---

[9] Lord, you are God's shepherd; Guard his animals loy-ally, Lead them to the field or the orchard, But lose them by no means, You will have good payment for your trouble Of guarding them well, and if you do not, You received this name in an evil hour.

A tel escot une seule journée
Ne me tiendroient, non une matinée." 10

Chapter XI

THE VISION OF DEATH

No other epoch has laid so much stress as the expiring
Middle Ages on the thought of death. An everlasting call
of *memento mori* resounds through life. Denis the Carthusian, in his *Directory of the Life of Nobles,* exhorts them:
"And when going to bed at night, he should consider how,
just as he now lies down himself, soon strange hands will
lay his body in the grave." In earlier times, too, religion
had insisted on the constant thought of death, but the pious
treatises of these ages only reached those who had already
turned away from the world. Since the thirteenth century,
the popular preaching of the mendicant orders had made
the eternal admonition to remember death swell into a
sombre chorus ringing throughout the world. Towards the
fifteenth century, a new means of inculcating the awful
thought into all minds was added to the words of the
preacher, namely, the popular woodcut. Now these two
means of expression, sermons and woodcuts, both addressing themselves to the multitude and limited to crude
effects, could only represent death in a simple and striking
form. All that the meditations on death of the monks of
yore had produced, was now condensed into a very primitive image. This vivid image, continually impressed upon
all minds, had hardly assimilated more than a single element of the great complex of ideas relating to death,
namely, the sense of the perishable nature of all things.

10 All the birds from here to Babylon With such a fare
a single day Would not keep me, no not one morning.

It would seem, at times, as if the soul of the declining Middle Ages only succeeded in seeing death under this aspect.

The endless complaint of the frailty of all earthly glory was sung to various melodies. Three motifs may be distinguished. The first is expressed by the question: where are now all those who once filled the world with their splendour? The second motif swells on the frightful spectacle of human beauty gone to decay. The third is the death-dance: death dragging along men of all conditions and ages.

Compared with the two others, the first of these themes is but a graceful and elegiac sigh. After having taken shape in Greek poetry, it was adopted by the Fathers, and pervaded the literature of all Christendom, and that of Islam also. Byron, too, used it in *Don Juan*. The Middle Ages cultivated it with special predilection. We find it in the heavy rhythm of the erudite poetry of the twelfth century:

"Est ubi gloria nunc Babylonia? nunc ubi dirus
  Nabugodonosor, et Darii vigor, illeque Cyrus? . . .
  Nunc ubi Regulus? aut ubi Romulus, aut ubi Remus?
  Stat rosa pristina nomine, nomina nuda tenemus." [1]

Franciscan poetry of the thirteenth century (if the following lines are not of an older date) still preserves an echo of these rhyming hexameters:

"Dic ubi Salomon, olim tam nobilis
   Vel Sampson ubi est, dux invincibilis,
   Et pulcher Absalon, vultu mirabilis,
   Aut dulcis Jonathas, multum amabilis?" [2]

[1] Where is now your glory, Babylon, where is now the terrible Nebuchadnezzar, and strong Darius and the famous Cyrus? Where is now Regulus, or where Romulus, or where Remus? The rose of yore is but a name, mere names are left to us.

[2] Say where is Solomon, once so noble, Or Samson where is he, the invincible chief, And fair Absalom of the wonderful face, Or sweet Jonathan, the most amiable?

Deschamps composed at least four of his ballads on this theme. Gerson worked it out in a sermon; Denis the Carthusian in his treatise, *De quattuor hominum novissimis* (on the four last things of man); Chastellain in a long poem entitled *Le Pas de la Mort*. Olivier de la Marche, in his *Parement et Triumphe des Dames* composed on it a lament over all the princesses who died in his time. Villon gives it a new accent of soft tenderness in his *Ballade des Dames du Temps fadis,* with the refrain:

> "Mais où sont lex neiges d'antan?"

And then he sprinkles it with irony in the *Ballad of the Lords* by adding to the series of kings, popes and princes of his time the words:

> "Helas! et le bon roy d'Espaigne
> Duquel je ne sçay pas le nom." [3]

However, the wistfulness of remembrance and the thought of frailty in itself do not satisfy the need of expressing, with violence, the shudder caused by death. The medieval soul demands a more concrete embodiment of the perishable: that of the putrefying corpse.

Ascetic meditation had, in all ages, dwelt on dust and worms. The treatises on the contempt of the world had, long since, evoked all the horrors of decomposition, but it is only towards the end of the fourteenth century that pictorial art, in its turn, seizes upon this motif. To render the horrible details of decomposition, a realistic force of expression was required, to which painting and sculpture only attained towards 1400. At the same time, the motif spread from ecclesiastical to popular literature. Until far into the sixteenth century, tombs are adorned with hideous images of a naked corpse with clenched hands and rigid feet, gaping mouth and bowels crawling with worms. The imagination of those times relished these horrors, without

[3] Alas! and the good king of Spain, Whose name I do not know.

ever looking one stage further, to see how corruption perishes in its turn, and flowers grow where it lay.

A thought which so strongly attaches to the earthly side of death can hardly be called truly pious. It would rather seem a kind of spasmodic reaction against an excessive sensuality. In exhibiting the horrors awaiting all human beauty, already lurking below the surface of corporeal charms, these preachers of contempt for the world express, indeed, a very materialistic sentiment, namely, that all beauty and all happiness are worthless *because* they are bound to end soon. Renunciation founded on disgust does not spring from Christian wisdom.

It is noteworthy that the pious exhortations to think of death and the profane exhortations to make the most of youth almost meet. A painting in the monastery of the Celestines at Avignon, now destroyed, attributed by tradition to the founder, King René himself, represented the body of a dead woman, standing, enveloped in a shroud, with her head dressed and worms gnawing her bowels. In the inscription at the foot of the picture the first lines read:

> "Une fois sur toute femme belle
> Mais par la mort suis devenu telle,
> Ma chair estoit très belle, fraische et tendre,
> Or, est-elle toute tournée en cendre.
> Mon corps estoit très plaisant et très gent,[4]
> Je me souloye souvent vestir de soye,
> Or en droict fault que toute nue je soys.
> Fourrée estois de gris et de menu vair,
> En grand palais me logeois à mon vueil,
> Or suis logée en ce petit cercueil.
> Ma chambre estoit de beaux tapis ornée,
> Or est d'aragnes ma fosse environnée." [5]

[4] It seems that two lines are missing after the lines 5 and 8.

[5] Once I was beautiful above all women But by death I became like this, My flesh was very beautiful, fresh and soft, Now it is altogether turned to ashes. My body was very pleasing and very pretty, I used frequently to dress in silk,

Here the *memento mori* still predominates. It tends imperceptibly to change into the quite worldly complaint of the woman who sees her charms fade, as in the following lines of the *Parement et Triumphe des Dames* by Olivier de la Marche.

> "Ces doulx regards, ces yeulx faiz pour plaisance,
> Pensez y bien, ilz perdront leur clarté,
> Nez et sourcilz, la bouche d'eloquence
> Se pourriront . . .
> Se vous vivez le droit cours de nature
> Dont LX ans est pour ung bien grant nombre,
> Vostre beaulté changera en laydure,
> Vostre santé en maladie obscure,
> Et ne ferez en ce monde que encombre.
> Se fille avez, vous luy serez ung umbre,
> Celle sera requise et demandée,
> Et de chascun la mère habandonnée." [6]

All pious purpose has disappeared in the ballads of Villon, where the old courtesan, "la belle heaulmière," calls to mind her irresistible beauty of former times and is deeply grieved at its sad decline.

> "Qu'est devenu ce front poly,
> Ces cheveulx blons, sourcils voultiz,
> Grant entroeil, le regart joly,
> Dont prenoie les plus soubtilz;

Now I must rightly be quite nude. I was dressed in grey fur and miniver, I lived in a great palace as I wished, Now I am lodged in this little coffin. My room was adorned with fine tapestry, Now my grave is enveloped by cobwebs.

[6] These sweet looks, these eyes made for pleasance, Remember, they will lose their lustre, Nose and eyelashes, the eloquent mouth Will putrefy. . . . If you live your natural lifetime, Of which sixty years is a great deal, Your beauty will change into ugliness, Your health into obscure malady, And you will only be in the way here below. If you have a daughter, you will be a shadow to her, She will be in request and asked for, And the mother will be abandoned by all.

Ce beau nez droit, grant ne petiz,
Ces petites joinctes oreilles,
Menton fourchu, cler vis traictiz
Et ces belles levres vermeilles?

.   .   .   .

Le front ridé, les cheveux gris,
Les sourcilz cheuz, les yeuls estains. . . ."[7]

This inability to free oneself from the attachment to
matter manifests itself in yet other forms. A result of the
same sentiment is to be found in the extreme importance
ascribed in the Middle Ages to the fact that the bodies of
certain saints had never decayed—that of Saint Rosa of
Viterbo, for example. The Assumption of the Holy Virgin
exempting her body from earthly corruption was on that
account regarded as the most precious of all graces. On
various occasions attempts were made to retard decomposition. The features of the corpse of Pierre de Luxembourg
were touched up with paint to preserve them intact until
the burial. The body of a heretic preacher of the sect of
the Turlupins, who died in prison, before sentence was
passed, was preserved in lime for a fortnight, that it might
be burned at the same time with a living heretical woman.

The importance attached to being buried in the soil of
one's own country gave rise to usages which the Church
had to interdict strictly as being contrary to the Christian
religion. In the twelfth and thirteenth centuries, when a
prince or a person of rank died far from his country, the
body was often cut up and boiled so as to extract the
bones, which were sent home in a chest, whereas the rest
was interred, not without ceremony, however, on the spot.
Emperors, kings and bishops have undergone this strange

[7] What has become of this smooth forehead, Fair hair,
curving eyelashes, Large space between the eyes, pretty
looks, Wherewith I caught the most subtle ones; That fine
straight nose, neither large nor small, These tiny ears close
to the head, The dimpled chin, well-shaped bright face,
And those beautiful vermilion lips? . . . The forehead
wrinkled, hair grey, The eyelashes come off, lack-lustre
eyes. . . .

operation. Pope Boniface VIII forbade it as *detestandae feritatis abusus, quam ex quodam more horribili nonnulli fideles improvide prosequuntur.*[8] Yet his successors sometimes granted dispensations. Numbers of Englishmen who fell in France in the Hundred Years' War enjoyed this privilege, notably Edward of York and the earl of Suffolk, who died at Agincourt; Henry V himself; William Glasdale, who perished at Orléans at the time of its relief; a nephew of Sir John Fastolfe, and others.

At the close of the Middle Ages the whole vision of death may be summed up in the word *macabre,* in its modern meaning. Of course, this meaning is the outcome of a long process. But the sentiment it embodies, of something gruesome and dismal, is precisely the conception of death which arose during the last centuries of the Middle Ages. This bizarre word appeared in French in the fourteenth century, under the form *macabré,* and, whatever may be its etymology, as a proper name. A line of the poet Jean Le Fèvre, "Je fis de Macabré la dance," which may be dated 1376, remains the birth-certificate of the word for us.

Towards 1400 the conception of death in art and literature took a spectral and fantastic shape. A new and vivid shudder was added to the great primitive horror of death. The macabre vision arose from deep psychological strata of fear; religious thought at once reduced it to a means of moral exhoration. As such it was a great cultural idea, till in its turn it went out of fashion, lingering on in epitaphs and symbols in village cemeteries.

The idea of the death-dance is the central point of a whole group of connected conceptions. The priority belongs to the motif of the three dead and three living men, which is found in French literature from the thirteenth century onward. Three young noblemen suddenly meet three hideous dead men, who tell them of their past gran-

[8] An abuse of abominable savagery, practised by some of the faithful in a horrible way and inconsiderately.

deur and warn them of their own near end. Art soon took
hold of this suggestive theme. We can see it still in the
striking frescoes of the *Campo santo* of Pisa. The sculpture
of the portal of the church of the Innocents at Paris, which
the duke of Berry had carved in 1408, but which has not
been preserved, represented the same subject. Miniature
painting and woodcuts spread it broadcast.

The theme of the three dead and three living men
connects the horrible motif of putrefaction with that of the
death-dance. This theme, too, seems to have originated in
France, but it is unknown whether the pictorial representation preceded the scenic or the reverse. The thesis of Monsieur Emile Mâle, according to which the sculptural and
pictorial motifs of the fifteenth century were supposed as a
rule to be derived from dramatic representations, has not
been able to keep its ground, on critical examination. It
may be, however, that we should make an exception in
favour of the death-dance. Anyhow, the Dance of the Dead
has been acted as well as painted and engraved. The duke
of Burgundy had it performed in his mansion at Bruges in
1449. If we could form an idea of the effect produced by
such a dance, with vague lights and shadows gliding over
the moving figures, we should no doubt be better able to
understand the horror inspired by the subject, than we
are by the aid of the pictures of Guyot Marchant or Holbein.

The woodcuts with which the Parisian printer, Guyot
Marchant, ornamented the first edition of the *Danse
Macabré* in 1485 were, very probably, imitated from the
most celebrated of these painted death-dances, namely,
that which, since 1424, covered the walls of the cloister of
the churchyard of the Innocents at Paris. The stanzas
printed by Marchant were those written under these mural
paintings; perhaps they even hail back to the lost poetry
of Jean Le Fèvre, who in his turn seems to have followed
a Latin model. The woodcuts of 1485 can give but a feeble
impression of the paintings of the Innocents, of which they
are not exact copies, as the costumes prove. To have a
notion of the effect of these frescoes, one should rather

look at the mural paintings of the church of La Chaise-Dieu, where the unfinished condition of the work heightens the spectral effect.

The dancing person whom we see coming back forty times to lead away the living, originally does not represent Death itself, but a corpse: the living man such as he will presently be. In the stanzas the dancer is called "the dead man" or "the dead woman." It is a dance of the dead and not of Death; the researches of Monsieur Gédéon Huet have made it probable that the primitive subject was a roundabout dance of dead people, come forth from their graves, a theme which Goethe revived in his *Totentanz*. The indefatigable dancer is the living man himself in his future shape, a frightful double of his person. "It is yourself," said the horrible vision to each of the spectators. It is only towards the end of the century that the figure of the great dancer, of a corpse with hollow and fleshless body, becomes a skeleton, as Holbein depicts it. Death in person has then replaced the individual dead man.

While it reminded the spectators of the frailty and the vanity of earthly things, the death-dance at the same time preached social equality as the Middle Ages understood it, Death levelling the various ranks and professions. At first only men appeared in the picture. The success of his publication, however, suggested to Guyot the idea of a dance macabre of women. Martial d'Auvergne wrote the poetry; an unknown artist, without equalling his model, completed the pictures by a series of feminine figures dragged along by a corpse. Now it was impossible to enumerate forty dignities and professions of women. After the queen, the abbess, the nun, the saleswoman, the nurse, and a few others, it was necessary to fall back on the different states of feminine life: the virgin, the beloved, the bride, the woman newly married, the woman with child. And here the sensual note reappears, to which we referred above. In lamenting the frailty of the lives of women, it is still the briefness of joy that is deplored, and with the grave tone of the *memento mori* is mixed the regret for lost beauty.

Nothing betrays more clearly the excessive fear of death felt in the Middle Ages than the popular belief, then widely spread, according to which Lazarus, after his resurrection, lived in a continual misery and horror at the thought that he should have again to pass through the gate of death. If the just had so much to fear, how could the sinner soothe himself? And then what motif was more poignant than the calling up of the agony of death? It appeared under two traditional forms: the *Ars moriendi* and the *Quattor hominum novissima,* that is, the four last experiences awaiting man, of which death was the first. These two subjects were largely propagated in the fifteenth century by the printing-press and by engravings. The Art of Dying, as well as the Last Four Things, comprised a description of the agony of death, in which it is easy to recognize a model supplied by the ecclesiastical literature of former centuries.

Chastellain, in a long-winded poem, *Le Pas de la Mort,* has assembled all the above motifs; he gives successively the image of putrefaction—the lament: Where are the great ones of the earth?—an outline of a death-dance—and the art of dying. Being prolix and heavy, he needs a great many lines to express what Villon presents in half a stanza. But in comparing them we recognize their common model. Chastellain writes:

> "Il n'a membre ne facture
> Qui ne sente sa pourreture.
> Avant que l'esperit soit hors,
> Le cœur qui veult crevier au corps
> Haulce et soulière la poitrine
> Qui se veult joindre à son eschine.
> —La face est tainte et apalie,
> Et les yeux treilliés en la teste.
> La parole luy est faillie,
> Car la langue au palais se lie.
> Le poulx tressault et sy halette.

>   . . . .

> Les os desjoindent à tous lez;
> Il n'a nerf qu'au rompre ne tende."[9]

And Villon:

> "La mort le fait fremir, pallir,
> Le nez courber, les vaines tendre,
> Le col enfler, la chair mollir,
> Joinctes et nerfs croistre et estendre. . . ."[10]

And again the sensual thought mingles with it:

> "Corps femenin, qui tant es tendre,
> Poly, souef, si precieux,
> Te fauldra il ces maulx attendre?
> Oy, ou tout vif aller es cieulx."[11]

Nowhere else were all the images tending to evoke the horror of death assembled so strikingly as in the churchyard of the Innocents at Paris. There the medieval soul, fond of a religious shudder, could take its fill of the horrible. Above all other saints, the remembrance of the saints of that spot, and of their bloody and pitiful martyrdom, was fitted to awake the crude compassion which was dear to the epoch. The fifteenth century honoured the Holy Innocents with special veneration. Louis XI presented to the church "a whole Innocent," encased in a crystal shrine. The cemetery was preferred to every other place of burial. A

[9] There is not a limb nor a form, Which does not smell of putrefaction. Before the soul is outside, The heart which wants to burst in the body Raises and lifts the chest Which nearly touches the backbone.—The face is discoloured and pale, And the eyes veiled in the head. Speech fails him, For the tongue cleaves to the palate. The pulse trembles and he pants. . . . The bones are disjointed on all sides; There is not a tendon which does not stretch as to burst.

[10] Death makes him shudder and turn pale, The nose to curve, the veins to swell, The neck to inflate, the flesh to soften, Joints and tendons to grow and swell.

[11] O female body, which is so soft, Smooth, suave, precious, Do these evils await you? Yes, or you must go to heaven quite alive.

bishop of Paris had a little of the earth of the churchyard of the Innocents put into his grave, as he could not be laid there. The poor and the rich were interred without distinction. They did not rest there long, for the cemetery was used so much, twenty parishes having a right of burial there, that it was necessary, in order to make room, to dig up the bones and sell the tombstones after a very short time. It was believed that in this earth a human body was decomposed to the bone in nine days. Skulls and bones were heaped up in charnel-houses along the cloisters enclosing the ground on three sides, and lay there open to the eye by thousands, preaching to all the lesson of equality. The noble Boucicaut, among others, had contributed to the construction of these "fine charnel-houses." Under the cloisters the death-dance exhibited its images and its stanzas. No place was better suited to the simian figure of grinning death, dragging along pope and emperor, monk and fool. The duke of Berry, who wished to be buried there, had the history of the three dead and the three living men carved at the portal of the church. A century later, this exhibition of funeral symbols was completed by a large statue of Death, now in the Louvre, and the only remnant of it all.

Such was the place which the Parisians of the fifteenth century frequented as a sort of lugubrious counterpart of the Palais Royal of 1789. Day after day, crowds of people walked under the cloisters, looking at the figures and reading the simple verses, which reminded them of the approaching end. In spite of the incessant burials and exhumations going on there, it was a public lounge and a rendezvous. Shops were established before the charnel-houses and prostitutes strolled under the cloisters. A female recluse was immured on one of the sides of the church. Frairs came to preach and processions were drawn up there. A procession of children only (12,500 strong, thinks the Burgher of Paris) assembled there, with tapers in their hands, to carry an Innocent to Notre Dame and back to the churchyard. Even feasts were given there. To such an extent had the horrible become familiar.

The desire to invent a visible image of all that apper-
tained to death entailed the neglecting of all those aspects
of it which were not suited to direct representation. Thus
the cruder conceptions of death, and these only, impressed themselves continually on the minds. The macabre
vision does not represent the emotions of tenderness or of
consolation. The elegiac note is wanting altogether. At bottom the macabre sentiment is self-seeking and earthly. It
is hardly the absence of the departed dear ones that is
deplored; it is the fear of one's own death, and this only
seen as the worst of evils. Neither the conception of death
the consoler, nor that of rest long wished for, of the end of
suffering, of the task performed or interrupted, have a
share in the funeral sentiment of that epoch. The soul of
the Middle Ages did not know the "divine depth of sorrow." Or, rather, it knew it only in connection with the
Passion of Christ.

In all these sombre lamentations about death the accents of true tenderness are extremely rare. They could,
however, hardly be wanting in relation to the death of
children. And, indeed, Martial d'Auvergne, in his death-
dance of women, makes the little girl, when led away by
death, say to her mother: "Take good care of my doll, my
knuckle-bones and my fine dress." But this touching note
is only heard exceptionally. The literature of the epoch
knew child-life so little! When Antoine de la Salle, in *Le
Reconfort de Madame du Fresne,* wishes to console a
mother for the death of her twelve-years-old son, he can
think of nothing better than citing a still more cruel loss:
the heart-rending case of a boy given as a hostage and
put to death. To overcome grief, the only advice he can
offer is to abstain from all earthly attachments. A doctri-
naire and dry consolation! La Salle, however, adds a second
short story. It is a version of the popular tale of the dead
child, who came back to beg its mother to weep no more,
that its shroud might dry. And here suddenly from this
simple story—not of his own invention—there arises a
poetical tenderness and beneficent wisdom, which we look
for in vain in the thousands of voices repeating in various

tones the awful *memento mori*. Folk-tale and folk-song, no doubt, in these ages preserved many sentiments which higher literature hardly knew.

The dominant thought, as expressed in the literature, both ecclesiastical and lay, of that period, hardly knew anything with regard to death but these two extremes: lamentation about the briefness of all earthly glory, and jubilation over the salvation of the soul. All that lay between—pity, resignation, longing, consolation—remained unexpressed and was, so to say, absorbed by the too much accentuated and too vivid representation of Death hideous and threatening. Living emotion stiffens amid the abused imagery of skeletons and worms.

Chapter XII

RELIGIOUS THOUGHT
CRYSTALLIZING INTO IMAGES

Towards the end of the Middle Ages two factors dominate religious life: the extreme saturation of the religious atmosphere, and a marked tendency of thought to embody itself in images.

Individual and social life, in all their manifestations, are imbued with the conceptions of faith. There is not an object nor an action, however trivial, that is not constantly correlated with Christ or salvation. All thinking tends to religious interpretation of individual things; there is an enormous unfolding of religion in daily life. This spiritual wakefulness, however, results in a dangerous state of tension, for the presupposed transcendental feelings are sometimes dormant, and whenever this is the case, all that is meant to stimulate spiritual consciousness is reduced to appalling commonplace profanity, to a startling worldliness in other-worldly guise. Only saints are capable of an attitude of mind in which the transcendental faculties are never in abeyance.

The spirit of the Middle Ages, still plastic and naïve, longs to give concrete shape to every conception. Every thought seeks expression in an image, but in this image it solidifies and becomes rigid. By this tendency to embodiment in visible forms all holy concepts are constantly exposed to the danger of hardening into mere externalism. For in assuming a definite figurative shape thought loses its ethereal and vague qualities, and pious feeling is apt to resolve itself in the image.

Even in the case of a sublime mystic, like Henry Suso, the craving for hallowing every action of daily life verges in our eyes on the ridiculous. He is sublime when, following the usages of profane love, he celebrates New Year's Day and May Day by offering a wreath and a song to his betrothed, Eternal Wisdom, or when, out of reverence for the Holy Virgin, he renders homage to all womankind and walks in the mud to let a beggar woman pass. But what are we to think of what follows? At table Suso eats three-quarters of an apple in the name of the Trinity and the remaining quarter in commemoration of "the love with which the heavenly Mother gave her tender child Jesus an apple to eat"; and for this reason he eats the last quarter with the paring, as little boys do not peel their apples. After Christmas he does not eat it, for then the infant Jesus was too young to eat apples. He drinks in five draughts because of the five wounds of the Lord, but as blood and water flowed from the side of Christ, he takes his last draught twice. This is, indeed, pushing the sanctification of life to extremes.

In so far as it concerns individual piety, this tendency to apply religious conceptions to all things and at all times is a deep source of saintly life. As a cultural phenomenon this same tendency harbours grave dangers. Religion penetrating all relations in life means a constant blending of the spheres of holy and of profane thought. Holy things will become too common to be deeply felt. The endless growth of observances, images, religious interpretations, signifies an augmentation in quantity at which serious divines grew alarmed, as they feared the quality would deteriorate proportionately. The warning which we find recurring in all reformist writings of the time of the schism and of the councils is—the Church is being overloaded.

Pierre d'Ailly, in condemning the novelties which were incessantly introduced into the liturgy and the sphere of belief, is less concerned about the piety of their character than about the steady increase itself. The signs of the ever-ready divine grace multiplied endlessly; a host of special benedictions sprang up side by side with the sacraments; in addition to relics we find amulets; the bizarre gallery of saints became ever more numerous and variegated. However emphatically divines insisted upon the difference between sacraments and *sacramentalia*, the people would still confound them. Gerson tells how he met a man at Auxerre, who maintained that All Fools' Day was as sacred as the day of the Virgin's Conception. Nicolas de Clemanges wrote a treatise, *De novis festivitatibus non instituendis*, in which he denounced the apocryphal nature of some among these new institutions. Pierre d'Ailly, in *De Reformatione*, deplores the ever-increasing number of churches, of festivals, of saints, of holy-days; he protests against the multitude of images and paintings, the prolixity of the Service, against the introduction of new hymns and prayers, against the augmentation of vigils and fasts. In short, what alarms him is the evil of superfluity.

There are too many religious orders, says d'Ailly, and this leads to a diversity of usages, to exclusiveness and rivalry, to pride and vanity. In particular he desired to impose restrictions on the mendicant orders, whose social utility he questions: they live to the detriment of the inmates of leper houses and hospitals, and other really poor and wretched people, who are truly entitled to beg (*ac aliis vere pauperibus et miserabilibus indigentibus quibus convenit jus et verus titulus mendicandi*). Let the sellers of indulgences be banished from the Church, which they soil with their lives and make ridiculous. Convents are built

on all sides, but sufficient funds are lacking. Where is this
to lead?

Pierre d'Ailly does not question the holy and pious character of all these practices in themselves, he only deplores
their endless multiplication; he sees the Church weighed
down under the load of particulars.

Religious customs tended to multiply in an almost mechanical way. A special office was instituted for every detail of the worship of the Virgin Mary. There were particular masses, afterwards abolished by the Church, in
honour of the piety of Mary, of her seven sorrows, of all
her festivals taken collectively, of her sisters—the two
other Marys—of the archangel Gabriel, of all the saints of
our Lord's genealogy. A curious example of this spontaneous accretion of religious usage is found in the weekly
observance of Innocents' Day. The 28th of December, the
day of the massacre at Bethlehem, was taken to be ill-
omened. This belief was the origin of a custom, widely
spread during the fifteenth century, of considering as a
black-letter day, all the year through, the day of the week
on which the preceding Innocents' Day fell. Consequently,
there was one day in every week on which people abstained from setting out upon a journey and beginning a
new task, and this day was called Innocents' Day, like
the festival itself. Louis XI observed this usage scrupulously. The coronation of Edward IV of England was repeated, as it had taken place on a Sunday, because the
28th of December of the previous year had been a Sunday
too. René de Lorraine had to give up his plan of fighting
a battle on the 17th of October, 1476, as his lansquenets
refused to encounter the enemy "on Innocents' Day."

This belief, of which we find some traces appearing in
England as late as the eighteenth century, called forth a
treatise from Gerson against superstition in general. His
penetrating mind had realized some of the danger with
which these excrescences of the creed menaced the purity
of religious thought. He was aware of their psychological
basis; according to him, these beliefs proceed *ex sola
hominum phantasiatione et melancholica imaginatione*; it is

a disorder of the imagination caused by some lesion of the brain, which in its turn is due to diabolic illusions.

The Church was constantly on her guard lest dogmatic truth should be confounded with this mass of facile beliefs, and lest the exuberance of popular fancy should degrade God. But was she able to stand against this strong need of giving a concrete form to all the emotions accompanying religious thought? It was an irresistible tendency to reduce the infinite to the finite, to disintegrate all mystery. The highest mysteries of the creed became covered with a crust of superficial piety. Even the profound faith in the eucharist expands into childish beliefs—for instance, that one cannot go blind or have a stroke of apoplexy on a day on which one has heard mass, or that one does not grow older during the time spent in attending mass. While herself offering so much food to the popular imagination, the Church could not claim to keep that imagination within the limits of a healthy and vigorous piety.

In this respect the case of Gerson is characteristic. He composed a treatise, *Contra vanam curiositatem*, by which he means the spirit of research which desires to scrutinize the secrets of nature. But whilst protesting against it, he himself becomes guilty of a curiosity which to us seems out of place and deplorable. Gerson was the great promoter of the adoration of Saint Joseph. His veneration for this saint makes him desirous of learning all that concerns him. He routs out all particulars of the married life of Joseph: his continence, his age, the way in which he learned of the Virgin's pregnancy. He is indignant at the caricature of a drudging and ridiculous Joseph, which the arts were inclined to make of him. In another passage Gerson indulges in a speculation on the bodily constitution of Saint John the Baptist: *Semen igitur materiale ex qua corpus compaginandum erat, nec durum nimis nec rursus fluidum abundantius fuit.*

Whether the Virgin had taken an active part in the supernatural conception, or, again, whether the body of Christ would have decomposed, if it had not been for the resurrection, were what the popular preacher Olivier

Maillard called "beautiful theological questions" to discuss before his auditors. The mixture of theological and embryological speculation to which the controversy about the immaculate conception of the Virgin gave rise shocked the minds of that period so little that grave divines did not scruple to treat the subject from the pulpit.

This familiarity with sacred things is, on the one hand, a sign of deep and ingenuous faith; on the other, it entails irreverence whenever mental contact with the infinite fails. Curiosity, ingenuous though it be, leads to profanation. In the fifteenth century people used to keep statuettes of the Virgin, of which the body opened and showed the Trinity within. The inventory of the treasure of the dukes of Burgundy makes mention of one made of gold inlaid with gems. Gerson saw one in the Carmelite monastery at Paris; he blames the brethren for it, not, however, because such a coarse picture of the miracle shocked him as irreverent, but because of the heresy of representing the Trinity as the fruit of Mary.

All life was saturated with religion to such an extent that the people were in constant danger of losing sight of the distinction between things spiritual and things temporal. If, on the one hand, all details of ordinary life may be raised to a sacred level, on the other hand, all that is holy sinks to the commonplace, by the fact of being blended with everyday life. In the Middle Ages the demarcation of the sphere of religious thought and that of worldly concerns was nearly obliterated. It occasionally happened that indulgences figured among the prizes of a lottery. When a prince was making a solemn entry, the altars at the corners of the streets, loaded with the precious reliquaries of the town and served by prelates, might be seen alternating with dumb shows of pagan goddesses or comic allegories.

Nothing is more characteristic in this respect than the fact of there being hardly any difference between the musical character of profane and sacred melodies. Till late in the sixteenth century profane melodies might be used indiscriminately for sacred use, and sacred for profane. It is notorious that Guillaume Dufay and others composed masses to the theme of love-songs, such as "Tant je me déduis,"[1] "Se la face ay pale,"[2] "L'omme armé."[3]

There was a constant interchange of religious and profane terms. No one felt offended by hearing the Day of Judgment compared to a settling of accounts, as in the verses formerly written over the door of the audit office at Lille.

"Lors ouvrira, au son de buysine
  Sa générale et grant chambre des comptes."[4]

A tournament, on the other hand, is called "des armes grantdisime pardon" (the great indulgence conferred by arms) as if it were a pilgrimage. By a chance coincidence the words *mysterium* and *ministerium* were blended in French into the form "mistère," and this homonymy must have helped to efface the true sense of the word "mystery" in everyday parlance, because even the most commonplace things might be called "mistère."

While religious symbolism represented the realities of nature and history as symbols or emblems of salvation, on the other hand religious metaphors were borrowed to express profane sentiments. People in the Middle Ages, standing in awe of royalty, do not shrink from using the language of adoration in praising princes. In the lawsuit about the murder of Louis of Orléans, the counsel for the defence makes the shade of the duke say to his son: "Look at my wounds and observe that *five* of them are particularly cruel and mortal." The bishop of Chalons, Jean Germain, in his *Liber de virtutibus Philippi ducis Burgundiae,* in his turn does not scruple to compare the victim of Montereau to the Lamb. The Emperor Frederick III, when sending his son Maximilian to the Low Countries to marry Mary of Burgundy, is compared by Molinet to God the Father. The

[1] So much I enjoy myself.
[2] If my face is pale.
[3] The armed man.
[4] Then to the sound of the trumpet God shall open His general and grand audit office.

same author makes the people of Brussels say, when they
wept with tenderness on seeing the emperor entering their
town with Maximilian and Philip le Beau: "Behold the
image of the Trinity, the Father, the Son and the Holy
Ghost." He offers a wreath of flowers to Mary of Burgundy,
a worthy image of Our Lady, "secluse la virginité." [5] "Non
point que je veuille déifier les princes!" [6] Molinet adds.

Although we may consider such formulæ of adulation
empty phrases, they show none the less the depreciation of
sacred imagery resulting from its hackneyed use. We can
hardly blame a court poet, when Gerson himself ascribes to
the royal auditors of his sermons guardian angels of a
higher rank in the celestial hierarchy than those of other
men.

The step from familiarity to irreverence is taken when
religious terms are applied to erotic relations. The subject
has been dealt with above. The author of the *Quinze Joyes
de Mariage* chose his title to accord with the joys of the
Virgin. The defender of the *Roman de la Rose* used sacred
terms to designate the *partes corporis inhonestas et peccata
immunda atque turpia.* No instance of this dangerous association of religious with amatory sentiments could be
more striking than the Madonna ascribed to Foucquet,
making part of a diptych which was formerly preserved at
Melun and is now partly at Antwerp and partly at Berlin;
Antwerp possessing the Madonna and Berlin the panel representing the donor, Etienne Chevalier, the king's treasurer, together with Saint Stephen. In the seventeenth
century Denis Godefroy noted down a tradition, then
already old, according to which the Madonna had the
features of Agnès Sorel, the royal mistress, for whom
Chevalier felt a passion that he did not trouble to conceal.
However this may be, the Madonna is, in fact, represented
here according to the canons of contemporary fashion:
there is the bulging shaven forehead, the rounded
breasts, placed high and wide apart, the high and slender

[5] Save the virginity.
[6] Not that I want to deify princes.

waist. The bizarre inscrutable expression of the Madonna's face, the red and blue cherubim surrounding her, all contribute to give this painting an air of decadent impiety in spite of the stalwart figure of the donor. Godefroy observed on the large frame of blue velvet E's done in pearls linked by love-knots of gold and silver thread. There is a flavour of blasphemous boldness about the whole, unsurpassed by any artist of the Renaissance.

The irreverence of daily religious practice was almost unbounded. Choristers, when chanting mass, did not scruple to sing the words of the profane songs that had served as a theme for the composition: *baisez-moi, rouges nez*.[7]

A startling piece of impudence is recorded of the father of the Frisian humanist Rodolph, Agricola, who received the news that his concubine had given birth to a son on the very day when he was elected abbot. "To-day I have twice become a father. God's blessing on it!" said he.

At the end of the fourteenth century people took the increasing irreverence to be an evil of recent date, which, indeed, is a common phenomenon at all times. Deschamps deplores it in the following lines:

> "On souloit estre ou temps passé
> En l'eglise benignement,
> A genoux en humilité
> Delez l'autel moult closement,
> Tout nu le chief piteusement,
> Maiz au jour d'uy, si come beste,
> On vient à l'autel bien souvent
> Chaperon et chapel en teste." [8]

On festal days, says Nicolas de Clemanges, few people go to mass. They do not stay till the end, and are content

[7] "Kiss me," "Red noses."
[8] In bygone times people used to be Gentle in church, On their knees in humility Close beside the altar, With meekly uncovered head, But at present, like beasts, They too often come to the altar With hood and hat on their heads.

with touching the holy water, bowing before Our Lady, or kissing the image of some saint. If they wait for the elevation of the Host, they pride themselves upon it, as if they had conferred a benefit on Christ. At matins and vespers the priest and his assistant are the only persons present. The squire of the village makes the priest wait to begin mass till he and his wife have risen and dressed. The most sacred festivals, even Christmas night, says Gerson, are passed in debauchery, playing at cards, swearing and blaspheming. When the people are admonished, they plead the example of the nobility and the clergy, who behave in like manner with impunity. Vigils likewise, says Clemanges, are kept with lascivious songs and dances, even in church; priests set the example by dicing as they watch. It may be said that moralists paint things in too dark colours; but in the accounts of Strassburg we find a yearly gift of 1,100 litres of wine granted by the council to whose who "watched in prayer" in church during the night of Saint Adolphus.

Denis the Carthusian wrote a treatise, *De modo agendi processiones,* at the request of an alderman, who asked him how one might remedy the dissoluteness and debauchery to which the annual procession, in which a greatly venerated relic was borne, gave rise. "How are we to put a stop to this?" asks the alderman. "You may be sure that the town council will not easily be persuaded to abolish it, for the procession brings large profits to the town, because of all the people who have to be fed and lodged. Besides, custom will have it so." "Alas, yes," sighs Denis; "he knows too well how processions were disgraced by ribaldry, mockery and drinking." A most vivid picture of this evil is found in Chastellain's description of the degradation into which the procession of the citizens of Ghent, with the shrine of Saint Liévin, to Houthem, had fallen. Formerly, he says, the notabilities were in the habit of carrying the holy body "with great and deep solemnity and reverence"; at present there is only "a mob of roughs, and boys of bad character"; they carry it singing and yelling, "with a hundred thousand gibes, and all are drunk."

They are armed, "and commit many offences where they pass, as if they were let loose and unchained; that day everything appears to be given up to them under the pretext of the body they carry."

We have already mentioned how much disturbance was caused during church services by people vying with each other in politeness. The usage of making a trysting-place of the church by young men and young women was so universal that only moralists were scandalized by it. The virtuous Christine de Pisan makes a lover say in all simplicity:

> "Se souvent vais ou moustier,
> C'est tout pour veoir la belle
> Fresche comme rose nouvelle." [9]

The Church suffered more serious profanation than the little love services of a young man who offered his fair one the "pax," or knelt by her side. According to the preacher Menot, prostitutes had the effrontery to come there in search of customers. Gerson tells that even in the churches and on festival days obscene pictures were sold *tanquam idola Belphegor*, which corrupted the young, while sermons were ineffective to remedy this evil.

As to pilgrimages, moralists and satirists are of one mind; people often go "pour folle plaisance." The Chevalier de la Tour Landry naïvely classes them with profane pleasures, and he entitles one of his chapters, "Of those who are fond of going to jousts and on pilgrimages."

On festal days, exclaims Nicolas de Clemanges, people go to visit distant churches, not so much to redeem a pledge of pilgrimage as to give themselves up to pleasure. Pilgrimages are the occasions of all kinds of debauchery; procuresses are always found there, people come for amorous purposes. It is a common incident in the *Quinze Joyes de Mariage*; the young wife, who wants a change, makes her husband believe that the baby is ill, because she has

[9] If I often go to church, It is all for seeing the fair one Fresh as a new-blown rose.

not yet accomplished her vow of pilgrimage, made during her confinement. The marriage of Charles VI with Isabella of Bavaria was preceded by a pilgrimage. It is far from surprising that the serious followers of the *devotio moderna* called the utility of pilgrimages in question. Those who often go on pilgrimages, says Thomas à Kempis, rarely become saints. One of his friends, Frederick of Heilo, wrote a special treatise, *Contra peregrinantes*.

The excesses and abuses resulting from an extreme familiarity with things holy, as well as the insolent mingling of pleasure with religion, are generally characteristic of periods of unshaken faith and of a deeply religious culture. The same people who in their daily life mechanically follow the routine of a rather degraded sort of worship will be capable of rising suddenly, at the ardent word of a preaching monk, to unparalleled heights of religious emotion. Even the stupid sin of blasphemy has its roots in a profound faith. It is a sort of perverted act of faith, affirming the omnipresence of God and His intervention in the minutest concerns. Only the idea of really daring Heaven gives blasphemy its sinful charm. As soon as an oath loses its character of an invocation of God, the habit of swearing changes its nature and becomes mere coarseness. At the end of the Middle Ages blasphemy is still a sort of daring diversion which belongs to the nobility. "What!" says the nobleman to the peasant in a treatise by Gerson, "you give your soul to the devil, you deny God without being noble?" Deschamps, on his part, notices that the habit of swearing tends to descend to people of low estate.

> "Si chétif n'y a qui ne die:
> Je renie Dieu et sa mère." [10]

People make a pastime of coining new and ingenious oaths, says Gerson: he who excels in this impious art is honoured as a master. Deschamps tells us that all France swore first after the Gascon and the English fashion, next

[10] There is none so mean but says, I deny God and His mother.

after the Breton, and finally after the Burgundian. He composed two ballads in succession made up of all the oaths
then in vogue strung together, and ended with a pious
phrase. The Burgundian oath was the worst of all. It was,
Je renie Dieu (I deny God), which was softened down to
Je renie de bottes (boots). The Burgundians had the reputation of being abominable swearers; for the rest, says
Gerson, the whole of France, for all her Christianity, suffers
more than any other country from the effects of this horrible
sin, which causes pestilence, war and famine. Even monks
were guilty of mild swearing. Gerson and d'Ailly expressly
call upon the authorities to combat the evil by renewing
the strict regulations everywhere, but imposing light penalties which may be really exacted. And a royal decree of
1397, in fact, re-established the old ones of 1269 and 1347,
but unfortunately also renewed the old penalties of lip-
slitting and cutting out of tongues, which bore witness, it
is true, to a holy horror of blasphemy, but which it was not
possible to enforce. In the margin of the register containing the ordinance, someone has noted: "At present, 1411,
all these oaths are in general use throughout the kingdom
without being punished."

Gerson, with his long experience as a confessor, knew the
psychological nature of the sin of blasphemy very well. On
the one hand, he says, there are the habitual swearers, who,
though culpable, are not perjurers, as it is not their intention to take an oath. On the other, we find young men of
a pure and simple nature who are irresistibly tempted to
blaspheme and to deny God. Their case reminds us of John
Bunyan's, whose disease took the form of "a propensity to
utter blasphemy, and especially to renounce his share in
the benefits of the redemption." Gerson counsels these
young men to give themselves up less to the contemplation
of God and the saints, as they lack the mental strength required.

It is impossible to draw the line of demarcation between
an ingenuous familiarity and conscious infidelity. As early
as the fifteenth century people liked to show themselves
esprits forts and to deride piety in others. The word

"papelard," meaning a hypocrite, was in frequent use with
lay writers of the time. "De jeune angelot vieux diable" (a
young saint makes an old devil), said the proverb, or, in
solemn Latin metre, *Angelicus juvenis senibus sathanizat in
annis.* "It is by such sayings," Gerson exclaims, "that youth
is perverted. A brazen face, scurrilous language and curses,
immodest looks and gestures, are praised in children. Well,
what is to be expected in old age of a *sathanizing* youth?"

The people, he says, do not know how to steer a middle
course between overt unbelief and the foolish credulity, of
which the clergy themselves set the example. They give
credence to all revelations and prophecies, which are often
but fancies of diseased people or lunatics, and yet when a
serious divine, who has been honoured by genuine revelations, is occasionally mistaken, he is called impostor and
"papelard," and the people henceforth refuse to listen to
any divine because all are considered hypocrites.

We not unfrequently find individual expressions of
avowed unbelief. "Beaux seigneurs," says Captain Bétisac
to his comrades when about to die, "I have attended to
my spiritual concerns and, in my conscience, I believe I
have greatly angered God, having for a long time already
erred against the faith, and I cannot believe a word about
the Trinity, nor that the Son of God has humbled Himself
to such an extent as to come down from Heaven into the
carnal body of a woman; and I believe and say that when
we die there is no such thing as a soul. . . . I have held
this opinion ever since I became self-conscious, and I shall
hold it till the end." The provost of Paris, Hugues Aubriot,
is a violent hater of the clergy; he does not believe in the
sacrament of the altar, he makes a mock of it; he does not
keep Easter, he does not go to confession. Jacques du
Clercq relates that several noblemen, in full possession of
their faculties, refused extreme unction. Perhaps we should
regard these isolated cases of unbelief less as wilful heresy
than as a spontaneous reaction against the incessant and
pressing call of the faith, arising from a culture overcharged
with religious images and concepts. In any case, they
should not be confounded either with the literary and su-

perficial paganism of the Renaissance, nor with the prudent epicureanism of some aristocratic circles from the thirteenth century downward, nor, above all, with the passionate negation of ignorant heretics who had passed the boundary-line between mysticism and pantheism.

The naïve religious conscience of the multitude had no need of intellectual proofs in matters of faith. The mere presence of a visible image of things holy sufficed to establish their truth. No doubts intervened between the sight of all those pictures and statues—the persons of the Trinity, the flames of hell, the innumerable saints—and belief in their reality. All these conceptions became matters of faith in the most direct manner; they passed straight from the state of images to that of convictions, taking root in the mind as pictures clearly outlined and vividly coloured, possessing all the reality claimed for them by the Church, and even a little more.

Now, when faith is too directly connected with a pictured representation of doctrine, it runs the risk of no longer making qualitative distinctions between the nature and the degree of sanctity of the different elements of religion. The image by itself does not teach the faithful that one should adore God and only venerate the saints. Its psychological function is limited to creating a deep conviction of reality and a lively feeling of respect. It therefore became the task of the Church to warn incessantly against want of discrimination in this respect, and to preserve the purity of doctrine by explaining precisely what the image stood for. In no other sphere was the danger of luxuriance of religious thought caused by a vivid imagination more obvious.

Now, the Church did not fail to teach that all honours rendered to the saints, to relics, to holy places, should have God for their object. Although the prohibition of images in the second commandment of the Decalogue was abrogated by the new law, or limited to God the Father alone, the Church purposed, nevertheless, to maintain intact the principle of *non adorabis ea neque coles*: Images were only meant to show simple-minded people what to believe. They

are the books of the illiterate, says Clemanges; a thought
which Villon has expressed in the touching lines which he
puts into his mother's mouth:

> "Femme je suis pourette et ancienne,
>   Qui riens ne sçai; oncques lettre ne leuz;
>   Au moustier voy dont suis paroissienne
>   Paradis paint, où sont harpes et luz,
>   Et ung enfer où dampnez sont boulluz:
>   L'ung me fait paour, l'autre joye et liesse . . ." [11]

The medieval Church was, however, rather heedless of
the danger of a deterioration of the faith caused by the
popular imagination roaming unchecked in the sphere of
hagiology. An abundance of pictorial fancy, after all, furnished to the simple mind quite as much matter for deviating from pure doctrine as any personal interpretation of
Holy Scripture. It is remarkable that the Church, so scrupulous in dogmatic matters, should have been so confiding
and indulgent towards those who, sinning out of ignorance, rendered more homage to images than was lawful.
It suffices, says Gerson, that they meant to do as the Church
requires.

Thus towards the end of the Middle Ages an ultra-real-
istic conception of all that related to the saints may be noticed in the popular faith. The saints had become so real
and such familiar characters of current religion that they
became bound up with all the more superficial religious
impulses. While profound devotion still centred on Christ
and His mother, quite a host of artless beliefs and fancies
clustered about the saints. Everything contributed to make
them familiar and life-like. They were dressed like the people themselves. Every day one met "Messires" Saint Roch
and Saint James in the persons of living plague patients and
pilgrims. Down to the Renaissance the costume of the saints

[11] I am a poor old woman who knows nothing; I never
could read. In my parish church I see Paradise painted,
where are harps and lutes, And a hell, where the damned
are boiled. The one frightens me, the other brings joy and
mirth.

always followed the fashion of the times. Only then did Sacred Art, by arraying the saints in classical draperies, withdraw them from the popular imagination and place them in a sphere where the fancy of the multitude could no longer contaminate the doctrine in its purity.

The distinctly corporeal conception of the saints was accentuated by the veneration of their relics, not only permitted by the Church but forming an integral part of religion. It was inevitable that this pious attachment to material things should draw all hagiolatry into a sphere of crude and primitive ideas, and lead to surprising extremes. In the matter of relics the deep and straightforward faith of the Middle Ages was never afraid of disillusionment or profanation through handling holy things coarsely. The spirit of the fifteenth century did not differ much from that of the Umbrian peasants, who, about the year 1000, wished to kill Saint Romuald, the hermit, in order to make sure of his precious bones; or of the monks of Fossanuova, who, after Saint Thomas Aquinas had died in their monastery, in their fear of losing the relic, did not shrink from decapitating, boiling and preserving the body. During the lying in state of Saint Elizabeth of Hungary, in 1231, a crowd of worshippers came and cut or tore strips of the linen enveloping her face; they cut off the hair, the nails, even the nipples. In 1392, King Charles VI of France, on the occasion of a solemn feast, was seen to distribute ribs of his ancestor, Saint Louis; to Pierre d'Ailly and to his uncles Berry and Burgundy he gave entire ribs; to the prelates one bone to divide between them, which they proceeded to do after the meal.

It may well be that this too corporeal and familiar aspect, this too clearly outlined shape, of the saints has been the very reason why they occupy so little space in the sphere of visions and supernatural experience. The whole domain of ghost-seeing, signs, spectres and apparitions, so crowded in the Middle Ages, lies mainly apart from the veneration of the saints. Of course, there are exceptions, such as Saint Michael, Saint Katherine and Saint Margaret appearing to Joan of Arc; and other instances might be added. But, generally speaking, popular phantasmagoria is full of angels, devils, shades of the dead, white women, but not of saints. Stories of apparitions of particular saints are, as a rule, suspect of having already undergone some ecclesiastical or literary interpretation. To the agitated beholder a phantom has no name and hardly a shape. In the famous vision of Frankenthal, in 1446, the young shepherd *sees* fourteen cherubim, all alike, who *tell* him they are the fourteen "Holy Martyrs," to whom Christian iconography attributed such distinct and marked appearances. Where a primitive superstition does attach to the veneration of some saint, it retains something of the vague and formless character that is essential to superstition, as in the case of Saint Bertulph at Ghent, who can be heard rapping the sides of his coffin in St. Peter's abbey "moult dru et moult fort" (very frequently and very loudly) as a warning of impending calamity.

The saint, with his clearly outlined figure, his well-known attributes and features as they were painted or carved in the churches, was wholly lacking in mystery. He did not inspire terror as do vague phantoms and the haunting unknown. The dread of the supernatural is due to the undefined character of its phenomena. As soon as they assume a clear-cut shape they are no longer horrible. The familiar figures of the saints produced the same sort of reassuring effect as the sight of a policeman in a foreign city. The complex of ideas connected with the saints constituted, so to say, a neutral zone of calm and domestic piety, between the ecstasy of contemplation and of the love of Christ on the one hand, and the horrors of demonomania on the other. It is perhaps not too bold to assert that the veneration of the saints, by draining off an overflow of religious effusion and of holy fear, acted on the exuberant piety of the Middle Ages as a salutary sedative.

The veneration of the saints has its place among the more outward manifestations of faith. It is subject to the influences of popular fancy rather than of theology, and they sometimes deprive it of its dignity. The special cult of Saint Joseph towards the end of the Middle Ages is characteristic

in this respect. It may be looked upon as the counterpart
of the passionate adoration of the Virgin. The curiosity with
which Joseph was regarded is a sort of reaction from the
fervent cult of Mary. The figure of the Virgin is exalted
more and more and that of Joseph becomes more and more
of a caricature. Art portrays him as a clown dressed in
rags; as such he appears in the diptych by Melchior
Broederlam at Dijon. Literature, which is always more explicit than the graphic arts, achieves the feat of making him
altogether ridiculous. Instead of admiring Joseph as the
man most highly favoured of all, Deschamps represents
him as the type of the drudging husband.

> "Vous qui servez a femme et a enfans
> Aiez Joseph toudis en remembrance;
> Femme servit toujours tristes, dolans,
> Et Jhesu Crist garda en son enfance;
> A piè trotoit, son fardel sur sa lance;
> En plusieurs liex est figuré ainsi,
> Lez un mulet, pour leur faire plaisance,
> Et si n'ot oncq feste en ce monde ci." [12]

And again, still more grossly:

> "Qu'ot Joseph de povreté
> De durté
> De maleurté
> Quant Dieux nasqui!
> Maintefois l'a comporté
> Et monté
> Par bonté
> Avec sa mère autressi,
> Sur sa mule les ravi:
> Je le vi

[12] You who serve a wife and children Always bear
Joseph in mind; He served his wife, gloomily and mourn-
fully, And he guarded Jesus Christ in his infancy; He went
on foot with his bundle slung on his staff; In several places
he is pictured thus, Beside a mule to give them pleasure,
And so he had never any amusement in this world.

Paint ainsi;
En Egipte en est alé.

"Le bonhomme est painturé
Tout lassé,
Et troussé
D'une cote et d'un barry:
Un baston au coul posé,
Vieil, usé
Et rusé.
Feste n'a en ce monde cy,
Mais de lui
Va le cri:
C'est Joseph le rassoté." [13]

This shows how familiarity led to irreverence of thought. Saint Joseph remained a comic type, in spite of the very special reverence paid to him. Doctor Eck, Luther's adversary, had to insist that he should not be brought on the stage, or at least that he should not be made to cook the porridge, *"ne ecclesia Dei irrideatur."* The union of Joseph and Mary always remained the object of a deplorable curiosity, in which profane speculation mingled with sincere piety. The Chevalier de la Tour Landry, a man of prosaic mind, explains it to himself in the following manner: "God wished that she should marry that saintly man Joseph, who was old and upright, for God wished to be born in wedlock, to comply with the current legal requirements, to avoid gossip."

[13] What poverty Joseph suffered What hardships What misery When God was born! Many a time he has carried him, And placed him In his goodness With his mother, too, On his mule, and took them with him: I saw him Painted thus; He went into Egypt.

The good man is painted Quite exhausted, And dressed in A frock and a striped garment, A stick across his shoulder, Old, spent And broken. For him there was no amusement in this world, But of him People say—That is Joseph, the fool.

An unpublished work of the fifteenth century[14] represents the mystic marriage of the soul with the celestial
spouse as if it were a middle-class wedding. "If it pleases
you," says Jesus to the Father, "I shall marry and shall have
a large bevy of children and relations." The Father fears a
misalliance, but the Angel succeeds in persuading him that
the betrothed-elect is worthy of the Son; on which the
Father gives his consent in these terms:

> "Prens la, car elle est plaisant
> Pour bien amer son doulx amant;
> Or prens de nos biens largement,
> Et luy en donne habondamment." [15]

There is no doubt of the seriously devout intention of this
treatise. It is only an instance of the degree of triviality
entailed by unbridled exuberance of fancy.

Every saint, by the possession of a distinct and vivid outward shape, had his own marked individuality, quite contrary to the angels, who, with the exception of the three
famous archangels, acquired no definite appearance. This
individual character of each saint was still more strongly
accentuated by the special functions attributed to many of
them. Now this specialization of the kind of aid given by
the various saints was apt to introduce a mechanical element into the veneration paid to them. If, for instance, Saint
Roch is specially invoked against the plague, almost inevitably too much stress came to be laid on his part in the
healing, and the idea required by sound doctrine, that the
saint wrought the cure only by means of his intercession
with God, came in danger of being lost sight of. This was
especially so in the case of the "Holy Martyrs" (les saints
auxiliaires), whose number is usually given as fourteen, and
sometimes as five, eight, ten, fifteen. Their veneration
arose and spread towards the end of the Middle Ages.

---

[14] *Le Livre de Crainte Amoureuse,* by Jean Berthelemy,
Bibliothèque Nationale, MS. français, 1875.

[15] Take her, for she is pleasing and fit To love her sweet
bridegroom; Now take plenty of our possessions, And give
them to her in abundance.

"Ilz sont cinq sains, en la genealogie,
    Et cinq sainctes, a qui Dieu octria
    Benignement a la fin de leur vie,
    Que quiconques de cuer les requerra
    En tous perilz, que Dieu essaucera
    Leurs prieres, pour quelconque mesaise.
    Saiges est donc qui ces cinq servira,
    Jorges, Denis, Christofle, Gille et Blaise." [16]

The Church had sanctioned the popular belief expressed
by Deschamps in these verses by instituting an office of the
Fourteen Auxiliary Saints. The binding character of their
intercession is clearly there expressed: "O God, who hast
distinguished Thy chosen saints, George, etc., etc., with
special privileges before all others, that all those who in
their need invoke their help, shall obtain the salutary fulfilment of their prayer, according to the promise of Thy
grace." So there had been a formal delegation of divine
omnipotence. The people could, therefore not be blamed
if, with regard to these privileged saints it forgot the pure
doctrine a little. The instantaneous effect of prayer addressed to them contributed still more to obscure their
part as intercessors; they seemed to be exercising divine
power by virtue of a power of attorney. Hence it is very
natural that the Church abolished this special office of the
Fourteen Auxiliary Saints after the Council of Trent. The
extraordinary function attributed to them had given rise to
the grossest superstition, such as the belief that it sufficed
to have looked at a Saint Christopher, painted or carved,
to be protected for the rest of the day from a fatal end.
This explains the countless number of the saints' images at
the entrances of churches.

[16] There are five saints in the genealogy, And five female saints to whom God granted Benignantly at the end
of their lives, That whosoever shall invoke their help with
all his heart In all dangers, that He will hear their
prayers, In all disorders whatsoever. He therefore is wise
who serves these five, George, Denis, Christopher, Giles
and Blaise.

As for the reason why this group was singled out among all the saints, it should be noticed that the greater number of them appear in art with some very striking attribute. Saint Achatius wore a crown of thorns; Saint Giles was accompanied by a hind, Saint George by a dragon; Saint Christopher was of gigantic stature; Saint Blaise was represented in a den of wild beasts; Saint Cyriac with a chained devil; Saint Denis carrying his head under his arm; Saint Erasmus being disembowelled by means of a windlass; Saint Eustace with a stag carrying a cross between its antlers; Saint Pantaleon with a lion; Saint Vitus in a cauldron; Saint Barbara with her tower; Saint Katherine with her wheel and sword; Saint Margaret with a dragon. It may well be that the special favour with which the Fourteen Auxiliary Saints were regarded was due, at least partially, to the very impressive character of their images.

The names of several saints were inseparably bound up with divers disorders, and even served to designate them. Thus various cutaneous diseases were called Saint Anthony's evil. Gout went by the name of Saint Maur's evil. The terrors of the plague called for more than one saintly protector; Saint Sebastian, Saint Roch, Saint Giles, Saint Christopher, Saint Valentine, Saint Adrian, were all honoured in this capacity by offices, processions and fraternities. Now here lurked another menace to the purity of the faith. As soon as the thought of the disease, charged with feelings of horror and fear, presented itself to the mind, the thought of the saint sprang up at the same instant. How easily, then, did the saint himself become the object of this fear, so that to him was ascribed the heavenly wrath that unchained the scourge. Instead of unfathomable divine justice, it was the anger of the saint which seemed the cause of the evil and required to be appeased. Since he healed the evil, why should he not be its author? On these lines the transition from Christian ethic to heathen magic was only too easy. The Church could not be held responsible, unless we are to blame her carelessness regarding the adulteration of the pure doctrine in the minds of the ignorant.

There are numerous testimonies to show that the people sometimes really regarded certain saints as the authors of disorders, though it would be hardly fair to consider as such those oaths which almost attributed to Saint Anthony the part of an evil fire-demon. "Que Saint Antoine me arde" (May Saint Anthony burn me!), "Saint Antoine arde le tripot," "Saint Antoine arde la monture" (Saint Anthony burn the brothel! Saint Anthony burn the beast!)—these are lines by Coquillart. So also Deschamps makes some poor fellow say:

> "Saint Antoine me vent trop chier
> Son mal, le feu ou corps me boute;" [17]

and thus apostrophizes a gouty beggar: "You cannot walk? All the better, you save the toll: Saint Mor ne te fera fremir" (Saint Maur will not make you tremble).

Robert Gaguin, who was not at all hostile to the veneration of the saints, in his *De validorum per Franciam mendicantium varia astucia,* describes beggars in these terms: "One falls on the ground expectorating malodorous spittle and attributes his condition to Saint John. Others are covered with ulcers through the fault of Saint Fiacrius, the hermit. You, O Damian, prevent them from making water, Saint Anthony burns their joints, Saint Pius makes them lame and paralysed."

In one of his Colloquies Erasmus makes fun of this belief. One of the interlocutors asks whether in Heaven the saints are more malevolent than they were on earth. "Yes," answers the other, "in the glory of Paradise the saints do not choose to be insulted. Who was sweeter than Saint Corneille, more compassionate than Saint Anthony, more patient than Saint John the Baptist, during their lives? And now what horrible maladies they send if they are not properly honoured!" Rabelais states that the lower class of preachers themselves represented Saint Sebastian to their congregation as the author of the plague and Saint

[17] Saint Anthony sells me his evil all too dear, He stokes the fire in my body.

Eutropius of dropsy. Henri Estienne has written of the same superstitions in the like manner. That they existed is thus clearly established.

The emotional constituents of the veneration of the saints had fastened so firmly on the forms and colours of their images that mere æsthetic perception was constantly threatening to obliterate the religious element. The vivid impression presented by the aspect of the images with their pious or ecstatic looks, rich gilding, and sumptuous apparel, all admirably reproduced by a very realistic art, left hardly any room for doctrinal reflection. Effusions of piety went out ardently towards those glorious beings, without a thought being given to the limits fixed by the Church. In the popular imagination the saints were living and were as gods. There is nothing surprising, therefore, in the fact that strict pietists like the Brethren of the Common Life and the Windesheim canons saw a certain danger to popular piety in the development of the veneration of the saints. It is very remarkable, however, that the same idea occurs to a man like Eustache Deschamps, a superficial poet and a commonplace mind, and for that very reason so faithful a mirror of the general aspirations of his time.

> "Ne faictes pas les dieux d'argent,
> D'or, de fust, de pierre ou d'arain,
> Qui font ydolatrer la gent. . . .
> Car l'ouvrage est forme plaisant;
> Leur painture dont je me plain,
> La beauté de l'or reluisant,
> Font croire à maint peuple incertain
> Que ce soient dieu pour certain,
> Et servent par pensées foles
> Telz ymages qui font caroles
> Es moustiers ou trop en mettons;
> C'est tresmal fait; a brief paroles,
> Telz simulacres n'aourons.
>
> .   .   .   .
>
> Prince, un Dieu croions seulement
> Et aourons parfaictement

> Aux champs, partout, car c'est raisons,
> Non pas faulz dieux, fer n'ayment,
> Pierres qui n'ont entendement:
> Telz simulacres n'aourons." [18]

Perhaps we may consider the diligent propagation of the cult of guardian angels towards the end of the Middle Ages as a sort of unconscious reaction against the motley crowd of popular hagiology. Too large a part of the living faith had crystallized in the veneration of the saints, and thus there arose a craving for something more spiritual as an object of reverence and a source of protection. In addressing itself to the angel, vaguely conceived and almost formless, piety restored contact with the supernatural and with mystery. Once more it is Jean Gerson, the indefatigable worker for the purity of faith, whom we find perpetually recommending the cult of the guardian angel. But here also he had to combat unbridled curiosity, which threatened to submerge piety under a mass of commonplace details. And it was just in connection with this subject of angels, which was more or less unbroken ground, that numbers of delicate questions obtruded themselves. Do they never leave us? Do they know beforehand whether we shall be saved or lost? Had Christ a guardian angel? Will the Antichrist have one? Can the angel speak to our soul without visions? Do the angels lead us to good as devils lead us to evil?—Leave these subtle speculations to divines, concludes Gerson; let the faithful keep to simple and wholesome worship.

[18] Do not make gods of silver, Of gold, of wood, of stone or of bronze, That lead people to idolatry. . . . Because the work has a pleasant shape; Their colouring of which I complain, The beauty of shining gold, Make many ignorant people believe That these are God for certain, And they serve by foolish thoughts Such images as stand about In churches where they place too many of them That is very ill done; in short Let us not adore such counterfeits. . . . Prince, let us only believe in one God And let us adore him to perfection In the fields, everywhere, for this is right, No false gods, of iron or of stone, Stones which have no understanding: Let us not adore such counterfeits.

A hundred years after Gerson wrote, the Reformation attacked the cult of the saints, and nowhere in the whole contested area did it meet with less resistance. In strong contrast with the belief in witchcraft and demonology, which fully maintained their ground in Protestant countries, both among the clergy and the laity, the saints fell without a blow being struck in their defence. This was possibly due to the fact that nearly everything connected with the saints had become *caput mortuum*. Piety had depleted itself in the image, the legend, the office. All its contents had been so completely expressed that mystic awe had evaporated. The cult of the saints was no longer rooted in the domain of the unimaginable. In the case of demonology, these roots remained as terribly strong as ever.

When, therefore, Catholic Reform had to re-establish the cult of the saints, its first task was to prune it; to cut down the whole luxuriant growth of medieval imagination and establish severer discipline, so as to prevent a reflorescence.

Chapter XIII

TYPES OF RELIGIOUS LIFE

In studying the history of religious life, we must beware of drawing the lines of demarcation too sharply. When we see side by side the most striking contrasts of passionate piety and mocking indifference, it is so easy to explain them by opposing, as if they made up distinct groups, the worldly to the devout, the intellectuals to the ignorant, the reformers to the conservatives. But, in so doing, we fail to take sufficient account of the marvellous complexity of the human soul and of the forms of culture. To explain the astonishing contrasts of religious life towards the end of the Middle Ages, we must start with the recognition of a general lack of balance in the religious temper, rendering

both individuals and masses liable to violent contradictions
and to sudden changes.

The general aspect presented by religious life in France
towards the end of the Middle Ages is that of a very mechanical and frequently very lax practice, chequered by
spasmodic effusions of ardent piety. France was a stranger
to that special form of pietism which sequesters itself in
small circles of fervent devotees, such as we find springing
up in the Netherlands: the "devotio moderna," dominated
by the figure of Thomas à Kempis. Still, the religious needs
which gave birth to this movement were not wanting in
France, only the devotees did not form a special organization. They found a refuge in the existing orders, or they
remained in secular life, without being distinguished from
the mass of believers. Perhaps the Latin soul endures more
easily than that of Northern peoples the conflicts with
which life in the world confronts the pious.

Of all the contradictions which religious life of the period presents, perhaps the most insoluble is that of an
avowed contempt of the clergy, a contempt seen as an un-
dercurrent throughout the Middle Ages, side by side with
the very great respect shown for the sanctity of the sacerdotal office. The soul of the masses, not yet completely
Christianized, had never altogether forgotten the aversion
felt by the savage for the man who may not fight and must
remain chaste. The feudal pride of the knight, the champion of courage and of love, was at one, in this, with the
primitive instinct of the people. The worldliness of the
higher ranks of the clergy and the deterioration of the lower
grades did the rest. Hence it was that nobles, burghers and
villeins had for a long time past been feeding their hatred
with spiteful jests at the expense of the incontinent monk
and the guzzling priest. Hatred is the right word to use in
this context, for hatred it was, latent, but general and persistent. The people never wearied of hearing the vices of
the clergy arraigned. A preacher who inveighed against
the ecclesiastical state was sure of being applauded. As
soon as a homilist broaches this subject, says Bernardino
of Siena, his hearers forget all the rest; there is no more

effective means of reviving attention when the congregation is dropping off to sleep, or suffering from heat or cold. Everybody instantly becomes attentive and cheerful.

Contempt and gibes are levelled especially at the mendicant orders. The types of unworthy priests in the *Cent Nouvelles Nouvelles*, like the starving chaplain who reads mass for three doits, or the confessor pledged to absolve the family of everything every year, in return for his board and lodging, are all of them mendicant friars. In a series of New Year's wishes Molinet rhymes thus:

"Prions Dieu que les Jacobins
Puissent manger les Augustins,
Et les Carmes soient pendus
Des cordes des Frères Menus." [1]

At the same time, the restoration of the mendicant orders caused a revival of popular preaching, which gave rise to those vehement outbursts of fervour and penitence which stamped so powerfully the religious life of the fifteenth century.

There is in this special hatred for the begging friars an indication of a most important change of ideas. The formal and dogmatic conception of poverty as extolled by Saint Francis of Assisi, and as observed by the mendicant orders, was no longer in harmony with the social sentiment which was just arising. People were beginning to regard poverty as a social evil instead of an apostolic virtue. Pierre d'Ailly opposed to the mendicant orders the "true poor"—*vere pauperes*. England, which, earlier than other nations, became alive to the economic aspect of things, gave, towards the end of the fourteenth century, the first expression to the sentiment of the sanctity of productive labour in that strangely fantastic and touching poem, *The Vision of William concerning Piers Plowman*.

Still, this general abuse of priests and monks goes hand

[1] Let us pray God that the Jacobins May eat the Augustinians, And that the Carmelites may be hanged With the cords of the Minorites.

in hand with a profound veneration for their sacred function. Ghillebert de Lannoy saw a priest at Rotterdam appease a tumult by raising the *Corpus Domini*.

The sudden transitions and the violent contrasts of the religious life of the ignorant masses reappear in that of cultured individuals. Often enlightenment comes like a thunderclap, as it did in the case of Saint Francis suddenly hearing the words of the Gospel as a compulsory command. A knight hears the baptismal ritual read: he has perhaps heard it twenty times before, but suddenly the miraculous virtue of these words pierces into his soul, and he promises himself henceforth to chase away the devil by the mere recollection of the baptism. Jean de Bueil is on the point of witnessing a duel, the adversaries are both going to swear to their good right on the Host. Suddenly the captain, seized by the thought that one of them must needs forswear himself and will be lost irrevocably, exclaims: "Do not swear; only fight for a wager of 500 crowns, without taking an oath."

As for the great lords, the basic unsoundness of their life of arrogant pomp and disordered enjoyment contributed to give a spasmodic character to their piety. They are devout by starts, for life is far too distracting. Charles V of France sometimes gives up the chase at the most exciting moments to hear mass. Ann of Burgundy, the wife of Bedford, now scandalizes the Parisians by splashing a procession by her mad riding, now leaves a court fête at midnight to attend the matins of the Celestines. She brought upon herself a premature death by visiting the sick of the Hôtel Dieu.

Among the princes and the lords of the fifteenth century, more than one presents the type of an almost inconceivable mixture of devotion and debauchery. Louis of Orléans, an insane lover of luxury and pleasure, addicted even to the sin of necromancy, has his cell in the common dormitory of the Celestines, where he shares the privations and duties of monastic life, rising at midnight and sometimes hearing five or six masses a day.

The coexistence in one person of devotion and worldli-

ness is displayed in a striking fashion in Philip the Good.
The duke, famous for his "moult belle compagnie" of bastards, his extravagant feasts, his grasping policy, and for a
pride not less violent than his temper, is at the same time
strictly devout. He was in the habit of remaining in his
oratory for a long time after mass, and living on bread and
water four days a week, as well as on all the vigils of Our
Lady and the apostles. He is often still fasting at four
o'clock in the afternoon. He gives alms on a great scale and
in secret. After the surprise of Luxembourg, he remains engrossed in his hours and special prayers of thanksgiving so
long that his escort, awaiting him on horseback, grow impatient, for the fight was not yet quite over. On being
warned of the danger, the duke replies: "If God has
granted me victory, He will keep it for me."

Gaston Phébus, count of Foix, King René, Charles of
Orléans, represent so many different types of a very worldly
and often frivolous temperament, coupled with a devotional
spirit which one shrinks from stigmatizing as hypocrisy or
bigotry. It has rather to be regarded as a kind of reconciliation, hardly conceivable to the modern mind, between
two moral extremes. Its possibility in the Middle Ages depends on the absolute dualism of the two conceptions,
which then dominated all thinking and living.

Men of the fifteenth century often couple with austere
devotion the love of bizarre splendour. The craving to
decorate faith with the magnificence of forms and colours
is displayed in other forms besides works of religious art; it
is sometimes found in the forms of spiritual life itself. When
Philippe de Mézières plans his Order of the Passion, which
was to save Christendom, he imagines a whole phantasmagoria of colours. The knights, according to their ranks,
will be dressed in red, green, scarlet and azure, with red
crosses and hoods of the same colour. The grand-master
will be all in white. If he saw but little of this splendour,
as his order was never established, he was at least able to
satisfy his artistic taste in the monastery of the Celestines
at Paris, which was the refuge of his last years. If the rules
of the order, which he followed as a lay-brother, were very

severe, the convent-church, on the other hand, a mauso-
leum of the princes of the time, was most sumptuous, all
sparkling with gold and precious stones; it was reputed
the most beautiful of Paris.

It is but a step from luxurious piety to theatrical displays
of hyperbolic humility. Olivier de la Marche remembered
to have seen in his youth the entry of Jacques de Bourbon,
the titular king of Naples, who had renounced the world
because of the exhortations of Saint Colette. The king,
miserably dressed, was carried in a sort of hand-barrow,
"not differing from the barrows in which dung and ordure
are usually carried." An elegant cortège followed closely.
"And I have heard it recounted and said"—says La Marche
—"that in all the towns where he came, he made similar
entries out of humility."

The minute directions given by a number of saintly persons concerning their burial bear witness to the same excessive humility. The blessed Pierre Thomas, improving
upon the example of Saint Francis of Assisi, leaves orders
to wrap him up in a sack, with a cord round his neck, and
so place him on the ground to die. "Bury me," he says,
"at the entrance of the choir, that every one may walk over
my body, even dogs and goats." Philippe de Mézières, his
disciple and friend, tries to go even further in fantastic
humility. In his dying hour a heavy iron chain is to be
placed round his neck. When he has given up the ghost,
he is to be dragged by his feet, naked, into the choir, where
he is to remain on the ground, his arms crossed, tied by
three ropes to a plank. Thus "this fine treasure for the
worms" is to wait till people come to carry it to the grave.
The plank is to take the place of the "sumptuous coffin,
ornamented with his vain and worldly coat of arms, which
would have been displayed at the interment of the unhappy pilgrim, if God had so much hated him that he had
let him die at the court of princes of this world." Dragged
along once more, his "carrion" is to be thrown, quite naked,
into the grave.

One is not surprised to hear that this lover of precise
specification made several wills. In the later ones details

of this kind are wanting; and at his death, which occurred in 1405, he was honourably buried in the frock of the Celestines, and two epitaphs, probably of his own composition, were carved on his tombstone.

The ideal of sanctity has always been incapable of much variation. The fifteenth century, in this respect, brings no new aspiration. Consequently, the Renaissance exercised hardly any influence on the conception of saintly life. The saint and the mystic remain almost wholly untouched by the changing times. The types of saints of the Counter-Reformation are still those of the later Middle Ages, who in their turn did not essentially differ from those of the preceding centuries. Both before and after the great turning of the tide, two types of saints stand out conspicuously: the men of fiery speech and energetic action, like Ignatius de Loyola, Francis Xavier, Charles Borromeo, who belong to the same class as Bernardino of Siena, John Capistrano and the blessed Vincent Ferrer, in earlier times; and the men absorbed in tranquil rapture, or practising extravagant humility, the poor in spirit, like Saint Francis of Paula and the blessed Pierre of Luxembourg in the fifteenth century, and Aloysius Gonzaga in the sixteenth.

It would not be unreasonable to compare to the romanticism of chivalry, as an element of medieval thought, a romanticism of saintliness, in the sense of a tendency to give the colours of fancy and the accents of enthusiasm to an ideal form of virtue and of duty. It is remarkable that this romanticism of saintliness always aims far more at miracles and excesses of humility and of asceticism, than at brilliant achievements in the service of religious policy. The Church has sometimes canonized the great men of action who have revived or purified religious culture, but popular imagination has been more impressed, in all ages, by the supernatural and by irrational excess.

It is not without interest to note some traits showing us the attitude of the aristocracy, refined and fastidious and engrossed in the chivalrous ideas, towards the ideal of saintly life. The princely families of France have produced later saints than Saint Louis. Charles of Blois, descended,

by his mother, from the house of Valois, found himself
charged, by his marriage with the heiress of Brittany, with
a war of succession, which filled the greater part of his
life. On marrying Jeanne de Penthièvre, he had promised
to adopt the arms and the battle-cry of the duchy, which
meant: to fight Jean de Montfort, the pretender supported
by England. The count of Blois waged the war like the best
of knights and captains of his time. He passed nine years in
captivity in England, and perished at Aurai in 1364, bat-
tling side by side with Bertrand du Guesclin and Beaumanoir.

Now this prince, whose career was altogether military,
had led, from his youth onward, the life of an ascetic. As a
child he plunged into the study of edifying books, a taste
which his father did his best to moderate, judging it un-
suitable to a future warrior. Later he used to sleep on straw
near the conjugal bed. After his death he was found to
have worn a hair-shirt under his armour. He confessed every evening, saying that no Christian ought to go to sleep
in the state of sin. As a prisoner in London he was in the
habit of entering the cemeteries to kneel down and say
the *de profundis*. The Breton squire whom he asks to say
the responses refused, saying: "No; there lie those who
have killed my parents and friends and have burnt their
houses." On being released, he resolved to undertake a
pilgrimage, barefooted, in the snow, from La Roche-
Derrien, where he had been captured, to the shrine of
Saint Yves at Tréguier. The people, hearing this, covered
the road with straw and blankets, but the count made a
detour and hurt his feet, so that for weeks he was unable
to walk.

Directly after his death his royal relations, especially his
son-in-law, Louis d'Anjou, a son of the king, took steps to
have him canonized. The proceedings, which took place at
Angers in 1371, ended in his beatification.

If we are to trust Froissart, this Charles of Blois would
seem to have had a bastard. "There was killed in good
style the aforesaid Lord Charles of Blois, with his face to
the enemy, and a bastard son of his called Jehans de Blois,

and several other knights and squires of Brittany." Was Froissart mistaken? Or are we to suppose that the mingling of piety and sensuality, which is so evident in the figures of Louis of Orléans and of Philip the Good, reappears in him in a still more astonishing degree?

No such question arises in the case of the blessed Pierre de Luxembourg, another ascetic sprung from court circles. This scion of the house of Luxembourg, which in its several branches held the imperial dignity and a preponderant place at the courts of France and Burgundy, is a striking representative of the type called by William James "the under-witted saint," a narrow mind, which can only live in a carefully isolated sphere of devotion. He died in his eighteenth year, in 1387, having been loaded from his childhood with ecclesiastical dignities, being bishop of Metz at fifteen and a cardinal soon after. His personality as it disengages itself from the narratives of the witnesses in the proceedings for his canonization is almost pitiful. He is of a consumptive disposition and has overgrown his strength. Even as a child he was wholly given up to austerity and devotion. He reprimands his brother when he laughs, because the Gospel does tell us that the Lord wept, but not that he laughed. "Sweet, courteous and debonair" —says Froissart—"virgin as to the body, a very great giver of alms. The greater part of the day and the night he spent in prayer. And in all his life there was nothing but humility." At first his noble parents tried to dissuade him from a life of religion. When he said he wished to go forth and preach, he was told: "You are much too tall, everybody would recognize you at once. You could not endure the cold, and as to preaching the crusade, how could you do that?" "I see," said Pierre—and here the very recesses of his narrow mind seem lighted up for a moment—"I see very well, that you want to lead me from the right road to the bad; but assuredly, if I once enter on it, I shall do so much that the whole world will talk of me."

When once his ascetic aspirations had overcome all attempts to extirpate them, his parents were clearly proud of having such a young saint in the family. Imagine, amidst

the unbridled luxury of the courts of Berry and Burgundy,
this sickly boy, horribly dirty and covered with vermin, as
the witnesses attest. He is ever occupied with his sins and
notes them down every day in a pocket-book. If he is prevented from doing this by a journey or some other reason,
he makes up for this neglect by writing for hours. At night
he is seen writing up or reading his pocket-books by the
light of a candle. He rises at midnight and awakes the
chaplains in order to confess; sometimes he knocks in vain
—they turn a deaf ear to his nocturnal call. If he obtains
a hearing, he reads out his lists of sins from his little scraps.
Towards the end of his life, he is shriven twice a day and
will not allow his confessor to leave him for a moment. After
his death a whole chest was found filled with these little
lists of sins.

The Luxembourgs and their friends immediately took
steps to get him canonized. The request was made at
Avignon by the king himself, and supported both by the
University of Paris and the Chapter of Notre Dame. The
greatest lords of France appeared as witnesses at the trial
in 1389: André de Luxembourg, Louis de Bourbon,
Enguerrand de Coucy. Though the canonization was not
obtained because of the pope's negligence (the beatification only took place in 1527), the veneration of Pierre de
Luxembourg was at once established, and miracles multiplied at Avignon, on the spot where he lay buried. The king
founded a Celestine monastery there after the model of
the one at Paris, which was the favourite sanctuary of the
high nobility, and which Pierre had also frequented in his
youth. The foundation-stone was laid by the dukes of Orléans, Berry and Burgundy.

There is another case which may serve to illustrate the
intercourse of princes with saints: Saint Francis of Paula at
the court of Louis XI. The very peculiar type of piety
which this king presents is too well known to be described
here at large. Louis XI, "who bought the grace of God and
of the Virgin Mary for more money than ever king did,"
displays all the qualities of the crudest fetishism. His passion for relics, pilgrimages and processions seems to us al-

most totally devoid of really pious sentiment, and even of respect. He used to handle the holy objects as if they were expensive medicines. At the approach of death he sent to all parts of the world for extraordinary relics. The pope sent him the corporal of Saint Peter. The Grand Turk actually offered him a collection of relics which were still at Constantinople. On the table beside his bed was the "Sainte Ampoule," the vase in which the holy oil for coronation was kept, and which had never left Reims before. According to Commines, the king wanted to try its miraculous virtue by having his whole body anointed. The cross of Saint Laud was specially sent for from Angers to take an oath upon, for Louis made a difference between oaths taken on one relic and on another. These are traits reminding us of the Merovingian times.

In him the fervent venerator of relics blends with the collector of curiosities. He corresponds with Lorenzo de Medici about the ring of Saint Zanobi and about an *Agnus Dei*, that is to say, one of these figures cut out of the fibrous trunk of an Asiatic fern, which were also called *Agnus Scythicus*, or Tartarian lamb, and to which rare medicinal virtues were attributed. At Plessis lès Tours the holy persons, summoned thither to say prayers for the king, rub shoulders with musicians of all sorts. "At that time the king had a great number of players of deep-toned and sweet instruments brought to him, whom he lodged at Saint-Cosme, near Tours, where they assembled, as many as a hundred and twenty, among whom there were many shepherds from the country of Poitou. Who often played before the king's mansion (but they did not see him), that the king might enjoy the aforesaid instruments as a pleasure and pastime and to prevent him from sleeping. And, on the other hand, he also sent for a great number of male and female bigots and devout people like hermits and saintly creatures, to pray God incessantly to allow that he should not die and that He might let him live longer."

Saint Francis of Paula, the Calabrian hermit, who surpassed the Minorite friars in humility by founding the order of the Minims, was literally a purchase of the royal

collector. After having failed with the king of Naples,
Louis's diplomacy succeeded, by the pope's intervention, in
securing the miraculous man. A noble escort bore him from
Italy, sorely against his will. His ferocious asceticism reminds us of the barbarous saints of the tenth century, Saint
Nil and Saint Romuald. He flies at the sight of a woman.
Since his youth he has never touched a piece of money.
He sleeps upright or in a leaning position; he lets his hair
and beard grow. He does not eat animal food and accepts
only roots. The king, who is already ill, took pains to procure the proper food for his rare saint. "Monsieur de Genas,
I beg you to send me lemons and sweet oranges, and
muscatel pears, and parsnips,[2] and it is for the holy man
who eats neither flesh nor fish; and you will do me a very
great pleasure." At court he was known only as "the holy
man," so that Commines appears not to have known his
name, although he often saw him. The mockers and sus-
picious persons also called him "holy man." The king himself, at the instigation of Jacques Coitier, his physician, began by setting spies on the man of God and by putting him
to the proof. Commines is prudently reserved about him.
Although declaring that he had never seen a man "of such
saintly life, nor one in whom the Holy Spirit seemed more
to speak through his mouth," he concludes: "He is still
alive, so that he may well change, for the better or for the
worse, so that I shall be silent, as many mocked at the
arrival of this hermit, whom they called 'holy man.'" It is
noteworthy that learned theologians like Jan Standonck
and Jean Quentin, having come from Paris to speak to
him about the founding of a monastery of Minims at Paris,
went back full of admiration.

It is a significant fact that the princes of the fifteenth
century often ask the advice of great visionaries and extravagant ascetics in political matters. Thus Saint Colette is
consulted by Philip the Good and by his mother, Marguerite of Bavaria, and acts as an intermediary in the con-

[2] Perhaps the king wrote by mistake, *pastenargues* for
pastèques = watermelons.

troversies between the houses of France, Savoy and Burgundy. Her canonization was demanded with pious insistence by the house of Burgundy.

More important still was the public part played by Denis the Carthusian. He also was frequently in touch with the house of Burgundy. Obsessed by the fear of imminent catastrophes, such as the conquest of Rome by the Turks, he urges the duke to undertake a crusade. He dedicates to him a treatise on princely government. He advises the duke of Guelders in the conflict with his son. Numbers of noblemen, clerks and burghers come to consult him in his cell at Ruremonde, where he is constantly engaged in resolving doubts, difficulties and questions of conscience.

Denys le Chartreux, or of Rickel, is the most complete type of religious enthusiast at the end of the Middle Ages. His mental range and many-sided energy are hardly conceivable. To mystic transports, ferocious asceticism, continual visions and revelations he unites immense activity as a theological writer. His works fill forty-five quarto volumes. All medieval divinity meets in him as the rivers of a continent flow together in an estuary. *Qui Dionysium legit nihil non legit,*[3] said sixteenth-century theology. He sums up, he concludes, but he does not create. All that his great predecessors have thought is reproduced by him in a simple and easy style. He wrote all his books himself, and revised, corrected, subdivided and illuminated them. At the end of his life, he deliberately laid down his pen. *Ad securae taciturnitatis portum me transferre intendo.*[4]

He never knew repose. Every day he recites the psalter almost entirely, and, at any rate, half. He prays continually, while dressing or while engaged in any other occupation. When others go to sleep again after matins, he remains awake. Big and strong, he exposes his body with impunity to all kinds of privations. I have a head of iron, he would say, and a stomach of brass. He feeds, for choice, on tainted victuals.

[3] He who reads Denis reads everything.
[4] I am now going to enter the haven of secure taciturnity.

The enormous amount of theological meditation and speculation which he achieved, was not the fruit of a peaceful and balanced life of study; it was carried out in the midst of intense emotions and violent shocks. Visions and revelations are with him ordinary experiences. Ecstasies come to him on all sorts of occasions, especially when he hears music, sometimes in the midst of noble company, who are listening to his wise advice. As a child he rose when the moon was shining brightly, thinking it was time to go to school. He is a stammerer. He sees the room of a dying woman full of demons who knock the stick out of his hand. He constantly converses with the dead. When asked if he often sees apparitions of deceased persons, he answers: "yes, hundreds of times." Although constantly occupied with his supernatural experiences, he does not like to speak about them, and is ashamed of the ecstasies which earned him among the laudatory surnames of the great theologians that of *Doctor ecstaticus.*

The great figure of Denis the Carthusian no more escaped suspicion and raillery than the miracle-worker of Louis XI. The slander and abuse of the world pursued him all his life. The mental attitude of the fifteenth century towards the highest religious manifestations of the age is made up equally of enthusiasm and distrust.

Chapter XIV

RELIGIOUS SENSIBILITY AND RELIGIOUS IMAGINATION

Ever since the gentle mysticism of Saint Bernard, in the twelfth century, had started the strain of pathetic tenderness about the Passion of Christ, the religious sensibility of the medieval soul had been increasing. The mind was saturated with the concepts of Christ and the cross. In early childhood the image of the cross was implanted on the sensitive heart, so grand and forbidding as to overshadow all other affections by its gloom. When Jean Gerson was a child, his father one day stood with his back against a wall, his arms outspread, saying: "Thus, child, was your God crucified, who made and saved you." This image of his father, he tells us, remained engraved on his mind, expanding as he grew older, even in his old age, and he blessed his pious father for it, who had died on the day of the Exaltation of the Cross. Saint Colette, when four years old, every day heard her mother in prayer lament and weep about the Passion, sharing the pain of contumely, blows, and torments. This recollection fixed itself in the supersensitive heart of Colette with such intensity, that she felt, all her life through, the most severe oppression of heart every day at the hour of the crucifixion; and at the reading of the Passion she suffered more than a woman in childbed.

A preacher sometimes paused to stand in silence, with his arms extended in the form of the cross, for a quarter of an hour.

The soul is so imbued with the conception of the Passion that the most remote analogy suffices to make the chord of the memory of Christ vibrate. A poor nun carrying wood to the kitchen imagines she carries the cross; a blind woman doing the washing takes the tub for the manger and the washhouse for the stable.

This extreme religious sensibility shows itself by copious weeping. Devotion, says Denis the Carthusian, is a sort of tenderness of heart, which easily moves to tears of piety. We should pray God to have "the daily baptism of tears." They are the wings of prayer and, according to Saint Bernard, the wine of angels. We should give ourselves up to the grace of meritorious tears, get ready for them and let ourselves be carried away by them all the year round, but especially during Lent, so that we may say with the psalmist: *Fuerunt mihi lacrimae meae panis die ac nocte.*[1] Sometimes they come so easily, that we pray sobbing and

---

[1] My tears have been my meat day and night.

groaning. If they do not come, we should not force them;
we should then content ourselves with the tears of the
heart. In the presence of others we should avoid these
signs of extraordinary devotion.

Vincent Ferrer shed so many tears every time he con-
secrated the Host that the whole congregation also wept,
insomuch that a general wailing was heard as if in the
house of one dead.

Popular devotion in France did not take a special form
as we notice in the Netherlands, where it was standardized,
so to say, in the pietistic movement of the Brethren of the
Common Life and the regular canons of the Congregation
of Windesheim. This was the circle whence proceeded the
"Imitation of Christ." The regulations which the Dutch devout bound themselves to obey, gave their piety a conventional form and preserved them from dangerous
excesses of fervour. French devotion, although very similar,
kept more of its passionate and spasmodic character, and
led more easily to fantastic aberrations, in those cases
where it did not speedily wear itself out.

Nowhere do we notice its character better than in the
writings of Gerson. The chancellor of the university was
the great dogmatic and moral censor of his time. His prudent, scrupulous, slightly academic mind was admirably
fitted to distinguish between true piety and exaggerated
religious manifestations. This was, indeed, his favourite occupation. Benevolent, sincere and pure, he had that meticulous carefulness in point of good style and form which
so often reminds us of his modest origin in the case of a
man who has raised himself by his own talents from humble circumstances to an aristocratic mentality. He was a
born psychologist and had a fine sense of style, which is
near akin to the craving for orthodoxy.

At the Council of Constance, Gerson defended the Dutch
Brethren of the Common Life against whom a Dominican
of Groningen brought a charge of heresy. He was, nevertheless, fully aware of the dangers threatening the Church
from a too exuberant popular devotion. It may therefore
appear strange that he often disapproved of manifestations

of piety in his own country, which reappear in that very "devotio moderna" of the Netherlands, over which he threw the mantle of his authority. The explanation is that the devout in France had no safe sheepfold of organization and of discipline to keep them within the limits of what the Church could tolerate.

The world, said Gerson, is approaching its end, and, like an old dotard, is exposed to all sorts of fancies, dreams and illusions which lead many a one to stray outside the pathway of truth. Mysticism is brought into the streets. Many people take to it, without suitable direction, and indulge in too rigid fasts, too protracted vigils, and too abundant tears, all of which disturb their brains. In vain they are advised to be moderate and to take heed lest they fall into the devil's snares. At Arras, he tells us, he visited a woman who won the admiration of the multitude by going completely without food during several consecutive days, against her husband's wishes. He talked to her and only found in her a vain and arrogant obstinacy; for, after her fasts, she ate with insatiable voracity. Her face betrayed imminent insanity. He also cites the case of an epileptic woman who thought that each twinge of pain in her corns was a sign that a soul descended to hell.

Gerson set little store by visions and revelations which were recent and universally spoken of, including even those of Bridget of Sweden and Catherine of Siena. He had heard so many stories of this sort that he had lost all belief in them. Someone or other would always be asserting that it had been revealed to him that he would be pope. A certain man, in particular, believed himself predestined, first, to become pope, then to be the Antichrist, so that he had thought of killing himself in order to save Christendom from such an evil.

There is nothing more dangerous, says Gerson, than ignorant devotion. The poor devout, learning that the heart of Mary exulted in her God, strain themselves to exult also; they call up all sorts of images without being able to distinguish between truth and delusion, and they take them all for miraculous proofs of their excellent devotion.

Contemplative life has great dangers, he continues; it has made numbers of people melancholy or mad. Gerson perceived the connection between fasting and hallucinations, and had a glimpse of the rôle played by fasting in the practice of magic.

Now, where was a man of Gerson's psychological subtlety to draw the line of demarcation in the manifestations of piety, between what is holy and laudable and what is inadmissible? The dogmatic point of view did not meet the case. It was easy for him, a theologian by profession, to point out deviations from dogma. But he felt that, as regards manifestations of piety, considerations of an ethical sort should guide our judgment, that it was a question of degree and of taste. There is no virtue, says Gerson, which is more neglected in these miserable times of schism than discretion.

The Church in the Middle Ages tolerated many religious extravagances, provided they did not lead up to novelties of a revolutionary sort, in morals or in doctrine. So long as it spent itself in hyperbolic fancies or in ecstasies, superabundant emotion was not a source of danger. Thus, many saints were conspicuous for their fanatical reverence for virginity, taking the form of a horror of all that relates to sex. Saint Colette is an instance of this. She is a typical representative of what has been called by William James the theopathic condition. Her supersensibility is extreme. She can endure neither the light nor the heat of fire, only the light of candles. She has an immoderate horror of flies, ants and slugs, and of all dirt and stenches of all kinds. Her abomination of sexual functions inspires her with repugnance for those saints who have passed through the matrimonial state, and leads her to oppose the admission of non-virginal persons to her congregation. The Church has ever praised such a disposition, judging it to be edifying and meritorious.

On the other hand, the same sentiment became dangerous, as soon as the fanatics of chastity, not content with shutting themselves up in their own sphere of purity, wanted to apply their principles to ecclesiastical and social life. The Church was repeatedly obliged to disown the violent assailants of the validity of the sacraments administered by priests living in fornication, for the double reason that sound catholic doctrine has always separated the sacredness of the office from the personal dignity of the bearer, and that she knew herself to be not strong enough to uproot the evil. Jean de Varennes had been a learned divine and a celebrated preacher. Chaplain to the youthful Cardinal of Luxembourg at Avignon, he seemed destined for the highest ecclesiastical career, when he suddenly threw up all his benefices, with the exception of a canonry of Notre Dame of Reims, gave up the great style of his life and went to Saint Lié, his birthplace, where he began to lead a saintly life and to preach. "And he was much visited by people who came to see him from all countries on account of the simple, very noble and most honest life he led." Soon he is called "the holy man of Saint Lié"; he is regarded as a future pope, a miraculous being, a messenger of God. All France talks of him.

Now, in the person of Jean de Varennes the passion of sexual purity assumes a revolutionary aspect. He reduces all the evils of the Church to the one evil of lust. His extremist programme for the re-establishment of chastity is not aimed only at the clergy. As to fornicating priests, he denies the efficacy of the sacraments they administer: an ancient and redoubtable thesis which the Church had encountered more than once. According to him, it was not permissible for a priest to live in the same house with his sister or with an elderly woman. Moreover, he attacks immorality in general. He ascribes twenty-three different sins to the matrimonial state. He demands that adultery shall be punished according to the Ancient Law; Christ Himself would have ordered the stoning of the adulterous woman, if He had been sure of her fault. He asserts that no woman in France is chaste, and that no bastard can live a good life and be saved. In his vehement indignation he preaches resistance to the ecclesiastical authorities, to the archbishop of Reims in particular. "A wolf, a wolf!" he cried to the people, who understood but too well who the wolf was, and repeated joyously: "Hahay, aus leus, mes bones gens, aus leus." The archbishop had Jean de Varennes locked up in a horrible prison.

This severity towards all revolutionary tendencies of a doctrinal kind contrasts with the indulgence shown by the Church for the extravagances of religious imagination, notably for ultra-sensuous fancies about divine love. It required the psychological perspicacity of a Gerson to be aware that there also the Faith was menaced by a moral and doctrinal danger.

The spiritual state called *dulcedo Dei*, the sweetness of the delights of the love of Christ, was towards the end of the Middle Ages one of the most active elements of religious life. The followers of the "devotio moderna" in the Netherlands had systematized it, and thereby made it more or less innocuous. Gerson, who distrusted it, has analysed it in his treatise, *De diversis diaboli tentationibus*, and elsewhere. "The day," he said, "would be too short if I were to enumerate the innumerable follies of the loving, nay, the raving, *amantium, immo et amentium*." He knew the peril by experience. For he can have only meant himself when he described the case of one of his acquaintances who had carried on a spiritual friendship with a nun, at first without any trace of carnal inclination, and without suspecting any sin, till a separation revealed to him the amorous nature of this relation. So that he drew the inference from it, *Amor spiritualis facile labitur in nudum carnalem amorem*,[2] and considered himself warned.

The devil, he says, sometimes inspires us with feelings of immense and marvellous sweetness which is very like devotion, so that we make the quest of this delight our object and want to love God only to attain it. Many have deceived themselves by immoderately cultivating such feelings; they have taken the mad excitement of their hearts for divine ardour, and were thus miserably led astray. Others strive to attain insensibility or complete passiveness, to become a perfect tool for God.

[2] Spiritual love easily falls into sheer carnal love.

It is this sensation of absolute annihilation of the individual, tasted by the mystics of all times, which Gerson, as a supporter of a moderate and prudent mysticism, could not tolerate. A female visionary told him that in the contemplation of God her mind had been annihilated, really annihilated, and then created anew. "How do you know?" he asked her. "I experienced it," she had answered. The logical absurdity of this reply had sufficed him to prove the reprehensible nature of these fancies.

It was dangerous to let such sensations express themselves by explicit formulas; the Church could only tolerate them in the form of images. Catherine of Siena might say that her heart had been changed into the heart of Christ. But Marguerite Porete, an adherent of the sect of the Brethren of the Free Spirit, who also believed that her soul had been annihilated in God, was burnt at Paris.

What the Church dreaded above all in the idea of the annihilation of the personality was the consequence, accepted by the extremist mystics of all religions, that the soul absorbed in God, and therefore, having no will, can no longer sin, even in following its carnal appetites. How many poor ignorant people had been dragged by such doctrines into the most abominable licence. Every time Gerson touches the question of the dangers of spiritual love, he remembers the excesses of the Bégards and of the Turlupins; he fears a truly satanic impiety, like that of the nobleman he mentions as having confessed to a Carthusian that the sin of lust did not prevent him from loving God; on the contrary, it inflamed him to seek for and taste more eagerly the sweetness of divine love.

So long as the transports of mysticism were translated into passionate imaginings of a symbolic nature, however vivid their colours might be, they caused but a relative danger. On becoming crystallized in images, they lost some of their noxiousness. In this way the exuberant imagery of the time, to a certain extent, diverted the most dangerous tendencies of the religious life of the epoch, however bizarre it may appear to us. Jan Brugman, a popular Dutch preacher, might with impunity compare Jesus, tak-

ing human form, to a drunkard, who forgets himself, sees
no danger, who gives away all he has. "Oh, was He not
truly drunk, when love urged Him to descend from the
highest heavens to this lowest valley of the earth?" He sees
Him in heaven, going about to pour out drinks for the
prophets, "and they drank till they were fit to burst, and
David with his harp, leaped before the table, just as if he
were the Lord's fool."

Not only the grotesque Brugman, the serene Ruysbroeck,
too, likes to represent divine love under the image of
drunkenness. Hunger also served as a figure to express the
relations of the soul with Christ. Ruysbroeck, in *The Adornment of the Spiritual Marriage*, says: "Here begins an
eternal hunger which is never appeased; it is an inner
craving and hankering of the loving power and the created
spirit for an uncreated good. . . . Those that experience it
are the poorest of men; for they are eager and greedy
and they have an insatiable hunger. Whatever they eat
and drink, they never become satiated by it, for this hunger
is eternal." The metaphor may be inverted, so that the
hunger is Christ's, as in *The Mirror of Eternal Salvation*.
"His hunger is immensely great; He consumes us entirely
to the bottom, for He is a greedy glutton with a voracious
hunger; He devours even the marrow of our bones. . . .
First He prepares His repast and in His love He burns up
all our sins and our faults. Next, when we are purified and
roasted by the fire of love, He opens his mouth like a
voracious being who wishes to swallow all."

A little insistence on the details of the metaphor will
make it ridiculous. "You will eat Him," says *Le Livre de
Crainte Amoureuse* of Jean Berthelemy, in speaking of the
Eucharist, "roasted at the fire, well baked, not at all over-
done or burnt. For just as the Easter lamb was properly
baked and roasted between two fires of wood or of char-
coal, thus was gentle Jesus on Good Friday placed on the
spit of the worthy cross, and tied between the two fires
of His very fearful death and passion, and of the very
ardent charity and love which He felt for our souls and our

salvation; He was, as it were, roasted and slowly baked to save us."

The infusion of divine grace is described under the image of the absorption of food, and also of being bathed. A nun feels quite deluged in the blood of Christ and faints. All the red and warm blood of the five wounds flowed through the mouth of Saint Henry Suso into his heart. Catherine of Siena drank from the wound in His side. Others drank of the Virgin's milk, like Saint Bernard, Henry Suso, Alain de la Roche.

The Breton, Alain de la Roche, a Dominican, born about 1428, is a very typical representative of this religious imagery, both ultra-concrete and ultra-fantastic. He was the zealous promoter of the use of the rosary, with a view to which he founded the Universal Brotherhood of the Psalter of Our Lady. The description of his numerous visions is characterized at the same time by an excess of sexual imagination and by the absence of all genuine emotion. The passionate tone which, in the grand mystics, makes these too sensuous images of hunger and thirst, of blood and voluptuousness, bearable, is altogether lacking. The symbolism of spiritual love has become with him a mere mechanical process. It is the decadence of the medieval spirit. We shall return to it shortly.

Now, whereas the celestial symbolism of Alain de la Roche seems artificial, his infernal visions are characterized by a hideous actuality. He sees the animals which represent the various sins equipped with horrible genitals, and emitting torrents of fire which obscure the earth with their smoke. He sees the prostitute of apostasy giving birth to apostates, now devouring them and vomiting them forth, now kissing them and petting them like a mother.

This is the reverse side of the suave fancies of spiritual love. Human imagination contained, as the inevitable complement of the sweetness of celestial visions, a black mass of demonological conceptions which also sought expression in language of ardent sensuality. Alain de la Roche forms the link between the placid and gentle pietism of the "devotio moderna" and the darkest horror produced by

the medieval spirit on the wane: the delusion of witchcraft, at that time fully developed into a fatally consistent
system of theological zeal and judicial severity. A faithful
friend of the regulars of Windesheim and the Brethren of
the Common Life, in whose house he died at Zwolle in
1475, he was at the same time the preceptor of Jacob
Sprenger, a Dominican like himself, not only one of the two
authors of the *Malleus maleficarum*, but also the propaga-
tor in Germany of the Brotherhood of the Rosary, founded
by Alain.

Chapter XV

SYMBOLISM IN ITS DECLINE

Thus religious emotion always tended to be transmuted into
images. Mystery seemed to become graspable by the mind
when invested with a perceptible form. The need of adoring the ineffable in visible shapes was continually creating
ever new figures. In the fourteenth century, the cross and
the lamb no longer sufficed for the effusions of overflowing
love offered to Jesus; to these is added the adoration of the
name of Jesus, which occasionally threatens to eclipse even
that of the cross. Henry Suso tattoos the name of Jesus
over his heart and compares himself to the lover who wears
the name of his beloved embroidered on his coat. Bernardino of Siena, at the end of a moving sermon, lights
two candles and shows the multitude a board a yard in
length, bearing on an azure ground the name Jesus in
golden letters, surrounded by the sun's rays. The people
filling the church kneel down and weep with emotion. The
custom spreads, especially with the Franciscan preachers.
Denis the Carthusian is represented in art holding such a
board in his uplifted hands. The sun as a crest above the
arms of Geneva is derived from this usage. The ecclesiastical authorities regarded the matter with suspicion; there

was some talk of superstition and of idolatry; there were
tumults for and against; Bernardino was summoned before the *curia*, and the usage was forbidden by Pope Martin V. About the same time a very similar form of adoring
Christ under a visible sign was successfully introduced into
the ritual, namely, that of the monstrance. To this also the
Church objected at first; the use of the monstrance was
originally forbidden except during the week of the Corpus
Christi. In taking, instead of the original form of a tower,
that of a radiant sun, the monstrance became very like the
board, bearing Jesus' name, of which the Church disapproved.

The abundance of images in which religious thought
threatened to dissolve itself would have only produced a
chaotic phantasmagoria, if symbolic conception had not
worked it all into a vast system, where every figure had
its place.

Of no great truth was the medieval mind more conscious
than of Saint Paul's phrase: *Videmus nunc per speculum in
aenigmate, tunc autem facie ad faciem.*[1] The Middle Ages
never forgot that all things would be absurd, if their meaning were exhausted in their function and their place in the
phenomenal world, if by their essence they did not reach
into a world beyond this. This idea of a deeper significance
in ordinary things is familiar to us as well, independently
of religious convictions: as an indefinite feeling which may
be called up at any moment, by the sound of raindrops on
the leaves or by the lamplight on a table. Such sensations
may take the form of a morbid oppression, so that all things
seem to be charged with a menace or a riddle which we
must solve at any cost. Or they may be experienced as a
source of tranquillity and assurance, by filling us with the
sense that our own life, too, is involved in this hidden meaning of the world. The more this perception converges upon
the absolute One, whence all things emanate, the sooner
it will tend to pass from the insight of a lucid moment to a

[1] For now we see through a glass darkly; but then face to
face.

permanent and formulated conviction. "By cultivating the continuous sense of our connection with the power that made things as they are, we are tempered more towardly for their reception. The outward face of nature need not alter, but the expressions of meaning in it alter. It was dead and is alive again. It is like the difference between looking on a person without love, or upon the same person with love. . . . When we see all things in God, and refer all things to Him, we read in common matters superior expressions of meaning." [2]

Here, then, is the psychological foundation from which symbolism arises. In God nothing is empty of sense: *nihil vacuum neque sine signo apud Deum,* said Saint Irenæus. So the conviction of a transcendental meaning in all things seeks to formulate itself. About the figure of the Divinity a majestic system of correlated figures crystallizes, which all have reference to Him, because all things derive their meaning from Him. The world unfolds itself like a vast whole of symbols, like a cathedral of ideas. It is the most richly rythmical conception of the world, a polyphonous expression of eternal harmony.

In the Middle Ages the symbolist attitude was much more in evidence than the causal or the genetic attitude. Not that this latter mode of conceiving the world, as a process of evolution, was wholly absent. Medieval thought, too, sought to understand things by means of their origin. But, destitute of experimental methods, and neglecting even observation and analysis, it was reduced, in order to state genetic relations, to abstract deduction. All notions of one thing proceeding from another took the naïve form of procreation or ramification. The image of a tree or a pedigree sufficed to represent any relations of origin and cause. An *arbor de origine juris et legum,* for example, classified all law in the form of a tree with numerous branches. Owing to its primitive methods, the evolutionist thought of the Middle Ages was bound to remain schematic, arbitrary and sterile.

[2] W. James: *Varieties of Religious Experience,* p. 474.

From the causal point of view, symbolism appears as a sort of short-circuit of thought. Instead of looking for the relation between two things by following the hidden detours of their causal connections, thought makes a leap and discovers their relation, not in a connection of cause or effects, but in a connection of signification or finality. Such a connection will at once appear convincing, provided only that the two things have an essential quality in common which can be referred to a general value. Expressed in terms of experimental psychology: all mental association based on a causal similitude whatever will immediately set up the idea of an essential and mystic connection. This may well seem a rather meagre mental function. Moreover, it reveals itself as a very primitive function, when envisaged from an ethnological point of view. Primitive thought is characterized by a general feebleness of perception of the exact demarcation between different concepts, so that it tends to incorporate into the notion of a definite something all the notions connected with it by any relation or similitude whatsoever. With this tendency the symbolizing function is closely related.

It is, however, possible to view symbolism in a more favourable light by abandoning for a while the point of view of modern science. Symbolism will lose this appearance of arbitrariness and abortiveness when we take into account the fact that it is indissolubly linked up with the conception of the world which was called Realism in the Middle Ages, and which modern philosophy prefers to call, though less correctly, Platonic Idealism.

Symbolic assimilation founded on common properties presupposes the idea that these properties are essential to things. The vision of white and red roses blooming among thorns at once calls up a symbolic assimilation in the medieval mind: for example, that of virgins and martyrs, shining with glory, in the midst of their persecutors. The assimilation is produced because the attributes are the same: the beauty, the tenderness, the purity, the colours of the roses, are also those of the virgins, their red colour that of the blood of the martyrs. But this similarity will only have a mystic meaning if the middle-term connecting the two terms of the symbolic concept expresses an essentiality common to both; in other words, if redness and whiteness are something more than names for a physical difference based on quantity, if they are conceived as essences, as realities. The mind of the savage, of the child, and of the poet never sees them otherwise.

Now, beauty, tenderness, whiteness, being realities, are also entities; consequently all that is beautiful, tender or white must have a common essence, the same reason of existence, the same significance before God.

In pointing out these very strong links between symbolism and realism (in the scholastic sense), we should be careful not to think too much of the quarrel about the universals. We know very well that the realism which declared *universalia ante rem*, and attributed essentiality and pre-existence to general ideas, did not dominate medieval thought without a struggle. Undoubtedly there were also nominalists. But it does not seem too bold to affirm that radical nominalism has never been anything but a reaction, an opposition, a countercurrent vainly disputing the ground with the fundamental tendencies of the medieval spirit. As philosophical formulæ, realism and nominalism had early made each other the necessary concessions. The new nominalism of the fourteenth century, that of the Occamites or Moderns, merely removed certain inconveniences of an extreme realism, which it left intact by relegating the domain of faith to a world beyond the philosophical speculations of reason.

Now, it is in the domain of faith that realism obtains, and here it is to be considered rather as the mental attitude of a whole age than as a philosophic opinion. In this larger sense it may be considered inherent in the civilization of the Middle Ages and as dominating all expressions of thought and of the imagination. Undoubtedly Neo-Platonism strongly influenced medieval theology, but was not the sole cause of the general "realist" trend of thought. Every primitive mind is realist, in the medieval sense, independently of all philosophic influence. To such a men-

tality everything that receives a name becomes an entity
and takes a shape which projects itself on the heavens. This
shape, in the majority of cases, will be the human shape.

All realism, in the medieval sense, leads to anthropomor-
phism. Having attributed a real existence to an idea, the
mind wants to see this idea alive, and can only effect this
by personifying it. In this way allegory is born. It is not
the same thing as symbolism. Symbolism expresses a mysterious connection between two ideas, allegory gives a visible form to the conception of such a connection. Symbolism
is a very profound function of the mind, allegory is a superficial one. It aids symbolic thought to express itself, but
endangers it at the same time by substituting a figure for
a living idea. The force of the symbol is easily lost in the
allegory.

So allegory in itself implies from the outset normalizing,
projecting on a surface, crystallizing. Moreover, medieval
literature had taken it in as a waif of decadent Antiquity.
Martianus Capella and Prudentius had been the models.
Allegory seldom loses an air of elderliness and pedantry.
Still, the use of it supplied a very earnest craving of the
medieval mind. How else can we explain the preference
which this form enjoyed so long?

These three modes of thought together—realism, symbolism and personification—have illuminated the medieval
mind with a flood of light. The ethic and æsthetic value
of the symbolical interpretation of the world was inesti-
mable. Embracing all nature and all history, symbolism
gave a conception of the world, of a still more rigorous
unity than that which modern science can offer. Symbolism's image of the world is distinguished by impeccable
order, architectonic structure, hierarchic subordination. For
each symbolic connection implies a difference of rank or
sanctity: two things of equal value are hardly capable of
a symbolic relationship with each other, unless they are
both connected with some third thing of a higher order.

Symbolist thought permits of an infinity of relations between things. Each thing may denote a number of distinct
ideas by its different special qualities, and a quality may

also have several symbolic meanings. The highest conceptions have symbols by the thousand. Nothing is too humble to represent and to glorify the sublime. The walnut signifies Christ; the sweet kernel is His divine nature, the green and pulpy outer peel is His humanity, the wooden shell between is the cross. Thus all things raise the thoughts to the eternal; being thought of as symbols of the highest, in a constant gradation, they are all transfused by the glory of divine majesty. Every precious stone, besides its natural splendour, sparkles with the brilliance of its symbolic values. The assimilation of roses and virginity is much more than a poetic comparison, for it reveals their common essence. As each notion arises in the mind the logic of symbolism creates a harmony of ideas. The special quality of each of them is lost in this ideal harmony and the rigour of rational conception is tempered by the presentment of some mystic unity.

A consistent concord reigns between all the spiritual domains. The Old Testament is the prefiguration of the New, profane history reflects the one and the other. About each idea other ideas group themselves, forming symmetrical figures, as in a kaleidoscope. Eventually all symbols group themselves about the central mystery of the Eucharist; here there is more than symbolic similitude, there is identity: the Host is Christ and the priest in eating it becomes truly the sepulchre of the Lord.

The world, objectionable in itself, became acceptable by its symbolic purport. For every object, each common trade had a mystical relation with the most holy, which ennobled it. Bonaventura identified the handicrafts symbolically with the eternal generation and incarnation of the Word, and with the covenant between God and the soul. Even profane love is attached by symbolic connection to divine love. In this way all individual suffering is but the shadow of divine suffering, and all virtue is as a partial realization of absolute goodness. Symbolism, in thus detaching personal suffering and virtue from the sphere of the individual in order to raise them to that of the universal, constituted a salutary counterpoise to the strong religious individualism, bent on personal salvation, which is characteristic of the Middle Ages.

Religious symbolism offered one cultural advantage more. To the letter of formulated dogma, rigid and explicit in itself, the flowering imagery of symbols formed, as it were, a musical accompaniment, which by its perfect harmony allowed the mind to transcend the deficiencies of logical expression.

Symbolism opened up all the wealth of religious conceptions to art, to be expressed in forms full of colour and melody, and yet vague and implicit, so that by these the profoundest intuitions might soar towards the ineffable.

In the later Middle Ages the decline of this mode of thought had already long set in. The representation of the Universe in a grand system of symbolical relations had long been complete. Still, the symbolizing habit maintained itself, adding ever new figures that were like petrified flowers. Symbolism at all times shows a tendency to become mechanical. Once accepted as a principle, it becomes a product, not of poetical enthusiasm only, but of subtle reasoning as well, and as such it grows to be a parasite clinging to thought, causing it to degenerate.

Symbolic assimilation is often only based on an equality of number. An immense perspective of ideal series of relationships is opened up in this way, but they amount to nothing more than arithmetical exercises. Thus the twelve months signified the apostles, the four seasons the evangelists, the year Christ. A regular cluster was formed of systems of seven. With the seven virtues correspond the seven supplications of the Lord's Prayer, the seven gifts of the Holy Spirit, the seven beatitudes and the seven penitential psalms. All these groups of seven are again connected with the seven moments of the Passion and the seven sacraments. Each of them is opposed to one of the seven deadly sins, which are represented by seven animals and followed by seven diseases.

A director of consciences like Gerson, from whom these examples are borrowed, is inclined to lay the stress on the moral and practical value of these symbolisms. In a visionary like Alain de la Roche the æsthetic element prevails. His symbolic speculations are very highly elaborated and somewhat factitious. In order to obtain a system in which the numbers fifteen and ten enter, representing the cycles of 150 Aves and of 15 Paters, which he prescribed to his Brotherhood of the Rosary, he adds the eleven celestial spheres and the four elements and then multiplies by the ten categories (substance, quality, etc.). As the product he obtained 150 natural habits. In the same way the multiplication of the ten commandments by fifteen virtues gives 150 moral habits. To arrive at the figure of fifteen virtues, he counts, besides the three theological virtues and the four cardinal virtues, seven capital virtues, which makes fourteen; there remain two other virtues: religion and penitence; that makes sixteen, which is one too many; but as temperance of the cardinal series is identical with abstinence of the capital series, we finally obtain the number fifteen. Each of these fifteen virtues is a queen having her nuptial bed in one of the divisions of the Pater Noster. Each of the words of the Ave signifies one of the fifteen perfections of the Virgin, and at the same time a precious stone, and is able to drive away a sin, or the animal which represents that sin. They represent other things as well: the branches of a tree which carries all the blessed ones; the steps of a staircase. To quote but two examples: the word *Ave* signifies the innocence of the Virgin and the diamond; it drives away pride, or the lion, which represents pride. The word *Maria* denotes her wisdom and the carbuncle; it drives away envy, symbolized by a black dog.

Sometimes Alain gets a little entangled in his very complicated system of symbolisms.

Symbolism was, in fact, played out. Finding symbols and allegories had become a meaningless intellectual pastime, shallow fancifulness resting on a single analogy. The sanctity of the object still gives it some small spiritual value. As soon as the craze of symbolism spreads to profane or simply moral matters, decadence is manifest. Froissart, in *Li Orloge amoureus,* compares all the details of love to the various parts of a timepiece. Chastellain and Molinet vie with each other in political symbolism. The three estates represent the qualities of the Virgin. The seven electors of the Empire signify the virtues; the five towns of Artois and Hainaut, which in 1477 remained faithful to the house of Burgundy, are the five wise virgins. In reality this is symbolism turned upside down; it uses things of the higher order as symbols of things of the lower order, for these authors in effect raise terrestrial things to the higher level by employing sacred conceptions merely to adorn them.

The *Donatus moralisatus,* sometimes, but erroneously, ascribed to Gerson, mixed up Latin grammar with theology: the noun-substantive is the man, the pronoun means that he is a sinner. The lowest grade of this kind of mental activity is represented by works like *Le Parement et Triumphe des Dames* of Olivier de la Marche, in which each article of female costume symbolizes a virtue—a theme also developed by Coquillart.

"De la pantouffle ne nous vient que santé
Et tout prouffit sans griefve maladie,
Pour luy donner tiltre d'auctorité
Je luy donne le nom d'humilité." [3]

In the same way shoes mean care and diligence, stockings perseverance, the garter resolution, etc.

It is clear that to the men of the fifteenth century this genre did not appear so silly as it does to us, otherwise they would not have cultivated it with so much gusto. We are thus led to conclude that, to the mind of the declining Middle Ages, symbolism and allegory had not yet lost all their living significance. The tendency to symbolize and to personify was so spontaneous that nearly every thought, of itself, took a figurative shape. Every idea being considered as an entity, and every quality as an essence, they were at once invested by the imagination with a personal form. Denis the Carthusian, in his revelations, sees the

[3] The slipper only gives us health And all profit without serious illness. To give it a title to authority I give it the name of humility.

Church in fully as personal a shape as when it was represented in an allegory on the stage. One of his revelations deals with the future reformation of the Church, such as fifteenth-century theology was hoping for: a Church cleansed from the evils that stained it. The spiritual beauty of this purified Church was revealed to his vision in the form of a superb and precious garment, with marvellous colours and ornaments. Another time he sees the persecuted Church: ugly, anæmic, enfeebled. God warns him that the Church is going to speak, and Denis then hears the inner voice as though it proceeded from the person of the Church *quasi ex persona Ecclesiae*. The figurative form that thinking assumes here is so direct and so sufficient to evoke the desired associations, that no need is felt to explain the allegory in detail. The idea of a splendid garment is fully adequate to express spiritual purity; thought here has resolved itself into an image, just as it can resolve itself into a melody.

Let us recall once more the allegorical personages of the *Roman de la Rose*. To us it requires an effort to picture to ourselves Bel-Accueil, Doulce Mercy, Humble Requeste. To the men of the Middle Ages, on the other hand, these figures had a very vivid æsthetic and sentimental value, which put them almost on a level with those divinities which the Romans conceived out of abstractions, like Pavor and Pallor, Concordia, etc. To the minds of the declining Middle Ages, Doux Penser, Honte, Souvenirs, and the rest, were endowed with a quasi-divine existence. Otherwise the *Roman de la Rose* would have been unreadable. One of the figures passed even from its original meaning to still more concrete signification: Danger in amorous parlance meant the jealous husband.

Allegory is often called in to express a thought of particular importance. Thus the bishop of Chalons, wishing to address a very serious political remonstrance to Philip the Good, gives it an allegorical form and presents it to the duke at Hesdin on Saint Andrew's Day, 1437. "Haultesse de Signourie," chased out of the Empire, having first fled to France, next to the court of Burgundy, is inconsolable,

and complains of being harrowed there, too, by "Carelessness of the prince, Feebleness of counsel, Envy of servants,
Exaction of the subjects," to drive away which it will be
necessary to oppose "Vigilance of the prince," etc., to them.
In short, the whole political argument has taken the form of
a *tableau vivant* instead of a newspaper leader, as it would
take with us. Evidently this was the way to create an impression, and it follows that allegory still had a suggestive
force which we find it very hard to realize.

The "Burgher of Paris" in his diary is a prosaic man, who
takes little trouble to ornament his style. Nevertheless,
when he comes to the most horrible events he has to relate,
that is to say, to the Burgundian murders in Paris, in June,
1418, he at once rises to allegory. "Then arose the goddess
of Discord, who lived in the tower of Evil Counsel, and
awoke Wrath, the mad woman, and Covetousness and
Rage and Vengeance, and they took up arms of all sorts
and cast out Reason, Justice, Remembrance of God and
Moderation most shamefully." His narrative of the atrocities
committed is entirely composed in the symbolic fashion.
"Then Madness the enraged, and Murder and Slaughter
killed, cut down, put to death, massacred all they found in
the prisons . . . and Covetousness tucked up her skirts
into her belt with Rapine, her daughter, and Larceny, her
son. . . . Afterwards the aforesaid people went by the
guidance of their goddesses, that is to say, Wrath, Covetousness and Vengeance, who led them through all the
public prisons of Paris, etc."

Why does the author use allegory here? To give his narrative a more solemn tone than the one he uses for the
daily events which he generally notes down in his diary.
He feels the necessity of regarding these atrocious events
as something more than the crimes of a few individual
malefactors; allegory is his way of expressing his sense of
tragedy.

It is just when allegory chafes us most that it fully reveals
its dominion over the medieval mind. We can bear it more
or less in a tableau vivant where conventional figures are
draped in a fantastical and unreal apparel. The fifteenth

century dresses up its allegorical figures, as well as its
saints, in the costume of the time and has the faculty of
creating new personages for each thought it wants to express. To tell the moral tale of a giddy young man, who is
led to ruin by the life at court, Charles de Rochefort, in
L'Abuzé en Court, invents a whole new series of personages, like those of the *Rose,* and these dim creations, Fol
cuidier, Folle bombance (Foolish credulity, Foolish show),
and the rest, are represented in the miniatures illustrating
the work like noblemen of the age. Time himself does not
require a beard or a scythe, and appears in doublets and
hose. The very commonplace aspect of these allegories is
precisely what shows their vitality.

We can understand that a human shape is ascribed to
virtues or to sentiments, but the spirit of the Middle Ages
does not hesitate to extend this process to notions which,
to us, have nothing personal. The personification of Lent
was a widely known type from 1300 onward. We find it
in the poem, *La Bataille de Karesme et de Charnage,* a
theme which Pieter Breughel was to take up much later
and illustrate with his mad fancy. A current proverb said:
Quaresme fait ses flans la nuit de Pasques.[4] In certain
towns of North Germany a doll, called Lent, was suspended in the choir of the church and taken down during mass on the Wednesday before Easter.

Was there a difference between the idea which people
formed of saints and that of purely symbolic personages?
Undoubtedly, the former were acknowledged by the
Church, they had a historical character and statues of wood
and stone, but the latter were in touch with living fancy,
and, after all, we may ask ourselves if to popular imagination Bel-Accueil or Faux Semblant did not appear as real
as Saint Barbara and Saint Christopher.

On the other hand, there is no real contrast between
medieval allegory and Renaissance mythology. There is
rather a fusion. The mythological figures are older than
the Renaissance. Venus and Fortune, for instance, had

---

[4] Lent bakes his cakes on Easter-night.

never completely died, and allegory, on the other hand, kept its vogue for a long time after the fifteenth century, nowhere stronger than in English literature. In the poetry of Froissart, Doux Semblant, Refus, Dangier and Escondit are seen contending, as it were, with mythological figures like Atropos, Clotho, Lachesis. At first the latter are less vivid and coloured than the allegories; they are dull and shadowy and there is nothing classic about them. Gradually Renaissance sentiment brings about a complete change. The Olympians and the nymphs get the better of the allegorical personages, who fade away, in proportion as the poetic glory of Antiquity is more intensely felt.

Symbolism, with its servant allegory, ultimately became an intellectual pastime. The symbolic mentality was an obstacle to the development of causal thought, as causal and genetic relations must needs look insignificant by the side of symbolic connections. Thus the sacred symbolism of the two luminaries and the two swords for a long time barred the road to historic and juridical criticism of papal authority. For the symbolizing of Papacy and Empire as the Sun and the Moon, or as the two swords brought by the Disciples, was to the medieval mind far more than a striking comparison; it revealed the mystic foundation of the two powers, and established directly the precedence of Saint Peter. Dante, in order to investigate the historical foundation of the pope's primacy, had first to deny the appropriateness of the symbolism.

The time was not distant when people were bound to awake to the dangers of symbolism; when arbitrary and futile allegories would become distasteful and be rejected as trammels of thought. Luther branded them in an invective which is aimed at the greatest lights of scholastic theology: Bonaventura, Guillaume Durand, Gerson and Denis the Carthusian. "These allegorical studies," he exclaims, "are the work of people who have too much leisure. Do you think I should find it difficult to play at allegory-making about any created thing whatsoever? Who is so feeble-witted that he could not try his hand at it?"

Symbolism was a defective translation into images of

secret connections dimly felt, such as music reveals to us. *Videmus nunc per speculum in aenigmate.* The human mind felt that it was face to face with an enigma, but none the less it kept on trying to discern the figures in the glass, explaining images by yet other images. Symbolism was like a second mirror held up to that of the phenomenal world itself.

Chapter XVI

THE EFFECTS OF REALISM

All that was thinkable had taken image-shape: conception had become almost entirely dependent on imagination. Now, a too systematic idealism (this is what realism meant in the Middle Ages) gives a certain rigidity to the conception of the world. Ideas, being conceived as entities and of importance only by virtue of their relation with the Absolute, easily range themselves as so many fixed stars on the firmament of thought. Once defined, they only lend themselves to classification, subdivision and distinction according to purely deductive norms. Apart from the rules of logic, there is never a corrective at hand to indicate a mistake in the classification, and this causes the mind to be deluded as to the value of its own operations and the certainty of the system.

If the medieval mind wants to know the nature or the reason of a thing, it neither looks into it, to analyse its structure, nor behind it, to inquire into its origin, but looks up to heaven, where it shines as an idea. Whether the question involved is political, social or moral, the first step taken is always to reduce it to its universal principle. Even quite trifling and ordinary things are regarded in this light. Thus a point is debated in the University of Paris: May examination fees be levied for intermediate degrees? The chancellor thinks so; Pierre d'Ailly intervenes to defend the opposite view. Now, he does not start from arguments based on law or tradition, but from an application of the text: *Radix omnium malorum cupiditas*,[1] and so he sets himself to prove by an entirely scholastic exposition that the aforesaid exaction is simoniacal, heretical, and contrary to natural and divine law. This is what so often disappoints and wearies us moderns in reading medieval demonstrations: they are directed heavenwards, and lose themselves from the very start in moral generalities and Scriptural cases.

This profound and systematic idealism betrays itself everywhere. There is an ideal and clearly defined conception of every trade, dignity or estate, to which the individual who belongs to it has to conform as best he may. Denis the Carthusian, in a series of treatises, *De vita et regimine episcoporum, archidiaconorum*, etc., etc., pointed out to all—bishops, canons, priests, scholars, princes, nobles, knights, merchants, husbands, widows, girls, friars—the ideal form of their professional duties, and the way to sanctify their calling or condition by living up to that ideal. His exposition of moral precepts, however, remains abstract and general; he never brings us into contact with the realities of the occupations or walks in life of which he speaks.

This tendency to reduce all things to a general type has been considered a fundamental weakness in the mentality of the Middle Ages, owing to which the power to discern and describe individual traits was never attained. Starting from this premise, the well-known summary of the Renaissance as the coming of individualism would be justified. But at bottom this antithesis is inexact and misleading. Whatever the faculty of seeing specific traits may have been in the Middle Ages, it must be noted that men disregarded the individual qualities and fine distinctions of things, deliberately and of set purpose, in order always to bring them under some general principle. This mental tendency is a result of their profound idealism. People feel an imperious need of always and especially seeing the general

---

[1] The root of all evil is covetousness.

sense, the connection with the absolute, the moral ideality, the ultimate significance of a thing. What is important is the impersonal. The mind is not in search of individual realities, but of models, examples, norms.

Every notion concerning the world or life had its fixed place in a vast hierarchic system of ideas, in which it is linked with ideas of a higher and more general order, on which it depends like a vassal on his lord. The proper business of the medieval mind is discrimination, displaying severally all concepts as if they were so many substantial things. Hence the faculty of detaching a conception from the ideal complex to which it belongs in order to regard it as a thing by itself. When Foulques de Toulouse is blamed for giving an alms to an Albigensian woman, he answers: "I do not give it to the heretic, but to the poor woman." Margaret of Scotland, queen of France, having kissed Alain Chartier, the poet, whom she found asleep, exculpates herself in these terms: "I did not kiss the man, but the precious mouth whence have issued and gone forth so many good words and virtuous sayings." It is the same turn of mind which, in the field of high theological speculation, distinguishes in God between an antecedent will, desiring the salvation of all, and a consequent will, extending only to the elect.

Without the brake of empirical observation, the habit of always subordinating and subdividing becomes automatic and sterile, mere numbering, and nothing else. No subject lent itself better to it than the category of virtues and of sins. Every sin has its fixed number of causes, species, noxious effects. There are, according to Denis the Carthusian, twelve follies, deceiving the sinner; each of them is illustrated, fixed and represented by Scripture texts and by symbols, so that the whole argument displays itself like a church portal ornamented with sculptures. The enormity of sin should be considered from seven points of view: that of God, that of the sinner, of matter, of circumstances, of the intention, of the nature of the sin and of its consequences. Next, every one of these seven points is subdivided, in its turn, into eight, or into fourteen. There are six infirmities of the mind which incline us to sin, etc. This systematizing of morality has its striking analogies in the sacred books of Buddhism.

Now, this everlasting classification, this anatomy of sin, would be apt to weaken the consciousness of sin which it should enhance, if it were not attended with an effort of the imagination directed to the gravity of the fault and the horrors of the chastisements. All moral conceptions are exaggerated, overcharged to excess, because they are always placed in direct connection with divine majesty. In every sin, even the least, the universe is concerned. No human soul can be fully conscious of the enormity of sin. All the saints and the just, the celestial spheres, the elements, the lower creatures and inanimate objects, cry for vengeance on the sinner. Denis strives to over-stimulate the fear of sin and of hell by detailed descriptions and terrifying images. Dante has touched with beauty the darkness of hell: Farinata and Ugolino are heroic, and Lucifer is majestic. But this monk, devoid of all poetic grace, draws a picture of devouring torment and nothing more; his very dullness makes the horror of it. "Let us imagine," he says, "a white-hot oven, and in this oven a naked man, never to be released from such a torment. Does not the mere sight of it appear insupportable? How miserable this man would seem to us! Let us think how he would sprawl in the oven, how he would yell and roar: in short, how he would *live*, and what would be his agony and his sorrow when he understood that this unbearable punishment was never to end."

The horrible cold, the loathsome worms, the stench, hunger and thirst, the darkness, the chains, the unspeakable filth, the endless cries, the sight of the demons, Denis calls up all this before us like a nightmare. Still more oppressive is the insistence on psychic suffering: the mourning, the fear, the empty feeling of everlasting separation from God, the inexpressible hatred of God, the envy of the bliss of the elect; the confusion of all sorts of errors and delusions in the brain. And the thought that this is to last in all eternity is by ingenious comparisons wrought up to the fever-point of horror.

The treatise *De quattuor hominum novissimis*, from which these details are borrowed, was the customary reading during meal-time at the convent of Windesheim. A truly bitter condiment! But medieval man always preferred drastic treatment. He was like an invalid who has been treated too long with heroic medicines, only the most powerful stimulants produced an effect on him. In order to make some virtue shine in all its splendour, the Middle Ages present it in an exaggerated form, which a sedater moralist would perhaps regard as a caricature. Saint Giles praying God not to allow his wound caused by an arrow to heal is their pattern of patience. Temperance finds its models in saints who always mix ashes with their food, chastity in those who tested their virtue by sleeping beside a woman. If it is not some extravagant act, it is the extreme youth of the saint which marks him out as a model, Saint Nicholas refusing his mother's milk on feast-days, or Saint Quiricus (a martyr, either three years or nine months old) refusing to be consoled by the prefect, and thrown into the abyss.

Here, again, it is the dominant idealism which makes people only relish the excellence of virtue in an extra strong dose. Virtue is conceived as an idea; its beauty shines more brightly in the hyperbolic perfection of its essence than in the imperfect practice of everyday life.

Nothing shows better the primitive character of the hyperidealist mentality, called realism in the Middle Ages, than the tendency to ascribe a sort of substantiality to abstract concepts. Though philosophic realism did never admit these materialist tendencies, and strove to avoid such consequences, it cannot be denied that medieval thought frequently yielded to the inclination to pass from pure idealism to a sort of magic idealism, in which the abstract tends to become concrete. Here the ties which bind the Middle Ages to a very remote cultural past are very clearly displayed.

It was about 1300 that the doctrine of the treasure of the

works of supererogation of Christ and the saints took a
fixed form. The idea itself of such a treasure, the common
possession of all the faithful, in so far as they are members
of the mystic body of Christ, which is the Church, was by
that time very ancient. But the way in which it was applied, in the sense that the superabundant good works
constitute an inexhaustible reserve, which the Church can
dispose of by retail, does not appear before the thirteenth
century. Alexandre de Halès was the first to use the word
thesaurus in the technical sense, which it has kept ever
since. The doctrine did not fail to excite resistance. In the
end, however, it prevailed and was officially formulated in
1343 in the bull *Unigenitus* of Clement VI. There the
treasure has altogether the form of a capital confided by
Christ to Saint Peter, and still increasing every day. For,
in proportion as men are more drawn to justice by the distribution of this treasure, the merits, of which it is composed, will go on accumulating.

The material conception of ethical categories made itself
felt more with regard to sin than to virtue. The Church, it
is true, has always explicitly taught that sin is not a thing
or an entity. But how could it have prevented the error,
when everything concurred to insinuate it into men's
minds? The primitive instinct which see sins as stuff which
soils or corrupts, which one should, therefore, wash away,
or destroy, was strengthened by the extreme systematizing
of sin, by their figurative representation, and even by the
penitentiary technique of the Church itself. In vain did
Denis the Carthusian remind the people that it was but
for the sake of comparison that he calls sin a fever, a cold
and corrupted humour—popular thought undoubtedly lost
sight of the restrictions of dogmatists. The terminology of
the law, less anxious than theology as to doctrinal purity,
did not hesitate, in England, to connect with felony the
notion of a corruption of the blood: this is the realistic conception in its spontaneous form.

On one special point the dogma itself demanded this perfectly realist conception: that is to say, with regard to the
blood of the Redeemer. The faithful are bound to con-

ceive it as absolutely material. A drop of the precious blood,
said Saint Bernard, would have sufficed to save the world,
but it was shed abundantly, as Saint Thomas Aquinas expresses it in a hymn:

> "Pie Pelicane, Jesu domine,
> Me immundum munda tuo sanguine,
> Cuius una stilla salvum facere
> Totum mundum quit ab omni scelere." [2]

Chapter XVII

RELIGIOUS THOUGHT BEYOND
THE LIMITS OF IMAGINATION

The imagination was continually striving, and in vain, to
express the ineffable by giving it shape and figure. To call
up the absolute, recourse is always had to the terminology
of extension in space, and the effort always fails. From the
pseudo-Dionysius the Areopagite onward, mystic authors
have piled up terms of immensity and infinity. It is always
infinite extension which has to serve for rendering the eternal accessible to reason. Mystics exert themselves to find
suggestive images. Imagine, says Denis the Carthusian, a
mountain of sand, as large as the universe; that every hundred thousand years a grain be taken from it. The mountain will disappear at last. But after such an inconceivable
space of time the sufferings of hell will not have diminished,
and will not be nearer to the end than when the first grain
was removed. And yet, if the damned knew that they

[2] Pious pelican, Lord Jesus, cleanse me, impure one, by
your blood, of which one drop can save all the world from
all iniquity.
   Compare Marlowe's *Faustus*: "See, where Christ's blood
streams in the firmament! One drop of blood will save me."

would be set free when the mountain had disappeared, it would be a great consolation to them.

If, to inculcate fear and horror, the imagination disposed of resources of appalling wealth, the expression of celestial joys, on the other hand, always remained extremely primitive and monotonous. Human language cannot provide a vision of absolute bliss. It has at its disposal only inadequate superlatives, which can do nothing but strengthen the idea arithmetically. What was the use of producing terms of height, or extension, or the inexhaustible? People never could progress beyond imagery, the reduction of the infinite to the finite, and the consequent weakening of the feeling of the absolute. Every sensation in expressing itself lost a little of its immediate force, every attribute ascribed to God robbed Him of a little of His majesty.

Thus begins the tremendous struggle of the spirit which yearns to rise above all imagery. It is the same at all epochs and with all races. Mystics, it has been said, have neither birthday nor native land. But the support of imagination cannot be given up all at once. The insufficiency of all modes of expression is gradually accepted. First the brilliant imagery of symbolism is abandoned, and the too concrete formulas of dogma are avoided. But still the contemplation of the absolute Being ever remains linked up with notions of extension or of light. Next these notions change into their negative opposites—silence, the void, obscurity. And as these latter formless conceptions, too, in their turn, prove insufficient, a constant joining of each to its contrary is tried. Finally, nothing remains to express the idea of divinity but pure negation.

Of course, these successive stages in the abandoning of imagery have not actually followed in strict chronological order. All had been reached already by Denis the Areopagite. In the following passage of Denis the Carthusian we find the greater number of these modes of expression united. In a revelation he hears the voice of God who is angry. "On hearing this answer the monk, collected within himself, and finding himself as transported into a region of immense light, most sweetly, in an intense tranquillity, by a secret call without external sound invoked the most secret and truly hidden, the incomprehensible God: O most over-lovable God, Thou in Thyself art the light and the region of light, in which Thy elect sweetly come to rest, repose, sleep. Thou art like a desert most over-vast, even and intraversable, where the truly pious heart, entirely purified of all individual affection, illumined from on high and inflamed by sacred ardour, deviates without erring and errs without deviating, happily fails and unfailingly convalesces."

We here find first the image of light, next that of sleep, then that of the desert, and, lastly, the opposites which cancel one another. The mystic imagination found a very impressive concept in adding to the image of the desert, that is to say, extension of surface—that of the abyss, or extension of depth. The sensation of giddiness is added to the feeling of infinite space. The German mystics, as well as Ruysbroeck, have made a very plastic use of this striking image.

Master Eckhart spoke of "the abyss without mode and without form of the silent and waste divinity." The fruition of bliss, says Ruysbroeck, "is so immense that God Himself is as swallowed up with all the blessed . . . in an absence of modes, which is a not-knowing, and in an eternal loss of self." And elsewhere: "The seventh degree, which follows next . . . is attained when, beyond all knowledge and all knowing, we discover in ourselves a bottomless not-knowing; when beyond all names given to God and to creatures, we come to expire and pass over in eternal namelessness, where we lose ourselves . . . and when we contemplate all these blessed spirits which are essentially sunken away, merged and lose in their super-essence, in an unknown darkness without mode."

Always the hopeless attempt to dispense with images and to attain "the state of void, that is mere absence of images." which only God can give. "He deprives us of all images and brings us back to the initial state where we find only wild and waste absoluteness, void of all form or image, for ever corresponding with eternity."

The contemplation of God, says Denis the Carthusian, is more adequately rendered by negations than by affirmations. "For, when I say: God is goodness, essence, life, I seem to indicate what God is, as if what He is had anything in common with, or any resemblance to, a creature, whereas it is certain, that He is incomprehensible and unknown, inscrutable and ineffable, and separated from all He works by an immeasurable and wholly incomparable difference and excellence." It is for this reason that the "uniting wisdom" was called by the Areopagite: unreasonable, insane and foolish.

But whether Denis or Ruysbroeck speak of light changed into darkness (a motif inspired by the Old Testament and which the pseudo-Areopagite had developed), or again of ignorance, forlornness or of death, they never get beyond images.

Without metaphors it is impossible to express a single thought. All effort to rise above images is doomed to fail. To speak of our most ardent aspirations only in negative terms does not satisfy the cravings of the heart, and where philosophy no longer finds expression, poetry comes in again. Mysticism has always rediscovered the road from the giddy heights of sublime contemplation to the flowery meadows of symbolism. The sweet lyricism of the older French mystics, Saint Bernard and the Victorines, will always come to the aid of the seer, when all the resources of expression have been exhausted. In the transports of ecstasy the colours and figures of allegory reappear. Henry Suso sees his betrothed, Eternal Wisdom: "She soared high above him in a sky with clouds, she was bright like the morning star and shone like the radiant sun; her crown was eternity, her robe beatitude, her speech sweetness, her kiss absolute delight; she was remote and near, high aloft and below; she was present and yet hidden; she let herself be approached and yet no one could grasp her."

The Church has always feared the excesses of mysticism, and with reason. For the fire of contemplative rapture, consuming all forms and images, must needs burn all formulæ, concepts, dogmas, and sacraments too. However, the very

nature of mystic transport implied a safeguard for the
Church. To be uplifted to the clarity of ecstasy, to wander
on the solitary heights of contemplation stripped of forms
and images, tasting union with the only and absolute principle, was to the mystic never more than the rare grace of
a single moment. He had to come down from the mountain-
tops. The extremists, it is true, with their following of
"enfants perdus," did deviate into pantheism and eccen-
tricities. The others, however—and it is among these that
we find the great mystics—never lost their way back to the
Church awaiting them with its wise and economic system
of mysteries fixed in the liturgy. It offered to everybody
the means to get into touch at a given moment with the
divine principle in all security and without danger of individual extravagances. It economized mystic energy, and
that is why it has always outlived unbridled mysticism and
the dangers it compassed.

"Unitive wisdom is unreasonable, insane and foolish."
The path of the mystic leading into the infinite leads to
unconsciousness. By denying all positive connection between the Deity and all that has form and a name, the
operation of transcendency is really abolished: "All creatures"—says Eckhart—"are mere nothing; I do not say that
they are little or aught: they are nothing. That which has
no entity, is not. All creatures have no being, for their being depends on the presence of God." Intensive mysticism
signifies return to a pre-intellectual mental life. All that is
culture is obliterated and annulled.

If, notwithstanding, mysticism has, at all times, borne
abundant fruit for civilization, it is because it always rises
by degrees, and because in its initial stages it is a powerful
element of spiritual development. Contemplation demands
a severe culture of moral perfection as a preparatory condition. The gentleness, the curbing of desires, the simplicity, the temperance, the labouriousness practised in mystical
circles, create about them an atmosphere of peace and of
pious fervour. All the great mystics have praised humble
labour and charity. In the Netherlands these concomitant
features of mysticism—moralism, pietism—became the es-

sence of a very important spiritual movement. From the preparatory phases of intensive mysticism of the few issued the extensive mysticism of the "devotio moderna" of the many. Instead of the solitary ecstasy of the blessed moment comes a constant and collective habit of earnestness and fervour, cultivated by simple townspeople in the friendly intercourse of their Fraterhouses and Windesheim convents. Theirs was mysticism by retail. They had "only received a spark." But in their midst the spirit lived which gave the world the work in which the soul of the declining Middle Ages found its most fruitful expression for the times to come: *The Imitation of Jesus Christ*. Thomas à Kempis was no theologian and no humanist, no philosopher and no poet, and hardly even a true mystic. Yet he wrote the book which was to console the ages. Perhaps here the abundant imagination of the medieval mind was conquered in the highest sense.

Thomas à Kempis leads us back to everyday life.

Chapter XVIII

THE FORMS OF THOUGHT AND PRACTICAL LIFE

The specific forms of the thought of an epoch should not only be studied as they reveal themselves in theological and philosophic speculations, or in the conceptions of creeds, but also as they appear in practical wisdom and everyday life. We may even say that the true character of the spirit of an age is better revealed in its mode of regarding and expressing trivial and commonplace things than in the high manifestations of philosophy and science. For all scholarly speculation, at least in Europe, is affiliated in a very complicated way to Greek, Hebrew, even Babylonian and Egyptian origins, whereas in everyday life the spirit of a race or of an epoch expresses itself naïvely and spontaneously.

The mental habits and forms characteristic of the high speculation of the Middle Ages nearly all reappear in the domain of ordinary life. Here, too, as we might expect, primitive idealism, which the schools called realism, is at the bottom of all mental activity. To take every idea by itself, to give it its formula, to treat it as an entity, next to combine the ideas, to classify them, to arrange them in hierarchic systems, always to build cathedrals with them, such, in practical life also, is the way in which the medieval mind proceeds.

All that acquires a fixed place in life is considered as having a reason for existence in the divine scheme. The most commonplace customs share this honour with the most exalted things. A very plain instance of this may be found in the treatment of rules of court etiquette, which we have touched upon already in another connection. Aliénor de Poitiers and Olivier de la Marche considered them wise laws, judiciously instituted by ancient kings and binding for all centuries to come. Aliénor speaks of them as of sacred monuments of the wisdom of ages: "And then I have heard it said by the ancients who knew . . ." etc. She sees with sorrow signs of decline. For a good many years the ladies of Flanders have been putting the bed of a woman newly delivered of a child before the fire, "at which people mocked a good deal," because formerly this was never done. What are we coming to? "But at present everybody does what he pleases: because of which we may well be afraid that all will go badly."—La Marche gravely asks the following question: Why has the "fruit-master," also the "wax-department" (le mestier de la cire), that is to say, illumination, among his attributes?—He answers, not less gravely: Because wax is extracted from flowers whence the fruit comes too: "so that this matter is very well ordained thus."

In matters of utility or of ceremony medieval authority creates a special organ for every function, because it regards the function as an idea and considers it as an actual thing. The "grand sergeanty" of the king of England comprised a dignitary whose office it was to hold the king's head when he crossed the Channel and was suffering with sea-sickness. A certain John Baker held this office in 1442, and after his death it passed to his two daughters.

Of the same nature is the custom, very ancient and very primitive, of giving a proper name to inanimate objects. We witnessed a revival of this usage when the big guns during the late war got names. During the Middle Ages it was much more frequent. Like the swords of the heroes in the *chansons de geste,* the stone mortars in the wars of the fourteenth and fifteenth centuries had names of their own: "Le Chien d'Orléans, la Gringade, la Bourgeoise, Dulle Griete." A few very celebrated diamonds are still known by proper names: this, too, is a survival of a widely spread custom. Several jewels of Charles the Bold had their names: "le sauny, les trois frères, la hôte, la balle de Flandres." If, at the present time, ships still have names, but bells and most houses have not, the reason lies in the fact that the ship preserves a sort of personality, also expressed in the English usage of making ships feminine. In the Middle Ages this tendency to personify things was much stronger; every house and every bell had its name.

In the minds of the Middle Ages every event, every case, fictitious or historic, tends to crystallize, to become a parable, an example, a proof, in order to be applied as a standing instance of a general moral truth. In the same way every utterance becomes a dictum, a maxim, a text. For every question of conduct Scripture, legends, history, literature, furnish a crowd of examples or of types, together making up a sort of moral clan, to which the matter in question belongs. If it is desired to make someone to pardon an offence, all the Biblical cases of pardon are enumerated to him; if to dissuade him from marrying, all the unhappy marriages of antiquity are cited. In order to free himself from blame for the murder of the duke of Orléans, Jean sans Peur compares himself to Joab and his victim to Absalom, rating himself as less guilty than Joab, because he

had not acted in open defiance of a royal warning. "Ainsy
avoit le bon duc Jehan attrait ce fait à moralité." [1]

In the Middle Ages everyone liked to base a serious
argument on a text, so as to give it a foundation. In 1406,
at the national council of Paris, where the question of the
schism was debated, the twelve propositions for and
against renouncing obedience to the pope of Avignon, all
started from a Biblical quotation. Profane orators, too, no
less than preachers, choose their text.

All the traits indicated are found united in striking fashion in the famous plea delivered on the 8th of March,
1408, at the hôtel de Saint Pol before a princely audience,
by Master Jean Petit, divine, preacher and poet, in order
to clear the duke of Burgundy of the charge of the murder
which the latter repented of having confessed. It is a real
masterpiece of political wickedness, built up with perfect
art and in a severe style on the text: *Radix omnium
malorum cupiditas* (the root of all evil is covetousness).
The whole is cunningly arranged in a scheme of scholastic
distinctions and complementary Biblical texts, illustrated
by Scriptural and historical examples and animated by a
fiendish verve. After having enumerated twelve reasons
obliging the duke of Burgundy to honour, love and avenge
the king of France, Maître Petit draws two applications
from his text: covetousness makes apostates and it makes
traitors. Apostasy and treason are divided and subdivided,
and then illustrated by three examples. Lucifer, Absalom
and Athalia rise up before the imagination of the hearers
as the archetypes of a traitor. Eight truths are brought
forward to justify tyrannicide. Referring to one of the eight,
he says: "I shall prove this truth by twelve reasons in honour of the twelve apostles." And he cites three sentences
of the doctors, three of the philosophers, three of the
jurists and three from Scripture. From the eight truths eight
corollaries are derived, completed by a ninth. By the aid
of allusions or insinuations he revives all the old suspicions

[1] Thus good duke John had drawn the moral inference
of the case.

which hung over the memory of the ambitious and de-
bauched prince: his responsibility for the disaster of the
"bal des ardents," where the young king's company, disguised as wild men, miserably perished by fire, while the
king himself narrowly escaped; his plans of murder and
poisoning, hatched in the Celestine monastery, in the
course of his conversations with "the sorcerer," Philippe de
Mézières. The notorious leaning of the duke towards
necromancy furnished an opportunity for describing very
picturesque scenes of horror. Maître Petit is even familiar
with the demons whom Orléans consulted; he knows their
names and the way in which they were dressed. He goes
so far as to ascribe a sinister meaning to the delirious utterances of the mad king.

All this makes up the major term of the syllogism. The
minor follows it, point by point. Grounding themselves on
the general propositions which had raised the case to the
plane of fundamental ethics and had artfully roused a sentiment of shuddering horror, the direct accusations burst
out in a flood of passionate hatred and defamation. The
pleading lasted for four hours, and at the end Jean sans
Peur pronounced the words: "I avouch you" (Je vous
avoue). The justification was written out in four costly
copies for the duke and his nearest relations, ornamented
with gilding and miniatures, and bound in pressed leather.
It was also for sale.

The tendency to give each particular case the character
of a moral sentence or of an example, so that it becomes
something substantial and unchallengeable, the crystallization of thought, in short, finds its most general and natural
expression in the proverb. In the thought of the Middle
Ages proverbs have performed a very living function.
There were hundreds in current use in every nation. The
greater number are striking and concise. Their tone is often
ironical, their accent always that of bonhomie and resignation. The wisdom we glean from them is sometimes profound and beneficent. They never preach resistance. "Les
grans poissons mangent les plus petis." "Les mal vestus
assiet on dos ou vent." "Nul n'est chaste si ne besongne."

"Au besoing on s'aide du diable." "Il n'est si ferré qui ne
glice." [2] To the laments of moralists about the depravity of
man the proverbs oppose a smiling detachment. The proverb always glozes over iniquity. Now it is naïvely pagan
and now almost evangelical. A people which has many
proverbs in current use will be less given to talking non-
sense, and so will avoid many confused arguments and
empty phrases. Leaving arguments to cultured people, it
is content with judging each case by referring to the
authority of some proverb. The crystallization of thought
in proverbs is therefore not without advantage to society.

Proverbs in their crude simplicity were thoroughly in
accordance with the general spirit of the literature of the
epoch. The level reached by authors was but little higher
than that of the proverbs. The dicta of Froissart often read
like proverbs gone wrong. "It is thus with feats of arms:
sometimes one loses, another time one wins." "There is
nothing of which one does not tire." It is therefore safer,
instead of hazarding moral sentences of one's own, to use
well-established proverbs like Geffroi de Paris, who lards
his rhyming chronicle with them. The literature of the time
is full of ballads of which each stanza ends with a proverb, as, for instance, the *Ballade de Fougères* of Alain
Chartier, the *Complaincte de Eco* of Coquillart, and several
poems by Jean Molinet, not to mention Villon's well-known
ballad which was entirely composed of them. The 171
stanzas of the *Passe Temps d'Oysiveté*, by Robert
Gaguin, nearly all end in some phrase looking like a proverb, although the greater number are not found in the
best-known collections. Did Gaguin invent them, then? In
that case we should have a still more curious indication of
the vital function of the proverb at this epoch, if we see
them here arising in an individual mind, *in statu nascendi*,
as it were.

[2] The big fishes eat the smaller. The badly dressed are
placed with their back to the wind. None is chaste if he
has no business. At need we let the devil help us. No horse
is so well shod that it never slips.

In political speeches and in sermons, proverbs are in frequent use. Gerson, Jean de Varennes, Jean Petit, Guillaume Fillastre, Olivier Maillard, take pains to strengthen their arguments by the most common ones. "Qui de tout se tait, de tout a paix.—Chef bien peigné porte mal bacinet.—Qui commun sert, nul ne l'en paye."[3]

Related to the proverb, in so far as it is a crystallized form of thought, is the motto, which the declining Middle Ages cultivated with marked predilection. It differs from it in that it is not, like the proverb, a wise adage of general application, but a personal maxim or exhortation. To adopt a motto is, so to say, to choose a text for the sermon of one's life. The motto is a symbol and a token. Marked in golden letters on every article of the wardrobe and of the equipment, it must have exercised a suggestive influence of no mean importance. The moral tone of these mottoes is mostly that of resignation, like that of the proverbs, or that of hope. The motto should be mysterious. "Quand sera ce?—Tost ou tard vienne.—Va oultre.—Autre fois mieulx.—Plus deuil que joye."[4] The greater number refer to love. "Aultre naray.—Vostre plaisir.—Souvienne vous.— Plus que toutes."[5] When of such a nature they were worn on armour and caparisons. Those engraved in rings have a more intimate note: "Mon cuer avez.—Je le desire.—Pour toujours.—Tout pour vous."[6]

A complement to mottoes is found in the emblem, like the knotty stick of Louis of Orléans with the motto "Je l'envie," a gambling term meaning "I challenge," to which Jean sans Peur replied with a plane and the words "Ic

[3] He who is silent about all things, is troubled by nothing.—A well-groomed head wears the helmet badly.—He who serves the common weal, is paid by none for his trouble.

[4] When will it be?—Soon or late it may come.—Onward. —Better next time.—More sorrow than joy.

[5] I shall have no other.—Your pleasure.—Remember.— More than all.

[6] You have my heart.—I desire it.—For ever.—All for you.

houd," that is to say, "accepted." Another instance is the
flint-and-steel of Philip the Good. With the emblem and
the motto we enter the sphere of heraldic thought, of which
the psychology is yet to be written. To the men of the
Middle Ages the coat of arms was undoubtedly more than
a matter of vanity or of genealogical interest. Heraldic
figures in their minds acquired a value almost like that of
a totem. Whole complexes of pride and ambition, of loyalty
and devotion, were condensed in the symbols of lions, lilies
or crosses, which thus marked and expressed intricate
mental contexts by means of an image.

The spirit of casuistry, which was greatly developed in
the Middle Ages, is another expression of the same tendency to isolate each thing as a special entity. It is another
effect of the dominant idealism. Every question which
presents itself must have its ideal solution, which will become apparent as soon as we have ascertained, by the aid
of formal rules, the relation of the case in question to the
eternal verities. Casuistry reigns in all the departments of
the mind: alike in morals and in law, and in matters of
ceremony, of etiquette, of tournaments and the chase, and,
above all, of love. We have already spoken of the influence
which chivalrous casuistry exercised on the origins of the
laws of war. Let us quote some more examples from the
Arbre des Batailles of Honoré Bonet. Should a member of
the clergy aid his father or his bishop? Is one bound to
make good borrowed armour which one has lost during
a battle? May one fight a battle on festal days? Is it better
to fight fasting or after a meal?

No subject lent itself better to the distinction of casuistry
than that of prisoners of war. To take noble and rich
prisoners was, at that time, the main point of the military
profession. In what circumstances may one escape from
captivity? What is a safe conduct worth? To whom does an
escaped and recaptured prisoner belong? May a prisoner
on parole fly, if his victor puts him in chains? Or may he do
so, if his captor forgot to ask his parole? In *Le Jouvencel*
two captains dispute for a prisoner before the commander-
in-chief. "I seized him first," says one, "by the arm and by

the right hand, and tore his glove from him." "But to me," says the other, "he gave that same hand with his parole."

Besides idealism, a strong formalism is at the bottom of all the traits enumerated. The innate belief in the transcendental reality of things brings about as a result that every notion is strictly defined and limited, isolated, as it were, in a plastic form, and it is this form which is all-important. Mortal sins are distinguished from venial sins according to fixed rules. In law, culpability is established in the first place by the formal nature of the deed. The ancient judicial adage, "The deed judges the man," had lost nothing of its force. Although jurisprudence had been long ago freed from the extreme formalism of primitive law, which knew no difference between the intentional and the involuntary deed and did not punish an attempt that had miscarried, yet traces of a severe formalism existed in great number at the close of the Middle Ages. Thus, there was a rule of long standing that a slip of the tongue in the formula of an oath rendered it null and void, the oath being a sacred thing. In the thirteenth century an exception was made in favour of foreign merchants who only knew the language of the country imperfectly, and it was conceded that their incorrect language in taking the oath should not lose them their rights.

The extreme sensibility to everything touching honour is an effect of the general formalism. A nobleman is blamed for having the caparison of his horse ornamented with his armorial bearings, because, if the horse, "a brute beast," should stumble at the joust, the coat of arms would be dragged through the sand and the whole family dishonoured.

The formal element occupied a large place in everything connected with vengeance, expiations, reparations for wounded honour. The right of vengeance, a very vital element in the customs of France and the Netherlands in the fifteenth century, was exercised more or less according to fixed rules. It is not always furious anger which urges people to acts of violence in pursuit of vengeance; amends for offended honour are sought according to a well-regulated plan. It is, above all, a question of shedding blood, not of killing; sometimes care is taken to wound the victim only in the face, the arms, or the thighs.

The satisfaction sought for, being formal, is symbolic. In political reconciliations in the fifteenth century, symbolic actions have a very large share: demolition of houses which recall the crime, erection of commemorative crosses or chapels, injunctions to block up a doorway, etc., not to mention expiatory processions and masses for the dead. After his reconciliation with his brother at Rouen in 1469, Louis XI's first care is to have the ring which the bishop of Lisieux gave to Charles in marrying him to Normandy as its duke, broken on an anvil in the presence of the notables.

The chronicle of Jean de Roye records a striking instance of this craving for symbols and forms. One Laurent Guernier had been hanged by mistake at Paris in 1478; he had obtained a reprieve, but his pardon arrived too late. A year later his brother obtained permission to have the body honourably buried. "And before this bier went four town criers of the aforesaid town sounding their rattles, and on their breasts were the arms of the aforesaid Guernier, and around that bier were four tapers and eight torches, carried by men dressed in mourning and bearing the aforesaid crest. And in this way it was carried, passing through the aforesaid city of Paris . . . as far as the gate of Saint Anthony, where the aforesaid corpse was placed on a cart draped in black to take it to Provins to be buried. And one of the aforesaid criers who walked before the aforesaid corpse, cried: 'Good people, say your pater nosters for the soul of the late Laurent Guernier, in his life an inhabitant of Provins, who was lately found *dead under an oak-tree!*"

The mentality of the declining Middle Ages often seems to us to display an incredible superficiality and feebleness. The complexity of things is ignored by it in a truly astounding manner. It proceeds to generalizations unhesitatingly on the strength of a single instance. Its liability to wrong judgment is extreme. Inexactitude, credulity, levity, inconsistency, are common features of medieval reasoning.

All these defects are rooted in its fundamental formalism. To explain a situation or an event, a single motive suffices, and, for choice, the most general motive, the most direct or the grossest. To Burgundian party-feeling, for example, there could be but a single ground which could have urged the duke of Burgundy to compass the murder of the duke of Orléans: he wished to avenge the (assumed) adultery of the queen with Orléans. In every controversy people would disregard all the features of the case save a few, whose significance they exaggerated at pleasure. Thus the presentment of a fact, in the minds of the epoch, is always like a primitive woodcut, with strong and simple lines and very clearly marked contours.

So much for "simplistic" habits of mind. As to ill-considered generalization, it manifests itself on every page of the literature of that time. From a single case of impartiality reported of the English of olden time, Olivier de la Marche concluded that at that period the English were virtuous, and because of that had been able to conquer France. The importance of a particular case is exaggerated, because it is seen in an ideal light. Moreover, every case can be paralleled in sacred history, and so be exalted to higher significance. In 1404 a procession of students at Paris was assaulted: two were wounded, the clothes of a third were torn. This was enough for the chancellor of the University, carried away by the heat of his indignation, and by a simple consonance, "Les enfants, les jolis escoliers comme agneaux innocens,"[7] to launch into comparison of the incident to the massacre of Bethlehem.

If for every particular case an explanation is so easily admitted, and, once admitted, takes root in the mind without meeting with resistance, then the danger of wrong judgments is extremely great. Nietzsche said that abstaining from wrong judgments would make life impossible, and it is probable that the intense life which we sometimes envy past centuries, was partly due to the facility of false judgments. In our own day too, in times which require the

[7] The children, the pretty scholars, like innocent lambs.

utmost exertion of national force, the nerves need the help of false judgment. The men of the Middle Ages lived in a continual mental crisis. They could not for a moment dispense with false judgments of the grossest kind. If, in the fifteenth century, the cause of the dukes of Burgundy could persuade so many Frenchmen first to breach of fealty and next to hostility to their country, this political sentiment can only be explained by a whole tissue of emotional conceptions and confused ideas.

It is in this light that the general and constant habit of ridiculously exaggerating the number of enemies killed in battle should be considered. Chastellain gives a loss of five nobles on the side of the duke at the battle of Gavre, as against twenty or thirty thousand of the Ghent rebels.

What are we to say, lastly, of the curious levity of the authors of the close of the Middle Ages, which often impresses us as an absolute lack of mental power? It sometimes seems as if they were content to present to their readers a series of vague pictures, and felt no need whatever of really hard thinking. Superficial description of outward circumstances—this is all we get from writers like Froissart and Monstrelet. Compared with Herodotus, to say nothing of Thucydides, their narrative is disjointed, empty, without pith or meaning. They do not distinguish the essential from the accidental. Their lack of precision is deplorable. Monstrelet was present at the interview of the duke of Burgundy with Joan or Arc, when a prisoner: he does not remember what was said. Thomas Basin himself, who conducted the process of rehabilitation, says in his chronicle that Joan was born at Vaucouleurs instead of Domremy, and that she was conducted to Tours by Baudricourt himself, whom he calls lord of the town instead of captain, while he is mistaken by three months as to the date of her first interview with the dauphin. Olivier de la Marche, master of the ceremonies and an impeccable courtier, constantly muddles the genealogy of the ducal family and goes so far as to make the marriage of Charles with Margaret of York take place after the siege of Neuss in 1475, though he was present at the wedding festivities in 1468. Even Commines is not exempt from surprising inexactitudes.

The credulity and the lack of critical spirit are too general and too well known to make it necessary to cite examples. It goes without saying that here the degree of erudition makes a great difference. Basin and Molinet treated the popular belief that Charles the Bold would come back as a fable. Ten years after the battle of Nancy, people were still lending money which was to be reimbursed on his return.

> "J'ay veu chose incongneue:
> Ung mort ressusciter,
> Et sur sa revenue
> Par milliers achapter.
> L'un dit: il est en vie,
> L'autre: ce n'est que vent.
> Tous bons cueurs sans envie
> Le regrettent souvent." [8]

A mentality, dominated like that of the declining Middle Ages by a lively imagination, by naïve idealism and by strong feeling, easily believes in the reality of every concept which presents itself to the mind. When once an idea has received a name and a form, its truth is presumed; it glides, so to say, into the system of spiritual figures and shares in their credibility.

On the one hand, their clear outlines and frequently anthropomorphic character give ideas a marked degree of fixity and immobility; on the other hand, the *meaning* of a conception runs a constant risk of being lost in the too vivid *form*. The principal person of the long allegorical and satirical poem of Eustache Deschamps, *Le Miroir de Mariage,* is called Franc Vouloir. Folly and Desire advise him to marry, Repertory of Science dissuades him. Now,

[8] I have seen an unknown thing: A dead man coming to life, And on his return Buy for thousands. The one says: he is alive. The other: it is but wind. All good hearts, void of envy, Regret his loss often.

if we ask ourselves what Deschamps wanted to express by the abstraction Franc Vouloir, it appears that the idea oscillates between the careless liberty of the bachelor and free will in a philosophic sense. The personification has more or less absorbed the idea which gave it birth. As undecided as the character of the central figure is the moral tone of the poem. The pious praise of the spiritual marriage and of the contemplative life contrasts strangely with the customary and rather vulgar mockery of women and of female virtue. The author sometimes puts exalted truths into the mouth of Folly and Desire, though their part is that of the devil's advocate. It is very hard to decide what was the personal conviction of the poet, and to what degree he was serious.

To distinguish clearly the serious element from pose and playfulness, is a problem that crops up in connection with nearly all the manifestations of the mentality of the Middle Ages. We saw it arise in connection with chivalry, and with the forms of love and of piety. We always have to remember that in more primitive cultural phases than ours, the line of demarcation between sincere conviction and "pretending" often seems to be wanting. What would be hypocrisy in a modern mind, is not always so in a medieval one.

The general want of balance, characterizing the soul of this epoch, in spite of the clear-cut form of its ideas, is especially felt in the domain of superstition. On the subject of sorcery, doubt and rationalistic interpretations alternate with the blindest credulity. We can never tell precisely to what degree this belief was sincere. Philippe de Mézières, in the *Songe du Vieil Pelerin*, tells that he himself learned the magic arts from a Spaniard. During more than ten years he did not succeed in forgetting his infamous knowledge. "A sa volenté ne povoit pas bien extirper de son cuer les dessusdits signes et l'effect d'iceulx contre Dieu." [9] At last, "though the grace of God, by dint

[9] He could not voluntarily extirpate from his mind the aforesaid signs and their effect against God.

of confessing and resisting, he was delivered from this great folly, which is an enemy to the Christian soul."

During the horrible campaign of persecution against sorcerers in 1461, known as the "Vauderie d'Arras," both the people and the magistrates gravely doubted the reality of the alleged crimes. Outside the town of Arras, says Jacques du Clercq, "not one person in a thousand believed that it was true that they practised the aforesaid sorcery. Such things were never before heard of happening in these countries." Nevertheless, the town suffered severely in consequence: people would no longer shelter its merchants or give them credit, for fear that, accused of witchcraft, on the morrow, perhaps, they might lose all their possessions by confiscation. One of the inquisitors, who claimed to be able to discover the guilty at sight, and went so far as to declare that it was impossible for a man to be wrongly accused of sorcery, afterwards went mad. A poem full of hatred accused the persecutors of having got up the whole affair out of covetousness, and the bishop himself called the persecution "a thing intended by some evil persons." Philip the Good, having asked the advice of the Faculty of Louvain, several of its members declared that the sorcery was not real. Upon which the duke, who, in spite of the archaic turn of his mind, was not superstitious, sent the king-at-arms of the Golden Fleece to Arras. Then the executions and the imprisonments ceased. Later on, all the processes were annulled, which fact the town celebrated by a joyful feast with representations of edifying "moralities."

The opinion that the rides through the air and the orgies of the witches' sabbath were but delusions which the devil suggested to the poor foolish women, was already rather widely spread in the fifteenth century. Froissart, describing the striking case of a Gascon nobleman and his familiar demon called Horton (he surpasses himself here in exactness and vividness of narrative), treats it as an "error." But it is an error caused by the devil, so the rationalizing interpretation, after all, goes only half-way. Gerson alone goes so far as to suggest the notion of a cerebral lesion, the others confine themselves to the hypothesis of diabolical illusions. Martin Lefranc, provost of the church of Lausanne, in the *Champion des Dames*, which he dedicated to Philip the Good in 1440, defended this opinion.

"Je ne croiray tant que je vive
Que femme corporellement
Voit par l'air comme merle ou grive,
—Dit le Champion prestement.—

. . . .

Quant la pourelle est en sa couche,
Pour y dormir et reposer,
L'ennemi qui point ne se couche
Se vient encoste allé poser.
Lors illusions composer
Lui scet sy tres soubtillement
Qu'elle croit faire ou proposer
Ce qu'elle songe seulement.
Force la vielle songera
Que sur un chat ou sur un chien
A l'assemblée s'en ira;
Mais certes il n'en sera rien:
Et sy n'est baston ne mesrien
Qui le peut ung pas enlever." [10]

In general the mental attitude towards supernatural facts was a vacillating one. Rational interpretation, timid credulity, or the suspicion of diabolical ruses, have the upper hand by turns. The Church did its best to combat

[10] As long as I live I shall not believe That a woman can bodily Travel through the air like blackbird or thrush, Said the Champion forthwith. . . . When the poor woman lies in her bed, In order to sleep and to rest there, The enemy who never lies down to sleep Comes and remains by her side. Then to call up illusions Before her he can so subtly, That she thinks she does or proposes to do What she only dreams. Perhaps the gammer will dream That on a cat or on a dog She will go to the meeting; But certainly nothing will happen; And there is neither a stick nor a beam Which could lift her a step.

superstitions. Friar Richard, the popular preacher at Paris, has the mandrakes brought to him to be burned, "which many foolish people kept in safe places, having such great faith in this ordure, that, indeed, they firmly believed, that so long as they had it (provided it were very neatly wrapped up in silk or linen folds) they would never be poor so long as they lived."

Dogmatic theology was always studious to inculcate the exact distinction between matters of faith and of superstition. Benedictions and conjurations, says Denis the Carthusian in his treatise *Contra vitia superstitionum*, have no effect in themselves. They operate only in so far as they are pronounced as humble prayers, with pious intention and placing one's hope in God. Since popular belief, nevertheless, attributes magical virtue to them, it would be better that the clergy forbade these practices altogether.

Unhappily, the zeal of the Church for the purity of the faith did not affect demonomania. Its own doctrine prevented it from uprooting belief in it. For it kept to the norm, fixed by the authority of Saint Augustine and Saint Thomas: *Omnia quae visibiliter fiunt in hoc mundo, possunt fieri per daemones.*[11] Conjurations, says Denis, continuing the argument we have just cited, often take effect in spite of the absence of a pious intention, because then the devil has taken a hand in it. This ambiguity left room for a good deal of uncertainty. The fear of sorcery and the blind fury of persecution continued to darken the mental atmosphere of the age. The official confirmation of both the theory and the practice of persecution was effected in the last quarter of the fifteenth century by the *Malleus maleficarum*, the Hammer for Witches, by two German Dominicans, which appeared in 1487, and by the bull, *Summis desiderantes*, of Pope Innocent VIII, of 1484.

So towards the end of the Middle Ages this dark system of delusion and cruelty grew slowly to completion. All the deficiencies of medieval thinking and its inherent tend-

[11] All that happens visibly in this world, can be done by demons.

ancies to gross error had contributed to its building. The fifteenth century transmitted it to the coming age like a horrible disease, which for a long time neither classical culture nor Protestant reformation nor the Catholic revival were able or even willing to cure.

Chapter XIX

ART AND LIFE

If a man of culture of 1840 had been asked to characterize French civilization in the fifteenth century in a few words, his answer would probably have been largely inspired by impressions from Barante's *Histoire des Ducs de Bourgogne* and Hugo's *Notre Dame de Paris*. The picture called up by these would have been grim and dark, scarcely illuminated by any ray of serenity and beauty.

The experiment repeated to-day would yield a very different result. People would now refer to Joan of Arc, to Villon's poetry, but above all to the works of art. The so-called primitive Flemish and French masters—Van Eyck, Rogier van der Weyden, Foucquet, Memling, with Claus Sluter, the sculptor, and the great musicians—would dominate their general idea of the epoch. The picture would altogether have changed its colour and tone. The aspect of mere cruelty and misery as conceived by romanticism, which derived its information chiefly from the chronicles, would have made room for a vision of pure and naïve beauty, of religious fervour and profound mystic peace.

It is a general phenomenon that the idea which works of art give us of an epoch is far more serene and happy than that which we glean in reading its chronicles, documents, or even literature. Plastic art does not lament. Even when giving expression to sorrow or pain it transports them to an elegiac sphere, where the bitter taste of suffering has passed away, whereas the poets and historians, voicing the endless griefs of life, always keep their immediate pungency and revive the harsh realities of bygone misery.

Now, our perception of former times, our historical organ, so to say, is more and more becoming visual. Most educated people of to-day owe their conception of Egypt, Greece, or the Middle Ages, much more to the sight of their monuments, either in the original or by reproductions, than to reading. The change of our ideas about the Middle Ages is due less to a weakening of the romantic sense than to the substitution of artistic for intellectual appreciation.

Still, this vision of an epoch resulting from the contemplation of works of art is always incomplete, always too favourable, and therefore fallacious. It has to be corrected in more than one sense. Confining ourselves to the period in question, we first have to take into consideration the fact that, proportionately, far more of the written documents than of the monuments of art have been preserved. The literature of the declining Middle Ages, with some few exceptions, is known to us fairly completely. We have products of all genres: the most elevated and the most vulgar, the serious and the comic, the pious and the profane. Our literary tradition reflects the whole life of the epoch. Written tradition, moreover, is not confined to literature: official records, in infinite number, enable us to augment almost indefinitely the accuracy of our picture.

Art, on the contrary, is by its very nature limited to a less complete and less direct expression of life. Moreover, we only possess a very special fraction of it. Outside ecclesiastical art very little remains. Profane art and applied art have only been preserved in rare specimens. This is a serious want, because these are just the forms of art which would have most clearly revealed to us the relation of artistic production to social life. The modest number of altar-pieces and tombs teaches us too little in this respect; the art of the epoch remains to us as a thing apart from the history of the time. Now, really to understand art, it is of great importance to form a notion of the function of art in life; and for that it does not suffice to admire surviving masterpieces, all that has been lost asks our attention too.

Art in those times was still wrapped up in life. Its function was to fill with beauty the forms assumed by life. These forms were marked and potent. Life was encompassed and measured by the rich efflorescence of the liturgy: the sacraments, the canonical hours of the day and the festivals of the ecclesiastical year. All the works and all the joys of life, whether dependent on religion, chivalry, trade or love, had their marked form. The task of art was to adorn all these concepts with charm and colour; it is not desired for its own sake, but to decorate life with the splendour which it could bestow. Art was not yet a means, as it is now, to step out of the routine of everyday life to pass some moments in contemplation; it had to be enjoyed as an element of life itself, as the expression of life's significance. Whether it served to sustain the flight of piety or to be an accompaniment to the delights of the world, it was not yet conceived as mere beauty.

Consequently, we might venture the paradox that the Middle Ages knew only applied art. They wanted works of art only to make them subservient to some practical use. Their purpose and their meaning always preponderated over their purely æsthetic value. We should add that the love of art for its own sake did not originate in an awakening of the craving for beauty, but developed as a result of superabundant artistic production. In the treasuries of princes and nobles, objects of art accumulated so as to form collections. No longer serving for practical use, they were admired as articles of luxury and of curiosity; thus the taste for art was born which the Renaissance was to develop consciously.

In the great works of art of the fifteenth century, notably in the altar-pieces and tombs, the nature of the subject was far more important than the question of beauty. Beauty was required because the subject was sacred or because the work was destined for some august purpose. This purpose is always of a more or less practical sort. The triptych served to intensify worship at the great festivals and to preserve the memory of the pious donors. The altarpiece of the Lamb by the brothers Van Eyck was opened at high festivals only. Religious pictures were not the only ones which served a practical purpose. The magistrates of the towns ordered representations of famous judgments to decorate the law courts, in order to solemnly exhort the judges to do their duty. Such are the judgment of Cambyses, by Gerard David, at Bruges; that of the Emperor Otto, by Dirk Bouts, at Louvain; and the lost pictures by Rogier van der Weyden, once at Brussels.

The following example may serve to illustrate the importance attached to the subjects represented. In 1384 an interview took place at Lelinghem for the purpose of bringing about an armistice between France and England. The duke of Berry had the naked walls of the old chapel, where the negotiating princes were to meet, covered with tapestry representing battles of antiquity. But John of Gaunt, duke of Lancaster, as soon as he saw them on entering, demanded that these pictures of war should be removed, because those who aspire to peace ought not to have scenes of combat and of destruction before their eyes. The tapestries were replaced by others representing the instruments of the Passion.

The importance of the subject is closely connected with the artistic value in the case of portraits, which even now preserve some moral significance, as souvenirs or heirlooms, because the sentiments determining their use are as vital as ever. In the Middle Ages portraits were ordered for all sorts of purposes, but rarely, we may be certain, to obtain a masterpiece of art. Besides gratifying family affection and pride, the portrait served to enable betrothed persons to make acquaintance. The embassy sent to Portugal by Philip the Good in 1428, to ask for the hand of a princess, was accompanied by Jan van Eyck, with orders to paint her portrait. Court chroniclers liked to keep up the fiction that the royal fiancé had fallen in love with the unknown princess on seeing her portrait—for instance, Richard II of England when courting the little Isabelle of France, aged six. Sometimes it is even said that a selection was made by comparing portraits of different parties. When a wife had to be found for the young Charles VI, according to the *Religieux de Saint Denis,* the choice lay between a Bavarian, an Austrian and a Lorraine duchess. A painter of talent was sent to the three courts; three portraits were submitted to the king, who chose the young Isabella of Bavaria, judging her by far the most beautiful.

Nowhere was the practical use of works of art weightier than in connection with tombs, by far the most important domain of the sculpture of the epoch. The wish to have an effigy of the deceased was so strong that it claimed satisfaction even before the construction of the tomb. At the burial of a man of rank, he is represented either by a living man or by an effigy. At the funeral service of Bertrand du Guesclin, at Saint Denis, "four men-at-arms, armed cap-à-pie, mounted on four chargers, well appointed and caparisoned, representing the dead man as he was alive," entered the church. An account of the Polignacs of 1375 relating to a funeral ceremony shows the item: "Six shillings to Blaise for representing the dead knight at the funeral." At royal interments a figure of leather, in state dress, represented the deceased. Great pains were taken to obtain a good likeness. Sometimes there is more than one of these effigies in the cortège. Visitors to Westminster Abbey know these figures. Perhaps the origin of making funeral masks, which began in France in the fifteenth century, is to be found here.

As all art was more or less applied art, the distinction between artists and craftsmen did not arise. The great masters in the service of the courts of Flanders, of Berry, or of Burgundy, each of them an artist of a very marked personality, did not confine themselves to painting pictures and to illuminating manuscripts; they were not above colouring statues, painting shields and staining banners, or designing costumes for tournaments and ceremonies. Thus Melchior Broederlam, court painter to the first duke of Burgundy, after holding the same position in the household of his father-in-law, the count of Flanders, puts the finishing touches to five sculptured chairs for the palace of the

counts. He repairs and paints some mechanical apparatus
at the castle of Hesdin, used for wetting the guests with
water by way of a surprise. He does work on a carriage for
the duchess. He directs the sumptuous decoration of the
fleet which the duke had assembled at Sluys in 1387 for an
expedition against the English, which, however, did not
take place. So, too, at wedding festivities and funeral ceremonies court painters were laid under contribution. Statues
were painted in Jan van Eyck's workshop. He himself made
a sort of map of the world for Duke Philip, on which the
towns and the countries were painted with marvellous
delicacy. Hugo van der Goes designed posters advertising a papal indulgence at Ghent. When the Archduke
Maximilian was a prisoner at Bruges in 1488, the painter
Gerard David was sent for, to decorate with pictures the
wickets and shutters of his prison.

Of all the handiwork of the masters of the fifteenth century, only a portion of a very special nature has survived:
some tombs, some altar-pieces and portraits, numerous
miniatures, also a certain number of objects of industrial
art, comprising vessels used in religious worship, sacerdotal
dress and church furniture, but of secular work, except
woodwork and chimneys, scarcely anything is left. How
much more should we know of the art of the fifteenth
century if we could compare the bathing and hunting
pieces of Jan van Eyck and Rogier van der Weyden with
their *pietàs* and madonnas. It is not only profane pictures
we lack. There are whole departments of applied art of
which we can hardly even form a conception. For this we
lack the power to compare with the priestly vestments that
have been preserved, the court costumes with their precious stones and tiny bells, that have perished: we lack the
actual sight of the brilliantly decorated war-ships of which
miniatures give us but a conventional and clumsy representation. Froissart, who, as a rule, is little susceptible to
impressions of beauty, fairly exults in his descriptions of the
splendours of a decked-out fleet, with its streamers, gay
with blazonry, floating from the mast-heads, and some
reaching to the water. The ship of Philippe le Hardi, dec-

orated by Broederlam, was painted azure and gold; large
heraldic shields surrounded the pavilion of the castle; the
sails were studded with daisies and the initials of the duke
and the duchess, and bore the motto *Il me tarde*. The
nobles vied with each other in lavishing money on the
decoration of their vessels. Painters had a good time of it,
says Froissart; there were not enough of them to go round,
and they got whatever prices they asked. According to
him, many nobles had their ship-masts entirely covered
with gold leaf. Guy de la Trémoïlle spent £2,000 on decorations. "And all this was paid by the poor people of
France. . . ."

These lost products of decorative art would have revealed to us, above all, extravagant sumptuousness. This
trait is characteristic of the epoch; it is to be found equally
in the works which we do possess, but as we study these
only for the sake of their beauty, we pay little attention to
this element of splendour and of pomp, which no longer
interests us, but which was just what people of that time
prized most.

Burgundo-French culture of the expiring Middle Ages
tends to oust beauty by magnificence. The art of this period
exactly reflects this spirit. All that we cited above as characteristic of the mental processes of the epoch: the craving
to give a definite form to every idea, and the overcrowding
of the mind with figures and forms systematically arranged—all this reappears in art. There, too, we find the
tendency to leave nothing without form, without figure,
without ornament. The flamboyant style of architecture is
like the postlude of an organist who cannot conclude. It
decomposes all the formal elements endlessly; it interlaces
all the details; there is not a line which has not its
counter-line. The form develops at the expense of the idea,
the ornament grows rank, hiding all the lines and all the
surfaces. A *horror vacui* reigns, always a symptom of artistic
decline.

All this means that the border-line between pomp and
beauty is being obliterated. Decoration and ornament no
longer serve to heighten the natural beauty of a thing;

they are overgrowing it and threaten to stifle it. The further
we get away from pure plastic art, the more this rankness
of formal decorative motifs is accentuated. This may be
very clearly observed in sculpture. In the creation of
isolated figures this overgrowth of forms does not occur:
the statues of Moses' well and the "plourants" of the tombs
are as sober as the figures of Donatello. But where sculpture is performing a decorative function we at once find
the overgrowth. In looking at the tabernacle of Dijon,
every one will be struck by a lack of harmony between
the sculpture of Jacques de Baerze and the painting of
Broederlam. The picture, painted for its own sake, is simple
and sober; the reliefs, on the contrary, in which the purpose is decorative, are complicated and overloaded. We
notice the same contrast between painting and tapestry.
Textile art, even when representing scenes and figures,
remains limited by its technique to decorative conception
and expression; hence we find the same craving for excessive ornamentation.

In the art of costume, the essential qualities of pure art,
that is to say, measure and harmony, vanish altogether,
because splendour and adornment are the sole objects
aimed at. Pride and vanity introduce a sensual element
incompatible with pure art. No epoch ever witnessed such
extravagance of fashion as that extending from 1350 to
1480. Here we can observe the unhampered expansion of
the æsthetic sense of the time. All the forms and dimensions of dress are ridiculously exaggerated. The female
head-dress assumes the conical shape of the "hennin," a
form evolved from the little coif, keeping the hair under the
kerchief. High and bombed foreheads are in fashion, with
the temples shaved. Low-necked dresses make their appearance. The male dress had features still more bizarre—
the immoderate length of the points of the shoes, called
"poulaines," which the knights at Nicopolis had to cut off,
to enable them to flee; the laced waists; the baloon-
shaped sleeves standing up at the shoulders; the too long
"houppelandes" and the too short doublets; the cylindrical
or pointed bonnets; the hoods draped about the head in

the form of a cock's comb or a flaming fire. A state costume was ornamented by hundreds of precious stones.

The taste for unbridled luxury culminated in the court fêtes. Every one has read the descriptions of the Burgundian festivities at Lille in 1454, at which the guests took the oath to undertake the crusade, and at Bruges in 1468, on the occasion of the marriage of Charles the Bold with Margaret of York. It is hard to imagine a more absolute contrast than that of these barbarous manifestations of arrogant pomp and the pictures of the brothers Van Eyck, Dirk Bouts and Rogier van der Weyden, with their sweet and tranquil serenity. Nothing could be more insipid and ugly then the "entremets," consisting of gigantic pies enclosing complete orchestras, full-rigged vessels, castles, monkeys and whales, giants and dwarfs, and all the boring absurdities of allegory. We find it difficult to regard these entertainments as something more than exhibitions of almost incredible bad taste.

Yet we must not exaggerate the distance separating the two extreme forms of the art of the fifteenth century. In the first place, it is important to realize the function of festivals in the society of that time. They still preserved something of the meaning they have in primitive societies, that of the supreme expression of their culture, the highest mode of a collective enjoyment and an assertion of solidarity. At epochs of great renovations of society, like that of the French Revolution, we see that festivals resume this social and æsthetic function.

Modern man is free, when he pleases, to seek his favourite distractions individually, in books, music, art or nature. On the other hand, at a time when the higher pleasures were neither numerous nor accessible to all, people felt the need of such collective rejoicings as festivals. The more crushing the misery of daily life, the stronger the stimulants that will be needed to produce that intoxication with beauty and delight without which life would be unbearable. The fifteenth century, profoundly pessimistic, a prey to continual depression, could not forgo the emphatic affirmation of the beauty of life, afforded by these splendid and solemn collective rejoicings. Books were expensive, the country was unsafe, art was rare; the individual lacked the means of distraction. All literary, musical and artistic enjoyment was more or less closely connected with festivals.

Now festivals, in so far as they are an element of culture, require other things than mere gaiety. Neither the elementary pleasures of gaming, drinking and love, nor luxury and pomp as such, are able to give them a framework. The festival requires style. If those of modern times have lost their cultural value, it is because they have lost style. In the Middle Ages the religious festival, because of its high qualities of style founded on the liturgy itself, for a long time dominated all the forms of collective cheerfulness. The popular festival, which had its own elements of beauty in song and dance, was linked up with those of the Church. It is towards the fifteenth century that an independent form of civil festival with a style of its own disengages itself from the ecclesiastical one. The "rhetoricians" of Northern France and the Netherlands are the representatives of this evolution. Till then only princely courts had been able to equip secular festivals with form and style, thanks to the resources of their wealth and the social conception of courtesy.

Nevertheless, the style of the courtly festival could not but remain greatly inferior to that of religious festivals. In the latter worship and rejoicing in common were always the expression of a sublime thought, which lent them a grace and dignity that even the excesses of their frequently burlesque details could not affect. On the other hand, the ideas glorified by the secular feast were nothing more than those of chivalry and of courtly love. The ritual of chivalry, no doubt, was rich enough to give these festivities a venerable and solemn style. There were the accolade, the vows, the chapters of the orders, the rules of the tournaments, the formalities of homage, service and precedence, all the dignified proceedings of kings-at-arms and heralds, all the brightness of blazonry and armour. But this did not suffice to satisfy all aspirations. The court fêtes were expected to visualize in its entirety the dream

of the heroic life. And here style failed. For in the fifteenth
century the apparatus of chivalrous fancy was no longer
anything but vain convention and mere literature.

The staging of the amazing festivities of Lille or of
Bruges is, so to say, applied literature. The ponderous-
ness of material representation destroyed the last remainder of charm which literature with the lightness of its
airy reveries had hitherto preserved. The unfaltering
seriousness with which these monstrous pageants were
organized is truly Burgundian. The ducal court seems to
have lost, by its contact with the North, some qualities of
the French spirit. For the preparation of the banquet of
Lille, which was to crown and conclude a series of banquets which the nobles provided, each in his turn, vying
with each other in magnificence, Philip the Good appointed a committee, presided over by a knight of the
Golden Fleece, Jean de Lannoy. The most trusted counsellors of the duke—Antoine de Croy, the chancellor Nicolas
Rolin himself—were frequently present at the sessions of
the committee, of which Olivier de la Marche was a
member. When the latter in his memoirs comes to this
chapter, a feeling of awe still comes over him. "Because
great and honourable achievements deserve a lasting renown and perpetual remembrance . . . ," thus he begins
the narrative of these memorable things. It is needless to
reprint it here, as it belongs to the *loci communes* of
historical literature.

Even from across the sea people came to view the gor-
geous spectacle. Besides the guests, a great number of
noble spectators were present at the feast, disguised for
the most part. First every one walked about to admire the
fixed show-pieces; later came the "entremets," that is to
say, representations of "personnages" and tableaux vivants.
Olivier himself played the important part of Holy Church,
making his appearance in a tower on the back of an ele-
phant, led by a gigantic Turk. The tables were loaded
with the most extravagant decorations. There were a
rigged and ornamented carack, a meadow surrounded by
trees with a fountain, rocks, and a statue of Saint Andrew,

the castle of Lusignan with the fairy Mélusine, a bird-shooting scene near a windmill, a wood in which wild beasts walked about, and, lastly, a church with an organ and singers, whose songs alternated with the music of the orchestra of twenty-eight persons, which was placed in a pie.

The problem for us is to determine the quality of taste or bad taste to which all this bears witness. It goes without saying that the mythological and allegorical tenor of these "entremets" cannot interest us. But what was the artistic execution worth? What people looked for most was extravagance and huge dimensions. The tower of Gorcum represented on the table of the banquet of Bruges in 1468 was 46 feet high. La Marche says of a whale, which also figured there: "And certainly this was a very fine entremets, *for* there were more than forty persons in it." People were also much attracted by mechanical marvels: living birds flying from the mouth of a dragon conquered by Hercules, and such-like curiosities, in which, to us, any idea of art is altogether lacking. The comic element was of a very low class: boars blow the trumpet in the tower of Gorcum; elsewhere goats sing a motet, wolves play the flute, four large donkeys appear as singers—and all this in honour of Charles the Bold, who was a good musician.

I would not, however, suggest that there may not have been many an artistic masterpiece among these pretentious and ridiculous curiosities. Let us not forget that the men who enjoyed these Gargantuan decorations were the patrons of the brothers Van Eyck and of Rogier van der Weyden—the duke himself, Rolin, the donor of the altars of Beaune and of Autun, Jean Chevrot, who commissioned Rogier to paint "The Seven Sacraments," now at Antwerp. What is more, it was the painters themselves who designed these show-pieces. If the records do not mention Jan van Eyck or Rogier as having contributed to similar festivities, they do give the names of the two Marmions and Jacques Daret. For the fête of 1468 the services of the whole corporation of painters were requisitioned; they were summoned in haste from Ghent, Brussels, Louvain, Tirlemont, Mons, Quesnoy, Valenciennes, Douai, Cambray, Arras, Lille, Ypres, Courtray, Oudenarde, to work at Bruges. It is impossible to believe that their handiwork was ugly. The thirty vessels decorated with the arms of the duke's domains, the sixty images of women dressed in the costumes of their country, "carrying fruit in baskets and birds in cages. . . ." I should be ready to give more than one mediocre church-picture to see them.

We may go further, at the risk of being thought paradoxical, and affirm that we have to take this art of showpieces, which has disappeared without leaving a trace, into account, if we would thoroughly understand the art of Claus Sluter.

Of all the forms of art, sepulchral sculpture is most fettered by the exigencies of its purpose. The sculptors charged with making the ducal tombs were not left free to create beautiful things; they had to exalt the glory of the deceased prince. The painter can always give free rein to his imagination; he is never obliged to limit himself strictly to commissioned work. It is probable, on the other hand, that the sculptor of this epoch rarely worked except on specified tasks. The motifs of his art, moreover, are limited in number and fixed by a rigorous tradition. It is true that painters and sculptors are equally servants of the ducal household; Jan van Eyck, as well as Sluter and his nephew, Claus de Werve, bore the title of "varlet de chambre," but for the two latter, the service is far more real than for the painters. The two great Dutchmen whom the irresistible attraction of French art life drew for good from their native country were completely monopolized by the duke of Burgundy. Claus Sluter inhabited a house at Dijon which the duke placed at his disposal; there he lived as a gentleman, but at the same time as a servant of the court. His nephew and successor, Claus de Werve, is the tragic type of an artist in the service of princes: kept back at Dijon year after year, to finish the tomb of Jean sans Peur, for which the financial means were never forthcoming, he saw his artistic career, so brilliantly begun, ruined by fruitless waiting.

Thus the art of the sculptor at this epoch is a servile art. On the other hand, sculpture is generally little influenced by the taste of an epoch, because its means, its material and its subjects are limited and little subject to change. When a great sculptor appears, he creates everywhere and always that *optimum* of purity and simplicity which we call classic. The human form and its drapery are susceptible of few variations. The masterpieces of carving of the different ages are very much alike, and, for us, Sluter's work shares this eternal identity of sculpture.

Nevertheless, on examining it more closely, we notice that especially the art of Sluter bears the marks of being influenced by the taste of the time (not to call it Burgundian taste) as far as the nature of sculpture permits. Sluter's works have not been preserved as they were, and as the master intended them to be. We must picture the well of Moses as it was in 1418, when the papal legate granted an indulgence to whosoever should come to visit it in a pious spirit. It must be remembered that the well is but a fragment, a part of a calvary with which the first duke of Burgundy of the house of Valois intended to crown the well of his Carthusian monastery of Champmol. The principal part, that is to say, the crucified Christ with the Virgin, Saint John and Mary Magdalen, had almost completely disappeared before the French Revolution. There remains only the pedestal, surrounded by the statues of the six prophets who predicted the death of the Saviour, with a cornice supported by angels. The whole composition is in the highest degree a representation, "une œuvre parlante," a show, closely related as such to the tableaux vivants or the "personnages" of the princely entries and of the banquets. There, too, the subjects were borrowed, for choice, from the prophecies relating to the coming of Christ. Like these "personnages," the figures surrounding the well hold scrolls containing the text of their predictions. It rarely happens in sculpture that the written word is of such importance. We can only fully realize the marvellous art here displayed in *hearing* these sacred and solemn words. *Immolabit eum universa multitudo filiorum Israel ad vesperum;* this is Moses' sentence. *Foderunt manus meas et pedes meos, dinumeraverunt omnia ossa mea;* this is David's. Jeremiah says: *O vos omnes qui transitis per viam, attendite et videte si est dolor sicut dolor meus.*[1] Isaiah, Daniel, Zachariah, all announce the death of the Lord. It is like a threnody of six voices rising up to the cross. Now in this feature lies the essence of the work. The gestures of the hands by which the attention is directed to the texts are so emphatic, and there is an expression of such poignant grief on the faces, that the whole is in some danger of losing the *ataraxia* which marks great sculpture. It appeals too directly to the spectator. Compared with the figures of Michelangelo, those of Sluter are too expressive, too personal. If more had come down to us of the calvary supported by the prophets than the head and the torso of Christ, of a stark majesty, this expressive character would be still more evident.

The spectacular character of the calvary of Champmol also came into prominence in the luxurious decorations of the work. We must picture it in all its polychrome splendour, for Jean Malouel, the artist, and Herman of Cologne, the gilder, were not sparing of vivid colours and brilliant effects. The pedestals were green, the mantles of the prophets were gilt, their tunics red and azure with golden stars. Isaiah, the gloomiest of all, wore a dress of gold-cloth. The open spaces were filled with golden suns and initials. The pride of blazonry displayed itself not only round the columns below the figures, but on the cross itself, which was entirely gilt. The extremities of the arms of the cross, shaped like capitals, bore the coats of arms of Burgundy and Flanders. Can one ask for better proof of the spirit in which the duke conceived this great monument of his piety? As a crowning "bizarrerie," a pair of spectacles

---

[1] Exodus xii. 6: "And the whole assembly of the congregation of Israel shall kill it in the evening." Psalm xxii. 16, 17: "They pierced My hands and My feet. They told all My bones." Lamentations of Jeremiah i. 12: "All ye that pass by, behold, and see if there be any sorrow like unto My sorrow."

of gilded brass, the work of Hannequin de Hacht, were placed on Jeremiah's nose.

This serfdom of a great art controlled by the will of a princely patron is tragic, but it is at the same time exalted by the heroic efforts of the great sculptor to shake off his shackles. The figures of the "plourants" around the sarcophagus had for a long time been an obligatory motif in Burgundian sepulchral art. These weeping figures were not meant to express grief in general; the sculptor was bound to give a faithful representation of the funeral cortège with the dignitaries present at the burial. But the genius of Sluter and his pupils succeeded in transforming this motif into the most profound expression of mourning known in art, a funeral march in stone.

Is it so certain, after all, that we are right in thinking of the artist as struggling with the lack of taste and refinement of his patron? It is quite possible that Sluter himself considered Jeremiah's spectacles a very happy find. In the men of that epoch artistic taste was still blended with the passion for what is rare or brilliant. In their simplicity they could enjoy the bizarre as if it were beauty. Objects of pure art and articles of luxury and curiosity were equally admired. Long after the Middle Ages the collections of princes contained works of art mixed up indiscriminately with knick-knacks made of shells and of hair, wax statues of celebrated dwarfs and such-like articles. At the castle of Hesdin, where side by side with art treasures the "engins d'esbatement" (contrivances for amusement) usual in princely pleasure-grounds were found in abundance, Caxton saw a room ornamented with pictures representing the history of Jason, the hero of the Golden Fleece. The artist is unknown, but was probably a distinguished master. To heighten the effect, a "machinerie" was annexed which could imitate lightning, thunder, snow and rain, in memory of the magic arts of Medea.

In the shows at the entries of princes inventive fancy stuck at nothing. When Isabella of Bavaria made her entry into Paris in 1389, there was a white deer with gilt antlers, and a wreath round its neck, stretched out on a "lit de justice," moving its eyes, antlers, feet, and at last raising a sword. At the moment when the queen crossed the bridge to the left of Notre Dame, an angel descended "by means of well-constructed engines" from one of the towers, passed through an opening of the hangings of blue taffeta with golden fleurs-de-lis which covered the bridge, and put a crown on her head. Then the angel "was pulled up again as if he had returned to heaven of his own accord." Philip the Good and Charles VIII were treated to similar descents. Lefèvre de Saint Remy greatly admired the spectacle of four trumpeters and twelve nobles on artificial horses, "sallying forth and caracoling in such a way that it was a fine thing to see."

Time the destroyer has made it easy for us to separate pure art from all these gewgaws and bizarre trappings, which have completely disappeared. This separation which our æsthetic sense insists upon, did not exist for the men of that time. Their artistic life was still enclosed within the forms of social life. Art was subservient to life. Its social function was to enhance the importance of a chapel, a donor, a patron, or a festival, but never that of the artist. Fully to realize its position and scope in this respect is now hardly possible. Too little of the material surroundings in which art was placed, and too few of the works of art themselves, have come down to us. Hence the priceless value of the few works by which private life, outside courts and outside the Church, is revealed to us. In this respect no painting can compare with the portrait of Jean Arnolfini and of his wife, by Jan van Eyck, in the National Gallery. The master, who, for once, need not portray the majesty of divine beings nor minister to aristocratic pride, here freely followed his own inspiration: it was his friends whom he was painting on the occasion of their marriage. Is it really the merchant of Lucca, Jean Arnoulphin, as he was called in Flanders, who is represented? Jan van Eyck painted this face twice (the other portrait is at Berlin); we can hardly imagine a less Italian-looking physiognomy, but the description of the picture in the inventory of Margaret of Austria, "Hernoul le fin with his wife in a chamber," leaves little room for doubt. However this may be, the persons represented were friends of Van Eyck; he himself witnesses to it by the ingenious and delicate way in which he signs his work, by an inscription over the mirror: *Johannes de Eyck fuit hic,* 1434.

"Jan van Eyck was here." Only a moment ago, one might think. The sound of his voice still seems to linger in the silence of this room. All that tenderness and profound peace, which only Rembrandt was to recapture, emanate from this picture. That serene twilight hour of an age, which we seemed to know and yet sought in vain in so many of the manifestations of its spirit, suddenly reveals itself here. And here at last this spirit proves itself happy, simple, noble and pure, in tune with the lofty church music and the touching folk-songs of the time.

So perhaps we imagine a Jan van Eyck escaping from the noisy gaiety and brutal passions of court life, a Jan van Eyck of the simple heart, a dreamer. It does not require a great effort of fancy to call up the "varlet de chambre" of the duke, serving the great lords against his will, suffering all the disgust of a great artist obliged to belie his sublime ideal of art by contributing to the mechanical devices of a festival.

Nothing, however, justifies us in forming such a conception of his personality. This art, which we admire, bloomed in the atmosphere of that aristocratic life, which repels us. The little we know of the lives of fifteenth-century painters shows them to us as men of the world and courtiers. The duke of Berry was on good terms with his artists. Froissart saw him in familiar conversation with André Beauneveu in his marvellous castle of Mehun sur Yevre. The three brothers of Limburg, the great illuminators, come to offer the duke, as a New Year's present, a surprise in the shape of a new illuminated manuscript, which turned out to be "a dummy book, made of a block of white wood painted to look like a book, in which there were no leaves and nothing was written." Jan van Eyck, without doubt, moved constantly in court circles. The secret diplomatic missions entrusted to him by the duke required a man of the world.

He passed, moreover, for a man of letters, reading classic authors and studying geometry. Did he not, by an innocent whim, disguise in Greek letters his modest device, *Als ik kan* (As I can)?

The intellectual and moral life of the fifteenth century seems to us to be divided into two clearly separated spheres. On the one hand, the civilization of the court, the nobility and the rich middle classes: ambitious, proud and grasping, passionate and luxurious. On the other hand, the tranquil sphere of the "devotio moderna," of the *Imitation of Christ,* of Ruysbroeck and of Saint Colette. One would like to place the peaceful and mystic art of the brothers Van Eyck in the second of these spheres, but it belongs rather to the other. Devout circles were hardly in touch with the great art that flourished at this time. In music they disapproved of counterpoint, and even of organs. The rule of Windesheim forbade the embellishment of the singing by modulations, and Thomas à Kempis said: "If you cannot sing like the nightingale and the lark, then sing like the crows and the frogs, which sing as God meant them to." The music of Dufay, Busnois, Okeghem, developed in the chapels of the courts. As to painting, the writers of the "devotio moderna" do not speak of it; it was outside their range of thought. They wanted their books in a simple form and without illuminations. They would probably have regarded the altar-piece of the Lamb as a mere work of pride, and actually did so regard the tower of Utrecht Cathedral.

The great artists generally worked for other circles than those of the devout townspeople. The art of the brothers Van Eyck and of their followers, though it sprang up in municipal surroundings and was fostered by town circles, cannot be called a bourgeois art. The court and the nobility exercised too powerful an attraction. Only the patronage of princes permitted the art of miniature to raise itself to the degree of artistic refinement which characterizes the work of the brothers of Limburg and the artists of the Hours of Turin. The employers of the great painters were, besides the princes themselves, the great lords, temporal or spiritual, and the great upstarts with whom the Burgundian epoch abounds, all gravitating towards the court. The ground for the difference between Franco-Flemish and Dutch art in this period lies in the fact that the latter still preserves some traits of simple soberness recalling the little out-of-the-way towns, such as Haarlem, where it was born. And even Dirk Bouts went south and painted at Louvain and Brussels.

Among the patrons of fifteenth-century art may be named Jean Chevrot, bishop of Tournay, whom a scutcheon designates as the donor of that work of touching and fervent piety, now at Antwerp, "The Seven Sacraments." Chevrot is the type of the court prelate; as a trusted counsellor of the duke, he was full of zeal for the affairs of the Golden Fleece and for the crusade. Another type of donor is represented by Pierre Bladelin, whose austere face is seen on the Middelburg altar-piece, now at Berlin. He was the great capitalist of those times; from the post of receiver of Bruges, his native town, he rose to be paymaster-general of the duke. He introduced control and economy into the ducal finances. He was appointed treasurer of the Golden Fleece and knighted. He was sent to England to ransom Charles of Orléans. The duke wished to charge him with the administration of the finances of the expedition against the Turks. He employed his wealth, which was the wonder of his contemporaries, on works of embankment and the founding of a new town in Flanders, to which he gave the name of Middelburg, after the town in Zeeland of that name.

Other notable donors—Judocus Vydt, the canon Van de Paele, the Croys, the Lannoys—belonged to the very rich, noble or burgher, ancient or new, of their time. Most famous of all is Nicolas Rolin, the chancellor, "sprung from little people," jurist, financier, diplomat. The great treaties of the dukes, from 1419 to 1435, are his work. "He used to govern everything quite alone and manage and bear the burden of all business by himself, be it of war, be it of peace, be it of matters of finance." By methods which were not above suspicion he amassed enormous wealth, which

he spent on all sorts of pious and charitable foundations.
Nevertheless, people spoke with hatred of his avarice and
pride, and had no faith in the devotional feelings which
inspired his pious works. This man whom we see in the
Louvre kneeling so devoutly in the picture painted for him
by Jan van Eyck for Autun, his native town, and again in
that by Rogier van der Weyden, destined for his hospital
of Beaune, passed for a mind only set on earthly things.
"He always harvested on earth," says Chastellain, "as
though the earth was to be his abode for ever, in which his
understanding erred and his prudence abased him, when
he would not set bounds to that, of which his great age
showed him the near end." This is corroborated by Jacques
du Clercq in these terms: "The aforesaid chancellor was
reputed one of the wise men of the kingdom, to speak
temporally; for as to spiritual matters, I shall be silent."

Are we, then, to look for a hypocritical expression in the
face of the donor of La Vierge au Chancelier Rolin? Let us
remember, before condemning him, the riddle presented
by the religious personality of so many other men of his
time, who also combined rigid piety with excesses of
pride, of avarice and of lust. The depths of these natures of
a past age are not easily sounded.

In the piety interpreted by the art of the fifteenth century, the extremes of mysticism and of gross materialism
meet. The faith pictured here is so direct that no earthly
figure is too sensual or too heavy to express it. Van Eyck
may drape his angels and divine personages with ponderous and stiff brocades, glittering with gold and precious
stones; to call up the celestial sphere he has no need of the
flowing garments and sprawling limbs of the baroque style.

Yet neither this art nor this faith is primitive. By using
the term primitive to designate the masters of the fifteenth
century we run the risk of a misunderstanding. They are
primitive in a purely chronological sense, in so far as, for us,
they are the first to come, and no older painting is known to
us. But if to this designation we attach the meaning of a
primitive spirit, we are egregiously mistaken. For the spirit
which this art denotes is the same which we pointed out in

religious life: a spirit rather decadent than primitive, a spirit involving the utmost elaboration, and even decomposition, of religious thought through the imagination.

In very early times the sacred figures had been seen as endlessly remote: awful and rigid. Then, from the twelfth century downward, the mysticism of Saint Bernard introduced a pathetic element into religion, which contained immense possibilities of growth. In the rapture of a new and overflowing piety people tried to share the sufferings of Christ by the aid of the imagination. They were no longer satisfied with the stark and motionless figures, infinitely distant, which romanesque art had given to Christ and His Mother. All the forms and colours which imagination drew from mundane reality were now lavished by it upon the celestial beings. Once let loose, pious fancy invaded the whole domain of faith and gave a minutely elaborate shape to every holy thing.

At first verbal expression had been in advance of pictorial and plastic art. Sculpture was still adhering to the formal rigidity of preceding ages, when literature undertook to describe all the details, both physical and mental, of the drama of the cross. A sort of pathetic naturalism arose, for which the *Meditationes vitae Christi*, early attributed to Saint Bonaventura, supplied the model. The nativity, the childhood, the descent from the cross, each received a fixed form, a vivid colouring. How Joseph of Arimathea mounted the ladder, how he had to press the hand of the Lord in order to draw out the nail, was all described in minute detail.

In the meantime, towards the end of the fourteenth century, pictorial technique had made so much progress that it more than overtook literature in the art of rendering these details. The naïve, and at the same time refined, naturalism of the brothers Van Eyck was a new form of pictorial expression; but viewed from the standpoint of culture in general, it was but another manifestation of the crystallizing tendency of thought which we noticed in all the aspects of the mentality of the declining Middle Ages. Instead of heralding the advent of the Renaissance, as is generally assumed, this naturalism is rather one of the ultimate forms of development of the medieval mind. The craving to turn every sacred idea into precise images, to give it a distinct and clearly outlined form, such as we observed in Gerson, in the *Roman de la Rose,* in Denis the Carthusian, controlled art, as it controlled popular beliefs and theology. The art of the brothers Van Eyck closes a period.

Chapter XX

THE ÆSTHETIC SENTIMENT

The study of the art of an epoch remains incomplete unless we try to ascertain also how this art was appreciated by contemporaries: what they admired in it, and by what standards they gauged beauty. Now, there are few subjects about which tradition is so defective as the æsthetic sentiment of past ages. The faculty and the need of expressing in words the sentiment of beauty have only been developed in recent times. What sort of admiration for the art of their time was felt by the men of the fifteenth century? Speaking generally, we may assert that two things impressed them especially: first, the dignity and sanctity of the subject; next, the astonishing mastery, the perfectly natural rendering of all the details. Thus we find, on the one hand, an appreciation which is rather religious than artistic; on the other hand, a naïve wonder, hardly entitled to rank as artistic emotion. The first to leave us critical observations on the painting of the brothers Van Eyck and Rogier van der Weyden was a Genoese man of letters, of the middle of the fifteenth century, Bartolomeo Fazio. Most of the pictures he speaks of are lost. He praises the beautiful and chaste figure of a Virgin, the hair of the archangel Gabriel, "surpassing real hair," the holy austerity expressed by the ascetic face of Saint John the Baptist, and a Saint Jerome who "seems to be alive." He admires the perspective of the cell of Jerome, a ray of light falling through a fissure, drops of sweat on the body of a woman in a bath, an image reflected by a mirror, a burning lamp, a landscape with mountains, woods, villages, castles, human figures, the distant horizon, and, once again, the mirror. The terms he uses to vent his enthusiasm betray merely a naïve curiosity, losing itself in the unlimited wealth of details, without arriving at a judgment on the beauty of the whole. Such is the appreciation of a medieval work by a mind which is still medieval.

A century later, after the triumph of the Renaissance, it is just this minuteness in the execution of details which is condemned as the fundamental fault of Flemish art. According to the Portuguese artist, Francesco de Holanda, Michelangelo spoke about it as follows:

"Flemish painting pleases all the devout better than Italian. The latter evokes no tears, the former makes them weep copiously. This is not a result of the merits of this art; the only cause is the extreme sensibility of the devout spectators. The Flemish pictures please women, especially the old and very young ones, and also monks and nuns, and lastly men of the world who are not capable of understanding true harmony. In Flanders they paint, before all things, to render exactly and deceptively the outward appearance of things. The painters choose, by preference, subjects provoking transports of piety, like the figures of saints or of prophets. But most of the time they paint what are called landscapes with plenty of figures. Though the eye is agreeably impressed, these pictures have neither art nor reason; neither symmetry nor proportion; neither choice of values nor grandeur. In short, this art is without power and without distinction; it aims at rendering minutely many things at the same time, of which a single one would have sufficed to call forth a man's whole application."

It was the medieval spirit itself which Michelangelo judged here. Those whom he called the devout are people of the medieval spirit. For him the ancient beauty has become a thing for the small and the feeble. Not all his contemporaries thought as he did. In the North many continued to venerate the art of their ancestors, among them Dürer and Quentin Metsys, and Jan Scorel, who is said to have kissed the altar-piece of the Lamb. But Michelangelo here truly represents the Renaissance as opposed to the Middle Ages. What he condemns in Flemish art are exactly the essential traits of the declining Middle Ages: the violent sentimentality, the tendency to see each thing as an independent entity, to get lost in the multiplicity of concepts. To this the spirit of the Renaissance is opposed, and, as always happens, only realizes its new conception of art and of life by temporally misjudging the beauties and the truths of the preceding age.

The consciousness of æsthetic pleasure and its expression are of tardy growth. A fifteenth-century scholar like Fazio, trying to vent his artistic admiration, does not get beyond the language of commonplace wonder. The very notion of artistic beauty is still wanting. The æsthetic sensation caused by the contemplation of art is lost always and at once either in pious emotion or a vague sense of well-being.

Denis the Carthusian wrote a treatise, *De venustate mundi et pulchritudine Dei*. The difference of the two words of the title at once indicates his point of view: true beauty only appertains to God, the world can only be *venustus*—pretty. All the beauties of creation, he says, are but brooks flowing from the source of supreme beauty. A creature may be called beautiful in so far as it shares in the beauty of the divine nature, and thereby attains some measure of harmony with it. As a starting-point of æsthetics, this is large and sublime, and might well serve as a basis for the analysis of all particular manifestations of beauty. Denis did not invent his fundamental idea: he founds himself on Saint Augustine and the pseudo-Areopagite, on Hugues de Saint Victor and Alexandre de Halès. But as soon as he tries really to analyse beauty, the deficiency of observation and expression is apparent. He borrows even his examples of earthly beauty from his predecessors, especially from Hugues and Richard de

Saint Victor: a leaf, the troubled sea with its changing hues, etc. His analysis is very superficial. Herbs are beautiful, because they are green; precious stones, because they sparkle; the human body, the dromedary and the camel, because they are appropriate to their purpose; the earth, because it is long and large; the heavenly bodies, because they are round and light. Mountains are admirable for their enormous dimensions, rivers for the length of their course, fields and woods for their vast surface, the earth for its immeasurable mass.

Medieval theory reduced the idea of beauty to that of perfection, proportion and splendour. Three things, says Saint Thomas, are required for beauty: first, integrity or perfection, because what is incomplete is ugly on that account; next, true proportion or consonance; lastly, brightness, because we call beautiful whatever has a brilliant colour. Denis the Carthusian tries to apply these standards, but he hardly succeeds: applied æsthetics are seldom successful. When the idea of beauty is so highly intellectualized, it is not surprising that the mind passes at once from earthly beauty to that of the angels and of the empyrean, or to that of abstract conceptions. There was no place, in this system, for the notion of artistic beauty, not even in connection with music, the effects of which, one would have supposed, could not fail to suggest the idea of beauty of a specific character.

Musical sensation was immediately absorbed in religious feeling. It would never have occurred to Denis that he might admire in music or painting any other beauty than that of holy things themselves.

One day, on entering the church of Saint John at Bois-le-Duc, while the organ was playing, he was instantly transported by the melody into a prolonged ecstasy.

Denis was one of those who objected to introducing the new polyphonous music into the church. Breaking the voice (*fractio vocis*), he says, seems to be the sign of a broken soul; it is like curled hair in a man or plaited garments in a woman: vanity, and nothing else. He does not mean that there are not devout people whom melody stim-

268 The Waning of the Middle Ages

ulates into contemplation, therefore the Church is right in tolerating organs; but he disapproves of artistic music which only serves to charm those who hear it, and especially to amuse the women. Certain people who practised singing in melodic parts assured him they experienced a certain pleasurable pride, and even a sort of lasciviousness of the heart (*lascivia animi*). In other words, to describe the exact nature of musical emotion the only terms he can find are those denoting dangerous sins.

From the earlier Middle Ages onward many treatises on the æsthetics of music were written, but these treatises, constructed according to the musical theories of antiquity, which were no longer understood, teach us little about the way in which the men of the Middle Ages really enjoyed music. In analysing musical beauty, fifteenth-century writers do not get beyond the vagueness and naïveness which also characterized their admiration of painting. Just as, in giving expression to the latter, they only praise the lofty character of the treatment and the perfect rendering of nature, so in music only sacred dignity and imitative ingenuity are appreciated. To the medieval spirit, musical emotion quite naturally took the form of an echo of celestial joy. "For music"—says the honest rhetorician Molinet, a great lover of music, like Charles the Bold—"is the resonance of the heavens, the voice of the angels, the joy of paradise, the hope of the air, the organ of the Church, the song of the little birds, the recreation of all gloomy and despairing hearts, the persecution and driving away of the devils." The ecstatic character of musical emotion, of course, did not escape them. "The power of harmony"—says Pierre d'Ailly—"is such that it withdraws the soul from other passions and from cares, nay, from itself."

The high valuation of the imitative element in art entailed graver dangers for music than for painting. Composition of the fourteenth and fifteenth centuries really suffered from the craze for naturalistic music, such as the *caccia* (whence English "catch"), originally representing a hunt with baying and yelping hounds and blowing horns. At the beginning of the sixteenth century, a pupil of

Josquin de Prés, Jannequin, composed several "Inventions" of this stamp, representing, amongst others, the battle of Marignano, the street-cries of Paris, the singing of birds and the chattering of women. Fortunately, the musical inspiration of the epoch was far too rich and alive to be enslaved by such an artificial theory; the masterpieces of Dufay, Binchois or Okeghem are free from imitative tricks.

Substituting for beauty the notions of measure, order and appropriateness offered a very defective explanation of it. One other means at least satisfied deeper æsthetic instincts: the reduction of beauty to the sensation of light and splendour. To define the beauty of spiritual things, Denis the Carthusian always compares them to light. Wisdom, science, art, are so many luminous essences, illuminating the mind by their brightness.

This tendency to explain beauty by light sprang from a strongly marked predilection of the medieval mind. When we leave definitions of the idea of beauty aside, and examine the æsthetic sense of the epoch in its spontaneous expressions, we notice that nearly always when men of the Middle Ages attempt to express æsthetic enjoyment, their emotions are caused by sensations of luminous brightness or of lively movement.

Froissart, for example, is not, as a rule, very susceptible to impressions of pure beauty. His endless narratives leave him no time for that. There are one or two spectacles, however, which never fail to enrapture him: that of vessels on the sea with their pavilions and streamers, with their rich decoration of many-coloured blazons, sparkling in the sunshine; or the play of reflected sunlight on the helmets and cuirasses, on the points of the lances, the gay colours of the pennons and banners, of a troop of cavaliers on the march. Eustache Deschamps has expressed his sense of the beauty of mills in movement and of a ray of sunlight scintillating in a dewdrop. La Marche was struck by the beauty of reflected sunlight on the blonde hair of a cavalcade of German and Bohemian noblemen. These displays of æsthetic sentiment are important, because in the fifteenth century they are extremely rare.

This fondness for all that glitters reappears in the general gaudiness of dress, especially in the excessive number of precious stones sewed on the garments. After the Middle Ages this sort of ornament will be replaced by ribbons and rosettes. Transferred to the domain of hearing, this partiality for brilliant things is shown by the naïve pleasure taken in tinkling or clicking sounds. La Hire wore a red mantle covered all over with little silver bells like cow-bells. At an entry in 1465, Captain Salazar was accompanied by twenty men-at-arms, the harness of whose horses was ornamented with large silver bells. The horses of the counts of Charolais and of Saint Pol were adorned in the same way, also those of the lord of Croy, at the entry of Louis XI into Paris in 1461. At festivals jingling florins or nobles were often sewn on to the dress.

To determine the taste in colours characteristic of the epoch would require a comprehensive and statistical research, embracing the chromatic scale of painting as well as the colours of costume and decorative art. Perhaps costume would prove to be the best clue to the nature of the taste for colour, because there it exhibits itself most spontaneously. Now, we have very few specimens of the materials used at that time, except in church vestments. Descriptions of costumes for tournaments and festivals, on the other hand, are very numerous. The following summary aims only at giving a provisional impression, based on an examination of these descriptions. It is necessary to observe that they refer to garments of state and of luxury, differing, as to colour, from ordinary costume, but showing the æsthetic sense more freely. When we consult the accounts published by Monsieur Couderc of a great Parisian tailor of the fifteenth century, we find that the quiet colours, grey, black and violet, occupy a large place, whereas in festal garments the most violent contrasts and the most vivid colours abound. Red predominates; at some princely entries all the accoutrements were in red. White comes next in popularity. Every combination of colours was allowed: red with blue, blue with violet. In an "entremets" described by La Marche a lady appeared in violet-coloured

silk on a hackney covered with a housing of blue silk, led
by three men in vermilion-tinted silk and in hoods of green
silk.

Black was already a favourite colour, even in state apparel, especially in velvets. Philip the Good, in his later
years, constantly dressed in black, and had his suite and
horses arrayed in the same colour. King René, who was
always in quest of what was refined and distinguished, combined grey and white with black. Together with grey and
violet, black was far more in vogue than blue and green,
whereas yellow and brown are, as yet, almost completely
wanting. Now, the relative rarity of blue and of green must
not be simply ascribed to an æsthetic predilection. The
symbolic meaning attached to blue and green was so
marked and peculiar as to make them almost unfit for usual
dress. They were the special colours of love. Blue signified
fidelity; green, amorous passion.

> "Il te fauldra de vert vestir,
>   C'est la livrée aux amoureux. . . ." [1]

Thus says a song of the fifteenth century. Deschamps
says of the lovers of a lady:

> "Li uns se vest pour li de vert,
> L'autre de bleu, l'autre de blanc,
> L'autre s'en vest vermeil com sanc,
> Et cilz qui plus la veult avoir
> Pour son grant dueil s'en vest de noir." [2]

Although other colours also had their meaning in amorous symbolism, a man exposed himself specially to raillery
by dressing in blue or in green, above all in blue, for a sug-
gestion of hypocrisy was mixed up with it. Christine de

[1] You will have to dress in green, It is the livery of
lovers. . .
[2] Some dress themselves for her in green, Another in
blue, another in white, Another dresses himself in vermilion
like blood, And he who desires her most Because of his
great sorrow, dresses in black.

Pisan makes a lady say to her lover who draws attention to
his blue dress:

> "Au bleu vestir ne tient mie le fait
> N'a devises porter, d'amer sa dame,
> Mais au servir de loyal cuer parfait
> Elle sans plus, et la garder de blasme.
> . . . Là gist l'amour, non pas au bleu porter,
> Mais puet estre que plusieurs le meffait
> De faulseté cuident couvrir soubz lame
> Par bleu porter. . . ." [3]

That is probably why, by a very curious transition, blue,
instead of being the colour of faithful love, came to mean
infidelity too, and next, besides the faithless wife, marked
the dupe. In Holland the blue cloak designated an adulterous woman, in France the "cote bleue" denotes a cuck-
old. At last blue was the colour of fools in general.

Whether the dislike of brown and yellow sprang from an
æsthetic aversion or from their symbolic signification remains undecided. Perhaps an unfavourable meaning was
attributed to them, because they were thought ugly.

> "Gris et tannée puis bien porter
> Car ennuyé suis d'espérance." [4]

Grey and brown were both colours of sadness, yet grey
was much in demand for festal apparel, whereas brown was
very rare.

Yellow meant hostility. Henry of Wurtemberg passed before Philip of Burgundy with all his retinue dressed in yellow, "and the duke was informed that it was meant for
him."

[3] To wear blue is no proof Nor to wear mottoes, of love
for one's lady, But to serve her with a perfectly loyal
heart And no others, and to keep her from blame. . . .
Love lies in that, not in wearing blue. But it may be that
many think To cover the offence of falsehood under a tombstone, By wearing blue. . . .

[4] I may well wear grey and tan For hope has only
brought me pain.

After the middle of the fifteenth century, there seems to be a temporary diminution of black and white in favour of blue and yellow. In the sixteenth century, at the same time when artists begin to avoid the naïve contrasts of primary colours, the habit of using bizarre and daring combinations of colours for costume vanishes too.

In so far as art is concerned, it might be supposed that this change was due to the influence of Italy, but the facts do not confirm this. Gerard David, who carries on most directly the tradition of the primitive school, already shows this refinement of colour-sentiment. It must therefore be regarded as a tendency of a more general character. Here is a domain in which the history of art and that of civilization have still a great deal to learn from each other.

Chapter XXI

VERBAL AND PLASTIC EXPRESSION COMPARED

1.   With each attempt to draw a sharp line of demarcation between the Middle Ages and the Renaissance, this borderline has receded further and further backward. Ideas and forms which one had been accustomed to regard as characteristic of the Renaissance proved to have existed as early as the thirteenth century. Accordingly, the word Renaissance has been so much extended by some as to include even Saint Francis of Assisi. But the term, thus understood, loses its genuine meaning. On the other hand, the Renaissance, when studied without preconceived ideas, is found to be full of elements, which were characteristic of the medieval spirit in its full bloom. Thus it has become nearly impossible to keep up the antithesis, and yet we cannot do without it, because Middle Ages and Renaissance by the usage of half a century have become terms which call up before us, by means of a single word, the difference be-

tween two epochs, a difference which we feel to be essential, though hard to define, just as it is impossible to express the difference of taste between a strawberry and an apple.

To avoid the inconvenience inherent in the unsettled nature of the two terms Middle Ages and Renaissance, the safest way is to reduce them, as much as possible, to the meaning they originally had—for instance, not to speak of Renaissance in reference to Saint Francis of Assisi or the ogival style.

Nor should the art of Claus Sluter and the brothers Van Eyck be called Renaissance. Both in form and in idea it is a product of the waning Middle Ages. If certain historians of art have discovered Renaissance elements in it, it is because they have confounded, very wrongly, realism and Renaissance. Now this scrupulous realism, this aspiration to render exactly all natural details, is the characteristic feature of the spirit of the expiring Middle Ages. It is the same tendency which we encountered in all the fields of the thought of the epoch, a sign of decline and not of rejuvenation. The triumph of the Renaissance was to consist in replacing this meticulous realism by breadth and simplicity.

The art and literature of the fifteenth century in France and in the Netherlands are almost exclusively concerned with giving a finished and ornate form to a system of ideas which had long since ceased to grow. They are the servants of an expiring mode of thought. Now, the literature and the art of a period in which artistic creation is almost limited to mere paraphrasing of ideas fully thought out, will differ widely from each other in their value for future ages. Let us consider roughly, for a moment, the impression left upon us, on the one hand, by the literature of the fifteenth century, and on the other hand by its painting. Villon and Charles d'Orléans apart, most of the poets will appear superficial, monotonous and tiresome. Always allegories with insipid personages and hackneyed moralizing, always the same themes repeated to satiety: the sleeper in the orchard, who, in a dream, sees a symbolic lady; the walk at daybreak in the month of May; the "debate" on a love case;

in short, an exasperating shallowness, cloying romanticism, vapid imagery. We shall rarely glean a thought there which is worth being remembered, or an expression which dwells in our memory. The artists, on the other hand, are not only very great, like Van Eyck, Foucquet, or the unknown who painted "The Man with the Glass of Wine," but nearly all, even the mediocre ones, arrest our attention by each detail of their work and hold us by their originality and freshness. Yet their contemporaries admired the poets much more than the artists. Why was the flavour lost in the one case and preserved in the other?

The explanation is that words and images have a totally different æsthetic function. If the painter does nothing but render exactly, by means of line and colour, the external aspect of an object, he yet always adds to this purely formal reproduction something inexpressible. The poet, on the contrary, if he only aims at formulating anew an already expressed concept, or describing some visible reality, will exhaust the whole treasure of the ineffable. Unless rhythm or accent save it by their own charms, the effect of the poem will depend solely on the echo which the subject, the thought in itself, awakens in the soul of the hearer. A contemporary will be thrilled by the poet's word, for the thought which the latter expresses also forms an integral part of his own life, and it will appear the more striking to him in so far as its form is more brilliant. A happy selection of terms will suffice to make the expression of it acceptable and charming to him. As soon, however, as this thought is worn out and no longer responds to the preoccupations of the soul of the period, nothing of value is left to the poem except its form. No doubt, that is of extreme value. Sometimes it is so fresh and so touching that it makes us forget the insignificance of the contents. A new beauty of form was already revealing itself in the literature of the fifteenth century; still, in the greater number of its productions, the form as well was worn out and the qualities of rhythm and tone are poor. In such a case, without novelty of thought or form, nought remains but an interminable postlude on hackneyed themes, a poetry without a future.

The painter of the same epoch and of the same mentality as the poet will have nothing to fear from time. For the inexpressible which he has put into his work will always be there as fresh as on the first day. Let us consider the portraits of Jan van Eyck, the somewhat pointed and pinched face of his wife, the aristocratic, impassible and morose head of Baudouin de Lannoy, the suffering and resigned visage of the Arnolfini at Berlin, the enigmatic candour of "Leal Souvenir" in the National Gallery. In each of these physiognomies the personality was probed to the last inch. It is the profoundest character-drawing possible. These characters were not analysed by the artist, but *seen* as a whole and then revealed to us by his picture. He could not have described them in words, even though he had been, at the same time, the greatest poet of his age. Painting, even when it professes no more than to render the outward appearance of things, preserves its mystery for all time to come.

Hence the art and the literature of the fifteenth century, though born of the same inspiration and the same spirit, inevitably produce on us quite different effects. Apart from this fundamental difference, it may be shown, by the comparison of particular specimens, that the literary and the pictorial expression have far more traits in common than might be supposed from our general appreciation of the one and the other.

Let us take the brothers Van Eyck as being the most eminent representatives of the art of the epoch. Who are the men of letters to be matched with them, in order to compare their inspiration, their modes of expression? We have to look for them in the same environment whence came the great painters, that is to say, as we demonstrated above, in the environment of the court, the nobility and the rich middle classes. There we may assume an affinity of spirit to exist. The literature which may be matched with the art of the brothers Van Eyck is that which the patrons of painting protected and admired.

At first sight the comparison seems to bring to light an essential difference. Whereas the subject-matter of the

artists is almost entirely religious, the profane genre preponderates in literature. Still, we must remember that the
profane element occupied a much larger place in painting
than might be supposed from what has been preserved. On
the other hand, we run some risk of overrating a little the
preponderance of profane literature. The history of literature, being naturally concerned with the tale, the romance,
the satire, the song, historical writings, might easily lead us
to forget that pious works always occupied the first and the
largest place in the libraries of the time. In order to make
a fair comparison between fifteenth-century painting and
literature, we must begin by imagining side by side with
the surviving altar-pieces and portraits all sorts of worldly
and even frivolous paintings, such as hunting or bathing
scenes. The above-named Fazio mentions a picture by
Rogier van der Weyden representing a woman in a sweat-
ing-bath, with two laughing young men peeping through
a chink.

Art and letters in the fifteenth century share the general
and essential tendency of the spirit of the expiring Middle
Ages: that of accentuating every detail, of developing every thought and every image to the end, of giving concrete form to every concept of the mind. Erasmus tells us
that he once heard a preacher in Paris preach during forty
days on the Parable of the Prodigal Son, so that he devoted
all Lent to it. He described his journeys on his setting out
and on his return, the bill of fare of his meals at the inns,
the mills he passed, his dicing, etc., torturing the texts of
prophets and evangelists to find some that might seem to
give some support to his twaddle. "And because of that the
ignorant multitude and the fat big-wigs considered him
almost a god."

To realize the place conceded to the minute execution of
details, it suffices to examine some paintings by Jan van
Eyck. Let us first take the Madonna of the chancellor Rolin,
at the Louvre. In any other artist the laborious exactness
with which the materials of the dresses are painted, also the
marble of the tiles and the columns, the reflections of the
windowpanes, and the chancellor's breviary, would give an

impression of pedantry. Even in him the exaggerated finish
of the details, as in the ornaments of the capitals, on which
a whole series of Biblical scenes is represented, is hurtful
to the general effect. But it is especially in the marvellous
perspective opened behind the figures of the Virgin and
the donor that his passion for details is given rein. "The
dumbfounded spectator," as Monsieur Durand-Gréville
says in describing this picture, "discovers between the head
of the divine child and the Virgin's shoulder, a town full
of pointed gables and elegant belfries, with a big church
with numerous buttresses, and a vast square, cut across all
its length by a staircase on which come and go and run
countless little touches of the brush, which are so many
living figures; his eye is next attracted by a curved bridge
swarming with groups of people who pass and repass; it
follows the meanderings of a river on which tiny barks
make ripples; and in the midst of which, on an island
smaller than the nail of a child's finger, rises up a lordly
castle with numerous turrets, surrounded by trees; it traces
on the left a quay planted with trees, and covered with
foot-passengers; it goes even further, passing beyond the
green hilltops, rests for a moment on the distant line of
snowy mountains, to lose itself, at last, in the infinite space
of a sky, which is hardly blue, where floating vapours are
vaguely discerned."

Are not unity and harmony lost in this aggregation of
details, as Michelangelo affirmed of Flemish art in general?
Having recently seen the picture again, I can no longer
deny it, as I formerly did on the strength of recollections
many years old.

Another work of the master, which lends itself particularly to the analysis of endless detail, is the "Annunciation"
in the National Gallery of Art, in Washington, D.C. If the
triptych of which this picture formed the right wing ever
existed as a whole, it must have been a superb creation.
Van Eyck here developed all the virtuosity of a master
conscious of his power to overcome all difficulties. Of all
his works it is the most hieratic and, at the same time, the
most refined. He followed the iconographic rules of the

past in using as a background for the apparition of the angel the ample space of a church and not the intimacy of a bedchamber, as he did in the altar-piece of the Lamb, where the scene is full of grace and tenderness. Here, on the contrary, the angel salutes Mary by a ceremonious bow; he is not represented with a spray of lilies and a narrow diadem; he carries a sceptre and a rich crown, and about his lips there is the stiff smile of the sculpture of Ægina. The splendour of the colours, the glitter of the pearls, the gold and the precious stones, surpass those of all the other angelic figures painted by Van Eyck. His coat is green and gold, his mantle of brocade is red and gold, his wings are covered with peacock feathers. The book of the Virgin and the cushion before her are executed with painstaking and minute care. In the church there is a profusion of anecdotal details. The tiles of the pavement are ornamented with the signs of the zodiac and scenes from the lives of Samson and of David. The wall of the apse is decorated with the figures of Isaac and of Jacob in the medallions between the arches, and that of Christ on the celestial globe between two seraphim in a window, besides other mural paintings representing the finding of the child Moses and the giving of the tables of the Law, all explained by legible inscriptions. Only the decoration of the wooden ceiling, though still discernible, remains indistinct.

This time unity and harmony are not lost in the accumulation of details. The twilight of the lofty edifice envelops all with mysterious shade, so that the eye can only with difficulty distinguish the anecdotal details.

It is the privilege of the painter that he can give the rein to his craving for endless elaboration of details (perhaps one ought to say, that he can comply with the most impossible demands of an ignorant donor) without sacrificing the general effect. The sight of this multitude of details fatigues us no more than the sight of reality itself. We only notice them if our attention has been directed to them, and we soon lose sight of them, so that they serve only to heighten effects of colouring or perspective.

When the same boundless passion for details is displayed

in literature, the effect is quite different. In the first place,
literature proceeds in another way; it sets itself to enumerate all the ideas and all the objects which the mind of the
poet associates with his subject. Most of the authors of the
fifteenth century are singularly prolix. They do not know
the value of omission, they fill the canvas of their composition with all the details that present themselves, but without giving, as does painting, an accurate image of their particular features—they confine themselves to enumerating
them. It is a strictly quantitative method, whereas that
of painting is qualitative.

Another difference between the two modes of expression
proceeds from the fact that the relation between the essential and the accidental is not the same in both. In painting
we can hardly distinguish between principal and accessory
elements. Everything is essential. The principal subject
may be of no interest to the spectator or in his opinion
badly rendered, without the work losing its charm, on that
account. Unless the religious sentiment preponderates over
æsthetic appreciation, the spectator before the altar-piece
of the Lamb will regard with as much, perhaps with more
profound emotion, the flowery field of the principal scene,
the procession of adorers of the Lamb, the towers behind
the trees in the background, as the central figures of the
composition in their august divinity. His glance will stray
from the rather uninteresting figures of God, the Virgin,
and Saint John the Baptist, to those of Adam and Eve, to
the portraits of the donors, to the charming perspective of
the sunlit street and the little brass kettle with the towel.
He will hardly ask if the mystery of the Eucharist has here
found its most appropriate expression, so much will he be
enchanted by the touching intimacy and the incredible
perfection of all these details, purely accessory in the eyes
of those who ordered and who executed the masterpiece.

Now, in the expression of details the artist is absolutely
free. Whereas he is tied down by rigid convention in the
composition of his principal theme he may give a free rein
to his imagination in all other respects. He may paint the
materials, the vegetation, the horizons, the faces, just as his

genius prompts him; the wealth of detail will no more over-
load his picture than flowers weigh down a dress which
they adorn.

In the poetry of the fifteenth century the relation of the
essential to the accident is reversed. The poet is generally
free as regards his principal subject; something novel is
expected from him. As to accessories, however, he is tied
down by tradition; there is a conventional way of expressing each detail, from which, though he may be unconscious
of it, he can hardly deviate; the flowers, the delights of
nature, sorrows and joys, all these are sung in a fashion
which varies but little. Moreover, the salutary limitation
which the dimension of his picture imposes upon the artist
does not exist for the poet, as a rule. Hence, to be worthy
of this liberty the poet should be relatively greater than the
artist. Even mediocre painters may delight posterity,
whereas the mediocre poet is forgotten.

To make the effect of the abuse of details in a fifteenth-
century poem felt, it would be necessary to quote it entirely. As this is impossible, we must content ourselves with
considering a few fragmentary specimens.

Alain Chartier in his day was held to be a great poet. He
was compared to Petrarch, and even Clement Marot placed
him in the first rank. We may, therefore, fairly compare his
work with that of the greatest painters of his time, and set
the description of nature with which his *Livre des Quatre
Dames* opens against the landscape of the altar-piece of
the Lamb.

One spring morning the poet goes out for a walk, to drive
away his persistent melancholy.

> "Pour oublier melencolie,
> Et pour faire chiere plus lie,
> Ung doulx matin aux champs issy,
> Au premier jour qu'amours ralie
> Les cueurs en la saison jolic. . . ."[1]

[1] To forget melancholy, And to cheer myself, One sweet
morning I went out into the fields On the first day on which
love joins Hearts in the beautiful season.

All this is conventional and without any special grace of rhythm or of accent. Then follows the description of a spring morning:

> "Tout autour oiseaulx voletoient,
> Et si très-doulcement chantoient
> Qu'il n'est cueur qui n'en fust joyeulx.
> Et en chantant en l'air montoient,
> Et puis l'un l'autre surmontoient
> A l'estrivée à qui mieulx mieulx.
> Le temps n'estoit mie nueux,
> De bleu estoient vestuz les cieux,
> Et le beau soleil cler luisoit." [2]

The mention of these delights would not have lacked charm if the author had known where to stop. But he was not so discreet; having gone through all the singing birds, he continues his enumeration at a jog-trot:

> "Les arbres regarday flourir,
> Et lièvres et connins courir.
> Du printemps tout s'esjouyssoit.
> Là sembloit amour seignourir.
> Nul n'y peult vieillir ne mourir,
> Ce me semble, tant qu'il y soit.
> Des erbes ung flair doulx issoit,
> Que l'air sery adoulcissoit,
> Et en bruiant par la valee
> Ung petit ruisselet passoit,
> Qui les pays amoitissoit,
> Dont l'eaue n'estoit pas salee.
> Là buvoient les oysillons,
> Après ce que des grisillons,

[2] All around birds were flying, And they sang so very sweetly That there is no heart that would not be gladdened by it. And while singing they rose up in the air, And then passed and repassed each other, Vying with each other as to which should rise highest. The weather was not cloudy at all. The heavens were clad in blue. And the beautiful sun was shining brightly.

Des mouschettes et papillons
Ilz avoient pris leur pasture.
Lasniers, aoutours, esmerillons
Vy, et mouches aux aguillons,
Qui de beau miel paveillons
Firent aux arbres par mesure.
De l'autre part fut la closture
D'ung pré gracieuz, ou nature
Sema les fleurs sur la verdure,
Blanches, jaunes, rouges et perses.
D'arbres flouriz fut la ceinture,
Aussi blancs que se neige pure
Les couvroit, ce sembloit painctnre,
Tant y eut de couleurs diverses." [3]

A brook brawls over pebbles, fishes swim in it, a grove spreads its twigs on the bank, forming a green curtain. And then the birds reappear: ducks, turtle-doves, pheasants and herons; all the birds from here to Babylon, as Villon would say.

The artist and the poet, both striving to render the beauty of nature, both dominated by the tendency to fasten on each detail, nevertheless arrive, because of the diversity of their methods, at a very different result. Unity and sim-

[3] I saw the trees blossom, And hares and rabbits run. Everything rejoiced at the spring. Love seemed to hold sway there. None could age or die, It seemed to me, so long as he was there. From the herbs arose a sweet smell, Which the clear air made sweeter still, And purling through the valley A little brook passed Moistening the lands Of which the water was not salt. There drank the little birds After they had fed upon crickets, Little flies and butterflies. I saw there lanners, hawks and merlins, And flies with a sting (wasps) Who made pavilions of fine honey In the trees by measure. In another part was the enclosure Of a charming meadow, where nature Strewed flowers on the verdure White, yellow, red and violet. It was encircled by blossoming trees As white as if pure snow Covered them, it looked like a painting, So many various colours there were.

plicity in the picture, in spite of the mass of details, monotony and formlessness in the poem.

But are we right in comparing poetry with painting, with respect to expressive power? Should we not rather take prose, less tied down to obligatory motifs, freer in its choice of means to give an exact vision of reality?

One of the fundamental traits of the mind of the declining Middle Ages is the predominance of the sense of sight, a predominance which is closely connected with the atrophy of thought. Thought takes the form of visual images. Really to impress the mind a concept has first to take a visible shape. The insipidity of allegory could be borne, because the satisfaction of the mind lay in the vision. This constant need of expressing the visible was far better fulfilled by pictorial than by literary means. And again better by prose than by poetry, because it conforms more easily to the visualizing turn of mind. The prose of the fifteenth century in general is superior to its poetry, because prose, like painting, could attain a high degree of direct and powerful realism, which was denied to poetry by its stage of development and by its proper nature.

There is one author, especially, who, by the eminent clearness of his vision of external things, reminds us of Van Eyck, namely, Georges Chastellain. He was a Fleming from the Alost district. Though he calls himself "a loyal Frenchman," "a Frenchman by birth," it is highly probable that Flemish was his mother-tongue. La Marche calls him "a born Fleming, though writing in the French language." He himself likes to lay stress on his rusticity; he speaks of "his coarse speech," he calls himself "a Flemish man, a man of the cattle-breeding marshes, rude, ignorant, stammering of tongue, greasy of mouth and of palate and quite bemired with other defects, proper to the nature of the land." His Flemish birth explains the heaviness of his flowery speech, his pompous and turgid grandiloquence; in short, his truly "Burgundian" style, which makes him almost unbearable to the French reader. It is a formal style, of somewhat elephantine character. But it is also to his Flemish cast of mind that Chastellain owes his lucid and penetrating vision and the richness of his colouring.

There are undeniable affinities between Chastellain and Jan van Eyck. In his best moments Chastellain equals Van Eyck at his worst, and that is saying a good deal. Let us recall the group of singing angels of the altar-piece of the Lamb. Those heavy dresses of red and gold brocade, loaded with precious stones, those too expressive grimaces, the somewhat puerile decoration of the lectern—all this in painting is the equivalent of the showy Burgundian prose. It is a rhetorician's style transferred to painting. Now, whereas this rhetorical element occupies but a small place in painting, it is the principal thing in Chastellain's prose, where the clear observation and the vivid realism are too often drowned in the flood of flowery phrases and stilted terms.

Only, when Chastellain describes an event which grips his visualizing mind, he evinces an imaginative strength, which makes him very interesting. He has no more ideas than his contemporaries and colleagues; his arsenal, like theirs, is stocked with nothing but moral, pious and chivalrous commonplaces; his speculations never go below the surface. But his powers of observation are remarkably keen and his descriptions very lively.

The portrait he drew of Duke Philip has all the vigour of a Van Eyck. He delights in the description of scenes of action and passion, displaying a degree of true and simple realism which would have made this chronicler an excellent novelist. Take, for instance, his narrative of a quarrel between the duke and his son Charles, which took place in 1457. His visual perception is nowhere so vivid as here; all the outward circumstances of the event are rendered with perfect clearness. A few rather long quotations are indispensable.

The difference arose in connection with a vacancy in the household of the young count of Charolais. The old duke wanted, contrary to his promise, to give the place to a member of the family of Croy, then in high favour. Charles,

who did not share his father's feelings for that family, had
destined it for one of his friends.

"Le duc donques par un lundy qui estoit le jour Saint-
Anthoine, après sa messe, aiant bien désir que sa maison
demorast paisible et sans discention entre ses serviteurs, et
que son fils aussi fist par son conceil et plaisir, apres que jà
avoit dit une grant part de ses heures et que la cappelle
estoit vuide de gens, il appela son fils à venir vers luy et lui
dist doucement: 'Charles de l'estrif qui est entre les sires de
Sempy et de Hémeries pour le lieu de chambrelen, je veuil
que vous y mettez cès et que le sire de Sempy obtiengne
le lieu vacant.' Adont dist le conte: 'Monseigneur, vous
m'avez baillié une fois vostre ordonnance en laquelle le sire
de Sempy n'est point, et monseigneur, s'il vous plaist, je
vous prie que ceste-là je la puisse garder.'—'Déa,' ce dit le
duc lors, 'ne vous chailliez des ordonnances, c'est à moy à
croistre et à diminuer, je veuil que le sire de Sempy y soit
mis.'—'Hahan!' ce dist le conte (car ainsi jurait tousjours),
'monseigneur, je vous prie, pardonnez-moy, car je ne le
pourroye faire, je me tiens à ce que vous m'avez ordonné.
Ce a fait le seigneur de Croy, qui m'a brassé cecy, je le
vois bien.'—'Comment,' ce dist le duc, 'me désobéyrez-
vous? ne ferez-vous pas ce que je veuil?'—'Monseigneur, je
vous obéyray volentiers, mais je ne feray point cela.' Et
le duc, à ces mots, enfelly de ire, respondit: 'Hà! garsson,
désobéyras-tu à ma volenté? va hors de mex yeux,' et le
sang, avecques les paroles, lui tira à cœur, et devint pâle
et puis à coup enflambé et si espoentable en son vis, comme
je l'oys recorder au clerc de la chapelle qui seul estoit
emprès luy, que hideur estoit à le regarder." . . .[4]

[4] The duke then, on a Monday, which was Saint Anthony's day, after mass, being very desirous that his house
should remain peaceful and without dissensions between
his servants, and that his son, too, should do his will and
pleasure, after he had already said a great part of his
hours, and the chapel was empty of people, called his son
to come to him and said to him gently: "Charles, the
quarrel which is going on between the lords of Sempy and
of Hémeries, about this place of chamberlain, I wish that
you put a stop to it, and that the lord of Sempy obtains

The duchess, who was present at this dispute, was so much frightened by her husband's look, that she tried to lead her son out of the oratory, and pushed him before her, to get out of range of his father's wrath. But they had to turn several corners before coming to the door of which the clerk had the key. "Caron, open the door for us," says the duchess, but the clerk falls at her feet, praying her to persuade her son to ask pardon, before leaving the chapel. In answer to his mother's urgent request, Charles answers in a loud voice: "Déa, madame, monseigneur m'a deffendu ses yeux et est indigné sur moy, par quoy, après avoir eu celle deffense, je ne m'y retourneray point si tost, ains m'en yray à la garde de Dieu, je ne scay où." [5] Then is heard the voice of the duke, who has remained in his seat, paralysed with fury . . . and the duchess in an agony of fear says to the clerk: "My friend, open the door quickly, quickly, we must be gone, or we are lost."

the vacancy." Then said the count: "Monseigneur, you once gave me your orders in which the lord of Sempy is not mentioned, and monseigneur, if you please, I pray you, that I may keep to them."—"Déa," this said the duke then, "do not trouble yourself about orders, it belongs to me to augment and to diminish, I wish that the lord of Sempy be placed there."—"Hahan!" this said the count (for he always swore like that), "monseigneur, I beg you, forgive me, for I could not do it, I abide by what you have ordered me. This was done by my lord of Croy, who played me this trick, I can see that."—"How," this said the duke, "will you disobey me? will you not do what I wish?"—"Monseigneur, I shall gladly obey you. But I shall not do this." And the duke, at these words, choking with anger, replied: "Hà! boy, will you disobey my will? Go out of my sight," and the blood with these words rushing to his heart, he turned pale and then all at once flushed and there came such a horrible expression on his face, as I heard from the clerk of the chapel, who alone was with him, that it was hideous to look at him. . . .

[5] Faith, madam, monseigneur has forbidden me to come into his sight and is indignant at me, so that, after this prohibition, I shall not return to him so soon, but under God's care, I shall go away, I do not know where.

On returning to his apartments, the old duke, beside himself with anger, fell into a fit of mental aberration; about nightfall he left Brussels alone, on horseback, insufficiently dressed and without warning anyone. "Les jours pour celle heurre d'alors estoient courts, et estoit jà basse vesprée quant ce prince droit-cy monta à cheval, et ne demandoit riens autre fors estre emmy les champs seul et à par luy. Sy porta ainsy l'aventure que ce propre jour-là, après un long et âpre gel, il faisoit un releng, et par une longue épaisse bruyne, qui avoit couru tout ce jour là, vesprée tourna en pluie bien menue, mais trés-mouillant et laquelle destrempoit les terres et rompoit glasces avecques vent qui s'y entrebouta." [6]

Both this passage, and the preceding one, are assuredly not lacking in simple and natural force. In the description which follows of the nocturnal ride of the duke, as he wanders through the fields and woods, Chastellain has mixed his pompous rhetoric with this spontaneous naturalism, which produces a very bizarre effect. Starving and tired, the old duke, having lost his way, vainly calls for help. He narrowly escapes falling into a river which he takes for a road. He is wounded by falling with his horse. He listens in vain for the crowing of a cock, or the barking of a dog, which might have indicated some habitation to him. At last he perceives a glimmer and tries to get to it; loses sight of it, finds it again and reaches it at last. "Mais plus l'approchoit, plus sambloit hideuse chose et espoentable, car feu partoit d'une mote d'en plus de mille lieux, avecques grosse fumière, dont nul ne pensast à celle heure fors que ce fust ou purgatoire d'aucune âme ou autre illusion de

[6] The days were short at that time, and it was already evening when that prince here mounted his horse, and asked nothing but to be alone out in the fields. It so happened that on that day after a long and sharp frost it had begun to thaw, and because of a lasting thick fog which had been about all day, in the evening a fine but very penetrating rain began to fall, which soaked the fields and broke the ice as did the wind which joined in.

l'ennemy. . . ." [7] Upon this he stops, but suddenly remembers that charcoal-burners are in the habit of lighting
such kilns in the depths of woods. However he does not
find a house anywhere near, and begins roaming about
once more. At last the barking of a dog directs him to the
hovel of a poor man, where he finds rest and food.

Other episodes furnished Chastellain with themes for
striking descriptions, such as the judicial duel between the
two burghers of Valenciennes, mentioned above; the nocturnal quarrel at the Hague, between the envoys of Friesland and some Burgundian noblemen whose sleep they disturb by playing at "touch and go" in the room above on
their pattens; the riot at Ghent in 1467, at the entry of the
new Duke Charles, which coincided with the fair of
Houthem, whither the people were in the habit of taking
the shrine of Saint Liévin in a procession. In all these pages
we admire the author's faculty of observation. A number of
spontaneous details betray his strongly visual perception.
The duke facing the rebels sees before him "a multitude
of faces in rusty helmets, framing the grinning beards of
villains, biting their lips." The lout who forces his way to
the window, by the duke's side, wears a gauntlet of blackened iron with which he strikes the window-sill to command silence.

The gift of finding the right and simple word accurately
to describe things seen is, at bottom, the same visual power
which enables Van Eyck to give his portraits their perfect
expression. Only, in literature, this realism remains enslaved
by conventional forms and suffocated under a heap of arid
rhetoric.

In this respect painting was greatly in advance of literature. It was already expert in the technique of rendering
the effects of light. Miniature-painters especially were oc-

---

[7] But the more he approached it, the more it seemed a
hideous and frightful thing, for fire came out of a mound in
more than a thousand places with thick smoke, and, at that
hour, anybody would think that it was the purgatory of
some soul or some other illusion of the devil.

cupied with the problem of fixing the light-effect of a moment. In painting, the effect of a light in the dark was first successfully achieved by Geertgen of Sint Jan of Haarlem, in his "Nativity," but long before this the illuminators had tried to render the light of the torches reflected on the cuirasses in the scene of the apprehension of Christ. The master who illuminated the *Cuer d'Amours espris* by King René had already succeeded in painting a sunrise and the most mysterious twilights, the master of the "Heures d'Ailly" a sun breaking through the clouds after a thunderstorm. On the other hand, the literary means for rendering the effects of light were still primitive. But, perhaps, we should seek in another direction the literary equivalent of this faculty for fixing the impression of a moment. It would rather seem to lie in the current use, in the literature of the fourteenth and fifteenth centuries, of *oratio recta*. At no other epoch has the effect of direct speech been so eagerly sought. The endless dialogues of which Froissart makes use, even to make a political situation clear, are often empty enough, nay, even tedious; still sometimes the impression of something immediate and instantaneous is produced in a very vivid manner, for instance in the following dialogue, which we should think of as being shouted. "Lors il entendi les nouvelles que leur ville estoit prise. 'Et de quel gens.' demande-il. Respondirent ceulx qui à luy parloient: 'Ce sont Bretons!'—'Ha,' dist-il, 'Bretons sont mal gent, ils pilleront et ardront la ville et puis partiront.' 'Et quel cry crient-ils?' dist le chevalier.—'Certes, sire, ils crient La Trimouille!'" [8]

To quicken the movement of the dialogue Froissart is rather too fond of the trick of making one interlocutor repeat with astonishment the last words of the other.—" 'Mon-

[8] Then he heard the news that their town was taken. "And by what people?" he asks. Those with whom he was speaking answered, "They are Bretons!" "Ha," says he, "Bretons are bad people, they will pillage and burn and afterwards depart." "And what war-cry do they cry?" said the knight. "Sure, my lord, they cry La Trimouille!"

seigneur, Gaston est mort.'—'Mort?' dist le conte.—'Certes, mort est-il pour vray, monseigneur.'" [9]

And elsewhere: "Si luy demanda, en cause d'amours et de lignaige, conseil.—'Conseil,' respondi l'archevesque, 'certes, beaux nieps, c'est trop tard. Vous voulés clore l'estable quand le cheval est perdu.'" [10]

Poetry, too, used the trick of short alternating sentences a good deal.

> "Mort, je me plaing—De qui?—De toy.
> —Que t'ay je fait?—Ma dame as pris.
> —C'est vérité.—Dy moy pour quoy.
> —Il me plaisoit—Tu as mespris." [11]

Here the means have become the object. The virtuosity of these jerky dialogues was carried to an extreme in the ballad of Jean Meschinot, in which France accuses Louis XI. In each of the thirty lines, questions and answers alternate, sometimes more than once. Still, this bizarre form does not destroy the effect of the political satire. This is the first stanza:

"Sire . . .—Que veux?—Entendez . . .—Quoy?—Mon cas.
—Or dy.—Je suys . . .—Qui?—La destruicte France!
—Par qui?—Par vous.—Comment?—En tous estats.
—Tu mens.—Non fais.—Qui le dit?—Ma souffrance.
—Que souffres tu?—Meschief—Quel?—A oultrance.
—Je n'en croy rien.—Bien y pert.—N'en dy plus!
—Las! si feray.—Tu perds temps.—Quelz abus!
—Qu'ay-je mal fait?—Contre paix—Et comment?

[9] "My lord, Gaston is dead." "Dead?" said the count. "Indeed, he is dead in sooth, my lord."
[10] So he asked him for counsel in matters of love and lineage. The archbishop answered, "Counsel, sure, good nephew, it is too late for that. You want to shut the stable when the horse is lost."
[11] Death, I complain. Of whom? Of you. What have I done to you? You have taken my lady. That is so. Tell me why? It pleased me. You mistook.

—Guerroyant . . .—Qui?—Vos amys et congnus.
—Parle plus beau—Je ne puis, bonnement." [12]

With Froissart the sober and accurate description of
outward circumstances sometimes acquires tragic force,
just because it leaves out all psychological speculation, as
for instance in the episode of the death of the young Gaston
Phébus, killed by his father in a fit of anger. Froissart's
soul was a photographic plate. Under the uniform surface
of his own style we may discern the qualities of the various
storytellers who communicated to him the endless number
of his items of news. For example, all that was told him by
his travelling companion, the knight Espaing du Lyon, has
been admirably rendered.

In short, whenever the literature of the period works by
means of direct observation, without conventional trammels, it approaches painting, without however rivalling it.
Therefore we should not look for the equivalents of painted
landscapes or interiors in literary descriptions of nature.
Painting of the fifteenth century produced marvels of perspective, because there the masters could let themselves
go, as landscapes were accessory and did not suffer from
the same severe restrictions as the principal subject. Notice the contrast between the principal scene and the background of the "Adoration of the Magi" in the "Trés riches
heures de Chantilly." The figures in the foreground are
affected and bizarre, the scene is overcrowded, whereas
the view of Bourges in the distance attains a perfect
serenity and harmony.

In literature, on the other hand, the feeling for nature

---

[12] Sire . . . What do you want? Listen . . . To what?
To my case. Speak out. I am . . . Who? Devastated
France! By whom? By you. How? In all estates. You lie.
I do not. Who says so? My sufferings. What do you suffer?
Misery. Which? The extremity of misery. I do not believe
a word of it. Evidently. Do not say any more about it.
Alas! I must. It is no use. What a shame! What have I
done ill? You have sinned against peace. And how? By
warring. With whom? With your friends and kinsmen.
Speak more pleasingly. I cannot, in truth.

was not free, neither was the manner of expressing it. Love of nature had taken the form of the pastoral and was therefore controlled by sentimental and æsthetic convention. The poems in which the beauty of flowers and the song of birds are sung proceed from an inspiration quite different from that which gave birth to painted landscapes. Literature in describing nature moves on another plane than painting.

Nevertheless it is in the pastoral that we can trace the development of the literary feeling for nature. Side by side with the poems of Alain Chartier, cited above, we may place those of the royal shepherd René singing in a disguised form his love for Jeanne de Laval, in the pastoral poem of *Regnault et Jehanneton*. There we find ingenuous gaiety and freshness; the king even tried, not without success, to render the effect of night closing in, but all this is far from being great art, like that of the calendars in the breviaries.

The pictures of the months in the calendar of the "Trés riches heures de Chantilly" enable us to compare the expression of the same motif in art and in literature, and that strongly in favour of the former. The reader will remember the glorious castles which ornament the background of the miniatures of the brothers of Limburg; September with the vintage in progress and the castle of Saumur, rising like a vision behind it, the steeples of the towers with their high weather-vanes, the pinnacles and the graceful chimneys, all shooting up like tall white flowers against the deep blue of the sky; or December and the sombre towers of Vincennes looming threateningly behind the leafless woods. What means or methods had a poet like Eustache Deschamps at his disposal to rival scenes like these when he produced a sort of literary counterpart to them in a series of poems, in praise of seven castles of Northern France? The description of architectural forms at which he tried his hand in the lines devoted to the castle of Bièvre was by no means successful. So he limited himself to enumerating the delights which these castles provided; thus, speaking of Beauté, he says:

"Son filz ainsné, daulphin de Viennois,
  Donna le nom à ce lieu de Beauté.
  Et c'est bien drois, car moult est delectables:
  L'en y oit bien le rossignol chanter;
  Marne l'ensaint, les haulz bois profitables
  Du noble parc puet l'en veoir branler. . . .
  Les prez sont pres, les jardins deduisables,
  Les beaus preaulx, fontenis bel et cler,
  Vignes aussi et les terres arables,
  Moulins tournans, beaus plains à regarder." [13]

What a difference between the effect of these lines and
that of the miniature! And yet the method is the same: it
is an enumeration of the things seen (or, in the case of the
poet, things heard). But the view of the artist embraces a
definite and limited space, in which he not merely has to
collect a number of things, but also to harmonize and blend
them into a single whole. In the miniature of February
Paul of Limburg assembled all the peculiarities of winter:
peasants warming themselves before the hearth, the wash
drying, crows on the snow, the sheepfold and beehives,
the barrels and the cart, and the wintry landscape in the
background with the tranquil village and the solitary
house on the hill. All this mass of details is worked into the
peaceful harmony of the landscape, and the unity of the
picture is perfect. The poet, on the other hand, suffers his
gaze to roam at will, but never concentrates it; and there
is no framework to compel him to give unity to his work.

In an epoch of pre-eminently visual inspiration, like the
fifteenth century, pictorial expression easily surpasses
literary expression. Although representing only the visible
forms of things, painting nevertheless expresses a profound

[13] His eldest son, the dauphin of Viennois, Gave this
spot the name of Beauty. And justly, for it is very delecta-
ble: One hears the nightingale sing there; The river Marne
surrounds it, the lofty pleasant woods Of the noble park
may be seen waving on the wind. Meadows are near,
pleasure-gardens, The fine lawns, beautiful and clear foun-
tains, Also vineyards and arable lands, Turning mills, plains
beautiful to view.

inner sense, which literature when it limits itself to describing externals wholly fails to do.

The poetry of the fifteenth century often gives us the impression of being almost devoid of new ideas. The inability to invent new fiction is general. The authors rarely go beyond the touching up, embellishing or modernizing of old subject-matter. What may be called a stagnation of thought prevails, as though the mind, exhausted after building up the spiritual fabric of the Middle Ages, had sunk into inertia. The poets themselves are aware of this feeling of fatigue. Deschamps laments:

> Hélas! on dit que je ne fais mès rien,
> Que jadis fis mainte chose nouvelle;
> La raison est que je n'ay pas merrien
> Dont je fisse chose bonne ne belle." [14]

In the fifteenth century the old romances of chivalry are recast from verse into very prolix prose. This "unrhyming"—"dérimage"—is another sign of the general stagnation of fancy. Nevertheless it marks at the same time an important broadening in the general conception of literature. In the more primitive stages of literature verse is the primary mode of expression. As late as the thirteenth century every subject, even natural history or medicine, seemed to lend itself to treatment in verse, because the principal mode of assimilating a written work was still hearing it recited and getting it by heart. Even the "chansons de geste," it seems, were chanted to a uniform melody. Individual and expressive declamation, as we understand it, was unknown in the Middle Ages. The growing predilection for prose means that reading was superseding recitation. Another custom, dating from the same epoch, testifies to this transition, namely the division of a work into small chapters with summaries, whereas formerly scarcely any division had been thought necessary. In fifteenth-

---

[14] Alas! it is said that I no longer make anything, I who formerly made many new things; The reason is that I have no subject-matter Of which to make good or fine things.

century literature prose was, to a certain degree, the more refined and artistic form.

The superiority of prose is, however, purely formal; it lacks novelty of thought just as much as poetry. Froissart is the type of this extreme shallowness of thought and facility of expression. The simplicity of his ideas is surprising. Only three or four motives or sentiments are known to him: fidelity, honour, cupidity, courage, and these in their simplest forms. He uses no allegorical or mythological figures, never touches on theology, and even moral reflections are almost wholly absent. He goes on narrating, without effort, correctly, and yet he remains empty, because he has but the mechanical exactitude of a cinematograph. His moral reflections, when they do occur, are so commonplace as to be almost bewildering. Certain conceptions are, with him, always accompanied by fixed judgments. He cannot speak of Germans without recalling their cupidity and their barbarous treatment of prisoners. Even the quotations from Froissart which are currently presented to us as piquant prove when read in their context to lack the point attributed to them. On reading his appreciation of the first Duke of Burgundy of the house of Valois, "sage, froid et imaginatif, et qui sur ses besognes veoit au loin,"[15] we think we have lighted upon a penetrating and concise analysis of character. Only, Froissart applied these terms to almost everybody!

The poverty and sterility of Froissart's mind, as compared with Chastellain's, for example, is all the more evident, as his style is wholly devoid of rhetorical qualities. Now it is rhetoric which in the literature of the fifteenth century signalizes the coming of the new spirit. For readers of that age lack of novelty in the matter was made up for by the æsthetic enjoyment of an ornate style. Everything seemed to them to be new when garbed in farfetched and turgid phrases. It is an error to suppose that only literature cultivated this stylistic ornamentation, and

[15] Wise, frigid and imaginative, and far-sighted in business.

that art was exempt from it. Art also displays the same pursuit of novelty and rich variety of expression. In the pictures of the brothers Van Eyck there are parts which might be called "rhetorician-like": for example, the figure of Saint George presenting Canon van de Paele to the Virgin at Bruges. The magnificent helmet, the gilt armour, in which a naïve classicism is apparent, the dramatic gesture of the saint, all this is closely akin to Chastellain's grandiloquence. The same tendency recurs in the figure of the archangel Michael in the small triptych of Dresden and in the group of angels singing and playing, on the altarpiece of the Lamb. It is also present in the work of the brothers of Limburg: for instance, in the bizarre magnificence of their "Adoration of the three Magi."

Unless the ornate form be so charming and so novel as to suffice in itself for giving life to a piece of verse, the poetry of the fifteenth century is happiest when it is not aspiring to express an important thought, nor aiming at elegance of style. When it is content to call up a simple image or scene, or to express a simple sentiment, it is not without vigour. Hence it is more successful in short pieces than in long-winded compositions and grave subjects. In the roundel and the ballad, constructed on a single airy theme, all grace depends on tone, rhythm and vision; in fact, the more the artistic song of the time approaches the popular song, the greater is its charm.

The end of the fourteenth century is a turning-point in the relations between music and lyrical poetry. The song of the preceding period was intimately linked with musical recitation. The common type of the lyrical poet of the Middle Ages is always the poet-composer. Guillaume de Machaut used to compose the melodies of his poems. He also fixed the customary lyrical forms of his time: roundels, ballads, etc. He invented the "débat," the contention of different parties on a moot point. His roundels and ballads are very airy, simple in form and thought; they have little colour; all these are merits, for a poem that is sung should not be too expressive. Here is an example:

> "Au departir de vous mon cuer vous lais
> Et je me'n vois dolans et esplourés.
> Pour vous servir, sans retraire jamais,
> Au departir de vous mon cuer vous lais.
> Et par m'ame, je n'arai bien ne pais,
> Jusqu'au retour, einsi desconfortés.
> Au departir de vous mon cuer vous lais
> Et je m'en vois dolans et esplourés." [16]

In Eustache Deschamps we no longer find composer and poet united. Hence his ballads are much more vivid and highly coloured than Machaut's, therefore often more interesting and yet of an inferior poetical style.

The roundel, because of its very structure, preserved the airy and fluent character of a song to be set to music, even after poets ceased to be composers.

> "M'aimerez-vous bien,
> Dictes, par vostre ame?
> Mais que je vous ame.
> Plus que nulle rien,
> M'aimerez-vous bien?
> Dieu mit tant de bien
> En vous, que c'est basme
> Pour ce je me clame
> Vostre. Mais combien
> M'aimerez-vous bien?" [17]

These lines are by Jean Meschinot. The simple and pure talent of Christine de Pisan lends itself admirably to these fugitive effects. She versified with the facility characteristic of the epoch, without much variety of form or thought,

[16] On parting from you I leave you my heart And I go away lamenting and weeping. To serve you without ever retracting. And by my soul, I shall indeed have no peace Till my return, being thus discomforted.

[17] Do you love me indeed? Tell me, by your soul. If I love you More than anything, Will you love me indeed? God put so much goodness In you that it is balm; Therefore I proclaim myself Yours. But how much Will you love me?

in a subdued tone and with a slight touch of melancholy.
Her poems remind us of those ivory tablets of the fourteenth century, which always represent the same motifs: a
hunting scene, episodes of the *Roman de la Rose* or of
Tristram and Yseult, yet always retain a certain freshness
and impeccable, though conventional gracefulness. When
in Christine courtly sweetness goes hand in hand with the
simplicity of the popular song, we hear an accent of the
most exquisite purity.

We print the dialogue of two lovers who meet after a
separation.

> "Tu soies le très bien venu,
> M'amour, or m'embrace et me baise
> Et comment t'es tu maintenu
> Puis ton départ? Sain et bien aise
> As tu esté toujours? Ça vien
> Costé moy, te sié et me conte
> Comment t'a esté, mal ou bien,
> Car de ce vueil savoir le compte.
>
> —Ma dame, a qui je suis tenu
> Plus que aultre, a nul n'en desplaise,
> Sachés que desir m'a tenu
> Si court qu'oncques n'oz tel mesaise,
> Ne plaisir ne prenoie en rien
> Loings de vous. Amours, qui cuers dompte,
> Me disoit: 'Loyauté me tien,
> Car de ce vueil savoir le compte.'
>
> —Dont m'as tu ton serment tenu,
> Bon gré t'en sçay par saint Nicaise;
> Et puis que sain es revenu
> Joye arons assez; or t'apaise
> Et me dis se scez de combien
> Le mal qu'en as eu a plus monte
> Que cil qu'a souffert le cuer mien,
> Car de ce vueil savoir le compte.

—Plus mal que vous, si com retien,
Ay eu, mais dites sanz mesconte,
Quans baisiers en aray je bien?
Car de ce vueil savoir le compte." [18]

Here is a girl deploring the absence of her lover:

"Il a au jour d'ui un mois
Que mon ami s'en ala.

Mon cuer remaint morne et cois,
Il a au jour d'ui un mois.

'A Dieu,' me dit, 'je m'en vois';
Ne puis a moy ne parla,
Il a au jour d'ui un mois." [19]

Here are words of consolation, addressed to a lover:

"Mon ami, ne plourez plus;
Car tant me faittes pitié

[18] You are most welcome, My love; now embrace me
and kiss me. And how have you been Since your departure? Healthy and at ease Have you always been? Here,
come Beside me; sit down and tell me How you have been,
well or not, For of this I want to have an account.
—Lady, to whom I am bound More than to any other,
may it displease no one, Know that desire so curbed me
That I never had such discomfort Nor did I take pleasure
in anything Far from you. Love, who tames hearts, Said to
me: "Remain faithful to me, For of this I want to have an
account."
—So you kept your oath to me, I thank you much for it
by saint Nicaise; And as you came back safe and sound
We shall have joy enough; now be appeased And tell me
if you know by how much The grief you had from it ex-
ceeds That which my heart has suffered, For of this I
want to have an account.
—More grief than you, as I think, I had, but tell me
without miscalculation, How many kisses shall I have for
it? For of this I want to have an account.
[19] It is a month to-day Since my lover departed. My
heart remains gloomy and silent. It is a month to-day.
"Good-bye," he said, "I am going"; Since then he has not
spoken to me. It is a month to-day.

> Que mon cuer se rent conclus
> A vostre doulce amistié.
> Reprenez autre maniere;
> Pour Dieu, plus ne vous doulez,
> Et me faittes bonne chiere:
> Je vueil quanque vous voulez." [20]

. . . . . .

What gives these verses their abiding womanly charm
is their spontaneous tenderness, their simplicity devoid of
all pomp and pretension. Christine was content to follow
the inspiration of her heart. But this is also the reason why
her poems so often show the defect, characteristic of the
poetry and music of all epochs of feeble inspiration, that of
exhausting all their vigour in the opening lines. How many
poems do we find with a fresh and striking theme, which
begin like a blackbird's song, only to lose themselves in
thin rhetoric after the first stanza! The poet (or in music,
the composer), after stating his theme, had come to the
end of his inspiration. We are constantly disillusioned in
this way by most of the fifteenth-century poets.

Here is an example taken from the ballads of Christine
de Pisan:

> "Quant chacun s'en revient de l'ost
> Pour quoy demeures tu derriere?
> Et si scez que m'amour entiere
> T'ay baillée en garde et depost." [21]

One expects the motif of the dead lover who reappears.
But we are deceived: after two more insignificant stanzas

[20] Friend, weep no more; For I am so touched with
pity That my heart gives itself up To your sweet friendship. Change your bearing; For God's sake, be sad no
longer. And show me a cheerful face: I am willing whatever you will.

[21] When everybody comes back from the army Why do
you stay behind? Yet you know that I pledged you My
loyal love to keep.

the poem finishes. What freshness there is in the first lines
of Froissart's *Debat dou Cheval et dou Levrier:*

> "Froissart d'Escoce revenoit
> Sus un cheval qui gris estoit,
> Un blanc levrier menoit en lasse.
> 'Las,' dist le levrier, 'je me lasse,
> Grisel, quant nous reposerons?
> Il est heure que nous mengons.'" [22]

After this the charm is lost; the author, in short, had
no other inspiration than a moment's vision of the two
animals conversing.

The motifs are occasionally of incomparable grandeur
and suggestive force, but the development remains most
feeble. The theme of Pierre Michault in his *Danse aux
Aveugles* was masterly; the everlasting dance of the human
race about the thrones of the three blind deities, Love,
Fortune, and Death. He only succeeded in working it up
into very mediocre poetry. An anonymous poem, entitled
Exclamacion des Os Sainct Innocent, begins by making the
charnel-houses of the famous churchya. ,peak:

> "Les os sommes des povres trespassez.
> Cy amassez par monceaulx compassez,
> Rompus, cassez, sans reigle ne compas. . . ." [23]

What an exordium for a weird lament! Yet what follows
is a most commonplace *memento mori.*

All these themes have only been realized visually. Such
vision may supply an artist with material for a most grand
conception and consummate execution; it is insufficient for
a poet.

[22] Froissart came back from Scotland On a horse which
was grey, He led a white greyhound in a leash. "Alas," said
the greyhound, "I am tired, Grisel, when shall we rest?
It is time we were feeding."
[23] We are the bones of the poor dead, Here heaped up
by measured mounds, Broken, fractured, without rule or
measure.

Chapter XXII

VERBAL AND PLASTIC EXPRESSION
COMPARED

II. The superiority of painting to literature in point of expressiveness is not, however, absolute and complete. There are regions where it does not exist, and these we must now consider.

The whole domain of the comic is much more open to literature than to plastic art. Unless it stoops to caricature, art can only express the comic in a slight degree. In art the comic tends at once to become serious again; we do not laugh on looking at Breughel, although we admire in him the same force of droll fancy which makes us laugh in reading Rabelais. Only where the comic forms but a slight accessory can pictorial expression rival the written word. We can observe it in what is called genre painting, which may be considered the most attenuated form of the comic.

The disproportionate refinement of details which we noticed above as being characteristic of the paintings of the epoch tends insensibly to change into the pleasure of relating petty curious facts. Whereas in the room of Arnolfini the minutiæ do not injure the solemn intimacy of the picture in the least, they have become mere curiosities in the master of Flémalle. His Joseph on the "Altar of Merode" is occupied with making mouse-traps. With him all the details are "genre," with an almost imperceptible flavour of the comic about them. Between his manner of painting an open window-shutter, a sideboard, a chimney, and that of Van Eyck, there is all the difference between purely pictorial vision and "genre" painting.

Now here comes to light a clear advantage of speech over pictorial representation. As soon as something more than mere vision has to be expressed, literature, thanks to its faculty of expressing moods explicitly, takes the lead. Let us remember again Deschamps' ballads, celebrating the beauty of the castles, which we compared with and found inferior to the perfect miniatures of the brothers of Limburg. These poems of Deschamps lack power and splendour; he has not succeeded in reproducing the vision of these glorious halls. But now compare the ballad in which he paints himself, lying ill in his poor little castle of Fismes, kept awake by the cries of barn-owls, starlings, crows and sparrows, nesting in his tower.

> "C'est une estrange melodie
>   Qui ne semble pas grant deduit
>   A gens qui sont en maladie.
>   Premiers les corbes font sçavoir
>   Pour certain si tost qu'il est jour:
>   De fort crier font leur pouoir,
>   Le gros, le gresle, sanz sejour;
>   Mieulx vauldroit le son d'un tabour
>   Que telz cris de divers oyseaulx,
>   Puis vient la proie; vaches, veaulx,
>   Crians, muyans, et tout ce nuit,
>   Quant on a le cervel trop vuit,
>   Joint du moustier la sonnerie,
>   Qui tout l'entendement destruit
>   A gens qui sont en maladie." [1]

At night the owls come with their sinister screeching, evoking thoughts of death:

[1] It is a strange melody, Which is not felt as a great amusement By people who are ill. First the ravens let us know For certain as soon as it is day: They cry aloud with all their might In deep and shrill tones, without interruption. Even the sound of a drum would be better Than those cries of various birds. Next come the cattle going to pasture, cows, calves, Bellowing, lowing, and all this is noxious When one has an empty brain, With the bells of the church chiming in, And destroying altogether the understanding Of people who are ill.

"C'est froit hostel et mal reduit
A gens qui sont en maladie." [2]

This trick of the mere enumeration of a multitude of
details loses its wearisome character, as soon as the faintest
trace of humour is mixed up with it. In the middle of a
very prolix allegorical poem, *L'Espinette amoureuse,* Froissart diverts us by the enumeration of some sixty games at
which he used to play at Valenciennes as a boy. The descriptions of burgher customs or of the female toilet, long
though they be, do not fatigue us, because they contain
a satirical element which was lacking in the poetical descriptions of the beauty of spring.

From the "genre" to the burlesque is but a step. But
here again painting may rival literature in expressive power.
Before 1400 art had already attained some mastery of
this element of burlesque vision which was to reach its
full growth in Pieter Breughel in the sixteenth century.
We find it in the figure of Joseph in the "Flight into
Egypt" by Broederlam at Dijon and, again, in the three
soldiers asleep in the picture of the "Three Marys at the
Sepulchre," at one time attributed to Hubert van Eyck.
Of the artists of the epoch none took more pleasure in
effects of bizarre jocularity than Paul of Limburg. A spectator of the "Purification of the Virgin" wears a kind of
bent wizard's cap, a yard long, and immoderately wide
sleeves. The font displays three monstrous masks, shooting
out their tongues. In the framework of the "Visitation,"
we see a soldier in a tower fighting with a snail, and a man
wheeling away on a barrow a pig playing the bagpipes.

The literature of the epoch is bizarre in nearly every
page, and very fond of burlesque. A vision worthy of
Breughel is called up by Deschamps in the ballad of the
watchman on the tower of Sluys; he sees the troops for
the expedition against England collecting on the beach;
they appear to him like an army of rats and mice.

[2] It is a cold hostelry and ill refuge For people who are
ill.

"Avant, avant! tirez-vous ça.
Je voy merveille, ce me semble.
 —'Et quoy, guette, que vois-tu là?'
Je voy dix mille rats ensemble
Et mainte souris qui s'assemble
Dessus la rive de la mer. . . ." [3]

On another occasion, sitting at table, absent-minded and gloomy, Deschamps suddenly began to notice the way in which the courtiers were eating: some chewing like pigs; some gnawing like mice, or using their teeth like a saw; others whose beards moved up and down or who made such horrible faces that they looked like devils.

As soon as literature sets to work to depict the life of the masses, it shows this realism full of vitality and good humour, which was to develop abundantly, but not till later, in painting. The peasant receiving in his hovel the duke of Burgundy, who has lost his way, reminds us, by the portrait which Chastellain draws of him, of Breughel's types. The Pastoral deviates from its central theme, which is sentimental and romantic, to find in the description of shepherds eating, dancing, and courting, matter for a naïve naturalism with a spice of burlesque.

Wherever the eye suffices for communicating the sense of the comic, however airy it may be, art is able to express it as well as, or better than, literature. Apart from this, pictorial art can never render the comic. Line and colour are impotent wherever the comic effect lies in a point of wit. Literature is incontestably sovereign both in the low-comedy genre of the farce and the fabliaux, and in the higher domain of irony.

It is especially in erotic poetry that irony developed; by adding its acrid flavour it refined the erotic genre; it purified it at the same time by introducing into it an element of a serious nature. Outside the pale of love-poetry

[3] Forward, forward, come here. I see a marvellous thing, it seems to me.—And what, watchman, do you see there?—I see ten thousand rats together And a multitude of mice collecting On the seashore. . . .

irony was still heavy and clumsy. It is worth remarking that a French writer of the fourteenth or fifteenth century, speaking ironically, often takes care to inform his reader of the fact. Deschamps praises his age; all is well, peace and justice reign everywhere:

"L'en me demande chascun jour
 Qu'il me semble du temps que voy,
 Et je respons: c'est tout honour,
 Loyauté, verité et foy,
 Largesce, prouesce et arroy,
 Charité et biens qui s'advance
 Pour le commun; mais, par ma loy,
 Je ne di pas quanque je pence." [4]

Another ballad, of the same tenor, has the refrain: "Tous ces poins a rebours retien"; [5] a third ends with the words:

"Prince, s'il est par tout generalment
 Comme je say, toute vertu habonde;
 Mais tel m'orroit qui diroit: 'Il se ment' . . ." [6]

A wit of the end of the fifteenth century entitles an epigram: "Soubz une meschante paincture faicte de mauvaises couleurs et du plus meschant peinctre du monde, par manière d'yronnie par maître Jehan Robertet." [7]

When dealing with love, on the other hand, irony had already often attained a high degree of refinement. In this region it blended with the gentle despondency and

[4] People ask me every day What I think of the present times, And I answer: it is all honour, Loyalty, truth and faith, Liberality, heroism and order, Charity and advancement Of the common weal; but, by my faith, I do not say what I think.

[5] Take all these points just the other way about.

[6] Prince, if it is generally everywhere As I know: every virtue abounds; But many a man hearing me will say: He lies.

[7] Under a bad picture done in bad colours and by the most paltry painter of the world, in an ironical manner by master Jehan Robertet.

the languishing tenderness which renewed the erotic
poetry of the fifteenth century. For the first time we hear
the poet voice his melancholy with a smile about his own
misfortune, such as Villon giving himself the air of "l'amant
remis et renié"[8] or Charles of Orléans singing his little
songs of disillusion. Nevertheless the figure "Je riz en
pleurs"[9] is not Villon's invention. Long before him the
scripture word, *risus dolore miscebitur et extrema gaudii
luctus occupat*,[10] had given a text for poetical application. Othe de Granson, for example, had said:

> "Veillier ou lit et jeuner à la table
> Rire plourant et en plaignant chanter."[11]

And again:

> "Je prins congié de ce tresdoulz enfant
> Les yeulx mouilliez et la bouche riant."[12]

Alain Chartier made use of the same motif in various
ways:

> "Je n'ay bouche qui puisse rire,
> Que les yeulx ne la desmentissent:
> Car le cueur l'en vouldroit desdire
> Par les lermes qui des yeulx issent."[13]

He says of a disconsolate lover:

> "De faire chiere s'efforçoit
> Et menoit une joye fainte,
> Et à chanter son cueur forçoit

[8] The shelved and rejected lover.
[9] I laugh in tears.
[10] Even in laughter the heart is sorrowful; and the end
of that mirth is heaviness.
[11] Lying abed awake and fasting at the board, Laughing
in tears and lamenting in song.
[12] I took leave of this most sweet child With tearful eyes
and a laughing mouth.
[13] My mouth cannot laugh, Without my eyes belying it:
For the heart would deny it By the tears issuing from the
eyes.

> Non pas pour plaisir, mais pour crainte,
> Car tousjours ung relaiz de plainte
> S'enlassoit au ton de sa voix,
> Et revenoit à son attainte
> Comme l'oysel au chant du bois." [14]

Very near akin to the motif of laughter and tears is that of the poet who at the end of his poem denies his own sorrow, as, for example, Alain Chartier:

> "Cest livret voult dicter et faire escripre
> Pour passer temps sans courage villain
> Ung simple clerc que l'en appelle Alain
> Qui parle ainsi d'amours pour oyr dire." [15]

Othe de Granson had already pretended to speak of secret love only "par devinaille." [16] King René treated this motif in a fantastic manner at the end of his *Cuer d'Amours espris*. His valet, with a candle in his hand, tries to find out if the king has really lost his heart, but finds no hole in his side.

> "Sy me dist tout en soubzriant
> Que je dormisse seulement
> Et que n'avoye nullement
> Pour ce mal garde de morir." [17]

By losing the impeccable gravity characteristic of them in preceding epochs, the ancient conventional forms of erotic poetry became penetrated by a new meaning.

---

[14] He constrained himself to be cheerful And showed a feigned joy, And forced his heart to sing Not for pleasure, but for fear, For ever a remainder of complaint Entwined itself with the tone of his voice, And reverted to its purpose Like the ousel singing in the wood.

[15] This booklet meant to dictate and to describe To pass the time without vulgar mood A simple clerk called Alain Who speaks thus of love by hearsay.

[16] By guessing.

[17] So he told me smiling That I should lie down and sleep And that I should not at all Be afraid to die of this evil.

Charles d'Orléans makes use of personifications and of allegories like all his predecessors, but, by some slight surplus
of stress, he adds an almost imperceptible flavour of
raillery, and this gives them an affecting note, which is
lacking in the graceful figures of the *Roman de la Rose*.
He sees his own heart as a double of himself.

"Je suys celluy au cueur vestu de noir. . . ."[18]

Occasionally in his extravagant personifications, the com-
ical element has the upper hand:

"Un jour à mon cueur devisoye
Qui en secret à moy parloit,
Et en parlant lui demandoye
Se point d'espargne fait avoit
D'aucuns biens quant Amours servoit:
Il me dist que très voulentiers
La verité m'en compteroit,
Mais qu'eust visité ses papiers.

"Quand ce m'eut dit, il print sa voye
Et d'avecques moy se partoit.
Après entrer je le véoye
En ung comptouer qu'il avoit:
Là, de ça et de là quéroit,
En cherchant plusieurs vieulx caïers
Car le vray monstrer me vouloit,
Mais qu'eust visitez ses papiers. . . ."[19]

---

[18] I am the wight whose heart is draped in black.
[19] One day I was talking with my heart Which secretly
spoke to me, And in talking I asked it If it had saved No
goods when serving Love: It said that quite willingly It
would tell me the truth about it, As soon as it had consulted its papers.

Having told me this it went away And from me departed.
Next I saw it enter In an office it had: There it rummaged
here and there In looking for several old writing-books, For
it would show me the truth, As soon as it had consulted
its papers.

Not always, however; in the following lines the comic is
not dominant:

"Ne hurtez plus à l'uis de ma pensée,
　Soing et Soucy, sans tant vous travailler;
　Car elle dort et ne veult s'esveiller,
　Toute la nuit en peine a despensée.

"En dangier est, s'elle n'est bien pansée;
　Cessez, cessez, laissez la sommeiller;
　Ne hurtez plus à l'uis de ma pensée,
　Soing et Soucy, sans tant vous travailler. . . ."[20]

For the spirit of the epoch nothing heightened so much
the acrid flavour of sad and sensitive love as the addition
of an element of profanation. Religious travesty has created
something better than the obscenities of the *Cent Nouvelles
Nouvelles;* it furnished the form for the tenderest love-
poem which that age produced: *L'Amant rendu Cordelier
à l'Observance d'Amours.*

Already the poetical club of Charles d'Orléans had imagined a literary brotherhood whose members, in analogy
to the reformed Franciscans, called themselves "amourex
de l'observance." The author of *L'Amant rendu Cordelier*
developed this motif. Who is this author? Is it really Martial
d'Auvergne? It is hard to believe it, so much does this
poem rise above the level of his work.

The poor disillusioned lover comes to renounce the
world in the strange convent, where only "the martyrs of
love" are received. He tells the Prior the touching story
of his despised love; the latter exhorts him to forget it.
Under a medieval guise we seem to perceive already the

[20] Do not knock at the door of my mind any more,
Anxiety and Care; do not give yourselves so much trouble;
For it sleeps and does not want to wake, It has passed all
the night in solicitude.
It will be in danger, if not well nursed; Stop, stop, let it
sleep; Do not knock at the door of my mind any more,
Anxiety and Care; do not give yourselves so much trouble.

genre of Watteau. Only the moonlight is wanting to remind us of Pierrot. "Was she not in the habit," asks the
Prior, "of giving you a sweet look or saying 'God save you'
in passing?"—"I had not got so far in her good graces,"
replies the lover; "but at night I stood about the door of
her house, and looked up at the eaves."

> "Et puis, quant je oyoye les verrières
> De la maison qui cliquetoient,
> Lors me sembloit que mes prières
> Exaussées d'elle sy estoient." [21]

"Were you quite sure that she noticed you?" asks the
Prior.

> "Se m'aist Dieu, j'estoye tant ravis,
> Que ne savoye mon sens ne estre,
> Car, sans parler, m'estoit advis
> Que le vent ventoit sa fenestre
> Et que m'avoit bien peu cognoistre,
> En disant bas: 'Doint bonne nuyt,'
> Et Dieu scet se j'estoye grant maistre
> Après cela toute la nuyt." [22]

Then he slept in glory.

> "Tellement estoie restauré
> Que, sans tourner ne travailler,
> Je faisoie un somme doré,
> Sans point la nuyt me resveiller,
> Et puis, avant que m'abiller,
> Pour en rendre à Amours louanges,

[21] And then, when I heard the window Of the house
which clattered, Then it seemed to me that my prayers
Had been heard by her.

[22] So help me God, I was so ravished That I was
scarcely conscious, For, without being told, it seemed to me
That the wind moved her window And she could well
have recognized me, Perhaps saying softly: "Good night,
then," and God knows I felt like a prince After this all night.

> Baisoie troys fois mon orillier,
> En riant à par moy aux anges." [23]

When he is solemnly received into the order, the lady who had despised him faints and a little gold heart enamelled with tears, which he had given her, falls from her dress.

> "Les aultres, pour leur mal couvrir
> A force leurs cueurs retenoient,
> Passans temps a clorre et rouvrir
> Les heures qu'en leurs mains tenoient,
> Dont souvent les feuillès tournoient
> En signe de devocion;
> Mais les deulz et pleurs que menoient
> Monstroient bien leur affection." [24]

The Prior enumerates his new duties to him, warning him never to listen to the nightingale's song, never to sleep under "eglantine and mayflower," and, above all, never to look a woman in the eyes. The exhortation ends in a long string of eight-lined stanzas, being variations to the theme "Sweet eyes."

> "Doux yeulx qui tousjours vont et viennent;
> Doux yeulx eschauffans le plisson,
> De ceulx qui amoureux deviennent. . . .

> "Doux yeulx a cler esperlissans,

[23] I felt so refreshed That without turning about or tossing, I enjoyed golden slumber, Without waking up all night, And then, before dressing To praise Love for it, I kissed my pillow thrice, While laughing silently at the angels.
[24] The others, to hide their affliction Controlled their hearts by force, Passing the time in closing and opening again The breviaries they held in their hands, Of which they often turned the leaves As a sign of devotion; But their sorrow and tears Clearly showed their emotion.

Qui dient: C'est fait quant tu vouldras,
A ceulx qu'ils sentent bien puissans. . . ." [25]

Towards the middle of the fifteenth century all the conventional genres of erotic poetry are of a languishing tenor, and bear the stamp of resigned melancholy. Even cynical contempt of woman grows refined. In the *Quinze Joyes de Mariage* the mischievous and gross purpose is tempered by wistful sentimentality. By its sober realism, by the elegance of its form and the subtlety of its psychology, this work is a precursor of the "novel of manners" of modern times.

In all that concerns the expression of love, literature profited by the models and the experience of a long series of past centuries. Masters of such diversity of spirit as Plato and Ovid, the troubadours and the wandering students, Dante and Jean de Meun, had bequeathed to it a perfected instrument. Pictorial art, on the contrary, having neither models nor tradition, was primitive in the strict sense of the word, in respect of erotic expression. Not till the eighteenth century was painting to overtake literature in point of delicate expression of love. The artist of the fifteenth century had not yet learned to be frivolous or sentimental. In the miniatures of that time the posture of lovers embracing remains hieratic and solemn. A portrait of a Dutch gentlewoman, Lysbet of Duvenvoorde, by an unknown master before 1430, shows a figure of such severe dignity that a modern scholar has taken the picture for a donor's portrait, omitting to read the words on the scroll she bears in her hand: "Mi verdriet lange te hopen, Wie is hi die syn hert hout open?" i.e.: "I am weary of hoping so long. Who is he who holds his heart open?" Pictorial expression knew no middle term between the chaste and the obscene. The rendering of erotic subjects was rare, and

[25] Sweet eyes that always come and go; Sweet eyes heating the fur coat Of those who fall in love. . . .
Sweet eyes of pearly clearness, That say: I am ready when you please, To those whom they feel to be powerful.

what there is of it, is naïve and innocent. Once more, however, we must bear in mind that the greater number of profane works have disappeared. It would be most interesting to be able to compare the nude of Van Eyck in his "Bath of Women," which Fazio saw, with that of his "Adam and Eve." As to the latter picture, it must not be imagined that the erotic element is lacking. Following the rules of the code of feminine beauty of his time, the artist made the breasts small and placed them too high; the arms are long and thin, the belly prominent. But he did so quite ingenuously and with no intention of giving sensual pleasure. A small picture in the Leipsic Gallery, occasionally designated as belonging to the "school of Jan van Eyck," represents a girl in a room; she is nude, as magical practices require, and is employing witchcraft to force her lover to show himself. Here the intention is present, and the artist has succeeded in expressing the erotic sentiment: the nude figure has the demure lasciviousness which reappears in those of Cranach.

It is most improbable that the restraint thus displayed in fifteenth-century art, in respect of erotic expression, was due to a sense of modesty, for in general an extreme licence was tolerated. Though pictorial art cultivated it very little as yet, the nude occupied a large place in the tableau vivant. The "personnages" of nude goddesses or nymphs played by real women were rarely wanting at the entries of princes. These exhibitions took place on platforms and occasionally even in the water, like that of the sirens who swam in the Lys "quite naked and dishevelled as they paint them," near the bridge over which Duke Philip had to pass, on his entry into Ghent in 1457. The Judgment of Paris was the favourite subject. These representations should be taken neither as proofs of high æsthetic taste nor gross licentiousness, but rather as naïve and popular sensuousness. Jean de Roye, speaking of sirens that were seen, not very far from a calvary, on the occasion of Louis XI's entry into Paris in 1461, says: "And there were also three very handsome girls, representing quite naked sirens, and one saw their beautiful turgid, separate, round and hard breasts, which was a very pleasant sight, and they recited little motets and bergerettes; and near them several deep-toned instruments were playing fine melodies." Molinet tells us of the pleasure which the people of Antwerp felt at the entry of Philip le Beau in 1494, when they saw the Judgment of Paris: "But the stand at which the people looked with the greatest pleasure was the history of the three goddesses represented nude by living women."

How far removed from the Greek sense of beauty was the parody of this theme got up for the entry of Charles the Bold at Lille in 1468, where were seen a corpulent Venus, a thin Juno and a hunchbacked Minerva, each wearing a gold crown.

These nude spectacles remained customary during the sixteenth century. Dürer, in the diary of his journey in the Netherlands, described the one he saw at Antwerp at the entry of Charles V in 1521, and as late as 1578 William of Orange, at his entry in Brussels, saw among other items a chained and nude Andromeda, "which one would have taken for a marble statue."

The inferiority of pictorial as compared with literary expression is not confined to the domain of the comic, the sentimental and the erotic. The expressive faculty of the art of this period fails as soon as it is no longer supported by that extraordinary turn for visualizing, which explains the marvels of its pictures. When more is required than the direct and accurate vision of reality, the superiority of pictorial expression at once vanishes, and then is felt the justice of Michelangelo's criticism: that this art aims at achieving several things at the same time, of which a single one would be important enough to demand the devotion of all its powers.

Let us once more consider a picture by Jan van Eyck. In so far as accurate observation suffices, his art is perfect, especially in facial expression, the material of the dresses, and the jewellery. As soon as it becomes necessary to reduce reality in some sort to a scheme, as is the case when buildings and landscapes have to be painted, certain weak-nesses appear. In spite of the charming intimacy of his perspectives, there is a certain incoherence, a defective grouping. The more the subject demands free composition and the creation of a new form, the more his powers fall short.

It cannot be denied that in the illuminated breviaries the calendar pages surpass in beauty those representing sacred subjects. To picture a month, it suffices to observe and reproduce accurately. On the other hand, to compose an important scene, full of movement, with many personages, needed the sense of rhythm and of unity which Giotto possessed and which Michaelangelo recaptured. Now, multiplicity was a characteristic of fifteenth-century art. It rarely succeeds in finding harmony and unity. The central part of the altar-piece of the Lamb does indeed show this harmony, in the severe rhythm in which the different processions of adorers are advancing towards the Lamb; but this effect has been obtained, so to say, by a purely arithmetical co-ordination. Van Eyck evaded the difficulties of the composition by grouping his personages in a very simple figure; the harmony is static, not dynamic.

The great distance separating Van Eyck from Rogier van der Weyden lies in the fact that the latter is aware of a problem of rhythmical composition. He limits himself in the use of detail, in order to find unity; it is true, without always succeeding.

There was a venerable and severe tradition regulating the representation of the most important sacred subjects. The artist had not to invent the composition of his picture; for some of these subjects rhythmical composition came, so to speak, of itself. It was impossible to paint a Descent from the Cross, a *pietà*, an Adoration of the Shepherds, without the composition assuming a certain rhythmical structure. It suffices to remember the Descent from the Cross by Rogier van der Weyden in the Escurial, his *pietà* at Madrid, or those of the Avignon school at the Louvre and at Brussels, those by Petrus Cristus, by Geertgen of Sint Jan, the "Belles heures d'Ailly." The very nature of the subject implied a simple and severe composition.

As soon as the scene to be represented required more movement, as in the case of Christ being mocked or bearing the cross, or in the Adoration of the Magi, the difficulties of the composition increase and a certain unrest and lack of harmony is the result. Here, however, iconographic tradition still supplies a model of a kind, but where it fails him altogether the artist of the fifteenth century is almost helpless. We need but notice the feebleness of composition in the scenes in courts of justice by Dirk Bouts and by Gerard David, though the solemnity of the subject itself called for an element of severity. The composition reaches an irritating pitch of clumsiness in scenes like the Martyrdom of Saint Erasmus at Louvain, and that of Saint Hippolytus, torn to pieces by horses, at Bruges.

And yet here we are still dealing with the representation of scenes borrowed from reality. When the whole has to be created by the unaided imagination, the art of the period cannot avoid the ridiculous. Pictures on the grand scale were saved by the solemnity of their subjects, but the illuminators could not evade the task of giving a shape to all the mythological and allegorical fancies of which literature was full. The illustrations by Jean Miélot for the *Epitre d'Othéa à Hector,* a mythological fancy of Christine de Pisan's, may serve as a sample. It is impossible to imagine anything more awkward.The Greek gods have large wings outside their ermine mantles and "houppelandes" of brocade. Saturn devouring his children, Midas awarding the prize, are simply ridiculous and devoid of all charm. Yet, whenever the illuminator sees a chance of enlivening the prospect by a little scene, such as a shepherd with his sheep, he shows the ability common to the period: within his province his hand is sure. The reason is that here we have come to the limit of the creative faculties of these artists. Easily masters of their craft, so long as observation of reality is their guide, their mastery fails at once when imaginative creation of new motifs is called for.

Imagination, both literary and artistic, had been led into a blind alley by allegory. The mind had grown accustomed simply to turn into pictorial presentments the allegorical ideas presenting themselves to the mind. Allegory linked the presentment to the thought and the thought to the presentment. The desire to describe accurately the allegorical vision caused all demands of artistic style to be lost sight of. The cardinal virtue of Temperance has to carry a clock to represent rule and measure. We see her with this attribute on a tomb, the work of Michel Colombe, in Nantes Cathedral, and on that of the cardinals of Amboise at Rouen. The illuminator of the *Epître d'Othéa*, to conform to this rule, simply puts on her head a timepiece resembling the one with which he ornaments the room of Philip the Good.

The allegorical figure can only be justified by a tradition which has become venerable. Invented all of a piece, it is rarely satisfactory. The more realistic the mind which creates it, the more bizarre and factitious its form will be. Chastellain, in his *Exposition sur vérité mal prise*, sees four ladies coming to accuse him. They call themselves "Indignation, Reprobation, Accusation, Vindication." This is how he describes the second. "This dame here appeared to have acrid conditions and very tart and biting reasons; she ground her teeth and bit her lips; often nodded her head; and showing signs of being argumentative, jumped on her feet and turned to this side and to that; she proved to be impatient and inclined to contradict; the right eye was closed and the other open; she had a bag full of books before her, of which she put some into her girdle, as if they were dear to her, the others she threw away spitefully; she tore up papers and leaves; she threw writing-books into the fire furiously; she smiled on some and kissed them; she spat on others out of meanness and trod them underfoot; she had a pen in her hand, full of ink, with which she crossed out many important writings . . . ; also with a sponge she blackened some pictures, she scratched out others with her nails, and others again she erased wholly and smoothed them as if to have them forgotten; and showed herself a hard and fell enemy to many respectable people, more arbitrarily than reasonably." Elsewhere he sees Dame Peace spread out her mantle and break up into four new ladies: Peace of Heart, Peace of Mouth, Seeming Peace, Peace of True Effect. Or he invents female figures which he calls "Importance of your lands, Various conditions and qualities of your several peoples, The envy and hatred of Frenchmen and of neighbouring nations," as if politics lent themselves to allegory. It is no living fancy, of course, which prompts him to imagine these quaint figures, but only reflection. All wear their names written on scrolls: he evidently imagines them as figures on tapestry, or in a picture or a show.

There is not a trace of true inspiration here. It is the pastime of an exhausted mind. Though the authors always place their action in the setting of a dream, their phantasmagorias never resemble real dreams, such as we find in Dante and Shakespeare. They do not even keep up the illusion of real vision: Chastellain naïvely calls himself in one of his poems "the inventor or the imaginer of this vision."

Only the note of raillery can still make the arid field of allegory flower again, as in these lines of Deschamps:

> "Phisicien, comment fait Droit?
> —Sur m'ame, il est en petit point. . . .
> —Que fait Raison? . . .
> Perdu a son entendement,
> Elle parle mais faiblement,
> Et Justice est toute ydiote. . . ."[26]

The different spheres of literary fancy are mixed up regardless of all homogeneity of style. The author of the *Pastoralet* dresses his political shepherds in a tabard ornamented with fleurs-de-lis and lions rampant; "shepherds in long cassocks" represent the clergy. Molinet muddles up

[26] Physician, what about Law?—By my soul, he is poorly. . . . How does Reason? . . . She is out of her mind, She speaks but feebly, And Justice is quite crazy.

religious, military, heraldic and amorous terms in a pro-
clamation of the Lord to all true lovers:

"Nous Dieu d'amours, créateur, roy de gloire
Salut à tous vrays amans d'humble affaire!
Comme il soit vrays que depuis la victoire
De nostre filz sur le mont de Calvaire
Plusieurs souldars par peu de cognoissance
De noz armes, font au dyable allyance. . . ." [27]

Therefore the true blazon is described to them:
escutcheon *argent*, chief *or* with five wounds—and the
Church militant is given full liberty to take all into her service who want to return to that blazon.

The feats which procured Molinet the reputation of an
excellent "rhétoriqueur" and poet appear to us rather as
the extreme degeneration of a literary form nearing its
end. He takes pleasure in the most insipid puns: "Et ainsi
demoura l'Escluse en paix qui lui fut incluse, car la guerre
fut d'elle excluse plus solitaire que rencluse." [28] In the
introduction to his prose version of the *Roman de la Rose*
he plays upon his name, Molinet. "Et affin que je ne perde
le froment de ma labeur, et que la farine que en sera
molue puisse avoir fleur salutaire, j'ay intencion, se Dieu
m'en donne la grace, de tourner et convertir soubz mes
rudes meulles le vicieux au vertueux, le corporel en
l'espirituel, la mondanité en divinité, et souverainement de
la moraliser. Et par ainsi nous tirerons le miel hors de la
dure pierre, et la rose vermeille hors de poignans espines,
où nous trouverons grain et graine, fruict, fleur et feuille,
très souefve odeur, odorant verdure, verdoyant floriture,

[27] We God of love, creator, king of glory All hail to all
true lovers of humble mind! As it is true that since the
victory Of our son on Mount Calvary Several soldiers
through lack of knowledge Of our arms, make an alliance
with the devil. . . .
[28] And so Sluys remained in peace that was included
with her, for war was excluded from her, lonelier than a
recluse.

florissant nourriture, nourrissant fruict et fructifiant pasture." [29]

When they do not play upon words, they play upon ideas. Meschinot makes Prudence and Justice the glasses of his *Lunettes des Princes*, Force the frame and Temperance the nail which keeps the whole together. The poet receives the aforesaid spectacles from Reason with directions how to use them. Sent by Heaven, Reason enters his mind and wants to feast there; but finds nothing "off which to dine well," for Despair has spoilt all.

Products like these would seem to betray mere decadence and senile decay. Thinking of Italian literature of the same period, the fresh and lovely poetry of the *quattrocento,* we may perhaps wonder how the form and spirit of the Renaissance can still seem so remote from the regions on this side of the Alps.

It requires some effort and some reflection to realize that exactly in these artifices of style and wit, we witness the coming of the Renaissance, in the shape it took outside Italy. To contemporaries this far-fetched form meant the renewal of art.

[29] And lest I lose the wheat of my labour, and that the meal into which it will be ground may have wholesome flour, I intend, if God gives me grace for it, to turn and convert under my rough mill-stones the vicious into the virtuous, the corporal into the spiritual, the worldly into the divine, and, above all, to moralize it. And in this way we shall gather honey from the hard stone and the vermeil rose from sharp thorns, where we shall find grains and seed, fruit, flower and leaf, very sweet odour, odoriferous verdure, verdant florescence, flourishing nurture, nourishing fruit and fruitful pasture.

Chapter XXIII

THE ADVENT OF THE NEW FORM

The transition from the spirit of the declining Middle Ages to humanism was far less simple than we are inclined to imagine it. Accustomed to oppose humanism to the Middle Ages, we would gladly believe that it was necessary to give up the one in order to embrace the other. We find it difficult to fancy the mind cultivating the ancient forms of medieval thought and expression while aspiring at the same time to antique wisdom and beauty. Yet this is just what we have to picture to ourselves. Classicism did not come as a sudden revelation, it grew up among the luxuriant vegetation of medieval thought. Humanism was a form before it was an inspiration. On the other hand, the characteristic modes of thought of the Middle Ages did not die out till long after the Renaissance.

In Italy the problem of humanism presents itself in a most simple form, because there men's minds had ever been predisposed to the reception of antique culture. The Italian spirit had never lost touch with classic harmony and simplicity. It could expand freely and naturally in the restored forms of classic expression. The *quattrocento* with its serenity makes the impression of a renewed culture, which has shaken off the fetters of medieval thought, until Savonarola reminds us that below the surface the Middle Ages still subsist.

The history of French civilization of the fifteenth century, on the contrary, does not permit us to forget the Middle Ages. France had been the mother land of all that was strongest and most beautiful in the products of the medieval spirit. All medieval forms—feudalism, the ideas of chivalry and courtesy, scholasticism, Gothic architecture—were rooted here much more firmly than ever they had been in Italy. In the fifteenth century they were dominating still. Instead of the full rich style, the blitheness and the harmony characteristic of Italy and the Renaissance, here it is bizarre pomp, cumbrous forms of expression, a worn-out fancy and an atmosphere of melancholy gravity which prevail. It is not the Middle Ages, it is the new coming culture, which might easily be forgotten.

In literature classical forms could appear without the spirit having changed. An interest in the refinement of Latin style was enough, it seems, to give birth to humanism. The proof of this is furnished by a group of French scholars about the year 1400. It was composed of ecclesiastics and magistrates, Jean de Monstreuil, canon of Lille and secretary to the king, Nicolas de Clemanges, the famous denouncer of abuses in the Church, Pierre et Gontier Col, the Milanese Ambrose de Miliis, also royal secretaries. The elegant and grave epistles they exchange are inferior in no respect—neither in the vagueness of thought, nor in the consequential air, nor in the tortured sentences, nor even in learned trifling—to the epistolary genre of later humanists. Jean de Monstreuil spins long dissertations on the subject of Latin spelling. He defends Cicero and Virgil against the criticism of his friend Ambrose de Miliis, who had accused the former of contradictions and preferred Ovid to the latter. On another occasion he writes to Clemanges: "If you do not come to my aid, dear master and brother, I shall have lost my reputation and be as one sentenced to death. I have just noticed that in my last letter to my lord and father, the bishop of Cambray, I wrote *proximior* instead of the comparative *propior*; so rash and careless is the pen. Kindly correct this, otherwise our detractors will write libels about it."

There are more charming passages in his correspondence than this: for example, his description of the monastery of Charlieu, near Senlis, where he speaks of the sparrows coming to share the monks' repast, the wren which behaves as if it were the abbot, and lastly, the gardener's donkey, which begs the author not to forget it in his letter.

We may hesitate whether to call this medieval naïvety or humanistic elegance.

It suffices to recall that we met Jean de Monstreuil and the brothers Col among the zealots of the *Roman de la Rose* and among the members of the Court of Love of 1401, to be convinced that this primitive French humanism was but a secondary element of their culture, the fruit of scholarly erudition, analogous to the so-called renaissances of classic latinity of earlier ages, notably the ninth and the twelfth century. The circle of Jean de Monstreuil had no immediate successors, and this early French humanism seems to disappear with the men who cultivated it. Still, in its origins it was to some extent connected with the great international movement of literary renovation. Petrarch was, in the eyes of Jean de Monstreuil and his friends, the illustrious initiator, and Coluccio Salutati, the Florentine chancellor who introduced classicism into official style, was not unknown to them either. Their zeal for classic refinement had evidently been roused not a little by Petrarch's taunt that there were no orators nor poets outside Italy. In France Petrarch's work had, so to say, been accepted in a medieval spirit and incorporated into medieval thought. He himself had personally known the leading spirits of the second half of the fourteenth century; the poet Philippe de Vitri, Nicolas Oresme, philosopher and politician, who had been a preceptor to the dauphin, probably also Philippe de Mézières. These men, in spite of the ideas which make Oresme one of the forerunners of modern science, were not humanists. As to Petrarch himself, we are always inclined to exaggerate the modern element in his mind and work, because we are accustomed to see him exclusively as the first of renovators. It is easy to imagine him emancipated from the ideas of his century. Nothing is further from the truth. He is most emphatically a man of his time. The themes of which he treated were those of the Middle Ages: *De contemptu mundi, De otio religiosorum, De vita solitaria*. It is only the form and the tone of his work which differ and are more highly finished. His glorification of antique virtue in his *De viris illustribus* and his *Rerum memorandarum libri* corresponds more or less with the chivalrous cult of the Nine Worthies. There is nothing surprising in his being found in touch with the founder of the Brethren of the Common Life, or cited as an authority on a dogmatic point by the fanatic Jean de Varennes. Denis the Carthusian borrowed laments from him about the loss of the Holy Sepulchre, a typically medieval subject. What contemporaries outside Italy saw in Petrarch was not at all the poet of the Sonnets or the *Trionfi*, but a moral philosopher, a Christian Cicero.

In a more limited field Boccaccio exercised an influence resembling that of Petrarch. His fame too was that of a moral philosopher, and by no means rested on the *Decamerone*. He was honoured as the "doctor of patience in adversity," as the author of *De casibus virorum illustrium* and of *De claris mulieribus*. Because of these queer writings treating of the inconstancy of human fate "messire Jehan Bocace" had made himself a sort of *impresario* of Fortune. As such he appears to Chastellain, who gave the name of *Le Temple de Bocace* to the bizarre treatise in which he endeavoured to console Queen Margaret, after her flight from England, by relating to her a series of the tragic destinies of his time. In recognizing in Boccaccio the strongly medieval spirit which was their own, these Burgundian spirits of a century later were not at all off the mark.

What distinguishes nascent Humanism in France from that of Italy, is a difference of erudition, skill and taste, rather than of tone or aspiration. To transplant antique form and sentiment into national literature the French had to overcome far more obstacles than the people born under the Tuscan sky or in the shadow of the Coliseum. France too, had her learned clerks, writing in Latin, who were capable at an early date of rising to the height of the epistolary style. But a blending of classicism and medievalism in the vernacular, such as was achieved by Boccaccio, was for a long time impossible in France. The old forms were too strong, and the general culture still lacked the proficiency in mythology and ancient history which was

current in Italy. Machaut, although a clerk, pitifully dis-
figures the names of the seven sages. Chastellain con-
founds Peleus with Pelias, La Marche Proteus with Piri-
thous. The author of the *Pastoralet* speaks of the "good
king Scipio of Africa." But at the same time his subject
inspires him with a description of the god Silvanus and a
prayer to Pan, in which the poetical imagination of the
Renaissance seems on the point of breaking forth. The
chroniclers were already trying their hand at military
speeches in Livy's manner, and adorning their narrative of
important events by mentioning portents, in close imitation
of Livy. Their attempts at classicism did not always succeed. Jean Germain's description of the Arras congress of
1435 is a veritable caricature of antique prose. The vision
of Antiquity was still very bizarre. At the funeral service
of Charles the Bold at Nancy, his conqueror, the young
duke of Lorraine, came to honour the corpse of his enemy,
dressed "in antique style," this is to say, wearing a long
golden beard which reached to his girdle. Thus got up to
represent one of the Nine Worthies, he prayed for a quarter
of an hour.

The word "antique" as conceived in France about 1400
belonged to the same group of ideas as "rhétorique,
orateur, poésie." No one would have thought of applying
the word "poésie" to a ballad or a song in the old French
form. This classical word, which evoked the idea of the
admired perfection of the Ancients, meant above all an
artificial form. The poets of this time are perfectly capable
of expressing heartfelt emotions in a simple form, but when
they wish to attain superior beauty, they hunt up mythology, employ pedantic latinized terms and then consider
themselves "rhetoricians." Christine de Pisan expressly
singles out a mythologic piece, which she calls "balade
pouétique," from her ordinary work. Eustache Deschamps,
wishing to air his talent, in sending his works to Chaucer,
his fellow-poet and admirer, adds the following lines:

> "O Socrates plains de philosophie,
> Seneque en meurs et Anglux en pratique,

Ovides grans en ta poeterie,
Bries en parler, saiges en rethorique
Aigles tres haulz, qui par ta théorique
Enlumines le regne d'Eneas,
L'Isle aux Geans, ceuls de Bruth, et qui as
Semé les fleurs et planté le rosier,
Aux ignorans de la langue pandras,
Grant translateur, noble Geoffroy Chaucier!

. . . .

A toy pour ce de la fontaine Helye
Requier avoir un buvraige autentique,
Dont la doys est du tout en ta baillie,
Pour rafrener d'elle ma soif ethique,
Qui en Gaul seray paralitique
Jusques a ce que tu m'abuveras." [1]

This is the beginning, modest as yet, of the ridiculous latinism which Villon and Rabelais satirized. This insufferable manner reappears whenever authors exert themselves to be exceptionally brilliant, in dedications, discourses, or literary correspondence. In this vein Chastellain will write "vostre très humble et obéissante serve et ancelle, la ville de Gand," "la viscérale intime douleur et tribulation," [2] La Marche "nostre francigène locution et langue vernacule," [3] Molinet "abreuvé de la doulce et melliflue

---

[1] O Socrates full of philosophy, Seneca in morals and Englishman in practice, Great Ovid in your poetry, Brief of speech, well-versed in rhetoric, Exalted eagle, who by your erudition Have illumined the reign of Eneas, The Island of the Giants, and that of Brut, and who have Sown flowers and planted the eglantine, For the ignorant of the language, you will pour yourself forth, Great translator, noble Geoffrey Chaucer!
From you therefore out of the fountain of Helye I ask to have an authentic draught, Of which the conduit is wholly in your power To slake my hectic thirst, I who in Gaul shall be paralysed Till you shall give me to drink.

[2] Your very humble and obedient slave and servant, the city of Ghent. The intestinal inward sorrow and tribulation.

[3] Our French-born locution and vernacular tongue.

liqueur procédant de la fontaine caballine," "ce vertueux duc scipionique," "gens de mulièbre courage." [4]

This far-fetched rhetoric testifies both to an ideal of literary conversation and to an ideal of style. Like the troubadours of yore, the rhetoricians and the humanists cultivated literature in the form of an all-round game. Literary correspondence of a rather strange kind springs up. A fervent admirer of Georges Chastellain, Jean Robertet, secretary to three dukes of Bourbon and to three kings of France, tried to enter into correspondence with the poet-historiographer of the Burgundian court, by the good offices of a certain Montferrant who lived at Bruges. The latter, to soften the old author, who was at first rather reserved, had recourse to the time-honoured device of allegory. He evoked the "twelve dames of rhetoric," Science, Eloquence, Gravity of Meaning, Profundity, etc., who appeared to him in a vision and told him to exert himself in behalf of the correspondence desired by Robertet. In the exchange of poetical and rhetorical compliments which followed, Chastellain's verses are sober, when compared with the hyperbolic effusions of Robertet.

> "Frappé en l'oeil d'une clarté terrible
> Attaint au cœur d'eloquence incrédible,
> A humain sens difficile à produire,
> Tout offusquié de lumière incendible
> Outre perçant de ray presqu'impossible
> Sur obscur corps qui jamais ne peut luire,
> Ravi, abstrait me trouve en mon déduire,
> En extase corps gisant à la terre,
> Foible esperit perplex à voye enquerre
> Pour trouver lieu et oportune yssue
> Du pas estroit où je suis mis en serre,
> Pris à la rets qu'amour vraye a tissue." [5]

[4] Having drunk from the sweet and mellifluous liquor proceeding from the equine fountain. This virtuous scipionic duke. People of muliebral courage.

[5] Struck in the eye by a terrible brightness, Touched in the heart by incredible eloquence, Difficult for the human

In these terms he describes the sensations which the arrival of a letter by Chastellain caused in him. And, continuing in prose, he asks his friend Montferrant (whom he calls "friend of the immortal gods, beloved of men, high Ulyssean breast, full of mellifluent eloquence"), "N'est-ce resplendeur équale au curre Phœbus?"[6] Does he not surpass Orpheus' lyre? and "la tube d'Amphion, la Mercuriale flute qui endormit Argus?" "Où est l'œil capable de tel objet visible, l'oreille pour ouyr le haut son argentin et tintinabule d'or?"[7]

Chastellain showed some scepticism as to this raving enthusiasm. Soon he had enough of it and wanted to bar the gate which had so long and widely been open to "Dame Vanity." "Robertet has quite soaked me by his cloud, of which the drops, congealing like hail, make my garments brilliant as with pearls; but what good is it to the dark body underneath, when my robe deceives the onlookers?" Therefore let him cease writing in this way, otherwise Chastellain will throw his letters into the fire without reading them. If he is willing to speak as beseems among friends, he may rest assured of Georges' affection.

Lucubrations of this sort by no means give us the feeling of the measure and harmony of the Renaissance. It all seems to us antiquated in sentiment and style. There is no doubt, however, that these wits considered themselves supremely modern. This Robertet had been in Italy, "a country greedy for renovation . . . on which the meteoric

mind to produce, Quite obscured by incendiary light Penetrating with almost unbearable rays, To a dark body that can never shine, Ravished, distraught, I find myself, in my delight, My body in ecstasy lying on the ground, My feeble spirit is at a loss to go in quest of a path In order to find a place and opportune exit From the narrow pass where I am hemmed in Caught in the toils which true love has netted.

[6] Is this not splendour equal to the car of Phœbus?

[7] The reed of Amphion, the Mercurial flute, which caused Argus to sleep? Where is the eye capable of seeing such a visible object, the ear to hear the high silver sound and golden tintinnabulation?

conditions operate to facilitate ornate speech, and towards which all elemental sweetness is drawn, there to resolve into harmony." He evidently believed that the secret of this harmony was in the "ornate speech" and that to rival the Italians it sufficed to bedeck the French style with the ornaments of classicism. Now, in Italy, where language and thought had never been entirely estranged from the pure Latin style, the social environment and the turn of mind were far more congenial to the humanistic tendencies than in France. Italian civilization had naturally developed the type of the humanist. The Italian language was not, like the French, corrupted by an influx of latinism; it absorbed it without difficulty. In France, on the contrary, the medieval foundations of social life were still solid; the language, much farther removed from Latin than Italian was, refused to be latinized. If, in English, erudite latinisms were to find an easy access, it was because of the very fact that here the language was not of Latin stock at all, so that no incongruity of expression made itself felt.

In so far as the French humanists of the fifteenth century wrote in Latin, the medieval subsoil of their culture is little in evidence. The more completely the classical style is imitated, the more the true spirit is concealed. The letters and the discourses of Robert Gaguin are not distinguishable from the works of other humanists. But Gaguin is, at the same time, a French poet of altogether medieval inspiration and of altogether national style. Whereas those who did not, and perhaps could not, write in Latin, spoiled their French by latinized forms, he, the accomplished latinist, when writing in French, disdained rhetorical effects. His *Débat du Laboureur, du Prestre et du Gendarme,* medieval in its subject, is also medieval in style. It is simple and vigorous, like Villon's poetry and Deschamps' best work.

Who are the true moderns in the French literature of the fifteenth century? Those, no doubt, whose works approach nearest to what the following century produced of beauty. Assuredly it is not, whatever their merits may have been, the grave and pompous representatives of the Bur-

gundian style: not Chastellain, La Marche, Molinet. The
novelties of form which they affected were too superficial,
the foundation of their thought too essentially medieval,
their classical whimsies too naïve. Should one look for the
modern element in the refinement of form? Sometimes this
form, though most artificial, has so much grace that the
sweet melody makes us forget the emptiness of meaning.

> "Plusiers bergiers sont en lacz mortelz telz
> Heurtez, boutez, que pou leur déduit duyt.
> Et leurs moutons en maux fortunez nez,
> Venez, vanez, de fers mal parez rez,
> Leurs bledz emblez, ayans sauf conduit vuyd,
> La nuit leur nuit, la mort qui destruit ruit,
> Leur fruit s'en fuit venant aperte perte:
> Mais Pan nous tient en asseurance experte." [8]

This was written by Jean Lemaire de Belges. Much more
might be said on this elaboration of a purely formal beauty
in poetry. But, taking all in all, it is not here that the future
of literature lies. If by moderns we understand those who
have most affinity with the later development of French
literature, the moderns are Villon, Charles of Orléans and
the poet of *L'Amant rendu Cordelier*, just those who kept
most aloof from classicism and who did not strain after
over-nice forms. The medieval character of their motifs
robs them not in the least of their aspect of youth and of
promise. It is the spontaneity of their expression which
makes them moderns.

Classicism then was not the controlling factor in the advent of the new spirit in literature. Neither was paganism.
The frequent use of pagan expressions or tropes has often
been considered the chief characteristic of the Renaissance.

---

[8] Several shepherds are in such mortal snares So much
knocked and pushed that it little tends to their delight. And
their sheep, born in an evil hour, Are hunted, exhausted,
shorn by ill-sharpened shears, Their corn is stolen, having
a fruitless safe-conduct, The night is noxious to them; de-
structive death rushes in, Their fruit flies, as open ruin
comes, But Pan holds us in his expert protection.

This practice, however, is far older. As early as the twelfth century mythological terms were employed to express concepts of the Christian faith, and this was not considered at all irreverent or impious. Deschamps speaking of "Jupiter come from paradise," Villon calling the Holy Virgin "high goddess," the humanists referring to God in terms like "princeps superum" and to Mary as "genetrix tonantis," are by no means pagans. Pastorals required some admixture of innocent paganism, by which no reader was duped. The author of the *Pastoralet* who calls the Celestine church at Paris "the temple in the high woods, where people pray to the gods," declares, to dispel all ambiguity, "If, to lend my Muse some strangeness, I speak of the pagan gods, the shepherds and myself are Christians all the same." In the same way Molinet excuses himself for having introduced Mars and Minerva, by quoting "Reason and Understanding," who said to him: "You should do it, not to instil faith in gods and goddesses, but because Our Lord alone inspires people as it pleases Him and frequently by various inspirations."

The purity of Faith was more seriously threatened when, as in the following lines, a certain respect for pagan cults, and notably of sacrifices, is manifested.

"Des dieux jadis les nations gentiles
  Quirent l'amour par humbles sacrifices,
  Lesquels, posé que ne fussent utiles,
  Furent nientmoins rendables et fertiles,
  De maint grant fruit et de haulx bénéfices,
  Monstrans par fait que d'amour les offices
  Et d'honneur humble, impartis où qu'ils soient
  Pour percer ciel et enfer suffisoient." [9]

[9] Formerly the gentile nations of the gods Craved love by humble sacrifices, Which, taken for granted that they were useless, Were nevertheless profitable and prolific Of much important fruit and of high benefits, Which shows by facts that offices of love And of humble homage, rendered wherever they were, Were sufficient to pierce heaven and hell.

This is a stanza of the *Dit de Vérité*, the best poem of Chastellain, which was inspired by his fidelity to the duke of Burgundy, and in which, forgetting his ordinary grandiloquence a little, he gives free rein to his political indignation.

To find paganism, there was no need for the spirit of the waning Middle Ages to revert to classic literature. The pagan spirit displayed itself, as amply as possible, in the *Roman de la Rose*. Not in the guise of some mythological phrases; it was not there that the danger lay, but in the whole erotic conception and inspiration of this most popular work of all. From the early Middle Ages onward Venus and Cupid had found a refuge in this domain. But the great pagan who called them to vigorous life and enthroned them was Jean de Meun. By blending with Christian conceptions of eternal bliss the boldest praise of voluptuousness, he had taught numerous generations a very ambiguous attitude towards Faith. He had dared to distort Genesis for his impious purposes by making Nature complain of men because they neglect her commandment of procreation, in the words:

> "Si m'aïst Diex li crucefis,
> Moult me repens dont homme fis." [10]

It is astonishing that the Church, which so rigorously repressed the slightest deviations from dogma of a speculative character, suffered the teaching of this breviary of the aristocracy (for the *Roman de la Rose* was nothing less) to be disseminated with impunity.

But the essence of the great renewal lies even less in paganism than in pure Latinity. Classic expression and imagery, and even sentiments borrowed from heathen Antiquity, might be a potent stimulus or an indispensable support in the process of cultural renovation, they never were its

[10] So help me God who was crucified, I much repent that I made man.

moving power. The soul of Western Christendom itself was outgrowing medieval forms and modes of thought that had become shackles. The Middle Ages had always lived in the shadow of Antiquity, always handled its treasurers, or what they had of them, interpreting it according to truly medieval principles: scholastic theology and chivalry, asceticism and courtesy. Now, by an inward ripening, the mind, after having been so long conversant with the forms of Antiquity, began to grasp its spirit. The incomparable simpleness and purity of the ancient culture, its exactitude of conception and of expression, its easy and natural thought and strong interest in men and in life,—all this began to dawn upon men's minds. Europe, after having lived in the shadow of Antiquity, lived in its sunshine once more.

This process of assimilation of the classic spirit, however, was intricate and full of incongruities. The new form and the new spirit do not yet coincide. The classical form may serve to express the old conceptions: more than one humanist chooses the sapphic strophe for a pious poem of purely medieval inspiration. Traditional forms, on the other hand, may contain the spirit of the coming age. Nothing is more erroneous than to identify classicism and modern culture.

The fifteenth century in France and the Netherlands is still medieval at heart. The diapason of life had not yet changed. Scholastic thought, with symbolism and strong formalism, the thoroughly dualistic conception of life and the world still dominated. The two poles of the mind continued to be chivalry and hierarchy. Profound pessimism spread a general gloom over life. The gothic principle prevailed in art. But all these forms and modes were on the wane. A high and strong culture is declining, but at the same time and in the same sphere new things are being born. The tide is turning, the tone of life is about to change.

BIBLIOGRAPHY

Achéry, Luc d' —, *Spicilegium*, nova ed., Paris, 1723, III, p. 730: *Statuts de l'ordre de l'Etoile.*

Acquoy, J. G. R. —, *Het klooster van Windesheim en zijn invloed*, 3 vols., Utrecht, 1875–80.

Acta Sanctorum, see Colette, François de Paule, Pierre de Luxembourg, Pierre Thomas, Vincent Ferrer.

Ailly, Pierre d' —, *De falsis prophetis*, in Gerson, *Opera* I, p. 538, *De Reformatione*, ibid. II, p. 911, *Tractatus I adversus cancellarium Parisiensem*, ibid. I, p. 723.

Alain de la Roche = Alanus de Rupe, Beatus Alanus redivivus, ed. J. A. Coppenstein, Naples, 1642.

Amant rendu cordelier à l'observance d'amours, L' —, poème attribué à Martial d'Auvergne, publié par A. de Montaiglon, Société des anciens textes français, 1881.

Anitchkoff, E., *L'esthétique au moyen âge*, Le Moyen Âge, vol. XX (1918), p. 221.

Baisieux, Jacques de —, *Des trois chevaliers et del chainse*, Scheler, Trouvères belges, vol. I, 1876.

Basin, Thomas —, *De rebus gestis Caroli VII et Ludovici XI historiarum libri XII*, ed. Quicherat, Société de l'histoire de France, 4 vols., 1855–59.

Baude, Les vers de maître Henri —, ed. Quicherat, Trésors des pièces rares ou inédites, 1856.

Beatis, Antonio de —, *Die Reise des Kardinals Luigi d'Aragona*, ed. L. von Pastor, Freiburg, 1905.

Becker, C. H. —, *Ubi sunt qui ante nos in mundo fuere*, Islamstudien I, 1924, p. 501.

Bertoni, G. —, *L'Orlando furioso e la rinascenza a Ferrara*, Modena, 1919.

Blois, Extraict de l'enqueste faite pour la canonization de Charles de—, in André du Chesne, *Histoire de la maison de Chastillon sur Marne*, Paris, 1621, Preuves, p. 223.

Bonaventura, Saint —, *Opera*, Paris, 1871.

Bonet, Honoré —, *L'arbre des batailles*, Paris, Michel le Noir, 1515.

Boucicaut, *Le livre des faicts du mareschal de* —, ed. Petitot, Collection de mémoires, VI.

Bourquelot, F. —, *Les Vaudois du quinzième siècle*, Bibliothèque de l'école des chartes, 2nd series, III, p. 109.

Burckhardt, J. —, *Die Kultur der Renaissance in Italien*, 10th edition, Leipzig, 1908.

Burckhardt, J. —, *Weltgeschichtliche Betrachtungen*, Berlin-Stuttgart, 1905.

Byvanck, W. G. C. —, *Spécimen d'un essai critique sur les œuvres de Villon*, Leyde, 1882.

——, *Un poète inconnu de la société de François Villon*, Paris, 1891.

Carnahan, D. H. —, *The "Ad Deum vadit" of Jean Gerson*, University of Illinois studies in language and literature, 1917, III, No. 1.

Caroli ducis Burgundiæ, De laudibus —, *De Morte* —, etc., *Chroniques relatives à l'histoire de la Belgique sous la domination des ducs de Bourgogne*, ed. Kervyn de Lettenhove, vol. III, Brussels, 1873.

Cartellieri, O. —, *Geschichte der Herzöge von Burgund, I Philipp der Kühne*, Leipzig, 1910.

——, *Beiträge zur Geschichte der Herzöge von Burgund*, Sitzungsberichte der Heidelberger Akademie der Wissenschaften, 1911, etc.

Cent ballades, Le livre des —, ed. G. Raynaud, Société des anciens textes français, 1905.

Cent nouvelles nouvelles, Les —, ed, Th. Wright, Bibliothèque elzévirienne, 2 vols., Paris, 1857–58.

Champion, P. —, *Vie de Charles d'Orléans, 1394–1465*, Paris, 1911.

——, *François Villon, sa vie et son temps*, Bibliothèque du XVᵉ siècle, 2 vols., Paris, 1913.

Chansons françaises du quinzième siècle, ed. G. Paris, Société des anciens textes français, 1875.

Charny, Geoffroy de —, see Piaget.

Chartier, Les œuvres de maistre Alain —, ed. A. Du Chesne Tourangeau, Paris, 1617.

Chartier, Jean —, *Histoire de Charles VII*, ed. D. Godefroy, Paris, 1661.

Chastellain, Œuvres de Georges —, ed. Kervyn de Lettenhove, 8 vols., Brussels, 1863–66. Especially Chronique I–V; Le miroer des nobles hommes en France, Le dit de vérité, Exposition sur vérité mal prise, La mort du roy Charles VII, vol. V; L'entrée du roy Loys en nouveau règne, Advertissement au duc Charles, Le livre de la paix, Recollection des merveilles, Le temple de Bocace, Les douze Dames de rhétorique, Le lyon rampant, Les hauts faits du duc de Bourgogne, La mort du duc Philippe, vol. VII, etc.

Chesne, André du —, *Histoire de la maison de Chastillon sur Marne*, Paris, 1621.

Chmelarz, E. —, *König René der Gute und die Handschrift seines Romanes "Cuer d'amours espris" in der K.K. Hofbibliothek*, Jahrbuch der kunsthist. Sammlungen des allerh. Kaiserhauses, XI, Vienna, 1890.

Chopinel, Jean —, see Roman.

Chronique de Berne, ed. H. Moranvillé, Société de l'histoire de France, 3 vols., 1891–97.

Chronique scandaleuse, see Roye.

Clemanges, Nicolas de —, *Opera*, ed. Lydius, Leyden, 1613.

Clercq, Jacques du —, *Mémoires (1448–1467)*, ed. de Reiffenberg, 4 vols., Brussels, 1823.

Clopinel, Jean —, see Roman.

Colette, Sainte —, *Acta Sanctorum Martii*, vol. I, 532–623.

Commines, Philippe de —, *Mémoires*, ed. B. de Mandrot, Collection de textes pour servir à l'enseignement de l'histoire, 2 vols., 1901–03.

Complainte du povre commun et des povres laboureurs de France, La —, in Monstrelet, *Chronique*, vol. VI, p. 176.

Coopland, G. W. —, *The Tree of Battles and some of its Sources*, Revue d'histoire du droit, V, 173, Haarlem, 1923.

Coquillart, G. —, *Œuvres*, ed. Ch. d'Héricault, Bibliothèque elzévirienne, 2 vols., 1857.

Couderc, C. —, *Les comptes d'un grand couturier parisien
au XVe siècle*, Bulletin de la société de l'histoire de Paris,
vol. XXXVIII (1911), p. 118.

Coville, A. —, *Les premiers Valois et la guerre de cent ans,
1328–1422*, in Lavisse, *Histoire de France*, vol. IV, 1.
———, *Le véritable texte de la justification du duc de
Bourgogne par Jean Petit*, Bibliothèque de l'école des
chartes, 1911, p. 57.

Débat des hérauts d'armes de France et d'Angleterre, Le
—, ed. L. Pannier et P. Meyer, Société des anciens textes
français, 1887.

Denifle, H. —, *La désolation des églises, etc., en France*,
2 vols., Paris, 1897–99.

Denifle, H. —, and Chatelain, Ae. —, *Chartularium universitatis Parisiensis*, 4+2 vols., Paris, 1889–97.

Déprez, E. —, *La bataille de Najera, 3 avril 1367*, Revue
historique, vol. CXXXVI (1921), p. 37.

Deschamps, Eustache —, *Œuvres complètes*, ed. De Queux
de Saint Hilaire et G. Raynaud, Société des anciens
textes français, 11 vols., 1878–1903.

Dionysius Cartusianus (or of Ryckel), *Opera omnia, cura
et labore monachorum sacr. ord. Cart.*, 41 vols., Montreuil and Tournay, 1896–1913. Especially Dialogion de
fide catholica, vol. 18; De quotidiano baptismate lacri-
marum, vol. 29; De munificentia et beneficiis Dei, vol.
34; De laudibus sanctæ et individuæ trinitatis, De
passione domini salvatoris dialogus, vol. 35; De mutua
cognitione, De modo agendi processiones, Contra vitia
superstitionum quibus circa cultum veri Dei erratur, vol.
36; De vita et regimine episcoporum, nobilium, etc.,
etc., vol. 37 ss; Inter Jesum et puerum dialogus, vol. 38;
Directorium vitæ nobilium, vol. 37; De vitiis et
virtutibus, vol. 39; De contemplatione, De quattuor
hominum novissimis, vol. 41.

Dixmude, Jan van —, *Chronike*, ed. J. J. Lambin, Ypres,
1839.

Douet d'Arcq, *Choix de pièces inédites relatives au règne*

de Charles VI, Société de l'histoire de France, 2 vols., 1863.

Doutrepont, G. —, *La littérature française à la cour des ducs de Bourgogne*, Bibliothèque du XVᵉ siècle, Paris, 1909.

Durand Gréville, E. —, *Hubert et Jean Van Eyck*, Bruxelles, 1910.

Durrieu, P. —, *Les très riches heures de Jean de France, duc de Berry*, Paris, 1904.

Durrieu, P. —, *Les belles heures du duc de Berry*, Gazette des beaux arts, 1906, vol. XXXV, p. 283.

—— *La Miniature flamande au temps de la cour de Bourgogne (1415–1530)*, Brussels, 1921.

——, *Un barbier de nom français à Bruges*, Comptes rendus de l'Académie des inscriptions et belles-lettres, 1917, p. 542.

Eckhart, Meister —, *Predigten*, ed. F. Pfeiffer, in *Deutsche Mystiker des XIV Jahrhunderts*, 2 vols., Leipzig, 1857.

Elisabeth, Saint —, Report of an autopsy of the body of — of Hungary by bishop Konrad of Hildesheim and abbot Hermann of Georgenthal, Historisches Jahrbuch der Görresgesellschaft, vol. XXVIII, p. 887.

Erasmus, Desiderius —, *Opera omnia*, ed. J. Clericus, 10 vols., Leyden, 1703–06.

——, *Opus epistolarum . . . denuo recognitum et auctum*, P. S. and H. M. Allen, 5 vols., Oxford 1906–24 (–1524).

——, *Ratio seu methodus compendio perveniendi ad veram theologiam*, ed. Basileæ, 1520.

——, *Colloquia*, ed. Elzevier, 1636.

Escouchy, Mathieu d' —, *Chronique*, ed. G. du Fresne de Beaucourt, Société de l'histoire de France, 3 vols., 1863–64.

Estienne, Henri —, *Apologie pour Hérodote*, ed. Ristelhuber, 2 vols., 1879.

Facius, Bartholomæus —, *De Viris illustribus liber*, ed. L. Mehus, Florence, 1745.

Fenin, Pierre de —, *Mémoires*, Petitot, Collection de mémoires, VII.

Ferrer, see Vincent.

Fierens Gevaert, *La renaissance septentrionale et les premiers maîtres des Flandres*, Brussels, 1905.

Fillastre, Guillaume —, *Le premier et Le second volume de la toison d'or*, Paris, Franc. Regnault, 1515–16.

François de Paule, Saint —, *Acta sanctorum Aprilis*, vol. I, pp. 103–234.

Fredericq, P., *Codex documentorum sacratissimarum Indulgentiarum Neerlandicarum*, Rijks geschiedkundige Publicatiën (small series), No. 21, The Hague, 1922.

Fresne de Beaucourt, G. du —, *Histoire de Charles VII*, 6 vols., Paris, 1881–91.

Froissart, Jean —, *Chroniques*, ed. S. Luce et G. Raynaud, Société de l'histoire de France, 11 vols., 1869–99 (–1385).

——, *Chroniques*, ed. Kervyn de Lettenhove, 29 vols., Brussels, 1867–77.

——, *Poésies*, ed. A. Scheler, Académie royale de Belgique, 3 vols., Brussels, 1870–72.

——, *Méliador*, ed. A. Longnon, Société des anciens textes français, 3 vols., 1895–99.

Gaguin, Robert —, *Epistolæ et orationes*, ed. L. Thuasne, Bibliothèque littéraire de la Renaissance, 2 vols., Paris, 1903.

——, *Compendium super Francorum gestis*, Paris, 1500.

Geffroi de Paris, *Chronique*, ed. De Wailly et Delisle, Bouquet, Recueil des historiens, vol. XXII.

Germain, Jean —, *Liber de virtutibus Philippi ducis Burgundiæ*, ed. Kervyn de Lettenhove, *Chron. rel. à l'hist. de la Belgique sous la dom. des ducs de Bourgogne*, vol. II.

Gerson, Jean —, *Opera omnia*, ed. L. Ellies du Pin, ed. II, Hagæ Comitis, 1728, 5 vols. Especially vol. I, De examinatione doctrinarum, De probatione spirituum, De distinctione verarum visionum a falsis, Epistola super librum Joh. Ruysbroeck, etc., Ep. contra libellum Joh. de Schonhavia, id. contra defensionem Joh. de Schonhavia, Contra vanam curiositatem, De libris caute legendis, De consolatione theologiæ, Contra superstitionem præsertim Innocentum, De erroribus circa

artem magicam, Compendium theologiæ, De decem
præceptis, De præceptis decalogi, De susceptione hu-
manitatis Christi, De falsis prophetis; vol. II, De nuptiis
Christi et ecclesiæ, Expostulatio adv. eos qui publice
volunt dogmatizare, etc., Contra impugnantes ordinem
Carthusiensium; vol. III, Liber de vita spirituali animæ,
Regulæ morales, De passionibus animæ, Centilogium de
impulsibus, Contra fœdam tentationem blasphemiæ, De
parvulis ad Christum trahendis, Expostulatio adversus
corruptionem juventutis per lascivas imagines, Discours
de l'excellence de virginité, Oratio ad bonum angelum
suum, De monte contemplationis, De via imitativa, Con-
sidérations sur Saint Joseph, De triplici theologia, Con-
sidérations sur le péché de blasphème, Contra gulam
sermo, Sermo contra luxuriem, Sermo de nativitate
Domini, Sermo de natalitate b. Mariæ Virginis, Sermones
in die S. Ludovici, Sermo de Angelis, Sermones de
defunctis, Sermo de S. Nicolao; vol. IV, Meditatio super
VII^{mo} psalmo pœnitentiali, Tractatus super Magnificat,
Querela nomine Universitatis, Sermo coram rege
Franciæ, Oratio ad regem Franciæ, Josephina.

Godefroy, Th. —, *Le cérémonial françois*, 2 vols., Paris,
1649.

Grandes chroniques de France Les —, ed. Paulin Paris, 6
vols., Paris, 1836–38.

Gratia Dei, Oratio Antonii —, ed. Kervyn de Lettenhove,
*Chron. rel. à l'hist. de Belg. sous la dom. des ducs de
Bourgogne*, vol. III.

Hanotaux, G. —, *Jeanne d'Arc*, Paris, 1911.

Hefele, K. —, *Der heilige Bernhardin von Siena und die
franziskanische Wanderpredigt in Italien*, Freiburg,
1912.

Hintzen, J. D. —, *De kruistochtplannen van Philips den
Goede*, Rotterdam, 1918.

Histoire littéraire de la France, XIVe siècle, vol. XXIV,
1862.

Hoepffner, E. —, *Frage- und Antwortspiele in der
französischen Literatur des 14. Jahrhunderts*, Zeitschrift
für romanische Philologie, vol. XXXIII, 1909.

Hospinianus, R. —, *De templis, hoc est de origine, progressu, usu et abusu templorum, etc.*, 2nd ed., Zürich, 1603.

Houwaert, J. B. —, *Declaratie van die triumphante incompst van den Prince van Oraingnien, etc.*, Antwerp, Plantijn, 1579.

Huet, G. —, *Notes d'histoire littéraire III*, in Le Moyen Âge, vol. XX, 1918.

Huizinga, J. —, *Uit de voorgeschiedenis van ons nationaal besef*, De Gids, 1912, III.

——, *Renaissancestudiën I: Het probleem*, De Gids, 1920, vol. IV.

James, W. —, *The Varieties of Religious Experience*, London, 1903.

Jorga, N. —, *Philippe de Mézières et la croisade au XIVe siècle*, Bibliothèque de l'école des hautes études, Fasc. CX, 1896.

Jouffroy, Jean —, *De Philippo duce oratio*, ed. Kervyn de Lettenhove, *Chron. rel. à l'hist. de Belg. sous la dom. des ducs de Bourgogne*, vol. III.

Journal d'un bourgeois de Paris, 1405–1449, ed. A. Tuetey, Publications de la société de l'histoire de Paris, doc. No. III, 1881.

Jouvencel, Le —, ed. C. Favre et L. Lecestre, Société de l'histoire de France, 2 vols., 1887–92.

Jouvenel des Ursins, Jean —, *Chronique*, ed. Michaud et Poujoulat, Nouvelle collection des mémoires, II.

Kempis, Thomas à —, *Opera omnia*, ed. M. J. Pohl, 7 vols., Freiburg, 1902–10.

Kleinclausz, A. —, *Histoire de Bourgogne*, Paris, 1909.

——, *L'art funéraire de la Bourgogne au moyen âge*, Gazette des beaux arts, vol. XXVII, 1902.

——, *Un atelier de sculpture au XVe siècle*, Gazette des beaux arts, vol. XXIX, 1903.

Krogh-Tonning, K. —, *Der letzte Scholastiker, Eine Apologie*, Freiburg, 1904.

Kurth, Betty —, *Die Blütezeit der Bildwirkerkunst zu Tournay und der burgundische Hof*, Jahrbuch der Kunstsammlungen des Kaiserhauses, XXXIV, 1917.

Laborde, L. de –, *Les ducs de Bourgogne, Etudes sur les lettres, les arts et l'industrie pendant le XV⁰ siècle,* 3 vols., Paris, 1849–53.

La Curne de Sainte Palaye, J. B. –, *Mémoires sur l'ancienne chevalerie,* 1781.

Lalaing, Le livre des faits du bon chevalier messire Jacques de –, ed. Kervyn de Lettenhove, in *Œuvres de Chastellain,* vol. VIII.

La Marche, Olivier de –, *Mémoires,* ed. Beaune et d'Arbaumont, Société de l'histoire de France, 4 vols., 1883–88.

——, *Estat de la maison du duc Charles de Bourgogne,* ibid., vol. IV.

——, *Rationarium aulæ et imperii Caroli Audacis ducis Burgundiæ,* ed. A. Matthæus, Analecta, I, pp. 357–494 (Middle Dutch translation of the preceding work).

——, *Le parement et triumphe des dames,* Paris, Michel le Noir, 1520.

Langlois, E. –, *Anciens proverbes français,* Bibliothèque de l'Ecole des chartes, vol. LX (1899), p. 569.

——, *Recueil d'arts de seconde rhétorique,* Documents inédits sur l'histoire de France, Paris, 1902.

Lannoy, Ghillebert de –, *Œuvres,* ed. Ch. Potvin, Louvain, 1878.

La Roche, see Alain.

La Salle, Antoine de la –, *La Salade,* Paris, Michel le Noir, 1521.

——, *Le reconfort de Madame du Fresne,* ed. J. Nève, Paris, 1903.

La Tour Landry, Le livre du chevalier de –, ed. A. de Montaiglon, Bibliothèque elzévirienne, Paris, 1854.

Lefèvre de Saint Remy, Jean, –, *Chronique,* ed. F. Morand, Société de l'histoire de France, 2 vols., 1876.

Leroux de Lincy, A. –, *Le livre des proverbes français,* 2nd ed., 2 vols., Paris, 1859.

Liber Karoleidos, ed. Kervyn de Lettenhove, Chron. rel. à l'hist. de Belg. sous la dom. des ducs de Bourgogne, vol. III.

Livre des trahisons, Le –, ed. id., ibid., vol. II.

Loër, Theodericus —, *Vita Dionysii Cartusiani*, in Dionysii Opera I, p. xlii.

Lorris, Guillaume de —, see Roman.

Louis XI, Lettres de —, ed. Vaesen, Charavay, De Mandrot, Société de l'histoire de France, 11 vols., 1883–1909.

Luce, S. —, *La France pendant la guerre de cent ans*, Paris, 1890.

Luther, Martin —, *De captivitate babylonica ecclesiæ præludium*, Werke, Weimar edition, vol. VI.

Luxembourg, see Pierre.

Machaut, Guillaume de —, *Le livre du Voir-dit*, ed. Paulin Paris, Société des bibliophiles françois, 1875.

——, *Œuvres*, ed. E. Hoepffner, Société des anciens textes français, 2 vols., 1908–11.

——, *Poésies lyriques*, ed. V. Chichmaref, Zapiski istoritcheski fil. fakulteta imp. S. Peterb. univers., vol. XCII, 1909.

Magnien, Ch. —, *Caxton à la cour de Charles le Téméraire*, Annuaire de la société d'archéologie de Bruxelles, vol. XXIII, 1912.

Maillard, Olivier —, *Sermones dominicales, etc.*, Paris, Jean Petit, 1515.

Mâle, E. —, *L'art religieux du treizème siècle en France*, Paris, 1902.

—— *L'art religieux à la fin du moyen âge en France*, Paris, 1908.

Mangeart, J. —, *Catalogue des manuscrits de la bibliothèque de Valenciennes*, 1860.

Martial (d'Auvergne), *Les poésies de Martial de Paris dit d'Auvergne*, 2 vols., Paris, 1724. See Amant.

Meschinot, Jean —, *sa vie et ses œuvres*, par A. de la Borderie, Bibliothèque de l'Ecole des chartes, vol. LVI, 1895.

Meyer, P. —, *Les neuf preux*, Bulletin de la société des anciens textes français, 1883, p. 45.

Michault, Pierre —, *La dance aux aveugles et autres poésies du XVᵉ siècle*, Lille, 1748.

Michel, André —, *Histoire de l'art*, vols. III and IV, Paris, 1907, etc.

Molinet, Jean, *Chronique,* ed. J. Buchon, Collection de chroniques nationales, 5 vols., 1827–28.

——, *Les faicts et dictz de messire Jehan —,* Paris, Jehan Petit, 1537.

Molinier, A. —, *Les sources de l'histoire de France, des origines aux guerres d'Italie* (1494), 6 vols., Paris, 1901–06.

Moll, W. —, *Kerkgeschiedenis van Nederland vóór de hervorming,* 5 parts, Utrecht, 1864–69.

Moll, W. —, *Johannes Brugman en het godsdienstig leven onzer vaderen in de vijftiende eeuw,* 2 vols., Amsterdam, 1854.

Monstrelet, Enguerrand de —, *Chroniques,* ed. Douet d'Arcq, Société de l'histoire de France, 6 vols., 1857–62.

Monstreuil, Jean de —, *Epistolæ,* ed. Martène et Durand, Amplissima collectio, II col., 1398.

Mougel, D. A. —, *Denys le Chartreux, sa vie, etc.,* Montreuil, 1896.

Nys, E. —, *Le droit de guerre et les précurseurs de Grotius,* Brussels and Leipzig, 1882.

——, *Etudes de droit international et de droit politique,* Brussels and Paris, 1896.

Ordonnances des rois de France, Paris, 1723–77.

Orléans, Charles d' —, *Poésies complètes,* 2 vols., Paris, 1874.

Oulmont, Ch. —, *Le verger, le temple et la cellule, Essai sur la sensualité dans les œuvres de mystique religieuse,* Paris, 1912.

Pannier, L. —, *Les joyaux du duc de Guyenne, recherches sur les goûts artistiques et la vie privée du dauphin Louis,* Revue archéologique, 1873.

Pastoralet, Le —, ed. Kervyn de Lettenhove, *Chron. rel. à l'hist. de Belg. sous la dom. des ducs de Bourgogne,* vol. II.

Pauli, Theodericus —, *De rebus actis sub ducibus Burgundiæ compendium,* ed. id., ibid., vol. III.

Petit Dutaillis, Ch. —, *Charles VII, Louis XI et les premières années de Charles VIII* (1422–1492), in Lavisse, *Histoire de France,* vol. IV, 2.

——, *Documents nouveaux sur les mœurs populaires et le droit de vengeance dans les Pays-Bas au XVᵉ siècle*, Bibliothèque du XVᵉ siècle, Paris, 1908.

Petit Jehan de Saintré, L'histoire et plaisante cronicque du —, ed. G. Hellény, Paris, 1890.

Petrarca, Francesco —, *Opera*, Basle edition, 1581.

Piaget, A. —, *Oton de Granson et ses poésies*, Romania, vol. XIX, 1890.

——, *La cour amoureuse dite de Charles VI*, Romania, vol. XX, 1891; XXI, 1892.

——, *Le livre messire Geoffroy de Charny*, Romania, vol. XXVI, 1897.

——, *Le chapel des fleurs de lis, par Philippe de Vitri*, Romania, vol. XXVII, 1898.

——, *Chronologie des épistres sur le Roman de la rose*, Etudes romanes dédiées à Gaston Paris, 1891, p. 113.

Pierre de Luxembourg, The Blessed —, *Acta sanctorum Julii*, vol. I, pp. 509–628.

Pierre Thomas, Carmelite, Saint —, *Acta sanctorum Januarii*, vol. II (his life by Philippe de Mézières).

Pirenne, H. —, *Histoire de Belgique*, 5 vols., Brussels, 1902–21.

Pisan, Christine de —, *Œuvres poétiques*, ed. M. Roy, Société des anciens textes français, 3 vols., 1886–96.

——, *Epitre d'Othéa à Hector*, Manuscrit 9392, de Jean Miélot, ed. J. van den Gheyn, Brussels, 1913.

Poésies françoises des XVᵉ et XVIᵉ siècles, Recueil de —, ed. A. de Montaiglon, Bibliothèque elzévirienne, Paris, 1856.

Poitiers, Aliénor de —, *Les honneurs de la cour*, ed. La Curne de Sainte Palaye, *Mémoires sur l'ancienne chevalerie*, 1781, II.

Polydorus Vergilius, *Anglicæ historiæ libri XXVI*, Basle, 1546.

Pool, J. C. —, *Frederik van Heilo en zijne schriften*, Amsterdam, 1866.

Quinze joyes de mariage, Les —, Paris, Marpon et Flammarion, without date.

Ramsay, J. H. –, *Lancaster and York, 1399–1485*, 2 vols., Oxford, 1892.

Raynaldus, *Annales ecclesiastici*, vol. III (= Baronius, vol. XXII).

Raynaud, G. –, *Rondeaux, etc., du XVe siècle*, Société des anciens textes français, 1889.

Religieux de Saint Denis, Chronique du –, ed. Bellaguet, Collection des documents inédits, 6 vols., 1839–52.

Renaudet, A. –, *Préréforme et humanisme à Paris, 1494–1517*, Paris, 1916.

René Œuvres du roi –, ed. De Quatrebarbes, 4 vols., Angers, 1845.

Roman de la Rose, Le –, ed. M. Méon, 4 vols., Paris, 1814.

——, ed. F. Michel, 2 vols., Paris, 1864.

——, ed. E. Langlois, Société des anciens textes français, 1914, I.

Rousselot, P. –, *Pour l'histoire du problème de l'amour*, Beiträge zur Geschichte der Philosophie im Mittelalter, ed. Bäumker and von Hertling, vol. VI, 1908.

Roye, Jean de –, *Journal dite Chronique scandaleuse*, ed. B. de Mandrot, Société de l'histoire de France, 2 vols., 1894–96.

Rozmital, Leo von –, *Reise durch die Abendlände, 1465–1467*, ed. Schmeller, Bibliothek des literarischen Vereins zu Stuttgart, vol. VII, 1844.

Ruelens, Ch. –, *Recueil de chansons, poèmes, etc. relatifs aux Pays-Bas*, 1878.

Ruusbroec, Johannes –, *Werken*, ed. David and Snellaert, Maetschappij der Vlaemsche bibliophilen, 1860–68. Especially II, Die chierheit der gheesteleker brulocht, Spieghel der ewigher salicheit; IV, Van seven trappen in den graet der gheestelicker minnen, Boec van der hoechster waerheit, Dat boec van seven sloten, Dat boec van den rike der ghelieven.

Ruysbroeck l'Admirable, Œuvres de –, Traduction du flamand par les Bénédictins de Saint Paul de Wisques, vols. I–III, Brussels and Paris, 1917–20.

Salmon, Pierre le Fruictier dit –, *Mémoires*, ed. Buchon,

Collection de chroniques nationales, 3e supplément de Froissart, vol. XV.

Schäfer, D. —, *Mittelalterlicher Brauch bei der Ueberführung von Leichen*, Sitzungsberichte der preussischen Akademie der Wissenschaften, 1920, p. 478.

Schmidt, C. —, *Der Prediger Olivier Maillard*, Zeitschrift für historische Theologie, 1856.

Seuse, Heinrich — (Suso), *Deutsche Schriften*, ed. K. Bihlmeyer, Stuttgart, 1907.

Sicard, *Mitrale sive de officiis ecclesiasticis summa*, Migne, Patr. lat., vol. CCXIII.

Stavelot, Jean de —, *Chronique*, ed. Borgnet, Collection des chroniques belges, Brussels, 1861.

Stein, H. —, *Etude sur Olivier de la Marche*, Mémoires couronnés de l'Académie royale de Belgique, vol. XLIX, 1888.

Tauler, Johannes —, *Predigten*, ed. F. Vetter, in *Deutsche Texte des Mittelalters*, vol. XI, Berlin, 1910.

Thomas Aquinas, Saint —, *Historia translationis corporis sanctissimi ecclesiæ doctoris divi Th. de Aq.*, *1368*, auct. fr. Raymundo Hugonis O.P., Acta sanctorum Martii, vol. I, p. 725.

Thomas, see Pierre.

Trahisons, see *Livre des* —.

Uhrig, H. —, *Dei vierzehn heiligen Nothelfer* (*XIV Auxiliatores*), Theologische Quartalschrift, vol. LXX, 1888.

Upton, Nicolas —, *De officio militari*, ed. E. Bysshe, London, 1654.

Valois, Noël —, *La France et le grand schisme d'occident*, 4 vols., Paris, 1896–1902.

Varennes, Jean de —, *Responsiones ad capitula accusationum, etc.*, in Gerson, *Opera*, I, pp. 906–943.

Vigneulles, Philippe de —, *Mémoires*, ed. H. Michelant, Bibliothek des lit. Vereins zu Stuttgart, vol. XXIV, 1852.

Villon, François —, *Œuvres*, ed. A. Longnon, Les classiques français du moyen âge, vol. II, Paris, 1914.

Vincent Ferrer, Saint —, *Vita*, auct. Petro Ranzano O.P., 1455, Acta sanctorum Aprilis, vol. I, pp. 82–512.

——, *Sermones quadragesimales*, Cologne, 1482.

Vitri, Philippe de —, *Le chapel des fleurs de lis*, ed. A. Piaget, Romania, vol. XXVII, 1898.

Vœux du héron, Les —, ed. Société des bibliophiles de Mons, No. 8, 1839.

Walsingham, Thomas —, *Historia Anglicana*, ed. H. T. Riley, in *Rer. brit. medii ævi scriptores* (Rolls series), 3 vols., London, 1864.

Weale, W. H. J. —, *Hubert and John van Eyck, their Life and Work*, London and New York, 1908.

Wielant, Philippe —, *Antiquités de Flandre*, ed. De Smet, Corpus chronicorum Flandriæ, vol. IV.

Wright, Th. —, *The Anglo-Latin Satirical Poets and Epigrammatists of the Twelfth Century*, in *Rerum britannicarum medii ævi scriptores* (Rolls series), 2 vols., London, 1872.

Zöckler, O. —, *Dionys des Kartäusers Schrift De venustate mundi, Beitrag zur Vorgeschichte der Asthetick*, Theologische Studien und Kritiken, 1881.

INDEX